WHAT PART OF *NO!* DON'T THEY UNDERSTAND?

C-51 C-52

Rescuing Food and Medicine from Government Abuse

A Manifesto

Helke Ferrie

KΩΣ Publishing

WHAT PART OF *NO!* DON'T THEY UNDERSTAND?

Rescuing Food and Medicine from Government Abuse

A Manifesto

The opinions expressed in this book are personal and those of the author alone. All medical information provided in this book is not to be taken as medical advice or as a substitute for consultation with a health practitioner. Any errors in fact are regretted and unintended. Corrections are most welcome and should be sent to the publisher whose address is given below.

National Library of Canada Cataloguing in Publication

ISBN-13: 978-0-9731945-8-6

First printing, 2008

Cover & Text Design/Layout, Print Production: Beth Crane, WeMakeBooks.ca

Published and distributed by KOS Publishing Inc.
1997 Beechgrove Road,
Caledon, ON Canada L7K 0N3
Tel: 519-927-1049
Fax: 519-927-9542
Website: www.kospublishing.com

Quantity discounts available

Printed and bound in Canada.

This book is dedicated to the following three Members of the 39th Parliament of Canada ....

Conservative Party member **Dr. James Lunney, MP** for Nanaimo-Alberni, British Columbia...for the courage and dedication to the truth of natural medicine and for permitting his 2003 *Vitality* article on Health Canada and his proposed bill C-420 to be reproduced in this book

NDP Party member **Judy Wasylycia-Leis, MP** for Winnipeg North, Manitoba...for her excellent grasp of the dark political underpinning of proposed Bills C-51 and C-52 and the eloquence and courage with which she presented these to the House of Commons

Liberal Party member **Robert Thibault, MP** for West Nova Scotia...for demanding the withdrawal of Bill C-51 on June 10, 2008, citing possible Contempt of Parliament due to proposed amendments after First Reading, before entering the Committee stage, instead of making those changes first and bringing the bill back for another First Reading, as required by parliamentary procedure

... for their efforts to keep democracy alive in Canada.

"If people let the government decide what foods they eat and what medicines they take, their bodies will soon be in as sorry a state as are the souls of those who live under tyranny."

—Thomas Jefferson (1743–1826)

"Globalization means corporations can decide to carry out a given industrial function in a given geographic region for economic reasons, notwithstanding any political considerations ... globalizations ignores political borders and merges economic spaces. And thus, on the margin of the state's area of responsibility there emerges a new anonymous and stateless power, a power that is intoxicating and fearsome. In this time of globalization, then, the vertical power of the state is gradually replaced by the horizontal power of the marketplace."

—Pierre Pettigrew

Former Canadian foreign affairs minister; from a lecture delivered to the Canadian Centre for Management Development on May 4, 2000.

"Without blushing or even without a second thought, we now talk of customers or clients in a way that would not have occurred to public servants three or four decades ago. Sometimes the results of this attempt to reinvent the public sector into the private sector are quite bizarre. I recently visited a well-meaning colleague who proudly presented to me the organizational renewal efforts of a high-priced foreign consultant that consisted in, among other things, the translation of all terms of public administration and parliamentary democracy into private sector equivalents, including the reinvention of members of Parliament as the shareholders of the corporation and Cabinet as the Board of Directors."

—Ralph Heintzman

From a lecture given to the Institute of Public Administration of Canada, August 31, 1999.

"By court government I do not mean the rise of the judicial power. Rather, I mean that effective political power now rests with the prime minister and a small group of carefully selected courtiers. I also mean a shift from formal decision-making processes in cabinet and, as a consequence, in the civil service, to informal processes involving only a handful of key actors."

—Donald J. Savoie

Court Government and the Collapse of Accountability in Canada and the United Kingdom, UTP, 2008. (All of the above from same.)

Table of Contents

An Open Letter to
Prime Minister Stephen Harper from Helke Ferrie

KOΣ Publishing Inc.
"Books on Medicine that Works!"
1997 Beechgrove Road
Caledon, Ontario, Canada L7K 0N3
Tel: 519-927-1049 | Fax: 519-927-9542
www.kospublishing.com | helke@sympatico.ca

June 15, 2008
793rd anniversary of the Magna Carta

The Right Honorable Stephen Harper
Office of the Prime Minister
80 Wellington Street
Ottawa, ON, K1A 0A2

Dear Mr. Prime Minister,

The *Globe & Mail* has on its masthead the following statement made by an 18th century British political thinker known only by his nom de plume, Junius: *"The subject who is truly loyal to the Chief Magistrate will neither advise nor submit to arbitrary measures."* It is in this spirit that I am writing to you about the proposed bills C-51 and C-52. Nobody knows who Junius was; he might have been anybody, as indeed I am—just a Canadian who is exceedingly alarmed and cannot help but feel protective towards this great nation in the face of a public health emergency. These two bills not only dramatically fail to address this crisis in public health, but actually threaten to increase this emergency to unmanageable levels, if passed. I am approaching your government in the spirit of Junius to advise against arbitrary measures and also to express clear resistance to such arbitrariness.

When a government falls into error, only the *governed* can correct that. It is my view, that in a parliamentary democracy it is the duty of the citizen to pay careful attention to government *and* to offer correction to government policy when necessary—but to do so *only* if able to provide supporting evidence to show that government is in error. In a democracy we neither want government to shoot off their mouths, nor should we be allowed to do so either. This book provides, I hope, that most significant supporting evidence for the contention that C-51 and C-52 are totally unacceptable, are impossible to amend, and must be withdrawn.

I should introduce myself first: For the past twelve years I have been researching medical politics and writing for various venues on a monthly basis. I also occasionally publish books written mostly by medical professionals who are especially concerned about environmental and nutritional medicine. This summer I am releasing Dr. Shiv Chopra's memoirs. Entitled *Corrupt to the Core —Memoirs of a Health Canada Whistleblower*. It is introduced by MP Paul Dewar (NDP), lawyer David Yazbeck, and three recipients of the Swedish Right Livelihood Award, namely public health scholar and oncologist Dr. Samuel S. Epstein, physicist Dr. Vandana Shiva, and Maude Barlow of the Council of Canadians. Dr. Chopra's book covers his four decades as a Health Canada regulator during which he determinedly fought to uphold the Food and Drugs Act and follow its Regulations, in order to protect the Canadian people from unsafe drugs.

As you will recall, he and his colleagues, Drs. Margaret Haydon and Gerard Lambert, managed to have that Act obeyed, against all political odds, so as to prevent bovine growth hormone (rBST—a carcinogen) from being passed in our food supply. For that service to the public, as you will also recall, they were fired in 2004 on grounds of insubordination by your predecessor, then Prime Minister Paul Martin.

At that time, given your campaign promises of transparency and accountability, many of us, myself included, had hoped and actually expected that you would take the necessary steps to reinstate these scientists and support them in their exercise of due diligence on behalf of public health. However, on May 20th this year, the Canadian Association of Journalists listed you as the top nominee for this year's Code of Silence Award for "having muzzled cabinet ministers, civil servants, and particularly professional scientists." Then you closed the data base for freedom-of-information inquiries, a research tool meant to help Canadians keep their governments accountable and transparent.

Most governments, once elected in sufficient numbers to form a government, only partly fulfill their campaign promises. In general, the electorate is as forgiving of the human inconsistencies in our friends and loved ones as they are of broken government promises. However, when the inconsistencies become too overwhelming, the relationship breaks down, usually irreparably, and the injured party resorts instinctively to self-defense. We may have reached that point.

These glaring inconsistencies between promise and action in your administration make it hard to trust the stated intent of bills C-51 and C-52; they are not difficult to understand. If passed into law, they would pose a threat to public health, the rule of law, and the freedom of scientific research. Both bills, to my mind, display an equally unparalleled disregard for the spirit, and most probably also the letter, of Canada's *Charter of Rights and Freedoms*.

The public has been repeatedly told that the government has only good intentions with regard to C-51 and C-52. Now, it seems to me that the contract between a people and its government cannot possibly ever be carried out on the basis of trust. Laws are guarantees. Pronouncements of intent mean literally nothing.

The most recent attempt at calming down the tens of thousands of angry Canadians who have made themselves heard since April 8, has been a proposal to amend C-51; this was presented by the Honorable Tony Clement on June 9, 2008. Those amendments appear to be of dubious parliamentary legality, as pointed out by MPs Marlene Jennings in her e-mails, and as was stated in the House by MP Robert Thibault who suggested this was possibly Contempt of Parliament. MP Jennings wrote: "I've been an MP eleven years. It is the first time that I see such a thing! Normally, the government does not table amendments at committee stage, only after all the experts and witnesses have been heard."

Worst of all, Health Canada arranged for so-called "stakeholder" meetings across the country to reassure outraged citizens about C-51; this exercise bordered on the absurd: people were invited to meet with representatives from the largest drug companies, who were co-sponsoring most of these events, in order to discuss public concerns about a government bill which is supposed to regulate those very companies. Just how scary can it get?

We are in the midst of a public health crisis caused by food contaminated with health hazards such as pesticides, genetically engineered food plants that we now know promote systemic disease, and pharmaceutical drugs based on fraudulent science and therefore having become the leading cause of death. This assertion is supported by verifiable, non-industry funded science from around the world—I was as amazed and shocked to discover this as everybody else. I myself used to wonder if the "natural health crowd" was just a bunch of tree-huggers , but it turns out they are often mainstream scientists, some even Nobel laureates, and many are outraged refugee scientists from the genetic engineering industry itself. Much of the evidence is presented in this book.

With regard to pharmaceutical drugs being the leading cause of death, this has been made public by the premier medical institutions in the world and since 1998 has been the subject of many research projects published in the world's "big five" medical journals, including the *Journal of the Canadian Medical Association*. In fact, this line of inquiry was first started, with the cooperation of the United States FDA, by Professor Bruce Pomerance of the University of Toronto. Ten years ago, he concluded that properly prescribed and correctly taken pharmaceutical drugs might be the fourth leading cause of death in North America. More recently, Johns Hopkins Medical School refined this research, largely due to the increasing death statistics which became available in the intervening years, so that now it is *the* leading cause of death, outpacing cancer and AIDS.

As reported in the CMAJ, in Canada, at least 23,000 people die every year from pharmaceutical drug-related problems; these are only the *reported* deaths. Both the FDA and Canadian experts believe the rate is much higher. Due to this constantly rising death toll, the CMAJ observed on January 4 and March 15, 2005, that Health Canada is not adequately monitoring the safety of marketed drugs and has "demonstrated a structural inability to do ongoing safety monitoring of new drugs and devices."

Unfortunately, bill C-51 does nothing to improve this situation because it does not even define safety, while the Food and Drugs Act, which supposedly requires "modernization," has very clear concepts of safety in its regulations—the very ones that allowed Dr. Chopra and his colleagues to identify those dangerous drugs they persistently opposed. The same is true for C-52, and both bills share the fact that they import into the regulation of foods, drugs, and hazardous products the wholly inappropriate concept of risk *management* instead of risk *assessment*.

The difference between these two concepts is that the first assumes there will be a body count and tolerates some exposure to hazardous substances; the decisions to be made under such *management* have to do with how many bodies and how much hazardous contamination the government can comfortably get away with. Risk *assessment*, on the other hand, determines the level at which people are harmed for the purpose of *banning* such substances.

Defining safety in both bills would result in a huge number of drugs and hazardous substances having to have their original marketing approval re-examined for purposes of assessment and potential withdrawal—as the European Union is doing now. Many would have to be recalled because the original approvals were not based on the available science and often granted under political pressure. In medicine, we even know with which ones to start the clean-up. The CMAJ told us so in their June 2, 2008 issue: they include especially the antipsychotics that Truehope so successfully replaced with safe natural products that also are so truly effective. These and many other potent pharmaceuticals also end up in the water and are ingested by people for whom they were not prescribed—something C-52 does not even address. About 14 million emergency room visits take place in Canada annually only due to adverse drug events. Given there are only roughly 30 million Canadians, this number is staggering and suggests that hundreds of thousands of people have more than one such experience per year.

It is my understanding, that government is mandated to manage health care with integrity. Therefore, I was astounded when I read in *The National Post* on May 6th, 2008, that your former communications director, Geoff Norquay, was directly involved with the lobbying efforts of pharmaceutical companies to restrict the availability of the far cheaper (and far safer because of proven post-marketing experience) generic drugs. I also find it hard to swallow that within a month after one of your close colleagues, Ken Boessenkool, registered as a lobbyist for Merck Frosst, your 2007 budget had $300 million allocated for their genital wart vaccine (marketed for cervical cancer) that seems to have the highest rate of deaths and complications reported for any vaccine, namely Gardasil. This is very disturbing optics.

Not a single death is known so far to have been caused by a natural health product. One of the overheads I frequently show at lectures is a chart provided by the World Health Organization showing that the most dangerous thing one can do in an industrialized country is to be admitted to hospital, while the chance of being harmed or killed by a natural health product is the same as being hit by a meteor. What complicates this drug crisis further is the fact that pharmaceutical drugs are the source of enormous wealth and that Canada's is one of the governments that has supported the increase of wealth from that source, not the decrease of the damage these products are causing .

Your policies appear to be falling into the error Junius advised against: *arbitrariness.* It is defined in the Oxford English Dictionary as: "Based solely on personal wishes, feelings, or perceptions rather than on objective facts, reasons, or principles."

Throughout C-51 and C-52, all sorts of enforcement provisions are relegated to Orders in Council—away from public scrutiny, unencumbered by messy parliamentary debate, and certainly free from probing questions from the press. Most surprising, and absolutely unacceptable, are those provisions that have to do with foreign governments and regulatory agencies—in which Canadians had no vote. I doubt this is legal. Unless Canadians read the *Canada Gazette* regularly, they would not even know that some deal has been struck with a foreign regulatory agency and that those foreign provisions have suddenly become law in Canada.

This is incomprehensible in view of your own publicly stated concern about Codex Alimentarius, for example, in 2003 when you were supporting MP James Lunney's bill C-420. Yet, as Prime Minister, you permitted this: I found on Health Canada's website that as of December 7 of last year, a "confidential" agreement already exists for such regulatory cross-Atlantic importation with the European

Union and the European Medicine Agency. The only thing that seems to be still needed to make this all legal is the passage of C-51.

The Honorable Tony Clement's attempt at introducing some accountability into C-51 by changing "may" to "shall" in C-51's section 20.4, so now "the Minister *shall* establish, committees for seeking advice" on complex issues of science in medicine, insults every Canadians' intelligence. Unless those committees are independently picked, and unless such exercises are open to the public, and unless the results are debated in Parliament, this proposed amendment does not at all ensure that the same old cherry-picking of suitable "tobacco scientists" won't continue to happen: in the provisions in C-51 the industry is included among those the Minister may pick from for advisory committees. However, it is the industry that is to be regulated . In any case, who cares if "may" is now "shall," because none of the Order in Council provisions have been removed, as they should be, if any transparency and accountability is to be guaranteed to the public.

The assurance that the government wishes to introduce a separate definition for natural health products, reported in the national press for the past few days, amounts to nothing at all in practice:

- natural health products are still part of the overall regulatory intent of bill C-51;
- the Natural Health Products Directorate of Health Canada did not incorporate the 53 Recommendations given by the Standing Committee on Health a decade ago, and C-51 is not correcting that blatant disregard of its own government advisers;
- all natural health products are still regulated as a "subcategory" of drugs and assessed within the drug model of approval, as the Minister himself has written in his many e-mails to Canadians;
- and Schedule A still stands prohibiting most diseases from being treated by natural health products (contrary to the mass of mainstream scientific evidence showing that they can);
- and the (sadly) most lucrative of all disease groups (depression, acute anxiety, including bi-polar disorder) was deliberately moved out of the category of diseases which may be treated with natural health products—even though none of them are Prozac-deficiencies and the Truehope clinical trials have proven that even the

most severe mental health conditions are ultimately disorders of nutrient absorption and nutrient metabolization.

Telling Canadians natural health products will be recognized as a special category of its own means nothing unless that category is on par with the pharmaceutical drug categories and entered into law as a choice patients can make—which is what about 70% of us want.

The entire damage-control exercise undertaken in the past couple of weeks leaves a very bad taste in the mouth and will inevitably cause the public anger to increase, once everybody has figured out that they have once again been had.

That brings me to the reasons provided both by the Honorable Tony Clement and the information found on Health Canada's website regarding the necessity for these bills. The examples given are of a batch of fluoridated toothpaste contaminated with some toxic chemical . A simple, classic contamination event that was cleared up without difficulty under the existing law. Yet, the *daily* poisoning of people and the environment with fluoridation continues unchecked—despite the scientific evidence . There is nothing in C-52 that could even begin to deal with this problem, nor is fluoride listed among the substances to be banned—as it should, if science was heeded or, at the very least, the precautionary principle was applied.

Also mentioned were cases of alleged liver toxicity caused by a botanical remedy derived from black cohosh, and the contamination of some herbal product with the active ingredient in drugs that treat erectile dysfunction. Canadians are supposed to believe that this immense legislative exercise is justified and prompted by these tempests in a teapot. Given the ongoing disaster of hundreds of deaths per day from Health Canada-approved pharmaceutical drugs, and given the fact that almost every drug listed in the CPS has some level of liver toxicity associated with it, these examples are like having an emergency room full of people bleeding to death while the government attends to a nosebleed, as a doctor recently said at a rally in Toronto organized to protest C-51.

You may be interested to know that the information your Health Minister used to defend C-51 is problematic. He was apparently relying on reports now about 4 years old, still posted on Health Canada's website (the links provided for verification purposes are no longer accessible), and still not updated or substantiated. So, I went to the National Institutes of Health, whose entry on black cohosh was updated on January 16 of this year and therefore is somewhat definitive. It turns out, that the NIH is currently funding a double-blind placebo-controlled cross-over study on this botanical for treatment of menopausal symptoms. Furthermore, the American College of Obstetricians and Gynecologists recommends it as helpful and safe in their most recent consensus opinion, cited by the NIH. It is so safe, that it is considered a food and unregulated in the US. The alleged liver damage occurred in people who were on all sorts of drugs, including teenagers experimenting with hard drugs at the time of sustaining liver damage; five deaths are recorded, one in Canada, but the information on the circumstances can no longer be accessed.

In light of this information, it will be difficult to convince menopausal female Canadians, who are well aware of the risk of cancer and heart attack from standard hormone replacement therapy with synthetic drugs, that C-51 is needed to protect us from black cohosh.

As for yohimbine, it has indeed many properties in common with the active ingredient of Viagra (sildenafil), but the fact is that it was first nature that created aphrodisiacs, then drug companies made the synthetic analogs. Consequently, it is not surprising that the more likely story behind this otherwise unimportant contamination event is the potentially embarrassing federal case against Health Canada brought by Strauss Herbal Co.

As for the references to toxic heavy metals, the current Food and Drugs Act is perfectly able to handle those types of emergencies and has done so in the past; heavy metals are known to be toxic since before even that act was written and have been one of the reasons public health legislation began in the 19th century.

Finally, the explanation given that we must protect people against contaminated foreign foods, from China for example, is really a good case of the mote in Chinese eyes and the beam making vision impossible in Canadian eyes: if the government was truly guided by published science of verifiable integrity, it would be *our* food supply that should be cleaned up from pesticides, genetic and prion contamination and the like, so we could sell it to Europe, where they don't want our food products; they have even defied World Trade Organization court rulings, when ordered to import Canadian foods because they know much of our food products carry the risk of cancer, the potential of Mad Cow Disease, and increased antibiotic resistance.

Thus, neither the Health Canada website, nor the communications that have so far come from the Honorable Tony Clement, have given Canadians any reasonable justification as to why we need our Food and Drugs Act urgently modernized. In contrast to the non-information coming from Health Canada and the Honorable Tony Clement, one of your own caucus members, Dr. James Lunney made some real sense when he spoke in the House on June 9. In 2003 you strongly and publicly supported him when he introduced bill C-420—a bill which was informed by a radically different spirit and completely unlike C-51. On June 9, Dr. Lunney read into the record the statement made by the members of the 39th International Congress on Nutritional Medicine which was then winding up in Vancouver. It was a resounding critique of the intent and purpose of C-51, all of which still applies after the attempts at damage control by the Ministry of Health.

It would be so much more reassuring if bill C-420 were brought back to life and you, too, would return to the principles that you stated in your letter of support at that time. This now defunct bill was one of the main reasons Canadians gave you a hesitant chance at running this country. Much of what you said before you were elected had the full support of the public; most of what you have done since, has not.

Bill C-51 also shows a remarkable disregard for the independence of scientific inquiry. Even clinical trials would be subject to the Minister's arbitrary powers, both in agriculture and medicine. Possibly this is the most appalling part of both bills: the cavalier readiness to manage even science as if it were a commodity. This lack of respect for the necessary independence of science is coupled with a contempt for the courts, as best illustrated in the Truehope case.

In December 2007, almost two years after you took office, Health Canada proceeded to raise accusations against Truehope Nutritional Support Ltd ***as if no court order had been given*** by Justice G. M. Maegher of the Alberta Provincial Court. The order required Health Canada to back off totally and for Truehope to continue its clinical trials involving the treatment of extreme bi-polar disorder in some 3,000 patients, and this order was given under the Criminal Code of Canada; Health Canada failed to appeal it because there were no grounds for appeal.

What should have happened, following the July 28, 2006, judgment, is that Health Canada should have immediately cleared the requisite natural health products used in this trial, especially in view of the fact that the astonishingly successful results of this trial had already been, and are continuing to be, reported in the leading mainstream psychiatric journals.

Your government may go down in medical history as having stood in the way of one of the greatest medical discoveries—how to treat successfully one of the most expensive and difficult mental health condition that affects about 18 million North Americans and costs $ 4 billion in direct medical costs annually.

The sense I get is that there is a misunderstanding with regard to what—for the want of a better term—one calls "job description." A Prime Minister is not a CEO. Members of Parliament are not shareholders. Citizens and the scientific enterprise are not stake-holders. Canada is not a terrain for prospectors seeking a fortune. Most importantly, whatever happens in our national home is established by the courts, not by a Cabinet that misunderstands itself as being a board of directors. If Canadians agreed with such changes to the very essence of government, changes to the Constitution will have to be made first—by public consultation.

Canada is first and foremost the home of some 30 million people who do not wish to be used as means towards ends that their elected government decides upon and then merely announced as Orders in Council in the *Canada Gazette*. It is not the job of government to redefine citizens into customers for enterprises chosen by government.

Some 97% of us do not want to eat genetically engineered food. The Royal College stated in 2004 that on no issue in the history of public polling has there been such overwhelming consensus as on the public's rejection of genetically engineered foods. Therefore, why does your government not immediately proceed to pass bill C-510 and C-448?

More than 70% of us prefer medical therapies that have been developed by mainstream medicine from substances that cannot be patented and which do not carry the demonstrated risk of organ and systemic injury or death. So, why does the government not implement the 53 Recommendations of its own Standing Committee on Health?

Some 83% of us do not want to have our regulatory systems harmonized with those of the US and Mexico (or any other country or regulatory agency such as Codex) as proposed by the Security and Prosperity Partnership (SPP). By what legal right or mandate do you support the harmonization of health care and health regulation with other countries and large corporations? Parliament makes laws, corporations do not. We did not elect those corporations and we are not even partners in this Security and Prosperity Partnership; in fact, we are deliberately excluded.

Following the February 23, 2007, SPP meeting in Ottawa, one of its members, Ron Covais of Lockheed Martin (the world's largest weapons manufacturer whose products are hardly good for anybody's health) told a reporter: "The guidance from the [government's] ministers was: *'Tell us what we need to do and we will make it happen.'*… [explaining that] rather than going through the legislative process in any country, the Security and Prosperity Partnership must be implemented in incremental changes by executive agencies, bureaucrats and regulators. *'We've decided not to recommend any things that require legislative changes, because we won't get anywhere.'*"

I certainly hope they won't! Before corporations make our parliament buildings into a five-star hotel, the Charter will have to disappear, doctors have to be stopped from free and independent scientific inquiry, and some 30 million of us will have to become zombies through enforced intake of antidepressant drugs. I certainly don't think that will happen either.

Since bill C-51 does nothing for medicine and C-52 does nothing for the environment and neither protects us against known health hazards, it is difficult not to conclude that bills C-51 and C-52 are instruments for those "incremental changes" corporations want for their own purposes.

However, there is that major difficulty that stands in the way like a mountain: the *Charter of Rights and Freedoms*. It is the contract the people of Canada have with you. It spells out the terms of a civilized relationship.

Yours respectfully,

Helke Ferrie
KOS Publishing Inc.

1

Rape as Government Policy

by Helke Ferrie

"The relationship between a regulator and the regulated... must never become one in which the regulator loses sight of the principle that it regulates only in the public interest and not in the interest of the regulated."

—JUSTICE KREVER
Commission of Inquiry on the Blood System in Canada, 1996

The Oxford English Dictionary informs us that the word "rape" was used for centuries to mean primarily: *"The act of taking anything by force; violent seizure (of goods), robbery."* Gradually, the word was used for any "*violent, destructive, or abusive treatment of something*" with sexual assault being one instance of such abuse. The word "rape" came to my mind when I read bills C-51 and 52 for the first time and tried to imagine them in action. To my mind they are a parliamentary act of rape; the assumptions and notions in this proposed legislation constitute an astounding regression back to some really dark and nasty centuries we thought we had survived. These bills attack both property rights and personal autonomy.

But that is not all. They also attack our Constitution.

All modern constitutions arose out the great debates of the 18th century Enlightenment about the power of the state in relation to all aspects of life, especially to slavery, the education of children, the economy, the relationship between church and state, who should be able to participate in shaping events, and what constitutes the wealth of a nation. The philosopher who most profoundly influenced the course of how constitutions eventually were written, starting with the American Constitution in the 1770s, was Emanuel Kant (1724–1804). His moral philosophy taught the ethical injunction: *"Recognize that human individuals are ends, and do not use them as mere means."* In the 18th century this insight became of *political* significance. One could say that the history of the 18th and 19th centuries is the long story about how politicians, and the captains of industry (a.k.a. slave traders and owners) attempted to obey or ignore this ethical law.

Today, Kant's ethical challenge is as relevant as it was two hundred years ago. Indeed, his injunction now includes all of nature. Kant could probably not have imagined the ruthlessness of biotechnology and medicine as a business. Our "intellectual property rights" treaties, the debates about public versus private ownership of natural resources, the notion of "competitiveness" as an unquestioned value, the push to establish the correctness of an action through "cost-benefit" considerations, the patenting of the genes of everything alive for purposes of biotechnological exploitation ("biopiracy," Vandana Shiva calls it), and the continuous attempt to obliterate the difference between risk *management* and risk *analysis*—all ultimately come up against Emanuel Kant's insistence that control, profit, and ownership become acts of violence when the end justifies the means. Invoking the crude vernacular, which nicely encompasses all aspects of the concept of rape, one can say that according to Kant, screwing people for your own benefit is not ethical.

Bills C-51 and C-52 hit one like a searing blast from the past—not just from the time when the use of power over others without consent, was questioned, as Kant did, but also from much earlier centuries during which the concept of fairness arose and the concepts of property rights and fair trials were consolidated.

About a thousand years ago, insights evolved that today we take for granted, the right to private property, the presumption of innocence, the right to a public trial, the right to a warrant before having one's property taken, the right to know what one is being accused of, and the right to appeal a decision to an impartial authority. Indeed, we are so used to these rights, which were included in our *Charter of Rights and Freedoms* without the slightest fuss almost thirty years ago, that we hardly seem to notice when they are being attacked. Reading the parliamentary debates about these two bills, as they transpired in April and May of this year during first reading for C-51 and first and second readings for C-52, is astonishing. Somebody should have got up and ripped those two bills in pieces in public and announced that proposing them in a civilized country is an utter disgrace.

Nobody did.

A thousand years of British Common Law has produced a sense of security and an assumption of fairness that is now close to sleepwalking. That more recent, thorny problem of how ends and means should relate is at the very heart of our Charter: all judicial fairness is founded on the assumption that in a civil society everybody is an end and may not, if at all possible, be treated as a means to an end.

In this chapter the reader is invited to study five important documents, rather than accept my personal outrage. See for yourself. Make up your own mind. A country is ultimately a large family in which every voice has only value if the person thinks critically. One does not need a law degree to understand these bills. They are exactly as bad as they appear.

The first item is a ***Quality Initiative Bulletin***. Readers who saw the National Film Board documentary movie, "The Genetic Takeover or Mutant Foods," will be familiar with it. It is shown and discussed in it by the film's producer, Professor Louise Vandelac. The film was made in 1999 and premiered on January 22, 2000, at McGill University in Montreal. That was the day now known as the famous "Montreal Event" which took place on one of the coldest days in decades (minus 50 degrees Celsius, with the wind chill): a huge demonstration forced the International Biosafety Protocol meeting, attended by delegates from 135 countries, to stop its deliberations which were intended to finalize the acceptance of the "substantial equivalence" of biotech foods on par with regular, natural foods. That day also, a national opinion poll released its finding that 92% of Canadians did not want GE foods—since then the polls show the number at 97%. (The 3% that want the stuff, must be the manufacturers.)

This is an internal government document which instructs Health Canada employees to rethink their role. Instead of *public* servants they are now *corporate* servants. Here is a stunning piece of evidence showing government policy dismissing the public interest as secondary. Safety of drugs and medical devices are considerations left essentially to the manufacturers. The drug disasters and unsustainable health care costs that resulted from this policy shift are now known to all. In this document, Canadians are gently and quietly re-defined as stakeholders, who admittedly have something to do with parliament, but really they are just the vast customer base for the manufacturers who guide government. The bulletin even reassures Health Canada employees that they need not have a troubled conscience about conflicts of interest—because all this is in the best interest of everybody. Without public debate, Canada became smoothly re-defined as a gold mine and its citizens as Klondike prospectors.

The four items that follow are informal legal discussions on the two bills by a lawyer with a great deal of experience with Health Canada, as well as the text of those bills exactly as they are now before Parliament. You may skip the two sections that follow, which are taken from articles I recently published on these issues and their evolution in our society, and read all these primary documents first, if you like. Then you might be able to assess my analysis of these bills yourself and decide whether I am alarmist.

Bills C-51 and C-52

"You've done enough. Have you no sense of decency, sir, at long last? Have you left no sense of decency?"

—Joseph Welch,
chief attorney for the US Army to Senator McCarthy at the Un-American Activities hearings, June 9, 1954

Do We Want This?

On April 8 the Harper government introduced bill C-51 as an amendment to the Food and Drugs Act. If passed into law, Canadians would no longer have the freedom to choose between pharmaceutical drugs and natural health products. The two categories we now have, namely drugs and natural health products, would be merged into "therapeutic products" and thereby become subject to toxicity testing and efficacy trials exactly the same as now required for artificial pharmaceutical drugs.

Neutraceuticals, derived from foods essential to life, would no longer be *presumed* safe unless harm is proven, but become subject to drug testing routines and prescription requirements. Only pharmaceutical drugs are currently presumed toxic until clinical trials show at what dosage they might have some demonstrable therapeutic benefit. This bill also changes the definition of "sell," so even health-related advice for which one doesn't get paid, might become subject to Health Canada's approval or be deemed a crime.

The government's website, www.healthycanadians.ca, categorically denies this in their terribly awkward and factually challenged attempt at damage-control. However, mere denials and insistence on good intentions are not the same as guaranteed rights anchored in law. Raulston Saul put it very well when he wrote in 1999: "To reassure us, they lie to us, and then treat us as idiots by insisting on things we all know are untrue. Not only does this prevent a reasonable debate from taking place, but it also creates a very unhealthy relationship between citizens and their elected representatives."

Health Canada inspectors would have powers of enforcement exceeding those of the police, such as entering your business without a warrant and removing anything they wish, making you pay for the cost of removal, freezing your bank account so you can't take legal action, and fining you up to $5 million for disobeying the orders of Health Canada inspectors. Customary recourse to the law is evaporated as well, leaving quite literally everything up to the health minister's discretion.

Furthermore, if the Minister believes it would be good for us to incorporate a foreign government's regulatory protocol, such as Codex or the currently evolving Security and Prosperity Partnership (SPP), they would become part of Canadian law without parliamentary debate, simply by a cabinet decision (Order in Council). The government is assumed to know best.

Any university or institution proposing research involving nutrition in the treatment of disease, would have to be approved by the Minister, who would decide whether the expected outcome of such research would be desirable in terms of risk-benefit considerations normally applied to toxic substances. It is important to remember that virtually all the science on which natural medicines are based comes from mainstream research in universities—their safety and efficacy having been established over and over again, unlike industry-funded drug research which is mostly secret and/or the product of manipulated data which themselves are protected by law as "proprietary information." If the Minister doesn't like a research project, it would simply not happen. The health minister is now assumed to be clairvoyant on matters of medical and nutritional science as well.

Bill C-51 is likely in violation of several sections of the Charter, of our criminal code, and certainly violates the independence of scientific research. Most significantly, it ignores some of the most important Supreme Court decisions of the last 20 years. Those decisions affirmed that *disobeying* the law is not a crime if such disobedience prevents more harm than would have occurred had the law been obeyed, as in the 2004 Truehope case. The extraordinarily lucid legal judgment is reproduced in its entirety in Chapter 2 below.

What this bill *does* do admirably well, however, is to prepare Canada for joining the ongoing international United Nations Codex efforts to regulate foods and drugs world-wide according to the one-size-fits all corporate model enforced by the World Trade Organization. It also serves the Security and Prosperity Partnership (SPP) process which has as one of its central requirements that Canada, the US, and Mexico "harmonize" their health care systems and especially the regulatory institutions governing therapeutic products. The latest polls indicate that 87% of Canadians are opposed to this process, especially with regard to health care and therapeutics.

History Lesson

Back in 1998, Chretien's Liberals tried to amend the Food and Drugs Act so that food-derived therapeutic products (i.e. vitamins, minerals, amino acids, herbal medicines, etc.) would have been classified as drugs, thereby starting the harmonization process with the United Nations' Codex Alimentarius (tobacco-science based) fantasies about maximum upper limits and their nonsensical requirement for toxicity tests—none of which is supported by science. Natural products would also have become drastically more expensive as many would have required prescriptions—from nutritionally clueless doctors trained to mistake Big Pharma propaganda for the practice of medicine. Nutritional science is not mandatory in medical training.

So, in 1998, under the rallying cry "Don't treat our foods as drugs!" Canadians caused what Truehope lawyer Shawn Buckley describes as "the most successful petition drive in Canadian history." Hit by an avalanche of outrage, Health Minister Alan Rock tossed this sizzling potato to the House Standing Committee on Health which came up with 53 excellent recommendations for amendments to the Food and Drugs Act to "reflect contemporary scientific thought [because] the weight of modern scientific evidence confirms the mitigation and prevention of many diseases … through the judicious use of Natural Health Products."

We are still waiting for those 53 recommendations to be implemented. Instead of implementing them, as democratic procedure required, they put their heads together and concocted C-51.

In 2003, Conservative MP Dr. James Lunney (Nanaimo-Albertini, BC), a chiropractor for more than twenty years, sponsored bill C-420 which would have removed all food-derived neutraceuticals from the drug category (and the reach of Codex). It was supported by more than 120,000 signatures. In his September 2003 *Vitality* article he called for action: "It's time to take the club out of the hand of hostile Health Canada bureaucrats who know nothing about health and care even less." His original article is reproduced in its entirety in Chapter 2 as well.

His comments came in the wake of Health Canada having shut down the Truehope research project run by the University of Calgary and a Harvard University psychiatrist involving some three thousand people being treated with vitamins and minerals for extreme manic depression. It was shut down even though preliminary published results in mainstream medical journals showed this treatment to be far superior to conventional drug therapy and without any side effects. This determination to maintain the drug-based medical model as the status quo, is now proposed to become the law with C-51.

Truehope disobeyed Health Canada orders and continued to provide the treatment to the trial participants in accordance with international medical law. Health Canada sued Truehope. The court found this disobedience to be legal, citing previous supportive Supreme Court judgments; Health Canada's conduct was found to be arbitrary and inhumane, and Truehope was ordered by the court to continue its program in accordance with the public interest. Bill C-51 would make Health Canada's treatment of Truehope the norm and allow it to ignore those Supreme Court decisions as well as medical law.

Lunney's bill C-420 had the full support of Stephen Harper, then the leader of the Opposition. On April 27, 2004, Harper wrote this to many Canadians, including to me: *"Your comments and concerns regarding unrestricted access to natural health products and* [about the dangers of the] *Codex Alimentarius are understandable. Please know that the Conserv-*

ative Party of Canada supports freedom of choice for complementary treatments and natural health products. We believe that Canadians should have access to a wide range of health treatments, as well as an assurance that the products available to them are safe and effective."

He sent out this letter to show his endorsement of MP James Lunney's intent "to put the brakes on a bureaucracy out of control." Harper's Conservatives proceeded to promise Canadians freedom of choice between Big Pharma toxic drugs and bio-identical and nutritional therapies that science (not funded by Big Pharma) has empirically shown actually work. C-420 died when the Martin government fell.

What Happened, Stephen?

Introduced by the government on April 8, 2008, bill C-51 is quite literally a Big Pharma bill. That's because Big Pharma (and the food industry) is Health Canada's employer—not only through their user fees for their new product evaluations to be done according to their own time-lines, but because our government actually put them in charge. The *Quality Initiative Bulletin* of February 1997 (reproduced below) makes that clear, and the user fee arrangement details can be found in the *Canada Gazette* of January 6 and March 12, 1996. This user fee arrangement was made part of the system without parliamentary debate, having been passed by an Order in Council.

Furthermore, what most people don't know is that virtually all the raw materials for vitamins, minerals, amino acids, and more are made by Big Pharma which sells these to the natural health products industry. Given the multi-billion dollar payments ordered by courts in many countries for drugs like Vioxx, which killed or harmed hundreds of thousands of people, it is Economics 101 to cut out the middle man. Forget the conspiracy theories—this is straight business strategy.

Remember, according to research from Johns Hopkins Medical School, properly prescribed drugs—not diseases—have become the leading cause of death. In the annually updated drug compendium (CPS), which Big Pharma provides on-line and to every doctor's office and pharmacy, almost every drug has a bold-lettered warning about the potential of sudden death or irreversible organ or central-nervous-system damage. This universally acknowledged toxicity is being proven to be true by those hundreds of thousands of patients who fell victim to this toxicity. Many more such cases are now making their way through the courts. Among the biological sciences, toxicology is considered to be an exact science—a fact that gives liability law its anchor.

Understandably, Big Pharma publications nowadays extol the virtues of "biologicals" and "biosimilars," usually referring to bio-identical compounds that are liver-friendly, or applications that by-pass the liver to reduce drug toxicity etc. If pharmaceutical companies hope to survive at all, they absolutely must make the transition into biologically-friendly therapies and drugs that don't become magnets for billion-dollar lawsuits. So, why sell those bio-identical raw materials to much smaller natural products companies when you could make expensive drugs from them yourself and continue to milk the system as well as keep your profits instead of paying them out to victims?

Big Pharma persuaded Australia to pass a law similar to our proposed C-51 some years ago which, as predicted, killed all small and mid-sized natural health product companies. Now Australia has only one large nutraceutical company producing high-priced poor-quality stuff; innovation is also dead. Big Pharma has the whole market there and appears to control the universities, too. Cartel replaces competition and innovation.

Due to the enormous liability problems associated with toxic drugs, pharmaceuticals are rapidly becoming as difficult to sell as gas-guzzling SUVs. Health Minister Tony Clement found that out personally: until recently he owned 25% of Prudential Chem Inc., a company that sells raw material chemicals to drug companies. He had a hard time getting rid of these after the government's ethics committee told him this was a conflict of interest. The major investment analysts have classified pharmaceuticals as "don't buy" or "sell" —another compelling reason to take over the natural products industry.

Meanwhile, when the going gets tough—advertise and grab the remaining gullible! No wonder C-51 even has a provision that would remove the current barriers against direct-to-consumer advertising. If this were to succeed, all those cases of illegal drug advertising already happening in Canada would escape prosecution. In the US, sales rose by more than 40% in one year when that happened there, and New Zealand (the only other country that permits DTCA) almost killed its health care system because of the increased cost of drugs billed to their health plan. Now they are reversing this policy.

About 70% of Canadians are taking bio-identical natural medicines free of deadly side effects and do not require additional medication. If you take SSRI antidepressants for a long time, you are highly likely to get diabetes or cancer—and that's very good for business. St. John's Wort and Inositol are natural, cannot be patented, have no side effects, and are likely to cure the depression—and that's not good for Big Pharma business. Obviously, something had to be done to scare the living daylights out of the natural products industry and to take over this potentially lucrative market. Bill C-51 does just that.

Health Canada's history is one of passing as okay a never-ending stream of carcinogens, neurotoxins, gender-benders, and ecologically disrupting substance. Medical practice and agriculture are now replete with drugs carrying deadly warnings, and we have agricultural practices so lethal, most of the rest of the world outlawed them decades ago. With natural health products under attack, Canada's Medicare, already close to collapse, is threatened to be totally overwhelmed as all those hundreds of thousands of Canadians relying on vitamins, minerals etc. will proceed to get sick or sicker. (Here's is great stuff for another documentary for you, Michael Moore!)

Faced with evidence of such abysmal stupidity, we cannot afford to leave our health to the sweet mercy of this (or any other) government. Fortunately, Canadians and nutraceutical producers are becoming increasingly noisy and articulate. Second reading of C-51 was scheduled for May 8, but mysteriously didn't happen. Google might have the answer for the government's timely hesitation: on May 7, Google had 60,000 entries for "Bill C-51 + Canada." By May 11 it was 70,500.

Sources:

S. Chopra, *Corrupt to the Core: Memoirs of a Health Canada Scientists*, Kos, 2008, in press, orders 519-927-1049

M.McBane, *Ill-Health Canada: Putting food and drug company profits ahead of safety*, CCPA, 2005

For information on Direct-to-Consumer-Advertising (DTCA) go to *Canadian Medical Association Journal* January 2, 2007, p.19, which explains the current legal action by CanWest against Health Canada to remove prohibitions against DTCA on the grounds of being a violation of the industry's Charter rights of free speech (Big Tobacco was defeated on that argument years ago). Bill C-51 proposes dropping Section 3 of the current Food and Drugs Act which would be dropping that prohibition. The experts on DTCA, its effects on public policy, health and Medicare are Joel Lexchin of York University, Barbara Mintzes of the University of British Columbia in Vancouver, and Alan Cassels of the same university and co-author (with Patrick Moynihan) of *Selling Sickness: How The World's Biggest Pharmaceutical Companies Are Turning Us All Into Patients*, Nation Books, 2004. Some of their research and published letters to the media are available on www.healthcoalition.ca.

Note: This is a shorter version of an article published first in *Vitality Magazine*, June 2008.

Government Hijacked by Industry

"The Panel identified... serious concerns about the undermining of the scientific basis for risk regulation in Canada due to... the conflict of interest created by giving to regulatory agencies the mandates both to promote the development of agricultural technologies and to regulate it...

—Royal Society of Canada
Expert Panel Report on the Future of Food Biotechnology, 2001

In 2005 this whole exercise was attempted by the Martin government. Industry and government have been trying for quite some time to circumvent or neutralize the nation state grounded in law. The approach taken in 2005 was first to eliminate the known opposition by finding some pretext to fire those civil servants who are likely to object to "modernizing" the law, then tiptoe around parliament calling it a "minor" modernization, hope that no MP wakes up, and warn your corporate friends so they can put their army of lobbyists on high alert.

That was The Plan in 2003, but in early 2005 some MPs woke up with a start, the Senate went into high gear and asked questions, the media didn't play corporate ball, and a conference was held in Ottawa hosted by the Canadian Health Coalition for the purpose of exposing The Plan's horrendous consequences. At this conference the Public Guardian Awards were presented to those very civil servants who had been fired to prevent them from protecting us, namely Drs. Shiv Chopra, Margaret Haydon, and Gerard Lambert: they had defied a series of administrations and stopped bovine growth hormone in Canada and Europe, exposed the dangers of genetically engineered crops, and refused to approve harmful antibiotics like the now banned Batryl. They were fired for "insubordination" as soon as Paul Martin became Prime Minister. The Senate, however, had all three testify in April and comment specifically on two bills. These scientists told the Senate of their many decades of fighting for safe food and drugs against an ever-growing tide of "corporatization of knowledge and the instituting of private interests ahead of the public good," as Dr. Chopra said; they also described the pressures brought to bear upon them by the Privy Council itself to conform to corporate interests, in flagrant violation of Canadian law. That whole story is now told in Dr. Chopra's 2008 book, *Corrupt to the Core*. See details at the end of this book.

The Plan was to get bills C-27 and C-28 passed. The first was to dissolve all independent oversight on the food industry, allowing the industry to regulate itself as well as eliminate accountability, if harm was done. Bill C-28 was to do the same for all drugs. *The Globe and Mail* pointed out on November 10, 2003, when these bills were introduced, that they would have the effect of "preventing Canadians from suing Health Canada for negligence, even for flagrant failures like those that occurred during the tainted-blood scandal [and] greatly increase the likelihood that unsafe drugs and hazardous products make their way to market"; it quoted Mike McBane of the Canadian Health Coalition: "The evidence indicates that federal health and safety regulatory agencies have been captured by industry."

Following second reading, during parliamentary committee hearings in April, Cathy Holtslander of the Beyond Factory Farming Coalition, observed that C-27 would force Canada to adopt regulatory practices of other countries without any debate here (why not pension off all our MPs right now?). Furthermore, this bill authorized the privatization of all food inspection services—just what the GMO business needed. Both bills shifted all regulation from the internationally supported "precautionary principle" to the corporate "risk management" approach which looks at the profits first: if profits are still reaped from a product that harms a certain percentage of people, the food or drug stays on the market. Bill C-28 specifically exempted agricultural chemicals, drugs in any combination, pest control products, and food additives which could not be identified as "adulteration." They were also to be allowed at residues higher than currently considered safe internationally. This "harmonized" Canada with the US, of course. The European Union took note and their reaction is described in my article at the start of Chapter 5.

Ottawa's *The Hill Times* wrote about these two bills on April 25, 2005: "Hocus-pocus, adulteration is not adulteration if the Minister of Health says so! The effect of bill C-28 is to eviscerate the Minister of Health's statutory duty to protect the public from health hazards and fraud... [even for those] drugs which are believed to be carcinogens like estradiol ... [also] used in beef production."

Holtslander's submission, and those of others, such as the Council of Canadians, cut through the verbal manure by pointing out that the government's "Smart Regulations," which interpret these two bills, are designed to totally integrate Canada's regulatory practices with those of the US. *Now Magazine*, in a masterful article by Adria Vasil (April 21, 2005) dubbed these regulations as being "Canada's version of No Lobbyist Left Behind." Indeed, Vasil reported, that Big Pharma and pesticide companies were so happy, they fired off celebratory press releases about this initiative "within moments" of Ottawa's announcement.

What made those corporations so happy is likely one specific sentence in the report by the committee that concocted what they called "Smart Regulations" supporting these two bills:. It states that " *...the government should adopt international approaches wherever possible and limit specific Canadian regulatory requirements.*" Of course "international" actually means the US and Canada—the EU has very different ideas about these issues.

Holtslander observed: "We would completely abandon our power to set and enforce independent rules," because these new regulations make it plain that bills C-27 and 28 "put trade ahead of public safety, and integration with the US ahead of democratic Canadian control of what we eat." Here was Paul Martin's blank cheque to industry and his love letter to President Bush. So, let's tear up the Charter and disband the Supreme Court, since these proposed laws, together with existing and proposed trade treaties, have the effect of superceding national law and the basic rights of Canadian citizens.

For some reason our current Prime Minister chooses to forget that his predecessor's attitude on these matters was one of the main reasons why Canadians no longer trusted the Liberals. At the time, Harper understood, otherwise he wouldn't have written that letter to all those outraged Canadians who wanted Lunney's bill C-420 passed.

What does this mean in the real world? University of Hawaii research shows that chemical preservatives in processed meats increase the risk of pancreatic cancer 67-fold, or 6,700 % (www.prnewswire.com, April 26, 2005). Such findings could not be used for a legal action against the meat-processing industry in Canada, if bills C-27 and 28 become law, because we would be perfectly aligned with the US. This is how:

These bills are timed so as to ensure Canada will be ready to hand over the nation when CAFTA, the next trade treaty, comes into force. We sold the farm, the city and the hamlet with NAFTA, but there was still something left to sell: our right to know what is in our foods and drugs and to demand responsibility for damage. There is perfect logic to all this: why maintain *two* corrupt regulatory bodies (Health Canada *and* the FDA) when *one* will do just as well to manage the free-trade flow of goods of mysterious and unknowable quality? In a true show of solidarity President Bush, perhaps after watching the documentary "Supersize Me" and realizing that a lot of loopholes were still open for true accountability to creep in and that they needed to be plugged, he introduced in May 2005 the "Personal Responsibility in Food Consumption Act" already dubbed "The Cheeseburger Bill." This bill would ensure nobody is able to sue food producers, sellers or distributors, even if harmful or addictive chemicals are intentionally added to foods.

In another supportive gesture, the US government gave Health Canada the FDA Award in May. Then Canadian Health Minister Ujjal Dosanjh explained that it celebrates the "dedication of Government of Canada staff in achieving our cultural goal of improving the health of citizens on our shared continent." Well, tell that to the 23,000 or so Canadians and some 700,000 Americans who die every year of properly prescribed drugs, as the Canadian and American Medical Associations tell us. Those drugs kill because Health Canada and the FDA ask few questions, have the questions they do ask muzzled, treat Big Pharma's dubious science as trade secrets, and yield to political pressure to pass drugs they know are unsafe.

It would spoil the party to mention mad cows caused by feeding slaughterhouse waste to them. One French researcher observes in the 1999 NFB documentary, "The Genetic Takeover or Mutant Fods" that "everyone worships the golden calf and then they turn into mad cows."

And then there are those GMOs which now, in 2008, are known to cause a host of health problems, as documented by Jeffrey Smith in his compilation of the science involved, *Genetic Roulette* (see the suggested reading list at the end of this book.) We also must not forget the cancer and asthma burden inflicted especially upon our children solely due to pesticides, as the Ontario College of Family Physicians report revealed in May 2004. However, in May of 2005, Health Canada, true to form, interpreted its mandate of "improving the health of citizens" as including the approval of the carcinogenic and neurotoxic herbicide 2,4 D at levels which exceed the World Health Organization's guidelines for children under five. If bills C-27 and 28 had passed, even complaining about the corporate abuse of human health would be futile. For Health Canada these bills would, of course, provide great relief since they are facing negligence lawsuits in the range of $ 13 billion.

The encouraging fact is that the persistence of the nutritional medicine doctors is beginning to pay off: the mainstream is finally getting it. Three examples: On May 5th Oxford University in the UK announced: "Foods affect behavior. To ignore the role of nutrition is indefensible," Dr. Patrick Holford of the UK-based Brain Bio Centre said. "We're seeing outrageous imbalances in brain chemistry caused by the kinds of foods that sadly millions of kids are eating, and no one's doing anything about it." (www.brainbiocentre.com) (Canada and the US are doing something about—they are trying to pass legislation that ensures kids continue eating this junk and that their parents can't complain about it either.)

The *American Journal of Psychiatry* reported in April 2005 that the chemical additives in junk food cause such serious deficiencies in zinc, iron and the B vitamins upon all of which the brain depends, that the dramatic increase in violence can be directly explained by the resulting altered brain chemistry. The study noted also that 80% of North Americans are chronically deficient in these brain foods (www.organicconsumers.org/school/agression040405.cfm). Is that why they go to war all the time? On April 22 Guelph University reported in the *Journal of Nutrition* the importance of essential fatty acids to the development of the human fetus and especially the brain, but that most pregnant Canadian women do not obtain the required amounts in their normal diet.

The truth is out there but requires eternal vigilance. Hopefully, not "eternal" if at all possible! Maybe if the current bills C-51 and 52 can be killed, this and future governments will get the message that we are not as stupid as advertising tends to assume people are.

Note: This is a short, updated version of an article published in *Vitality Magazine*, September 2005.

DRUGS AND MEDICAL DEVICES PROGRAM QUALITY INITIATIVE BULLETIN

This is a second in a series of one-page bulletins on the Quality Initiative

QUESTIONS AND ANSWERS – Who is our client?

WHY DO I NEED TO KNOW WHO MY CLIENT IS?

- **All of the work we do should be of value to a client, otherwise where is the reason to do the work. To best meet the client's needs, you need to know who your client is and what they require.**

WHO IS YOUR CLIENT?

- **Your client is the direct recipient of your services. In many cases this is the person or the company who pays for the services.**

………………..

BUT WHAT ABOUT THE PUBLIC AS MY CLIENT?

- **In some cases, your direct client is a stakeholder. For example, when handling public complaints or providing information to the public.**

- **However, society at large is better described by the term stakeholder. The public could also be called a beneficiary of your work. Although they are not your direct client in most cases, the public has an important role in determining government policy. This drives the delivery of the service.**

HOW DOES A CLIENT FOCUS FIT IN A REGULATORY ENVIRONMENT?

- **Client satisfaction depends on both what your deliver (policies, products, and services) and how you deliver them.**

……………

- **There is no conflict of interest between delivering a service to a stakeholder and functioning in a regulatory environment. As you move toward a client service you are also ensuring the integrity of the programs determined by government policy. However, you are delivering that program in a client-centered manner.**

Bulletin # 2 February 1997

Source: Health Canada *Quality Initiative Bulletin* No 2, February 1997

DRAFT DISCUSSION PAPER ON Bill C-51

Prepared by Shawn Buckley, president of the NHPPA on April 9, 2008.

Purpose of the Paper

Yesterday the Minister of Health introduced Bill C-51 into the House of Commons. The Bill passed first reading. The following is a link to a version of the Bill:
http://www2.parl.gc.ca/HousePublications/Publication.aspx?DocId=3398126&

Although this only occurred yesterday, upon our reading of the Bill it became apparent that it may have wide ranging negative implications for the Natural Health Product industry. We are of the opinion that it would be prudent to draft an initial discussion paper to be circulated to stakeholders and more importantly to other stakeholder groups to begin discussion on the issues raised in this Bill.

Need for a Broad Consensus

We feel that Bill C-51 has such broad implications for the Natural Health Product Industry that it would be prudent for all of the various stakeholder groups to collaborate to see if an industry consensus can be reached in how to approach Bill C-51. If Bill C-51 poses a threat to the industry, unless there is consensus, efforts to protect the industry will fail.

Discussion Paper Only

This is a discussion paper only and does not reflect the position of the NHPPA or of the NHPPA advisory board. The thoughts and comments are those of the author, Mr. Shawn Buckley and are intended to foster discussion.

The NHPPA will formulate its position after industry feedback.

Source: Discussion Paper on C-51 by Shawn Buckley LLD

Invitation to Other Stakeholder Groups

We will be forwarding this discussion paper to other stakeholder groups such as the CHFA and consumer groups.

We would like the other stakeholder groups to analyze the Bill. We would then like to get representatives of the various groups together to see if a consensus can be reached concerning Bill C-51. We believe that it is important for the various stakeholder groups to take a leading role with their members on this issue in the event that their leadership is required to protect the industry.

Initial Points of Discussion

Scope of Discussion Points

Because we feel it is necessary to get this Discussion Paper out immediately to stimulate examination and discussion on Bill C-51, I will only focus on what I consider to be major points. I fully expect that as others examine this Bill and take part in the discussion that they will identify other significant issues.

Preamble to the Act

The preamble to the Act is not part of the Act and does not become law if the Bill is passed. What the preamble does is explain why the Bill is necessary.

The second last paragraph of the preamble reads:

> "Whereas the Parliament of Canada recognizes that it is the responsibility of regulated persons to ensure that only products that meet legislative requirements are available to the public;"

My initial thoughts is that this is a classic case of what George Orwell calls doublespeak. That is, a case of saying the opposite of what you are doing.

What is communicated:

> that it is the responsibility of "regulated persons" to ensure that only products that meet the legislative requirements are available to the public.

Source: Discussion Paper on C-51 by Shawn Buckley LLD

What the Act does:

> the Act gives broad power and responsibility to Health Canada inspectors to force "regulated persons" to take whatever measures the inspectors deem necessary to ensure safety. For example, see section 23.8 of the Bill.

I am troubled by this due to the following scenario developing:

1) currently roughly 60% of natural health product license applications are failing. The majority of these license applications are for single ingredient products which are easier to licence then multi-ingredient products. The percentage of failed license applications is expected to increase as more multi-ingredient product license applications are considered. My estimate is an overall failure rate of 70%. **This means that over 60% of the natural health products on the market will fail the licensing process and will become illegal.** At that point the manufacturer can wilfully withdraw them from the market or Health Canada can take enforcement action;

2) the NHPD has been given more resources to process license applications which means that the majority of the products will become illegal sooner rather than later;

3) Health Canada is currently going to universities to recruit university graduates as inspectors because Health Canada anticipates an increased need for enforcement, and

4) Bill C-51 gives inspectors new powers to force products off of the market.

I am not aware of Health Canada having enforcement problems with chemical drug pharmaceutical companies. My belief is that when Health Canada asks a pharmaceutical company to take a product off of the market, the pharmaceutical company does. I expect that this occurs because pharmaceutical companies would face huge liability issues if they failed to comply with a Health Canada request and then someone was injured. **If I am incorrect in this I am inviting correction as it is important for us to determine "who" the new enforcement powers are directed to.**

If Health Canada is not having compliance problems with pharmaceutical companies, then should we interpret the new powers in Bill C-51 as necessary to force the natural health product industry into compliance? I do not know the answer to this. I would ask you to analyse this as you work through the Bill.

Source: Discussion Paper on C-51 by Shawn Buckley LLD

The Move to the term "Therapeutic Products"

Bill C-51 moves away from the use of the term "drug" and introduces the term "therapeutic products". Indeed even the name of the "Food and Drugs Act" will be changed to "An Act respecting foods, therapeutic products and cosmetics."

The definition of "drug" remains unchanged but a new definition of "therapeutic product" is added which includes drugs, medical devices and cells, tissues or organs. However, the term "drug" is replaced throughout the old Food and Drugs Act with the term "therapeutic products".

Natural Health Products remain "drugs" under the Act. The only change is that now all drugs are referred to as "therapeutic products" in the Act instead of as drugs.

I have found this to be a very interesting change, and perhaps the most significant of all of the changes. I think this is perhaps the most significant of all changes as I asked myself the following questions:

1) why is a language change away from the word "drug" and to the term "therapeutic product" important to Health Canada, and

2) what part of the industry is this change for?

We think and communicate in language. The terms we use to define and refer to things affect how we think about them. That is why advertising firms exist.

The term "drug" in the Food and Drugs Act is not substance specific in that any substance is considered a "drug" if sold or manufactured for a therapeutic purpose. However, many people think of the word "drug" as referring to chemical drugs as opposed to plants sold for therapeutic purposes.

There is no confusion in the public's mind concerning pharmaceutical drugs. When the public thinks of pharmaceutical drugs they are comfortable with the word "drug".

There is confusion when the word "drug" is applied to natural health products.

Because there was no confusion concerning pharmaceutical drugs and the word "drug", is the change of terminology directed at the Natural Health Product industry or are there other reasons?

Source: Discussion Paper on C-51 by Shawn Buckley LLD

The change certainly affects the dynamics of the debate over regulating NHPs as foods or as a third category separate from drugs. Let's use the NHPPA's position on regulatory change as an example. The NHPPA Advisory Board has given the NHPPA the goal of obtaining a regulatory environment where:

(1) NHPs are presumed to be safe. A NHP cannot be taken off of the market unless the Government can prove that it is unsafe;

(2) there are different claims structures so that:

a) manufacturers do not have to make claims;
b) manufacturers can make limited claims, such as structure function claims with a low evidence threshold, and
c) manufacturers can make specific health claims if they can meet a higher evidence threshold;

(3) NHPs are not regulated as drugs. They are either regulated as food or as a third category separate from drugs and food;

(4) there are Good Manufacturing Processes that are appropriate for the low risk profile of NHPs, and

(5) there is a conflict resolution mechanism to settle disputes between the Government and industry members.

The last time consumers and the industry rebelled against Health Canada enforcement actions against NHPs, the rallying cry was "don't treat our foods as drugs". That rallying cry created the most successful petition drive in Canadian history. It was a large factor leading then Minister of Health Allan Rock to refer the issue to the Standing Committee on Health. The result was the 53 Recommendations which the industry would still like to see implemented.

Would the rallying cry have been successful with the new term: "don't treat our foods as therapeutic products"? Or to be more accurate: "don't treat or natural health products as therapeutic products"?

My point in all of this is simply to communicate that terms and language are important as they determine the parameters of how we think and can affect debate. The change in terms is being introduced deliberately by Health Canada and we need to consider what the implications for the industry are.

Source: Discussion Paper on C-51 by Shawn Buckley LLD

Expanded Definition of "Sell"

The old definition of "sell" is:

> "'sell' includes offer for sale, expose for sale, have in possession for sale and distribute, whether or not the distribution is made for consideration."

The new definition of "sell" is"

> "'sell' includes offer for sale, expose for sale or have in possession for sale or distribute **to one or more persons**, whether or not the distribution is made for consideration and in relation to a device, includes lease, offer for lease, expose for lease or have in possession for lease."
>
> (emphasis added).

The lease provision is not going to affect the NHP industry.

The change that is interesting is the new if you distribute to "one or more persons" you can be prosecuted for selling under the Act. Under the old definition, although you did not have to get paid if you gave product away, it is fair to say that the definition of "sell", especially when considered in the context of the Act as a whole, would be considered to be referring to a commercial venture. So for example a manufacturer giving out free samples would be selling.

Now the term "selling" will apply to a single isolated giving of a therapeutic product. So if I give my child a natural health product I am now selling under the Act and can be prosecuted. I doubt that the intention is to prosecute parents for giving their children NHPs, although that could happen under the new definition. Rather, as a lawyer who defends people and companies charged with violating the Act and Regulations, I see this as an open door to prosecute natural health practitioners, including naturopathic and homeopathic doctors.

Changes to legislation are supposed to solve a problem. When we analyse this change to the definition of "sell" we need to ask, what is the problem that Health Canada feels needs to be addressed by significantly widening the scope of selling under the Act?

It is going to be vital to obtain the input of natural health practitioners concerning this change.

Source: Discussion Paper on C-51 by Shawn Buckley LLD

Introduction of the term "Controlled Activity"

The Bill creates the following term:

"'controlled activity' means

(a) in relation to a therapeutic product manufacturing, collecting, processing, preserving, labelling, packaging, importing for sale, distributing, wholesaling or testing, and
(b) in relation to a designated therapeutic product manufacturing collecting, processing, preserving, labelling, packaging, importing, distributing or testing.

My initial thoughts on the introduction of this term is that it is again directed at natural health practitioners such as naturopathic and homeopathic doctors.

The Bill introduces the following section:

"13. No person shall conduct a **controlled activity** unless they are authorized by an establishment license to do so."

The change from our current regulatory scheme is the expansion of the site licence requirements. Section 27 of the Natural Health Products Regulations does not include: collecting, processing, preserving. Section 27 already includes manufacturing. By adding processing and preserving Health Canada is targeting something other than manufacturing.

Allowing Trade Agreements to become law without Parliamentary Approval – and the Sharing of Confidential Information with Foreign Governments and Agencies.

The following term is added to the Act:

"'government' means any of the following **or their institutions**, as applicable:
(a) the federal government;
(b) a corporation named in Schedule III to 10 of the Financial Administration Act,

Source: Discussion Paper on C-51 by Shawn Buckley LLD

(c) a provincial government **or a public body** established under an Act of the legislature of a province,
(d) an aboriginal government as defined in subsection 13(3) of the Access to Information Act,
(e) **a government of a foreign state or of a subdivision of a foreign state, or**
(f) **an international organization of states.**

(emphasis added).

Defining "government" to include foreign states or international organizations of states such as the United Nations, is important because of a change to section 30 of the Act. Bill C-51 adds the following to the regulation making power of the federal government:

"30(7) A regulation may incorporate by reference documents produced by a person or body other than the Minister of the Canadian Food Inspection Agency including
(a) an organization established for the purpose of writing standards, including an organization accredited by the Standards Council of Canada;
(b) an industrial or trade organization; or
(c) **a government**."

This addition allows the federal government to make documents prepared by foreign governments or bodies law in Canada by simply passing a regulation incorporating the document. **So for example, the CODEX treaty could become law without Parliamentary approval by simply passing a regulation saying it is now part of our regulations.**

Just so that everyone understands what this means I will explain the difference between Acts and Regulations. Acts are documents introduced into either the House of Commons or the Senate. They must pass three readings in both before they can become law. This process ensures that Canadians and their representatives become aware of proposed changes, have them debated in Parliament, and have time to contest them.

Regulations on the other hand are simply published in the Canada Gazette twice and then can be signed into law. Parliament does not vote on regulations.

This change to allow the federal cabinet to incorporate documents from foreign governments or organizations as law by referring to them in

Source: Discussion Paper on C-51 by Shawn Buckley LLD

regulations will remove Parliamentary scrutiny on issues that could fundamentally change the ground rules for our industry.

Because these changes were not made by accident, the questions are raised:

> **what purpose is served by removing Parliamentary scrutiny to the adoption of documents from foreign governments and institutions into Canadian Law, and**
>
> **does the federal cabinet already have specific foreign documents in mind?**

There are also significant confidentiality issues associated with the new term of "government" in the Act. Bill C-51 also gives the Minister authority to disclose personal and business information without consent to a person or "government" that carries out functions relating to the protection or promotion of human health (see sections 20.9, 21 and 21.1). There are some safeguards, but at the same time the Minister has new power to share personal and confidential business information with a wide range of bodies, both Canadian and foreign, without consent.

Product Monographs are "Deemed" to be part of your Label

Bill C-51 adds:

> 2.1 For the purposes of this Act,
> a) a product monograph of a therapeutic product is deemed to be a label even if it is not attached or included in or does not accompany the therapeutic product;

Approaching this from a defence counsel perspective, my immediate concern is that this will subject companies to misrepresentation and fraud charges.

I will need input from industry stakeholders concerning the implications when manufacturers disagree with the Health Canada monographs.

It would also be helpful to get feed-back as to why Health Canada wants this change. Put another way, what is broken that this is intended to fix?

Source: Discussion Paper on C-51 by Shawn Buckley LLD

A New Purpose of The Act

The Food and Drugs Act (i.e. the Food and Therapeutic Products Act) is given a new purpose which is:

> 2.3 The purpose of this Act is to protect and promote the health and safety of the public **and encourage accurate and consistent product representation** by prohibiting and regulating certain activities in relation to foods, therapeutic products and cosmetics.
>
> (emphasis added).

Section 3 Prohibiting Schedule A Claims is Removed

Section 3 of the Act which prohibited Schedule A claims is removed. I expect that this is in response to the CanWest lawsuit to have s. 3 declared unconstitutional.

New Restrictions on the Importation and Transportation of Food

Section 4 of the Act is amended to include restrictions on the "import for sale" of foods that are poisonous, unfit, injurious or adulterated. I do not see a difficulty with this.

This is part of a general change in the Act towards prohibiting importation and shipping.

Sections 5.1 to 5.4 are added which place restrictions on "prescribed food". A prescribed food will be a food put on a list by the federal cabinet. These sections prevent the importation from another country and the shipping across provincial borders of a prescribed food unless they have a "registration or a license". These foods can only be sent to registered establishments.

It is not clear to me at this point what danger or purpose these new provisions are directed to addressing. What foods currently need these types of restrictions?

Bill C-51 represents a tightening of restrictions and the increasing of Health Canada powers in all areas covered by the Act.

Source: Discussion Paper on C-51 by Shawn Buckley LLD

Importing is added to prohibitions in the former sections 8 and 9.

The new sections 8 and 9 are similar in nature to the old ones except that the prohibitions are expanded to include importing and conveying for sale.

Is Health Canada Approval now required for clinical trials involving food?

Prior to the creation of the NHPD universities did not get Health Canada approval to do nutrition research. So for example, if a university wanted to run a clinical trial to better understand the effect limes have on scurvy, they did not get Health Canada approval. Even with the creation of the NHPD, it is not clear to me that Health Canada approval would be necessary to study the effect of limes on scurvy.

It has also been the case that some clinical trial businesses did not feel they needed Health Canada approval for natural health products that had been in the food chain for a long period of time.

The new Act adds a definition of "clinical trial" as well as a prohibition on conducting a clinical trial for a therapeutic product without Health Canada authorization.

As I read the new provisions, I think that a study of limes for scurvy would now require Health Canada approval.

I would like input as to whether the current regime needs to be widened?

The need for pre-market approval becomes part of the Act as opposed to part of the Regulations – And the Criteria Changes.

The new section 12 provides:

> 12(1) No person shall advertise, sell or import for sale a therapeutic product that does not have a market authorization or is not a designated therapeutic product.

Source: Discussion Paper on C-51 by Shawn Buckley LLD

The Act does not currently require Health Canada pre-approval for the sale of drugs. For there to be a pre-approval requirement, it has to be added in the Regulations. So for example, the NHP Regulations require pre-approval.

This change will mean that there is a blanket need for pre-approval and any exception needs to be added to the Regulations.

What has changed is that the Act will now presume that all "therapeutic products" are dangerous and need pre-approval unless specifically exempted.

Again part of the general tightening in Bill C-51.

Concerning the criteria change: section 18.7 will only enable Health Canada to issue market authorization if satisfied "that the benefits that are associated with the therapeutic product outweigh the risks." Risks are not defined and so it is unclear if Health Canada will continue to use risk factors such the risk people will not seek "proper" (i.e. read mainstream medical) treatment if they take an NHP.

This criteria change is legislating an efficacy requirement. The NHPD will have to have evidence of efficacy before they can determine that the benefits outweigh any risks.

This balancing is appropriate for chemical drugs that carry a high risk profile. The industry will have to discuss whether it is appropriate for the NHP industry which has never caused a single death in Canadian history. **In any event, if Bill C-51 passes, the goal posts for the NHP industry will change which should require re-licensing of NHPs.**

After the Act is changed to require NHPs to demonstrate their benefits outweigh their risks, NHPs can only be exempted from this requirement if the federal cabinet is satisfied that their nature is such that a risk assessment is not necessary

I have just discussed how the Act will now require proof of efficacy before a product can be licensed unless it is specifically exempted. It needs to be appreciated, however, that there are limits on exempting products from this requirement. The new subsection 30(1.1) contains this limit as follows:

Source: Discussion Paper on C-51 by Shawn Buckley LLD

> 30 (1.1) a regulation may be made under paragraph (1)(d) [the section governing the designation of therapeutic products] **only if** the Governor in Council is satisfied that the therapeutic product is one that by its nature does not need to be the subject of an assessment of its benefits and risks.

This means that the federal cabinet could only exempt NHPs or a class of NHPs from the new proof of efficacy requirement "if" they are satisfied that "by its nature" it does not need to be subject to a benefit and risk analysis. This is very vague and there is no mechanism in place for making submissions to the cabinet.

If Bill C-51 passes, those in the industry such as our advisory board who would like to see NHPs to be presumed safe until proven to be dangerous will be disappointed. It would require a change to the new Act as opposed to a change to the regulations.

"Import for sale" is added to the old drug provisions.

The old drug provisions of the Act which are now the "therapeutic product" provisions now include a prohibition for importing for sale although this addition is not highlighted in the proposed Bill as other changes are.

A Prohibition against selling prescription "therapeutic products" without a prescription is added to the Act.

The Regulations currently provide that prescription drugs (that is those listed in Schedule F of the Regulations) are only available by those authorized to write prescriptions. This is now being put as part of the Act as opposed to the Regulations.

There are other changes and it is not clear to me yet whether or not it will now be Health Canada as opposed to the provinces who will be determining who is eligible to write prescriptions, although I view that as an area of provincial jurisdiction.

Why the prescription drug issue is important to the NHP industry is that Health Canada currently has a policy that if you can extract a prescription drug substance from a plant or animal, then that plant or animal can only be sold by prescription. So for example, green and black tea contain a prescription substance but Health Canada has not yet started attacking NHPs with tea as an ingredient.

Source: Discussion Paper on C-51 by Shawn Buckley LLD

Again part of the general tightening in Bill C-51.

Inspection and Seizure Powers are Increased

The inspection and seizure powers found in s. 23 of the Act are increased to:

give inspectors authority to enter private property to prevent non-compliance with the Act or Regulations;

enter conveyances for the purposes of inspections;

enter places where even a document relating to the Act and Regulations may be located. Currently inspectors are restricted to places where articles to which the Act or regulations apply are manufactured, prepared, preserved, packaged or stored. Note that document is defined in Bill C-51 to include information that can be read by a computer or device so if your blackberry is in your car the car can be searched;

take samples free of charge. This is interesting for two reasons. First, there is no limit to the value of the samples. Second, although the current wording of the section does not state that Health Canada should pay for samples they take, it was clearly the intention of the government that they do pay for them. Prior to the current wording the Act specifically set out that Health Canada had to pay fair value for samples they took. When the new wording was introduced the Minister made it clear that although the wording changed that the samples were to be paid for. This can be found in the Hansard for April 21, 1953 where the Minister is asked:

Q. In the matter of taking samples, the section says that the inspector may take samples and examine them. No provision is made in section 21 for leaving the sample. Later on in the bill we are going to come to the point of a court case on the analysis of a sample.
A. When an inspector takes the sample he pays for it, of course.

There is a general principle that the government cannot take property without compensating the owner. Is it necessary to abandon that principle in this case?

seize and detain **for any time** anything connected to the Act and Regulations, such as your products and equipment. This is a significant change. Currently, an inspector can only seize if he/she "believes on

Source: Discussion Paper on C-51 by Shawn Buckley LLD

Section 31 is amended to make it an offence not to do something that the Minister or an inspector directs you to do. Similarly it is an offence to do something the Minister or an inspector tells you not to do.

As discussed above, this is particularly problematic for natural health practitioners who would be violating the new Act if they failed to take health decision advice from an inspector.

An incredible increase in penalties for violating the Act or Regulations along with New Offences.

There are two types of offences under the Act: indictable offences and summary conviction offences. Indictable offences are considered more serious than summary conviction offences.

The current penalties are:

> for summary conviction offences a fine of up to $500 and/or imprisonment of up to 3 months for a first offence, and a fine of up to $1,000 and/or up to 6 months incarceration for subsequent offences, and
>
> for indictable offences a fine of up to $5,000 and/or imprisonment for up to 3 years.

The new penalties are:

> for summary conviction offences a fine of up to $250,000 and/or imprisonment of up to 6 months for a first offence, and a fine of up to $500,000 and/or up to 18 months of incarceration for subsequent offences, and
>
> For indictable offences a fine of up to $5,000,000 and/or imprisonment of up to 2 years.

This is not a doubling or tripling of fines. In the case of indictable offences the fine is increased by a multiple of 1000 times. In the case of summary conviction offences the fine is increased by a multiple of 500 times.

This raises the question as to why it is necessary to raise the primary penalty by multiples of 500 and 1000. This is probably unprecedented in Canadian history.

Source: Discussion Paper on C-51 by Shawn Buckley LLD

purposes Health Canada was going to have difficulty proving ownership. Now if in doubt Health Canada can simply seize enough of your property that you will go bankrupt if you do not claim it and hence solve the proof of ownership issue. It is highly unusual for their to be forfeiture without a Court order. The costs of destruction can be charged to the owner or person entitled to possession.

Inspectors are given apparently unlimited powers to direct your actions and do "anything" for even the slightest suspected violation of the Act or Regulations

The new section 23.8 gives inspectors extremely broad powers. If the inspector believes on reasonable grounds there is a contravention of the Act or Regulations they can direct you to:

a) stop doing something that is in contravention of the Act or the regulations or cause it to be stopped; or

b) take a measure that is necessary to identify or respond to a risk of injury to health that is related to the activity that is the subject of the contravention.

This means that if an inspector who does not understand the NHP industry, and who is not qualified to make health decisions tells a manufacturer to stop selling an essential product, or tells a natural health practitioner not to provide a product their patients rely upon, that the manufacturer or natural health practitioner is committing an offence if they do not comply.

The new section 24 also gives Health Canada the authority to require a product recall. Currently Health Canada cannot require a recall.

I am of the opinion that the recall provision is directed at the NHP industry. As discussed above, I do not think there is a problem with the chemical pharmaceutical industry recalling when Health Canada asks them to recall.

There are problems in the NHP industry with companies refusing to recall. This is because often it is dangerous for a NHP company to issue a recall. The most obvious example is that of Truehope Nutritional Support. The Alberta Court found that Truehope would have caused suicides and hospitalizations if they had listened to Health Canada's demand to take the product off of the market. The decision can be found at: http://www2.albertacourts.ab.ca/jdb%5C2003-%5Cpc%5Ccriminal%5C2006%5C2006abpc0196.pdf

Source: Discussion Paper on C-51 by Shawn Buckley LLD

When a NHP manufacturer asks me whether they should follow a Health Canada demand for a recall, I have to first get information from them as to whether or not any Canadians rely upon the product for their health. If they do then I have to advise them about the Criminal Code criminal negligence provisions which would make them liable to criminal prosecution if they removed a product from the market that people relied upon, and for which there were not obvious alternatives.

When Health Canada inspectors demand that NHPs be recalled or removed, they are in effect making decisions that affect people's health. In determining whether these inspectors should be given blanket power to recall and seize products, we need to consider whether we want untrained persons making health decisions. Currently to force a recall Health Canada would need to seek an injunction in Court. Under this procedure the Court would consider the risk of removing the NHP before making an order. In assessing these new powers, we need to consider whether we want to remove the Court's oversight which is currently required.

Bill C-51 adds the right to apply to a Court for an injunction. This right already exists under the Federal Court Act and so this is not a significant change except that it may enable provincial superior courts to consider injunction applications.

You are now told where to keep your documents, which includes computer records

The new section 25 and 26 require you to keep your documents "in Canada at a prescribed place". Remember documents is defined to include electronic documents and would also cover your web-sites.

Again part of the general tightening in Bill C-51.

Expanded powers to make regulations

For the purpose of this discussion paper I am not going to go into the specifics of the expanded powers except to comment that the Minister's powers to make regulations is expanded.

The new offence of not listening to an inspector

Source: Discussion Paper on C-51 by Shawn Buckley LLD

Section 31 is amended to make it an offence not to do something that the Minister or an inspector directs you to do. Similarly it is an offence to do something the Minister or an inspector tells you not to do.

As discussed above, this is particularly problematic for natural health practitioners who would be violating the new Act if they failed to take health decision advice from an inspector.

An incredible increase in penalties for violating the Act or Regulations along with New Offences.

There are two types of offences under the Act: indictable offences and summary conviction offences. Indictable offences are considered more serious than summary conviction offences.

The current penalties are:

> for summary conviction offences a fine of up to $500 and/or imprisonment of up to 3 months for a first offence, and a fine of up to $1,000 and/or up to 6 months incarceration for subsequent offences, and
>
> for indictable offences a fine of up to $5,000 and/or imprisonment for up to 3 years.

The new penalties are:

> for summary conviction offences a fine of up to $250,000 and/or imprisonment of up to 6 months for a first offence, and a fine of up to $500,000 and/or up to 18 months of incarceration for subsequent offences, and
>
> For indictable offences a fine of up to $5,000,000 and/or imprisonment of up to 2 years.

This is not a doubling or tripling of fines. In the case of indictable offences the fine is increased by a multiple of 1000 times. In the case of summary conviction offences the fine is increased by a multiple of 500 times.

This raises the question as to why it is necessary to raise the primary penalty by multiples of 500 and 1000. This is probably unprecedented in Canadian history.

Source: Discussion Paper on C-51 by Shawn Buckley LLD

Again, we need to ask who the changes are directed towards and whether they will be beneficial for the industry.

There are also new offences for wilfully or recklessly violating the Act or Regulations or not listening to the Minister or an inspector. The penalties for these new wilful or reckless offences are higher. They are:

> For summary conviction offences a fine of up to $500,000 and/or imprisonment for up to 18 months for a first offence, and a fine of up to $1,000,000 and/or imprisonment of up to two years for subsequent offences, and
>
> for indictable offences "a fine the amount of which is at the discretion of the court or to imprisonment for a term of not more than five years or to both".

Please note that in all of my years defending companies in Court, I have never seen Health Canada charge only one offence. In one case there were 73 charges. Under ten would be an exception. So when considering whether a company could survive sentencing, do not calculate a single fine for a single offence. Rather assume multiple fines for multiple offences.

These are penalties that few manufacturers or natural health practitioners could survive. **Small and medium manufacturers along with natural health practitioners now face bankruptcy for violations of the Act or Regulations.**

Directors and officers of corporations are now also personally responsible for violations of the Act and Regulations and so are also facing personal bankruptcy if there is any violation of the Act or Regulations.

Need for input

This draft document is admittedly only a cursory consideration of Bill C-51. However, because the Bill presents significant changes that may be extremely damaging to the NHP industry, we felt that it was necessary to prepare an initial discussion document to get the various stakeholders aware of the issues presented by the Bill.

It is essential that stakeholders and stakeholder groups take the time to examine Bill C-51 and to draw their own conclusions.

Source: Discussion Paper on C-51 by Shawn Buckley LLD

We will be inviting the various stakeholder groups to discuss the issues to see if there is consensus on how the industry should proceed and how they can take a leadership role in protecting the industry.

I anticipate that my very quick analysis will contain errors and that some of you will correct them. I thank you in advance for your input. I am also looking forward to issues that I missed or avoided being brought forward.

Shawn Buckley

Source: Discussion Paper on C-51 by Shawn Buckley LLD

nhppa
NATURAL HEALTH PRODUCTS PROTECTION ASSOCIATION

Draft Discussion Paper on Bill C-52 the Canada Consumer Product Safety Act

Prepared by Shawn Buckley, president of the Natural Health Products Protection Association on May 14, 2008.

Purpose of the Paper

On April 8, 2008, Prime Minister Stephan Harper introduced Bill C-52 in the House of Commons. A copy of the Bill can be found at http://www2.parl.gc.ca/HousePublications/Publication.aspx?DocId=3397415&Language=e&Mode=1&File=29. The stated purpose of the Bill is to protect consumers. The Federal Government has been aggressively advertising to convince Canadians that the new law will protect them.

The Government advertising is targeted at the strong emotion we share to protect children. The first half-page ad that I saw in my local paper began "Your Family's Safety – Our Government's Priority". The ad featured pictures of vulnerable children, which was successful in evoking an emotional reaction for me to support the Bill to protect my children.

The NHPPA has asked me to prepare this Discussion Paper on Bill C-52 out of a concern that the Bill may represent an unprecedented encroachment on freedoms currently enjoyed by Canadians. The NHPPA is focussed on protecting Canadians' access to Natural Health Products. Although Bill C-52 does not specifically target Natural Health Products, the NHPPA is concerned that Bill C-52 sets a precedent where Canadians will accept the removal of their rights in the name of safety. **Also, if Bill C-51 is defeated but Bill C-52 passes, Bill C-52 could be made applicable to Natural Health Products by way of a regulatory amendment to Schedule I of Bill C-52.**

Summary of Points Discussed In This Paper

Bill C-52 is being advertised as necessary to protect our families.

info@nhppa.org www.nhppa.org

Source: Discussion Paper on C-52 by Shawn Buckley LLD

nhppa
NATURAL HEALTH PRODUCTS
PROTECTION ASSOCIATION

Under the existing law the State can already:

- ban or restrict any consumer product under threat of million dollar fines and two year jail sentences under the *Hazardous Products Act*;
- make immediate orders banning or restricting any consumer product if there is a significant risk to health or safety. In addition to fines and imprisonment for non-compliance, the State can apply to the Court for an injunction which brings police enforcement of the order, and
- prosecute for criminal negligence or homicide under the *Criminal Code*. In some cases this can result in penalties of life imprisonment.

The real change brought about by Bill C-52 is not that it protects consumers, as the current law already grants the State significant powers to protect safety. Rather the real change is the abolition of procedural safeguards citizens currently enjoy.

Bill C-52 abolishes the law of trespass thus allowing the State access onto private property without any legal recourse.

Bill C-52 allows the State to seize property without a Court order, without reporting the seizure to a Court, and for an indefinite period.

Bill C-52 allows the State to assume control over the movement of private property without a Court order and without a safety concern.

The search and seizure powers in Bill C-52 are probably unconstitutional for violating the right found in section 8 of the *Canadian Charter of Rights and Freedoms* to be free from unreasonable search and seizure.

Persons can be fined and have property forfeited to the State for administrative violations. Persons so charged have no right to have a Court determine their guilt or innocence. Guilt is determined by the Minister. There is no defence of due diligence or of honest but mistaken belief. There does not have to be a safety risk to be charged with an administrative

info@nhppa.org www.nhppa.org

Source: Discussion Paper on C-52 by Shawn Buckley LLD

nhppa
NATURAL HEALTH PRODUCTS
PROTECTION ASSOCIATION

offence. The Minister who determines your guilt or innocence can keep seized property if he/she finds you guilty.

Discussion Paper Only

This is a discussion paper only and does not reflect the position of the NHPPA or of the NHPPA Advisory Board. The thoughts and comments are those of the author, Mr. Shawn Buckley and are intended to encourage Canadians to read Bill C-52 and to foster discussion.

This is an initial discussion paper only. The author expects that as feedback is received and further study of the Bill is undertaken, that the opinion of the author will broaden.

The NHPPA is inviting comments on this discussion paper. Feedback and comments can be forwarded to the attention of Shawn Buckley or Peter Helgason at info@nhppa.org.

For media enquiries only, contact Peter Helgason at (250) 318-5005.

The Property and Privacy Rights Affected by the Bill are Broad in Scope

The Bill has a very wide application. Section 2 of the Act contains the following definitions:

> "consumer product" means a product, including its components, parts or accessories, that can reasonably be expected to be obtained by an individual to be used for non-commercial purposes, including for domestic, recreational and sports purposes, and includes its packaging.
>
> "article to which this Act or the regulations apply" means
>
> (a) a consumer product;

info@nhppa.org www.nhppa.org

Source: Discussion Paper on C-52 by Shawn Buckley LLD

(b) anything used in the manufacturing, importation, packaging, storing, advertising, selling, labelling, testing or transportation of a consumer product; and

(c) a document that is related to any of those activities or a consumer product.

"Consumer product" covers anything from start to finish that makes its way into the hands of consumers, even if it is just a part of a consumer product. **A product remains a "consumer product" after it is purchased by the consumer**. The definition is not limited to apply only to consumer products prior to sale to consumers.

"Article to which this Act or regulations apply" covers all consumer products and all property including equipment, buildings, vehicles, media outlets, and labs that are used in the manufacturing, importation, packaging, storing, advertising, selling, labelling, testing or transportation of a consumer product.

In discussing the broad powers the new law gives the State to seize and destroy property without any compensation, it is important for Canadians to realize that the new law applies to:

> **most items purchased by consumers regardless of cost to the consumer, and**
>
> **a very wide range of commercial property including buildings, media outlets and vehicles that are not themselves "consumer products" and which pose no risk to the consumer.**

Consumers are not being told that as the new law is currently written, products they purchased may be subject to seizure without compensation.

Business owners are not being told that the new law gives the State sweeping powers to control and seize their property without a warrant and without having to report to a Court.

Context for the New Law – is it necessary to take away freedoms to protect us?

Source: Discussion Paper on C-52 by Shawn Buckley LLD

nhppa
NATURAL HEALTH PRODUCTS PROTECTION ASSOCIATION

New laws are supposed to serve a public purpose. In this case the State is advertising that the new law is necessary to protect our families from dangerous consumer products.

This raises the question: **are we so unsafe without the new law that we legitimately need the new law to protect us?**

For citizens to form a realistic opinion on this, it is necessary to understand the powers the State currently has to protect consumers from dangerous products. As outlined below the State currently can:

> ban or restrict any consumer product under threat of million dollar fines and two year jail sentences under the *Hazardous Products Act*;
>
> make immediate orders banning or restricting any consumer product if there is a significant risk to health or safety. In addition to fines and imprisonment for non-compliance, the State can apply to the Court for an injunction which brings police enforcement of the order, and
>
> prosecute for criminal negligence or homicide under the *Criminal Code*. In some cases this can result in penalties of life imprisonment.

With these tools already in place, the question arises as to what "other" powers are necessary to protect us?

Bill C-52 adds new powers. However, the real significance is that it allows the State to control and destroy private property without the review and supervision of the Courts or of other independent review boards. This raises another question: considering the sweeping powers the State already has to "protect" us, is it necessary to take away the independent supervision of the Courts that citizens have traditionally relied upon to "protect" citizens from the State?

Put another way: if the State already has all the powers necessary to ensure that consumer products are safe, how are we protected by allowing the State to control, seize and destroy private property without the independent supervision of the Courts that citizens currently enjoy?

info@nhppa.org www.nhppa.org

Source: Discussion Paper on C-52 by Shawn Buckley LLD

NATURAL HEALTH PRODUCTS PROTECTION ASSOCIATION

These are questions of fundamental importance that need to be addressed as people read and consider the need for the sweeping State powers found in Bill C-52. We look forward to input on these questions as we try to formulate answers.

The Hazardous Products Act.

This Act can be found at http://laws.justice.gc.ca/en/ShowFullDoc/cs/H-3//20080514/en?command=HOME&caller=SI&search_type=all&shorttitle=%22hazardous%20products%20act%22&day=14&month=5&year=2008&search_domain=cs&showall=L&statuteyear=all&lengthannual=50&length=50.

The *Hazardous Products Act* (the "HPA") currently gives the State significant powers to protect consumers. Under this Act the State can:

> prohibit the advertising, sale or importation of any consumer product;
>
> put restrictions on the advertising, sale or importation of any consumer product;
>
> if there is a significant risk to health or safety, **make an order prohibiting or restricting the advertising, sale or importation of any consumer product**, and
>
> demand any information from a manufacturer to determine the safety of a product.

Although the State has broad powers to make immediate orders to stop the sale of any hazardous product, the HPA also protects the property owner by having procedural safeguards that comply with the rule of law. These include provisions that:

> orders made for safety reasons expire after 14 days unless they are approved by the Governor in Council (i.e. the Federal Cabinet). This gives the State 14 days to determine if there really is a health risk in the situation where an order was made as a precaution;
>
> the order must be tabled in Parliament for review, and

info@nhppa.org www.nhppa.org

Source: Discussion Paper on C-52 by Shawn Buckley LLD

nhppa
NATURAL HEALTH PRODUCTS
PROTECTION ASSOCIATION

if the order is confirmed the property owner can apply to an independent Review Board to contest the order. In this way the rule of law is respected. The State cannot affect property rights without an independent review.

It is an offence under the HPA to ignore an interim order. Penalties include fines of up to a million dollars and/or imprisonment of up to two years for each violation.

Although there are significant penalties under the HPA to ensure compliance with orders made to protect consumer safety, it needs to also be kept in mind that the State can apply to the Federal Court for an injunction if an order is ignored. This can be done quickly. It enables police intervention to enforce the Court's order. The property owner is protected as the Court will consider all of the evidence concerning safety and can compensate the property owner if it is eventually determined that there was not a safety risk.

For the purposes of this Discussion Paper I should add that I am not certain that the Board of Review provisions would apply to an interim order under the HPA. There is some ambiguity in the wording of that Act. I have only done cursory research and have not found a case to resolve that ambiguity. It is my current opinion based on the wording of the HPA that the Board of Review provisions apply to interim orders. I look forward to feedback on this issue.

The Criminal Code Criminal Negligence Provisions

Under section 219 of the *Criminal Code*, a person or company commits criminal negligence if they do anything or fail to do anything it is their duty to do which "shows wanton or reckless disregard for the lives or safety of other persons." This means that if a person or company sold a consumer product which they knew was not safe or which they should have known was unsafe, they are committing a criminal offence and are subject to the penalties for criminal negligence found in the *Criminal Code*.

The penalties for criminal negligence vary depending upon the harm caused. If bodily harm is caused the maximum penalty is imprisonment for 10 years. If death is caused the maximum penalty is imprisonment for life. Persons who cause death by criminal negligence can also be charged with homicide under section 222(5)(b) of the *Criminal Code*. The penalties for homicide vary depending upon whether the homicide is characterized as murder, manslaughter or infanticide. If

info@nhppa.org www.nhppa.org

Source: Discussion Paper on C-52 by Shawn Buckley LLD

NATURAL HEALTH PRODUCTS PROTECTION ASSOCIATION

the criminal negligence is characterized as murder, the minimum penalty is life imprisonment.

The *Criminal Code* penalty of life imprisonment for criminal negligence and murder is the most severe penalty permitted in our Justice System.

Civil Penalties

Anyone harmed by a consumer product can sue for damages. Arguably it is the threat of bankruptcy posed by law suits that have historically ensured that consumer products are safe. Any person or company that sells a dangerous product faces bankruptcy regardless of whether they knew the product was unsafe.

The Abolition of the Law of Trespass

As a British Colony we inherited the British Common Law on trespass. Indeed, it has been one of the foundations of our right to own and enjoy property that no one, including the police, can come onto our property or interfere with our property. We consider this to be such a fundamental freedom that when suing for trespass upon our land, we do not even have to prove we suffered any damage or loss. The law has traditionally held the right to private enjoyment of our land to be so significant, that the mere trespass upon it is enough to get a civil judgment.

Our right to enjoy property free of trespass is not limited to land. We have the right to enjoy our personal property without interference. Anyone who interferes with our personal property commits trespass.

We hold the right to the private enjoyment of property as so important, that we have placed specific provisions in the *Criminal Code* to protect it. These include:

> section 177 which makes it a criminal offence to trespass near a private home at night;
>
> section 38 which makes it an offence to take away our personal property. It also allows us to prevent a trespasser from taking our personal property without worrying about being charged with assault;

Source: Discussion Paper on C-52 by Shawn Buckley LLD

nhppa
NATURAL HEALTH PRODUCTS
PROTECTION ASSOCIATION

section 39 which protects us from criminal prosecution for defending our personal property;

section 40 which enables us to use as much force as is necessary to prevent trespassers from entering our homes, and

section 41 which deem trespassers to commit assault if they resist attempts to remove them from a house or land. This section also allows persons to use force to remove persons from their homes or land.

Bill C-52 abolishes the law of trespass. Subsection 21(3) provides:

> An inspector who is carrying out their functions may enter on or pass through or over private property **without being liable for doing so and without the owner of the property having the right to object to that use of the property.**

Note that under subsection 21(3), an inspector is not limited to investigating the property owner. An inspector can trespass on your property if investigating another person's property and you have no recourse.

Currently consumer safety is protected under the *Hazardous Products Act*, the *Criminal Code* and Civil Law while respecting the law of trespass. **This raises the question as to whether it is necessary to abolish fundamental property rights under the justification of "consumer protection".** I look forward to comments on this question.

The Right to Seize Property Without a Court Order, Without Reporting the Seizure to a Court, and for an Indefinite Period

Section 21 provides in part:

> 21(1) Subject to subsection 22(1), an inspector may, **for the purpose of verifying compliance or preventing non-compliance with this Act or the regulations**, at any reasonable time enter a place, including a conveyance, in which the inspector believes on reasonable grounds that a

info@nhppa.org www.nhppa.org

Source: Discussion Paper on C-52 by Shawn Buckley LLD

NATURAL HEALTH PRODUCTS PROTECTION ASSOCIATION

consumer product is manufactured, imported, packaged, stored, advertised, sold, labelled, tested or transported, or a document relating to the administration of this Act or the regulations is located.

21(2) The inspector may

(a) examine or test anything – and take samples free of charge of an article to which this Act or the regulations apply – that is found in the place;

(d) seize and detain for any time that may be necessary

(i) an article to which this Act or the regulations apply that is found in that place, or
(ii) a conveyance;

Please note that these sections do not allow an inspector to enter into your home. To enter a private home an inspector has to apply for a warrant (see section 22).

These sections provide that, with the exception of a private home, inspectors can enter on any property in which the inspector believes a consumer product is manufactured, imported, packaged, stored, advertised, sold, labelled, tested or transported. This would include:

all media outlets that accept advertising of consumer products;

private property (excluding homes) in which a consumer product is stored;

all commercial property which is in any way connected with consumer products or parts of consumer products, and

conveyances such as trains and trucks.

Subparagraph 21(2)(a) permits the seizure of samples for testing. This means that subparagraph 21(2)(d) is not referring to the taking of samples for testing.

Under subparagraph 21(2)(d) there is no limit to:

how much property can be seized, and

info@nhppa.org www.nhppa.org

Source: Discussion Paper on C-52 by Shawn Buckley LLD

nhppa
NATURAL HEALTH PRODUCTS
PROTECTION ASSOCIATION

how long the property can be seized.

There is also:

no requirement for a warrant prior to seizure;

no requirement to report the seizure to a Court;

no mechanism to have the seizure and on-going detention reviewed by a Court or independent review board (as in the *Hazardous Products Act*), and most importantly

THERE DOES NOT HAVE TO BE A HEALTH RISK BEFORE THERE IS A SEIZURE AND DETENTION. All that is required is that the seizure be for the purpose of verifying compliance or preventing non-compliance.

Considering that the stated purpose of the Act is to protect our safety, it is curious that there does not have to be a health risk for there to be a seizure. If we are being asked to surrender our property rights in the name of safety, we should consider when analysing this Bill whether there should be a safety requirement for there to be a seizure and unlimited detention.

The State can Assume Control over the Movement of Private Property Without a Court Order and Without a Safety Concern

Section 23 of the Bill reads:

> 23. An inspector may order the owner or person having possession, care or control of an article to which this Act or the regulations apply to not move it – or to restrict its movement – for as long as, in the opinion of the inspector, is necessary for the purposes referred to in subsection 21(1).

Section 26 of the Act Reads:

info@nhppa.org www.nhppa.org

Source: Discussion Paper on C-52 by Shawn Buckley LLD

nhppa
NATURAL HEALTH PRODUCTS
PROTECTION ASSOCIATION

> 26 An inspector who seizes a thing under this Act shall release it if they are satisfied that the provisions of this Act and the regulations with respect to it have been complied with.

The purpose set out in subsection 21(1) is "the purpose of verifying compliance or preventing non-compliance with this Act or the regulations".

As outlined above an "article to which this Act or the regulations apply" includes all consumer products and all property including equipment, buildings, vehicles, media outlets, and labs that are used in the manufacturing, importation, packaging, storing, advertising, selling, labelling, testing or transportation of a consumer product.

This means that an inspector can tell property owners to not move private property to check compliance or to prevent non-compliance regardless of how trivial the compliance issue is and regardless of whether or not there is a health risk. I would expect that property owners would be surprised that the movement of their property can be restricted without the presence of even an imagined health risk.

The State can Assume Control of Private Property, Including Land, Without a Court Order and Without a Safety Concern

Bill C-52 enables the State to shut down businesses and to control public property for non-health reasons such as over a testing disagreement with the State or if the State believes there is a contravention of the Act or Regulations. The "contravention" does not have to be one that creates a health risk.

For greater clarity, these new powers permit the State to take control of business and of private property for trivial violations of the Act or Regulations even if those violations do not in any way pose a safety problem. Currently the State has to apply to a Court for a warrant to gain control of private property for alleged offences. The property owner is currently protected as the Court will only issue a warrant on evidence under oath that meets a legal test. Property seized under a warrant has to be promptly reported to the Court. The Court then supervises the holding of the property

info@nhppa.org www.nhppa.org

Source: Discussion Paper on C-52 by Shawn Buckley LLD

nhppa
NATURAL HEALTH PRODUCTS
PROTECTION ASSOCIATION

to ensure it is returned if proper to do so. Bill C-52 removes these fundamental safeguards. In effect, Bill C-52 moves us away from the rule of law. The sections to review are:

> **32.** (1) If an inspector believes on reasonable grounds that a consumer product is a danger to human health or safety, they may order a person who manufactures, imports or sells the product for commercial purposes to recall it.
>
> (2) The order shall be provided in the form of a written notice and must include
>
> *(a)* a statement of the reasons for the recall; and
>
> *(b)* the time and manner in which the recall is to be carried out.
>
> **33.** (1) An inspector may order a person who manufactures, imports, advertises or sells a consumer product to take any measure referred to in subsection (2) if
>
> *(a)* that person does not comply with an order made under **section 12** [section 12 concerns orders by the Minister for testing and/or the production of documents] with respect to the product;
>
> *(b)* the inspector has made an order under section 32 with respect to the product;
>
> *(c)* the inspector believes on reasonable grounds that the product is the subject of a measure or recall undertaken voluntarily by the manufacturer or importer; or
>
> *(d)* the inspector believes on reasonable grounds that there is a contravention of this Act or the regulations in relation to the product.
>
> (2) **The measures include**
>
> (b) **stopping the manufacturing, importation, packaging, storing, advertising, selling, labelling, testing or transportation** of the consumer product or causing any of those activities to be stopped; and

info@nhppa.org www.nhppa.org

Source: Discussion Paper on C-52 by Shawn Buckley LLD

(c) **any measure** that the inspector considers necessary **to remedy a non-compliance with this Act or the regulations, including any measure that relates to the product that the inspector considers necessary in order for the product to meet the requirements of the regulations** or to address or prevent a danger to human health or safety that the product poses.

(3) The order shall be provided in the form of a written notice and must include

(a) a statement of the reasons for the measure; and

(*b*) the time and manner in which the measure is to be carried out.

34. If a person does not comply with an order made under section 32 or 33 in the time specified, **the inspector may**, on their own initiative and at that person's expense, carry out the recall or measure required.

The Move Away from the "Significant Risk" Test

As outlined immediately above, sections 32 to 34 appear to permit the State to take control over businesses and private property. This can be to address a "danger to human health or safety" or "to prevent a danger to human health or safety".

At first this sounds reasonable as the entire purpose is to protect safety. One concern may be, however, that "danger" is not qualified. Many consumer products inherently pose a danger, firearms and some sporting equipment being obvious examples. As written the State can take control of businesses and private property for **any danger, however trivial.** This raises the question as to whether or not the State should be able to override private property rights for trivial safety concerns.

Under the *Hazardous Products Act*, the State cannot make orders unless there is a "significant risk, direct or indirect, to health or safety". By requiring the risk to be "significant", the *Hazardous Products Act* protects property owners by ensuring

Source: Discussion Paper on C-52 by Shawn Buckley LLD

nhppa
NATURAL HEALTH PRODUCTS
PROTECTION ASSOCIATION

that the State can only override their property rights when there is a "significant" danger. In analysing Bill C-52 the question needs to be addressed as to: whether the State should be allowed to take control of private property without there being a significant risk, as is currently the case.

In considering whether Inspectors should have the power to control private property without a "significant" risk, it should be kept in mind that Bill C-52 permits the Minister to make the same interim orders that can be made under the *Hazardous Products Act* if there is a "significant" risk.

The Abolition of the Independent Review Board

Under the *Hazardous Products Act*, State actions and orders affecting private property can be appealed to a Board of Review (see section 8 and 9).

An appeal to the Board of Review under the *Hazardous Products Act* is like an appeal to a Court. The Board of Review has the power to:

compel witnesses to attend before the Board of Review;

compel persons to produce documents;

compel witnesses to testify under oath;

hire experts to assist it to make a fair determination, and

employ clerks and court reporters as necessary to ensure a proper hearing.

It is clear that under the *Hazardous Products Act* property owners are protected by having an independent Board of Review which acts like an independent Court to adjudicate between the State and the property owner. In this way the current system upholds the rule of law.

Bill C-52 does not have the Board of Review procedural safeguard. There are two types of orders under Bill C-52: inspector orders and Minister orders (see ss. 32, 33, and 39). The Ministerial orders are a repetition of the power to make

info@nhppa.org www.nhppa.org

Source: Discussion Paper on C-52 by Shawn Buckley LLD

nhppa
NATURAL HEALTH PRODUCTS
PROTECTION ASSOCIATION

orders found in the *Hazardous Products Act.* However, unlike *the Hazardous Products Act,* there is no Board of Review.

Under Bill C-52 property owners can ask for a review of inspector's orders. However, that review is not conducted by an independent Board of Review with Court powers to ensure a fair hearing. Rather, reviews are to be done by "review officers". Subsection 36(5) suggests that "review officers" will be inspectors other than the inspector who made the original order. This is like asking one police officer to review the order of another police officer in the same department.

The review officer does not have any of the powers the Board of Review has under the *Hazardous Products Act.* They cannot compel witnesses to testify. They cannot compel the production of documents. They cannot take evidence under oath. They are not given the authority to hire experts.

There is also a very short time limitation in Bill C-52 which may prevent property owners from fairly stating their case. Under the current *Hazardous Products Act* a person has 60 days to ask for a review. They can ask for a review sooner. However, if they need 60 days to get the necessary evidence together, they can take that time. Under Bill C-52, property owners now only have a **maximum of 7 days to put their case together or "any shorter period that may be specified in the order"** (see s. 36(2)). Seven days or less is a very short period of time for which to gather and submit evidence for review of decisions that can destroy a business and which can involve the seizure of private property.

In assessing the removal of the Board of Review safeguard that we currently enjoy, the question needs to be asked as to: whether it is necessary to restrict property owners to 7 days or less to present a case as to why their property should not be seized or their businesses impacted?

Are the Powers to Take Control of Businesses and to Seize Private Property for Alleged Contraventions Legal?

Section 8 of the *Canadian Charter of Rights and Freedoms* gives us the right to be free from unreasonable searches and seizures. These rights apply to both individuals and to businesses.

Source: Discussion Paper on C-52 by Shawn Buckley LLD

nhppa
NATURAL HEALTH PRODUCTS PROTECTION ASSOCIATION

In determining whether State rights to seize property are "reasonable", Courts have drawn a distinction between administrative and criminal seizures. Administrative seizures are seizures that are necessary for the State to check to see if the rules are being followed. So for example, the taking of samples for testing is generally considered to be a legitimate administrative seizure.

For administrative seizures the State is not taking control of business premises or stock. Rather, small samples are taken to check for compliance. Courts generally do not require search warrants for administrative seizures.

Criminal seizures are seizures made by the State when the State believes that an offence has or is occurring. Criminal seizures usually involve the taking control of private property for evidence and/or to prevent the continuation of an offence. Criminal seizures are by nature intrusive.

Because criminal seizures encroach upon the property owner's rights, Court have found that to be "reasonable" criminal seizures can only occur if:

> there is a search warrant or other prior authorization for the search and seizure;
>
> the warrant or other prior authorization must be given by an independent person who is capable of acting judicially, and
>
> the issuance of the warrant or other authorization is based on an objective standard. Search warrants cannot be issued because an individual subjectively feels one should be issued.

The leading case on this point is *Hunter v. Southam*, [1984] 2 S.C.R. 145.

Because Bill C-52 allows the State to take control of businesses and to seize property when "the inspector believes on reasonable grounds that there is a contravention of this Act or the regulations in relation to the product", it probably violates the *Charter of Rights and Freedoms*.

I suggest that Bill C-52 probably violates the *Charter of Rights and Freedoms* because it authorizes a criminal seizure without a warrant issued by an independent person based on an objective standard.

info@nhppa.org www.nhppa.org

Source: Discussion Paper on C-52 by Shawn Buckley LLD

nhppa
NATURAL HEALTH PRODUCTS PROTECTION ASSOCIATION

It is important to note that an almost identical seizure power was declared unconstitutional in the case of *C.E. Jamieson & Co. (Dominion) v. Canada (Attorney General)*, [1987] F.C.J. No. 826 (T.D.). This means that the Government is currently trying to pass a law giving the State authority to seize private property in a way that has been found to be unconstitutional. When reviewing Bill C-52 the question should be asked as to: **why we would support a law which probably violates our right to be free from unreasonable search and seizure?**

An ancillary question would be: is it necessary to give up the current protection we have whereby the State has to apply for a warrant prior to seizing our property. In considering this question, it is important to note that it is not difficult for the State to apply for warrants. Indeed, an inspector does not even have to go to Court. They can fax or phone in under what is called the telewarrant process. This process is designed to enable inspectors to act quickly, while at the same time maintaining the rule of law.

The Creation of Administrative Offences

Bill C-52 creates two types of offences: criminal and administrative.

The new administrative offences create some interesting ramifications for property owners.

Section 59 sets out that for administrative offences **you cannot** defend yourself by saying you exercised due diligence or were honestly and reasonably mistaken.

Due diligence is defined in Black's Law Dictionary as:

> "such a measure of prudence, activity, or assiduity, as is properly to be expected from, and ordinarily exercised by, a reasonable and prudent man under the particularly circumstances".

All of this means that you can be convicted of an administrative offence even if:

> you were doing everything that a responsible business person would be expected to do, and
>
> you honestly believed there was no violation of the Acts or Regulations.

info@nhppa.org www.nhppa.org

Source: Discussion Paper on C-52 by Shawn Buckley LLD

NATURAL HEALTH PRODUCTS PROTECTION ASSOCIATION

Further, to convict you the State does not have to prove guilt on the usual standard of guilt beyond a reasonable doubt. Rather the standard is the lower civil standard of the balance of probabilities (see s. 60).

Aside from being convicted and penalized:

> when acting responsibly;
>
> without knowledge of any wrongdoing, and
>
> on the lower civil standard of a balance of probabilities,

where the administrative penalties get interesting is that they allow the State to keep private property upon an administrative conviction. This is found at section 64 which provides:

> **64.** Anything seized under this Act in relation to a violation is, at the election of Her Majesty in right of Canada, immediately forfeited to Her Majesty in right of Canada and may be disposed of, at the expense of its owner or the person entitled to possess it at the time of its seizure, if
>
> (*a*) the person is deemed by this Act to have committed the violation; or
>
> (*b*) the Minister, on the basis of a review under this Act, has determined that the person has committed a violation.

Finally, it is the Minister who determines if you are guilty of an administrative offence. Once you are served with a notice of violation you have to request a review by the Minister to contest the charges (see s. 52). **You do not get to go to Court to have an impartial Judge determine whether or not you are guilty or innocent.** Rather, the Minister makes the decision. Remember it is the Minister who gets to keep your property if he/she finds you guilty.

Under the administrative provisions you can be fined and have your property permanently taken by the State without a Court finding you guilty. Indeed, you have no right to a Court hearing.

info@nhppa.org www.nhppa.org

Source: Discussion Paper on C-52 by Shawn Buckley LLD

NATURAL HEALTH PRODUCTS PROTECTION ASSOCIATION

This is in stark contrast to the current *Hazardous Products Act* under which Courts determine guilt or innocence and property issues.

Administrative violations relate to any violation of the Act or Regulations. There does not have to be a safety risk.

In assessing these administrative provisions there should be dialogue concerning whether the State should be allowed to fine property owners and keep property without determinations of guilt by a Court as is currently required.

We are Responsible for the Costs of Seizures and Detentions Regardless of Whether the Seizures and Detentions were Justified

There is a long-standing principle in Canadian law that the State cannot take a citizen's property without compensation. It is also unprecedented for the State to invoice citizens for the State's cost in seizing our property. Bill C-52 moves away from this tradition with the following provisions:

s. 21(2)(a) allows the State to take samples for testing "free of charge";

s. 25 makes the property owner responsible for the State's cost in seizing, removing and storing the property owner's property. Alternately, the State can direct the property owner to move and store the owner's property at a place directed by an inspector at the owner's expense;

s. 27 makes the property owner responsible for the cost of destroying property that is forfeited to the State under that section;

s. 29 makes the property owner responsible for the cost of destroying seized property under s. 29;

s. 34 makes the property owner responsible for the State's cost in forcing a recall or taking other measures such as taking control of

info@nhppa.org www.nhppa.org

Source: Discussion Paper on C-52 by Shawn Buckley LLD

business premises. This is the case even if it turns out that the State was wrong in forcing a recall or taking other measures, and

s. 64 makes the property owner responsible for the cost of destroying property that is forfeited to the State under that section.

When one considers that there is no limit to the amount or value of property seized, or for the length of time the State can hold the property, it is clear that the costs to the property owner could be significant. By placing the cost on the property owner, there is no incentive for the State to move quickly concerning stored property, as there is no expense to the State.

Aside from the significant financial damage that consumers or businesses face if their property is seized and detained, these changes raise some interesting philosophical issues. Under the *Hazardous Products Act* the State does not currently have the power to charge citizens for the costs of seizing, storing and destroying private property. Are we currently facing such serious safety issues that it is necessary for us to give up the fundamental right we have to compensation if the State takes our property? I look forward to comments on this issue. I also look forward to comments on all of the other issues raised in this Discussion Paper.

Source: Discussion Paper on C-52 by Shawn Buckley LLD

C-51

Second Session, Thirty-ninth Parliament,
56-57 Elizabeth II, 2007-2008

HOUSE OF COMMONS OF CANADA

BILL C-51

An Act to amend the Food and Drugs Act and to make consequential amendments to other Acts

---

FIRST READING, APRIL 8, 2008

Source: Bill C-51

RECOMMENDATION

Her Excellency the Governor General recommends to the House of Commons the appropriation of public revenue under the circumstances, in the manner and for the purposes set out in a measure entitled "*An Act to amend the Food and Drugs Act and to make consequential amendments to other Acts*".

SUMMARY

This enactment amends the *Food and Drugs Act* to modernize the regulatory system for foods and therapeutic products, to strengthen the oversight of the benefits and risks of therapeutic products throughout their life cycle, to support effective compliance and enforcement actions and to enable a greater transparency and openness of the regulatory system.

It also amends other Acts in consequence and includes transitional provisions and coordinating amendments.

Source: Bill C-51

2nd Session, 39th Parliament,
56-57 Elizabeth II, 2007-2008

HOUSE OF COMMONS OF CANADA

BILL C-51

An Act to amend the Food and Drugs Act and to make consequential amendments to other Acts

Preamble

Whereas the Parliament of Canada recognizes the objectives of protecting, promoting and improving human health;

Whereas the Parliament of Canada recognizes that those objectives can only be realized through a continued commitment to the health and safety of the public;

Whereas the Parliament of Canada recognizes that ongoing assessment of information about a therapeutic product over its life cycle is required both before and after it reaches the market in order to support its safe use;

Whereas the Parliament of Canada recognizes that cooperation among regulators of foods, therapeutic products and cosmetics contributes to the health and safety of the public;

Whereas the Parliament of Canada recognizes that the assessment of benefits and risks is to be based on scientific and objective evidence;

Whereas the Parliament of Canada recognizes that a lack of full scientific certainty is not to be used as a reason for postponing measures that prevent adverse effects on human health if those effects could be serious or irreversible;

Whereas the Parliament of Canada recognizes the objective of promoting accurate and consistent product representation;

Source: Bill C-51

Whereas the Parliament of Canada recognizes that it is the responsibility of regulated persons to ensure that only products that meet legislative requirements are available to the public;

And whereas the Parliament of Canada recognizes that openness and transparency, including the sharing of information and the meaningful involvement of the public in seeking the input of those impacted by regulatory decisions, help advance understanding of risks and benefits and enhance the credibility of and public trust in decision-making;

Now, therefore, Her Majesty, by and with the advice and consent of the Senate and House of Commons of Canada, enacts as follows:

R.S., c. F-27

FOOD AND DRUGS ACT

1. The long title of the *Food and Drugs Act* is replaced by the following:

An Act respecting foods, therapeutic products and cosmetics

2. The heading before section 2 of the French version of the Act is replaced by the following:

DÉFINITIONS ET INTERPRÉTATION

3. (1) The definition "contraceptive device" in section 2 of the Act is repealed.

(2) The definition ""publicité" ou "annonce"" in section 2 of the French version of the Act is repealed.

Source: Bill C-51

R.S., c. 27 (1st Supp.), s. 191; 1993, c. 34, ss. 71(2)(F) and (3); 1996, c. 8, par. 32(1)(*g*); 1997, c. 6, s. 62

(3) The definitions “analyst”, “device”, “inspector”, “label”, “Minister”, “package”, “sell” and “unsanitary conditions” in section 2 of the Act are replaced by the following:

“analyst” « *analyste* »

“analyst” means an individual designated as an analyst under section 28 or under subsection 13(3) of the *Canadian Food Inspection Agency Act*;

“device” « *instrument* »

“device” means an article, instrument, apparatus or contrivance — including a component, part or accessory of one — that is manufactured, sold or represented for use in

(*a*) the diagnosis, treatment, mitigation or prevention of a disease, disorder or abnormal physical state, or its symptoms, in human beings or animals,

(*b*) restoring, correcting or modifying the body structure of human beings or animals or the functioning of parts of the bodies of human beings or animals,

(*c*) the diagnosis of pregnancy in human beings or animals,

(*d*) the care of human beings or animals during pregnancy or at or after the birth of the offspring, including care of the offspring, or

(*e*) the prevention of conception in human beings or animals;

“inspector” « *inspecteur* »

“inspector” means an individual designated as an inspector under subsection 22(1) or under subsection 13(3) of the *Canadian Food Inspection Agency Act*;

“label” « *étiquette* »

“label” includes a legend, word or mark that is attached to, is included in or accompanies a food, therapeutic product, cosmetic or package;

“Minister” « *ministre* »

“Minister” means the Minister of Health or, for the purposes of the responsibilities set out in subsection 11(3) of the *Canadian Food Inspection Agency Act*, the Minister of Agriculture and Agri-Food;

“package” « *emballage* »

“package” includes anything in which a food, therapeutic product or cosmetic is wholly or partly contained or packed;

Source: Bill C-51

"sell" *« vente »*

"sell" includes offer for sale, expose for sale or have in possession for sale — or distribute to one or more persons, whether or not the distribution is made for consideration — and, in relation to a device, includes lease, offer for lease, expose for lease or have in possession for lease;

"unsanitary conditions" *« conditions non hygiéniques »*

"unsanitary conditions" means conditions or circumstances that could contaminate with dirt or filth, or render injurious to health, a food, therapeutic product or cosmetic.

(4) The definition "advertisement" in section 2 of the English version of the Act is replaced by the following:

"advertisement" *« publicité »*

"advertisement" includes a representation by any means for the purpose of promoting directly or indirectly the sale of a food, therapeutic product or cosmetic;

(5) Paragraph (*c*) of the definition "drug" in section 2 of the Act is replaced by the following:

(*c*) disinfection of premises in which a food is manufactured, prepared or kept;

(6) Section 2 of the Act is amended by adding the following in alphabetical order:

"article to which this Act or the regulations apply" *« article visé par la présente loi ou les règlements »*

"article to which this Act or the regulations apply" includes

(*a*) a food, therapeutic product or cosmetic, and

(*b*) anything, including a document, that is used in an activity that is governed by this Act or the regulations;

"clinical trial" *« essai clinique »*

"clinical trial" means

(*a*) an investigation in respect of a therapeutic product for use in human beings that involves human subjects and that is intended to discover or verify the therapeutic product's

Source: Bill C-51

clinical, pharmacological or pharmacodynamic effects, to identify adverse events in respect of the therapeutic product, to study the absorption, distribution, metabolism or excretion of the therapeutic product or to ascertain its safety or efficacy, or

(*b*) an investigation in respect of a drug for use in animals that produce food, that are intended for consumption as food or in which the use of the drug could affect human health;

"clinical trial authorization" « *autorisation d'essai clinique* »

"clinical trial authorization" means an authorization issued under section 18.2;

"confidential business information" « *renseignements commerciaux confidentiels* »

"confidential business information" — in respect of a person to whose business or affairs the information relates — means, subject to the regulations, business information

(*a*) that is not publicly available,

(*b*) in respect of which the person has taken measures that are reasonable in the circumstances to ensure that it remains not publicly available, and

(*c*) that has actual or potential economic value to the person or their competitors because it is not publicly available and its disclosure would result in a material financial loss to the person or a material financial gain to their competitors;

"controlled activity" « *activité contrôlée* »

"controlled activity" means

(*a*) in relation to a therapeutic product — manufacturing, collecting, processing, preserving, labelling, packaging, importing for sale, distributing, wholesaling or testing, and

(*b*) in relation to a designated therapeutic product — manufacturing, collecting, processing, preserving, labelling, packaging, importing, distributing or testing;

"designated therapeutic product" « *produit thérapeutique*

"designated therapeutic product" means a therapeutic product designated as such by regulations made under paragraph 30(1)(*d*);

Source: Bill C-51

"document"
« *document* »

"document" means anything on which information is recorded or marked and that is capable of being understood by a person or read by a computer or other device;

"establishment licence"
« *licence d'établissement* »

"establishment licence" means a licence issued under section 19.2;

"government"
« *administration* »

"government" means any of the following or their institutions, as applicable:

(*a*) the federal government,

(*b*) a corporation named in Schedule III to the *Financial Administration Act*,

(*c*) a provincial government or a public body established under an Act of the legislature of a province,

(*d*) an aboriginal government as defined in subsection 13(3) of the *Access to Information Act*,

(*e*) a government of a foreign state or of a subdivision of a foreign state, or

(*f*) an international organization of states;

"market authorization"
« *autorisation de mise en marché* »

"market authorization" means an authorization issued under section 18.7;

"person"
« *personne* »

"person" means an individual or an organization as defined in section 2 of the *Criminal Code*;

"personal information"
« *renseignements personnels* »

"personal information" has the same meaning as in section 3 of the *Privacy Act*;

"practitioner"
« *praticien* »

"practitioner" means an individual who is authorized under the law of a province to prescribe or dispense prescription therapeutic products;

"prescription therapeutic product"
« *produit thérapeutique sur ordonnance* »

"prescription therapeutic product" means a therapeutic product designated as such by an order made under subsection 15.1(4);

"therapeutic product"
« *produit thérapeutique* »

"therapeutic product" means

(*a*) a drug,

(*b*) a device,

Source: Bill C-51

(*c*) cells, tissues or organs that are distributed or represented for use in

(i) the diagnosis, treatment, mitigation or prevention of a disease, disorder or abnormal physical state, or its symptoms, in human beings or animals, or

(ii) restoring, correcting or modifying the body structure of human beings or animals or the functioning of parts of the bodies of human beings or animals, or

(*d*) a combination of two or more of the things referred to in paragraphs (*a*) to (*c*);

(7) Section 2 of the French version of the Act is amended by adding the following in alphabetical order:

« publicité » *"advertisement"*

« publicité » S'entend notamment de toute présentation visant par un moyen quelconque à encourager directement ou indirectement la vente d'un aliment, d'un produit thérapeutique ou d'un cosmétique.

1993, c. 34, s. 72(F)

4. The headings before section 3 and sections 3 and 4 of the Act are replaced by the following:

Product monographs and contact lenses

2.1 For the purposes of this Act,

(*a*) a product monograph of a therapeutic product is deemed to be a label even if it is not attached to or included in or does not accompany the therapeutic product; and

(*b*) a contact lens is deemed to be a device.

Clinical trial authorization or market authorization

2.2 For the purposes of this Act, a therapeutic product has a clinical trial authorization or a market authorization if, at the relevant time, a person is the holder of a clinical trial authorization or a market authorization in respect of the therapeutic product.

PURPOSE

Purpose

2.3 The purpose of this Act is to protect and promote the health and safety of the public and encourage accurate and consistent product representation by prohibiting and regulating certain activities in relation to foods, therapeutic products and cosmetics.

Source: Bill C-51

PROHIBITIONS

GENERAL

False or misleading information

3. No person shall knowingly provide the Minister with false or misleading information in relation to a matter under this Act or the regulations, including in relation to an application for a licence, registration or authorization.

Tampering

3.1 (1) No person shall tamper with a food, therapeutic product or cosmetic — or its label or package — with the intent to

(*a*) render the food, therapeutic product or cosmetic injurious to human health; or

(*b*) cause a reasonable apprehension in others that the food, therapeutic product or cosmetic is injurious to human health without themself believing that it is so.

Selling or importing for sale

(2) No person shall sell or import for sale a food, therapeutic product or cosmetic that was tampered with in order to render it injurious to human health.

Threats

(3) No person shall threaten to tamper with a food, therapeutic product or cosmetic in order to render it injurious to human health.

Hoaxes

3.2 No person shall — knowing information to be false or being reckless as to its truth — communicate or cause to be communicated that information with the intent to cause a reasonable apprehension in others that a food, therapeutic product or cosmetic is adulterated, was manufactured, processed, prepared, preserved, packaged, stored or conveyed under unsanitary conditions or was tampered with in order to render it injurious to human health.

FOODS

Prohibited sales and imports

4. No person shall sell or import for sale a food that

(*a*) has a poisonous or harmful substance in or on it;

(*b*) is unfit for human consumption;

(*c*) is injurious to human health;

(*d*) is adulterated; or

Source: Bill C-51

(*e*) was manufactured, processed, prepared, preserved, packaged, stored or conveyed under unsanitary conditions.

5. (1) Subsection 5(1) of the Act is replaced by the following:

Deception, etc.

5. (1) No person shall manufacture, process, label, package, sell, import for sale or advertise a food in a manner that is false, misleading or deceptive or is likely to create an erroneous impression regarding its character, value, quantity, composition, merit, safety or origin.

(2) Subsection 5(2) of the English version of the Act is replaced by the following:

Labelled or packaged contrary to regulations

(2) A food that is not labelled or packaged as required by, or is labelled or packaged contrary to, the regulations is deemed to be labelled or packaged contrary to subsection (1).

6. The Act is amended by adding the following after section 5:

Importation

5.1 No person shall import a prescribed food for sale unless they are authorized by a registration or licence to do so.

Interprovincial trade — licence or registration required

5.2 No person shall send or convey from one province to another a prescribed food that is intended for sale unless they are authorized by a registration or licence to do so.

Interprovincial trade — persons conducting prescribed activities

5.3 No person shall send or convey from one province to another a prescribed food that is intended for sale unless the persons who conduct prescribed activities relating to the prescribed food are authorized by a registration or licence to do so.

Interprovincial trade — establishments

5.4 No person shall send or convey from one province to another a prescribed food that is intended for sale unless the establishments in which prescribed activities relating to the prescribed food are conducted are registered.

R.S., c. 27 (3rd Supp.), s. 1

7. Subsection 6(2) of the Act is repealed.

Source: Bill C-51

8. Sections 7 to 21 and the headings after section 21 of the Act are replaced by the following:

Unsanitary conditions

7. No person shall manufacture, process, prepare, preserve, package, store or convey for sale any food under unsanitary conditions.

THERAPEUTIC PRODUCTS

Adulterated products

8. No person shall sell or import for sale a therapeutic product that is adulterated.

Unsanitary conditions — manufacture, etc.

9. (1) No person shall manufacture, collect, process, prepare, preserve, package, store or convey for sale a therapeutic product under unsanitary conditions.

Unsanitary conditions — sell, etc.

(2) No person shall sell or import for sale a therapeutic product that was manufactured, collected, processed, prepared, preserved, packaged, stored or conveyed under unsanitary conditions.

No clinical trial without authorization

10. No person shall conduct a clinical trial in respect of a therapeutic product that does not have a market authorization unless they are authorized by a clinical trial authorization to do so.

No clinical trial contrary to regulations

11. No person shall conduct a clinical trial in respect of a therapeutic product unless they do so in accordance with the regulations.

Selling, advertising and importing

12. (1) No person shall advertise, sell or import for sale a therapeutic product that does not have a market authorization or is not a designated therapeutic product.

Exception

(2) A person does not contravene subsection (1) if

(*a*) they are the holder of a clinical trial authorization and the advertising, selling or importing is for the purpose of a clinical trial to which the authorization relates; or

(*b*) they sell the therapeutic product to a person who is the holder of a clinical trial authorization or they import it for sale to that person.

Source: Bill C-51

Conducting controlled activity

13. No person shall conduct a controlled activity unless they are authorized by an establishment licence to do so.

Deception, etc.

14. No person shall manufacture, process, label, package, sell, import for sale or advertise a therapeutic product in a manner that is false, misleading or deceptive or is likely to create an erroneous impression regarding its benefits, risks, conditions of use, quality, quantity, composition, design, construction, performance, origin or authorization status.

Counterfeiting

15. No person shall manufacture, label, package, sell, import for sale or advertise a therapeutic product that resembles one that has a market authorization or establishment licence and is likely to be mistaken for the one that has a market authorization or establishment licence.

Prescription therapeutic products — unauthorized sale

15.1 (1) No person shall sell a prescription therapeutic product unless

(*a*) they are a practitioner who is authorized to prescribe the prescription therapeutic product;

(*b*) the sale is made under a prescription that was received by or transferred to them in the prescribed manner;

(*c*) the sale is to a person who belongs to a prescribed class of persons; or

(*d*) the sale is made in the prescribed circumstances.

Unauthorized advertising

(2) No person shall advertise a prescription therapeutic product to a person other than a practitioner unless they are authorized by the regulations to do so.

Importation

(3) No person shall import a prescription therapeutic product unless

(*a*) they belong to a prescribed class of persons;

(*b*) they are a practitioner;

(*c*) they are an individual, the product is on their person at the time that it is imported, the product is for their use or the use of an

Source: Bill C-51

accompanying dependant and the quantity does not exceed the quantity required for a 90-day period; or

(*d*) the importation is made in the prescribed circumstances.

Designation

(4) Subject to the regulations, the Minister may, by order, designate a therapeutic product — either individually or by class — as a prescription therapeutic product for the purposes of this section.

Samples — drugs

15.2 (1) No person shall distribute or cause to be distributed a drug as a sample.

Exception

(2) Subsection (1) does not apply to the distribution under prescribed conditions of a sample of a drug by or to a practitioner.

Prohibited sales and imports

16. No person shall sell or import for sale a cosmetic that

(*a*) presents a significant risk of injury to health if it is used according to directions or under customary or usual conditions;

(*b*) is adulterated; or

(*c*) was manufactured, processed, prepared, preserved, packaged, stored or conveyed under unsanitary conditions.

Deception, etc.

16.1 No person shall manufacture, process, label, package, sell, import for sale or advertise a cosmetic in a manner that is false, misleading or deceptive or is likely to create an erroneous impression regarding its character, value, quantity, composition, merit or safety.

If standard prescribed

17. If a standard has been prescribed for a cosmetic, no person shall label, package, sell, import for sale or advertise anything in a manner such that it is likely to be mistaken for the cosmetic unless it complies with the prescribed standard.

Source: Bill C-51

Unsanitary conditions

18. No person shall manufacture, process, prepare, preserve, package, store or convey for sale a cosmetic under unsanitary conditions.

AUTHORIZATIONS AND LICENCES

FOODS

Ministerial authorization

18.1 (1) Subject to the regulations, the Minister may, on application

(*a*) register a person, or issue a licence to a person, authorizing them to import a prescribed food for sale;

(*b*) register a person, or issue a licence to a person, authorizing them to send or convey from one province to another a prescribed food that is intended for sale;

(*c*) register a person, or issue a licence to a person, authorizing them to conduct a prescribed activity in relation to a prescribed food that is intended for sale and is to be sent or conveyed from one province to another; or

(*d*) register an establishment authorizing a person to conduct a prescribed activity in the establishment in relation to a prescribed food that is intended for sale and is to be sent or conveyed from one province to another.

Terms and conditions — regulations

(2) A registration or licence is deemed to be subject to the terms and conditions that are prescribed from time to time.

Terms and conditions — Minister

(3) A registration or licence is subject to the additional terms and conditions that the Minister considers appropriate.

Obligation to comply

(4) The person who is authorized to conduct an activity under subsection (1) shall comply with the terms and conditions to which the registration or licence, as the case may be, is subject.

Source: Bill C-51

CLINICAL TRIAL AUTHORIZATIONS

Issuance

18.2 (1) Subject to the regulations, the Minister may, on application, issue a clinical trial authorization to a person in respect of therapeutic products.

Terms and conditions — regulations

(2) The clinical trial authorization is deemed to be subject to the terms and conditions that are prescribed from time to time.

Terms and conditions — Minister

(3) The Minister may issue the clinical trial authorization subject to the additional terms and conditions that he or she considers appropriate.

Obligation to comply

(4) The holder of the clinical trial authorization shall comply with the terms and conditions to which the authorization is subject.

No transfer without consent

18.3 A clinical trial authorization is not transferable without the Minister's consent.

Amendment

18.4 (1) Subject to the regulations, the Minister may, on his or her own initiative or on the application of the holder of the authorization, amend a clinical trial authorization or the terms and conditions to which it is subject other than a prescribed term or condition.

Representations

(2) The Minister may not make an amendment on his or her own initiative unless he or she first gives the holder an opportunity to make representations to the Minister.

Suspension — contravention or prevention of injury

18.5 (1) Subject to the regulations, the Minister may, after giving the holder of the authorization an opportunity to make representations, suspend a clinical trial authorization if the Minister is of the opinion that

(*a*) the holder has contravened this Act or the regulations in respect of a therapeutic product to which the authorization relates;

(*b*) the holder has contravened a term or condition of the authorization; or

(*c*) the suspension is necessary to prevent injury to the health of a clinical trial subject or a person who is involved in the clinical trial.

Immediate suspension

(2) Subject to the regulations, the Minister may, without having to give the holder of the authorization an opportunity to make represen-

Source: Bill C-51

tations, suspend a clinical trial authorization if the Minister is of the opinion that an immediate suspension is necessary to respond to a serious and imminent risk of injury to the health of a clinical trial subject or a person who is involved in the clinical trial.

Revocation — contravention

18.6 (1) Subject to the regulations, the Minister may, after giving the holder of the authorization an opportunity to make representations, revoke a clinical trial authorization if the Minister believes on reasonable grounds that

(*a*) the holder has contravened this Act or the regulations in respect of a therapeutic product to which the authorization relates; or

(*b*) the holder has contravened a term or condition of the authorization.

Revocation — unacceptable risks

(2) Subject to the regulations, the Minister may — after requesting the holder of the authorization to establish within the time specified by the Minister that the risks, to the health of a clinical trial subject or to a person who is involved in the clinical trial, that are associated with the therapeutic product to which the authorization relates are not unacceptable — revoke a clinical trial authorization if the Minister is of the opinion that the holder has failed to do so.

Revocation with consent

(3) The Minister may revoke a clinical trial authorization with the consent of its holder.

MARKET AUTHORIZATIONS

Issuance

18.7 (1) Subject to the regulations, the Minister may, on application, issue a market authorization to a person in respect of a therapeutic product other than a designated therapeutic product if the Minister is of the opinion that the person has established that the benefits that are associated with the therapeutic product outweigh the risks.

Terms and conditions — regulations

(2) The market authorization is deemed to be subject to the terms and conditions that are prescribed from time to time.

Terms and conditions — Minister

(3) The Minister may issue the market authorization subject to the additional terms and conditions that he or she considers appropriate.

Source: Bill C-51

Obligation to comply

(4) The holder of the market authorization shall comply with the terms and conditions to which the authorization is subject.

No transfer without consent

18.8 A market authorization is not transferable without the Minister's consent.

Amendment

18.9 (1) Subject to the regulations, the Minister may, on his or her own initiative or on application of the holder of the authorization, amend a market authorization or the terms and conditions to which it is subject other than a prescribed term or condition.

Representations

(2) The Minister may not make an amendment on his or her own initiative unless he or she first gives the holder a reasonable opportunity to make representations to the Minister.

Suspension — contravention or risks

19. (1) Subject to the regulations, the Minister may, after giving the holder of the authorization an opportunity to make representations, suspend a market authorization if the Minister is of the opinion that

(*a*) the holder has contravened this Act or the regulations in respect of a therapeutic product to which the authorization relates;

(*b*) the holder has contravened a term or condition of the authorization; or

(*c*) the risks that are associated with the therapeutic product to which the authorization relates outweigh the benefits.

Immediate suspension

(2) Subject to the regulations, the Minister may, without having to give the holder of the authorization an opportunity to make representations, suspend a market authorization if the Minister is of the opinion that an immediate suspension is necessary to respond to a serious and imminent risk of injury to health.

Revocation — contravention

19.1 (1) Subject to the regulations, the Minister may, after giving the holder of the authorization an opportunity to make representations, revoke a market authorization if the Minister believes on reasonable grounds that

(*a*) the holder has contravened this Act or the regulations in respect of a therapeutic product to which the authorization relates; or

Source: Bill C-51

(*b*) the holder has contravened a term or condition of the authorization.

Revocation — benefits outweighing risks not established

(2) Subject to the regulations, the Minister may — after requesting the holder of the authorization to establish within the time specified by the Minister that the benefits that are associated with the therapeutic product to which the authorization relates outweigh the risks — revoke a market authorization if the Minister is of the opinion that the holder has failed to do so.

Revocation with consent

(3) The Minister may revoke a market authorization with the consent of its holder.

ESTABLISHMENT LICENCES

Issuance

19.2 (1) Subject to the regulations, the Minister may, on application, issue an establishment licence to a person authorizing them to conduct, in respect of the one or more therapeutic products or classes of therapeutic products specified in the licence, the specified controlled activity in the specified premises.

Terms and conditions — regulations

(2) The establishment licence is deemed to be subject to the terms and conditions that are prescribed from time to time.

Terms and conditions — Minister

(3) The Minister may issue the establishment licence subject to the additional terms and conditions that he or she considers appropriate.

Obligation to comply

(4) The holder of the establishment licence shall comply with the terms and conditions to which the licence is subject.

Period of validity

19.3 An establishment licence is valid for the period that the Minister specifies in it.

No transfer without consent

19.4 An establishment licence is not transferable without the Minister's consent.

Amendment

19.5 (1) Subject to the regulations, the Minister may, on his or her own initiative or on the application of the holder of the licence, amend an establishment licence or the terms and conditions to which it is subject other than a prescribed term or condition.

Source: Bill C-51

Representations

(2) The Minister may not make an amendment on his or her own initiative unless he or she first gives the holder a reasonable opportunity to make representations to the Minister.

Suspension — contravention or prevention of injury

19.6 (1) Subject to the regulations, the Minister may, after giving the holder of the licence an opportunity to make representations, suspend an establishment licence if the Minister is of the opinion that

(*a*) the holder has contravened this Act or the regulations in relation to an activity that the holder is authorized to conduct under the licence;

(*b*) the holder has contravened a term or condition of the licence; or

(*c*) the suspension is necessary to prevent injury to health.

Immediate suspension

(2) Subject to the regulations, the Minister may, without having to give the holder of the licence an opportunity to make representations, suspend an establishment licence if the Minister is of the opinion that an immediate suspension is necessary to respond to a serious and imminent risk of injury to health.

Revocation — contravention

19.7 (1) Subject to the regulations, the Minister may, after giving the holder of the licence an opportunity to make representations, revoke an establishment licence if the Minister believes on reasonable grounds that

(*a*) the holder has contravened this Act or the regulations in relation to an activity that the holder is authorized to conduct under the licence; or

(*b*) the holder has contravened a term or condition of the licence.

Revocation — risk of injury to health

(2) Subject to the regulations, the Minister may — after requesting the holder of the licence to establish within the time specified by the Minister that allowing the licence to continue in force would not present a risk of injury to health — revoke an establishment licence if the Minister is of the opinion that the holder has failed to do so.

Revocation — consent

(3) The Minister may revoke an establishment licence with the consent of its holder.

Source: Bill C-51

POWERS OF THE MINISTER

Power to require information

19.8 Subject to the regulations, the Minister may direct the holder of a clinical trial authorization, market authorization or establishment licence to provide the Minister with the information that is in their control and that the Minister considers necessary for the administration of this Act.

Power to require tests or studies, etc.

19.9 Subject to the regulations, the Minister may direct the holder of a market authorization or establishment licence to

(*a*) compile information, conduct tests or studies or monitor experience in respect of a therapeutic product to which the authorization or licence relates for the purpose of obtaining additional information about its effects on health or safety; or

(*b*) report the information or the results of the tests, studies or monitoring to the Minister.

Power to require information — after discontinuance or revocation

20. If the clinical trials that are authorized by a clinical trial authorization are discontinued or the clinical trial authorization is revoked, the Minister may, subject to the regulations, direct the holder or former holder of the authorization to provide the Minister with the information that they receive about the therapeutic product to which the authorization relates.

Power to require labels to be revised

20.1 Subject to the regulations, the Minister may direct the holder of a clinical trial authorization, market authorization or establishment licence to revise the label of a therapeutic product to which the authorization or licence relates to reflect the information that the Minister considers necessary to prevent injury to health.

Power to require reassessment

20.2 Subject to the regulations, the Minister may direct the holder of a market authorization to conduct a reassessment of the therapeutic product to which the authorization relates or provide the Minister with the results of the reassessment within the time specified by the Minister.

Source: Bill C-51

Power to disclose risk information

20.3 The Minister may disclose to the public information about the risks or benefits that are associated with a therapeutic product.

GENERAL PROVISIONS

CONSULTATION

Committees

20.4 (1) The Minister may establish committees for the purpose of seeking advice.

Remuneration and travel and living expenses

(2) Committee members may be paid remuneration up to the amount that is fixed by the Governor in Council and are entitled to the reasonable travel and living expenses that they incur while performing their duties away from their ordinary place of residence.

INFORMATION

Required information — serious risk

20.5 If the Minister is of the opinion that a food, therapeutic product or cosmetic may present a serious risk to human health, the Minister may direct a person to provide the Minister with information that is in the person's control and that is necessary for the Minister to determine whether it presents that risk.

Required information — s. 19(1) of the *Canadian Food Inspection Agency Act*

20.6 The Minister may direct a person referred to in subsection 19(1) of the *Canadian Food Inspection Agency Act* to provide the Minister with information that is in the person's control and that is necessary for the purposes of that subsection.

Required information — health care institutions

20.7 A health care institution that belongs to a prescribed class of health care institutions shall provide the Minister with information about the adverse reactions of individuals who receive medical treatment from them that are associated with the use of therapeutic products.

Register

20.8 The Minister is to establish and maintain a publicly accessible register in which is to be kept the prescribed information about therapeutic products.

PERSONAL INFORMATION

Disclosure — serious risk

20.9 The Minister may disclose personal information to a person or government that carries out functions relating to the protection or promotion of human health without the consent of the individual to whom the personal

Source: Bill C-51

information relates if the disclosure is necessary to identify or respond to a serious risk to human health. The exercise of the Minister's power is subject to the making of regulations respecting the disclosure of personal information.

Disclosure — foods

21. The Minister may disclose personal information to a person or government that carries out functions relating to the protection or promotion of human health without the consent of the individual to whom the personal information relates if the disclosure is necessary for the purposes of subsection 19(1) of the *Canadian Food Inspection Agency Act.*

CONFIDENTIAL BUSINESS INFORMATION

Disclosure — agreement

21.1 The Minister may disclose confidential business information to a government or to the following persons, without the consent of the person to whose business or affairs the information relates and without notifying that person, for a purpose that is related to the protection or promotion of the health or safety of the public, if the government or person agrees in writing to maintain the confidentiality of the information:

(*a*) a person from whom the Minister seeks advice; and

(*b*) a person who carries out functions relating to the assessment of the safety of a food, therapeutic product or cosmetic, of the nutritional quality of a food, of the effectiveness, cost effectiveness or appropriate use of a therapeutic product or cosmetic or of the risks or benefits associated with a therapeutic product or cosmetic.

Disclosure — risk

21.2 (1) The Minister may, without the consent of the person to whose business or affairs the information relates and without notifying that person, disclose confidential business information if

(*a*) the information is about a food, therapeutic product or cosmetic that presents a serious and imminent risk of injury to health; or

Source: Bill C-51

(*b*) the disclosure is necessary for the purposes of subsection 19(1) of the *Canadian Food Inspection Agency Act*.

Disclosure — other confidential business information

(2) The Minister may, without the consent of the person to whose business or affairs the information relates, disclose other confidential business information if the disclosure is authorized by the regulations.

ADMINISTRATION AND ENFORCEMENT

INSPECTION

9. Subsection 22(1) of the Act is replaced by the following:

Inspectors

22. (1) The Minister may designate an individual as an inspector for the purpose of the administration and enforcement of this Act and the regulations.

R.S., c. 31 (1st Supp.), s. 11; R.S., c. 27 (3rd Supp.), s. 2; 1997, c. 6, s. 64

10. Section 23 to 28 of the Act are replaced by the following:

Authority to enter a place

23. (1) Subject to subsection 23.1(1), an inspector may, for the purpose of verifying compliance or preventing non-compliance with this Act or the regulations, at any reasonable time enter a place, including a conveyance, in which the inspector believes on reasonable grounds that an activity that is governed by this Act or the regulations is conducted or a document relating to the administration of this Act is located.

Powers of inspectors

(2) The inspector may

(*a*) examine or test anything — and take samples free of charge of an article to which this Act or the regulations apply — that is found in the place;

(*b*) open a receptacle or package that is found in the place;

(*c*) examine a document that is found in the place, make a copy of it or take an extract from it;

(*d*) seize and detain for any time that may be necessary

Source: Bill C-51

(i) an article to which this Act or the regulations apply that is found in the place, or

(ii) a conveyance;

(*e*) direct the owner or the person having possession, care or control of a conveyance to move it;

(*f*) use or cause to be used a computer or other device that is at the place to examine a document that is contained in or available to a computer system or reproduce it or cause it to be reproduced in the form of a printout or other intelligible output and remove the output for examination or copying;

(*g*) use or cause to be used copying equipment that is at the place and remove the copies for examination;

(*h*) take photographs or make recordings or sketches; and

(*i*) direct the owner or person in charge of the place or a person who conducts an activity that is governed by this Act or the regulations at the place

(i) to establish their identity to the inspector's satisfaction, or

(ii) to stop or start the activity.

Assistance and information to be given to inspector

(3) The owner or person in charge of the place and a person found in the place shall give an inspector who is carrying out their functions all reasonable assistance and provide them with the information that they may reasonably require.

Private property

(4) An inspector who is carrying out their functions may enter on or pass through or over private property without being liable for doing so and without the owner of the property having the right to object to that use of the property.

Dwelling-house

23.1 (1) If the place referred to in subsection 23(1) is a dwelling-house, an inspector may not enter it without the consent of the occupant except under the authority of a warrant issued under subsection (2).

Source: Bill C-51

Authority to issue warrant

(2) A justice of the peace may, on *ex parte* application, issue a warrant authorizing, subject to the conditions specified in the warrant, the inspector named in it to enter a dwelling-house if the justice of the peace is satisfied by information on oath that

(*a*) the dwelling-house is a place referred to in subsection 23(1);

(*b*) entry to the dwelling-house is necessary for a purpose referred to in subsection 23(1); and

(*c*) entry to the dwelling-house was refused or there are reasonable grounds to believe that it will be refused.

Use of force

(3) In executing a warrant issued under subsection (2), the inspector may not use force unless the inspector is accompanied by a peace officer and the use of force is authorized in the warrant.

Telewarrant

(4) If an inspector believes that it would not be practical to appear personally to make an application for a warrant under subsection (2), a warrant may be issued by telephone or other means of telecommunication on application submitted by telephone or other means of telecommunication and section 487.1 of the *Criminal Code* applies for that purpose, with the necessary modifications.

Restriction on movement

23.2 An inspector may direct the owner or person having possession, care or control of an article to which this Act or the regulations apply to not move it — or to restrict its movement — for as long as is in the opinion of the inspector necessary for the purposes referred to in subsection 23(1).

SEIZURE

Disposition of things seized

23.3 An inspector who seizes a thing under this Act may

(*a*) on notice to and at the expense of its owner — or the person having possession, care or control of the thing at the time of its seizure — store it or move it to another place;

Source: Bill C-51

(*b*) direct its owner or the person having possession, care or control of it at the time of its seizure to store the thing or move it to another place at their expense; or

(*c*) if the inspector believes on reasonable grounds that the thing could be injurious to human health,

(i) dispose of it on notice to and at the expense of its owner or the person having possession, care or control of it at the time of its seizure, or

(ii) direct its owner or the person having possession, care or control of it at the time of its seizure to dispose of it at their expense.

Release of seized things

23.4 An inspector who seizes a thing under this Act shall release it if they are satisfied that the provisions of this Act and the regulations with respect to it have been complied with.

FORFEITURE

Thing unclaimed

23.5 (1) A seized thing is, at Her election, forfeited to Her Majesty in right of Canada if

(*a*) within 60 days after the seizure, no person is identified as its owner or as a person who is entitled to possess it; or

(*b*) within 60 days after the day on which the owner or person who is entitled to possess it is notified that the inspector has released it, they do not claim it.

Exception

(2) Subsection (1) does not apply if proceedings are instituted in respect of an offence that relates to the seized thing.

Disposition

(3) A seized thing that is forfeited may be disposed of at the expense of its owner or the person who was entitled to possess it at the time of its seizure.

Conviction for offence

23.6 (1) If a person is convicted of an offence under this Act, the court may order that a seized thing by means of or in relation to which the offence was committed be forfeited to Her Majesty in right of Canada.

Source: Bill C-51

Disposition

(2) A seized thing that is forfeited may be disposed of at the expense of its owner or the person who was entitled to possess it at the time of its seizure.

Consent

23.7 If the owner of a seized thing consents to its forfeiture, it is forfeited to Her Majesty in right of Canada and may be disposed of at the owner's expense.

OTHER MEASURES

Measures

23.8 (1) If an inspector believes on reasonable grounds that there is a contravention of this Act or the regulations, the inspector may, among other things, direct a person to

(*a*) stop doing something that is in contravention of this Act or the regulations or cause it to be stopped; or

(*b*) take a measure that is necessary to identify or respond to a risk of injury to health that is related to the activity that is the subject of the contravention.

Operation

(2) The inspector may direct that a requirement established under subsection (1) apply for a specified period or until the inspector is satisfied that no further contravention is likely to take place.

Court has same powers as inspector

(3) If a person is charged with an offence relating to the contravention, the court may confirm, vary or rescind the requirement.

Removal of unlawful imports

23.9 An inspector who believes on reasonable grounds that a food, therapeutic product or cosmetic that was imported for sale does not meet the requirements established under this Act, or was imported for sale in contravention of a requirement established under this Act, may direct its owner or importer or the person having possession, care or control of it to remove it from Canada at their expense even if the inspector does not seize it.

Recall — therapeutic product or cosmetic

24. (1) If, in the opinion of the Minister, a therapeutic product or cosmetic presents a serious or imminent risk of injury to health,

Source: Bill C-51

the Minister may direct a person who sells it to recall it and if necessary to have it sent to the place designated by the Minister.

Prohibition

(2) Subject to subsection (3), no person shall sell a therapeutic product or cosmetic that the Minister directs a person to recall.

Exception to recall

(3) The Minister may authorize a person to sell a therapeutic product or cosmetic even if the Minister has directed a person to recall it.

Injunction

24.1 (1) If, on the application of the Minister, it appears to a court of competent jurisdiction that a person did or is about or likely to do an act or thing that constitutes or is directed toward the commission of an offence under this Act, the court may order the person named in the application to

(*a*) refrain from doing an act or thing that it appears to the court may constitute or be directed toward the commission of an offence under this Act;

(*b*) do an act or thing that it appears to the court may prevent the commission of an offence under this Act; or

(*c*) take a measure referred to in subsection 23.8(1).

Notice

(2) No injunction shall be issued under subsection (1) unless 48 hours' notice is given to the person named in the application or the urgency of the situation is such that giving notice would not be in the public interest.

Obstruction and false statements

24.2 (1) No person shall obstruct or hinder, or knowingly make a false or misleading statement either orally or in writing to, an inspector who is carrying out their functions.

Interference

(2) Except with the authority of an inspector, no person shall remove, alter or interfere in any way with anything seized under this Act.

Source: Bill C-51

DOCUMENTS

Maintenance and production of documents

25. Subject to section 26, a person who is required to maintain documents shall keep them in Canada at a prescribed place, or at the person's place of business if there is no prescribed place, and shall on request provide an inspector with them.

Outside Canada

26. The Minister may, subject to the terms and conditions that he or she specifies, exempt a person or class of persons from a requirement to keep documents in Canada if he or she considers it unnecessary or impracticable for them to keep them in Canada.

Prohibition

27. No person shall falsify a document that they are required to maintain or provide or — with intent to mislead — alter, destroy, erase or obliterate one.

ANALYSIS

Analysts

28. The Minister may designate an individual as an analyst for the purpose of the administration and enforcement of this Act and the regulations.

1994, c. 47, s. 117; 1999, c. 33, s. 347

11. (1) Subsections 30(1) to (3) of the Act are replaced by the following:

Regulations

30. (1) The Governor in Council may make regulations for carrying the purposes and provisions of this Act into effect, including regulations

(*a*) declaring that foods, therapeutic products or cosmetics are adulterated if a prescribed substance or class of prescribed substances is present or was added to them or extracted or omitted from them;

(*b*) defining, in respect of a food, therapeutic product or cosmetic or a class of foods, therapeutic products or cosmetics, "collect", "manufacture", "prepare", "prescription", "preserve", "process", "product monograph", "test" or "wholesale";

(*c*) specifying, for the purposes of the definition "confidential business information" in section 2, the business information that is not confidential business information and

Source: Bill C-51

respecting the circumstances in which business information ceases to be confidential business information;

(*d*) subject to subsection (1.1), designating therapeutic products or classes of therapeutic products as designated therapeutic products, including designating them as such if they are used only by a specified class of persons;

(*e*) respecting the preparation or retention of anything that the Governor in Council considers necessary for the administration or enforcement of this Act or the regulations — including specifying the documents or classes of documents that are to be prepared or retained and requiring a class of persons to prepare or retain documents or to provide the Minister or an inspector with them or with access to them — or specifying the period for which they are to be kept;

(*f*) requiring persons who sell or import for sale foods, therapeutic products or cosmetics to establish tracing systems that would enable them to ascertain their place of origin or destination, recall them or provide persons who could be affected by them with information;

(*g*) respecting the tracing systems that are required by regulations made under paragraph (*f*);

(*h*) respecting

(i) the labelling, packaging or advertising — or the offering or exposing for sale — of foods, therapeutic products or cosmetics,

(ii) the size, dimensions or fill of, or other specifications for, packages of foods, therapeutic products or cosmetics,

(iii) the sale or the conditions of sale of a food, therapeutic product or cosmetic, or

(iv) the use of a substance as an ingredient in a food, therapeutic product or cosmetic;

(*i*) establishing — in respect of a food, therapeutic product or cosmetic — a standard of composition, strength, potency, purity, quality or another property;

Source: Bill C-51

(*j*) respecting the importation of foods, therapeutic products or cosmetics;

(*k*) respecting the manufacturing, collecting, processing, preparation, preserving, storing, conveying or testing of foods, therapeutic products or cosmetics;

(*l*) establishing pre-clearance or in-transit requirements in respect of a food, therapeutic product or cosmetic that is or is to be imported into Canada or in respect of a package, document, label or other thing that is imported with it;

(*m*) respecting the recognition of foreign inspection bodies, foreign inspection or preparation systems, foreign preparation facilities or foreign inspection results;

(*n*) establishing requirements for quality management programs, quality control programs, safety programs or other similar programs relating to foods, therapeutic products or cosmetics;

(*o*) specifying, for the purposes of subsection 5(1) and sections 14 and 16.1, what is considered to be a manner that is false, misleading or deceptive or is likely to create an erroneous impression;

(*p*) respecting the conduct of a controlled activity;

(*q*) respecting the designation of prescription therapeutic products;

(*r*) respecting the distribution or the conditions of distribution of samples of a therapeutic product;

(*s*) specifying the terms and conditions to which registrations or licences referred to in section 18.1, clinical trial authorizations, market authorizations or establishment licences are subject;

(*t*) respecting the registration of persons or establishments or the issuance of licences to persons under section 18.1 and respecting applications for registration or for licences or the amendment, suspension, revocation, reinstatement or transfer of registrations or licences;

Source: Bill C-51

(*u*) respecting the manner in which information, notices or documents that are required under this Act are to be sent;

(*v*) in the case of information, notices or documents that are required to be sent in electronic form,

(i) specifying the persons or classes of persons who may transmit them in electronic form,

(ii) respecting signatures in electronic or other form and respecting their execution, adoption or authorization in a manner that is to have the same effect as a signature, or

(iii) respecting the time at which or the circumstances in which information, notices or documents are deemed to be sent or received or the place at which they are deemed to be sent or received;

(*w*) respecting the conduct of clinical trials;

(*x*) establishing classes of clinical trial authorizations, market authorizations or establishment licences and specifying the class or classes of therapeutic products to which each class relates;

(*y*) respecting applications for or the issuance, amendment, suspension, revocation or transfer of clinical trial authorizations, market authorizations or establishment licences;

(*z*) respecting the designation or recognition of persons who are authorized to certify compliance with requirements or standards in relation to clinical trial authorizations, market authorizations or establishment licences and respecting their functions in relation to that certification;

(*z.1*) specifying the circumstances in which the Minister is bound or ceases to be bound by statements made in writing to applicants for or holders of clinical trial authorizations, market authorizations or establishment licences;

(*z.2*) respecting the exercise of the Minister's powers under sections 19.8 to 20.3, 20.5 and 20.6 or the circumstances in which the Minister may exercise those powers;

Source: Bill C-51

(*z.3*) respecting the reassessments referred to in section 20.2;

(*z.4*) respecting the membership, functions or operation of committees established under subsection 20.4(1);

(*z.5*) respecting public consultations in respect of foods, therapeutic products or cosmetics;

(*z.6*) for the purposes of section 20.7, respecting the information that is to be provided by health care institutions;

(*z.7*) respecting the collection, use or disclosure of personal information or confidential business information by the Minister, including its disclosure to the public;

(*z.8*) respecting the exercise of analysts' or inspectors' functions or the circumstances in which an inspector may exercise their powers;

(*z.9*) respecting the taking of samples or the seizure, detention, forfeiture or disposition of anything under this Act;

(*z.10*) respecting the measures referred to in sections 23.2, 23.8 and 23.9;

(*z.11*) respecting, for the purposes of section 24, the recall of a therapeutic product or cosmetic or the sale of one that was recalled;

(*z.12*) respecting the requirements for the application of section 37, including the labelling, packaging, storage or advertising of a food, therapeutic product or cosmetic that is manufactured for the purpose of being exported;

(*z.13*) exempting from the application of this Act or the regulations or a provision of this Act or the regulations a food, therapeutic product or cosmetic or class of foods, therapeutic products or cosmetics and fixing the conditions of the exemption;

(*z.14*) exempting a person or class of persons from the application of this Act or the regulations or a provision of this Act or the regulations in relation to a food, therapeutic

Source: Bill C-51

product or cosmetic or class of foods, therapeutic products or cosmetics and fixing the conditions of the exemption;

(*z.15*) exempting an activity or class of activities from the application of this Act or the regulations or a provision of this Act or the regulations in relation to a food, therapeutic product or cosmetic or class of foods, therapeutic products or cosmetics and fixing the conditions of the exemption;

(*z.16*) respecting the assessment of the effect on the environment or on human life or health of the release into the environment of a food, therapeutic product or cosmetic and the measures to take before importing or selling a food, therapeutic product or cosmetic that was assessed; and

(*z.17*) prescribing anything that by this Act is to be prescribed.

Restriction — designated therapeutic products

(1.1) A regulation may be made under paragraph (1)(*d*) only if the Governor in Council is satisfied that the therapeutic product is one that by its nature does not need to be the subject of an assessment of its benefits and risks.

Restriction — indefinite retention

(1.2) In specifying a period for the purposes of paragraph (1)(*e*), the Governor in Council may specify an indefinite period in relation to a class of documents or other things only if, in the opinion of the Governor in Council, the indefinite retention of those documents or other things is required in order to enable the identification or tracking of transmissible diseases or disease agents.

Source: Bill C-51

Regulations — drugs manufactured outside Canada

(2) Without limiting or restricting the authority conferred by any other provisions of this Act for carrying into effect the purposes and provisions of this Act, the Governor in Council may make the regulations — governing, regulating or prohibiting the sale or importation of a drug or class of drugs that is manufactured outside Canada — that the Governor in Council considers necessary for the protection of the public in relation to the safety and quality of a drug or class of drugs.

Regulations — North American Free Trade Agreement and WTO Agreement

(3) Without limiting or restricting the authority conferred by any other provisions of this Act for carrying into effect the purposes and provisions of this Act, the Governor in Council may make the regulations that the Governor in Council considers necessary for the purpose of implementing, in relation to drugs, Article 1711 of the North American Free Trade Agreement or paragraph 3 of Article 39 of the Agreement on Trade-related Aspects of Intellectual Property Rights set out in Annex 1C to the WTO Agreement.

2004, c. 23, s. 2

(2) Subsection 30(5) of the Act is replaced by the following:

Regulations — General Council Decision

(5) Without limiting or restricting the authority conferred by any other provisions of this Act for carrying into effect the purposes and provisions of this Act, the Governor in Council may make the regulations that the Governor in Council considers necessary for the purpose of implementing the General Council Decision.

(3) Section 30 of the Act is amended by adding the following after subsection (6):

Externally produced documents

(7) A regulation may incorporate by reference documents produced by a person or body — other than the Minister or the Canadian Food Inspection Agency — including

(*a*) an organization established for the purpose of writing standards, including an organization accredited by the Standards Council of Canada;

(*b*) an industrial or trade organization; or

(*c*) a government.

Source: Bill C-51

Reproduced or translated documents

(8) A regulation may incorporate by reference documents that the Minister reproduces or translates from documents produced by a person or body other than the Minister or the Canadian Food Inspection Agency

(*a*) with any adaptations of form or reference that would facilitate their incorporation into the regulation; or

(*b*) in a form that sets out only the parts of them that apply for the purposes of the regulation.

Jointly produced documents

(9) A regulation may incorporate by reference documents that the Minister or the Canadian Food Inspection Agency produces jointly with another government for the purpose of harmonizing the regulation with other laws.

Internally produced standards

(10) A regulation may incorporate by reference technical or explanatory documents that the Minister or the Canadian Food Inspection Agency produces, including

(*a*) specifications, classifications, illustrations, graphs or other information of a technical nature; and

(*b*) test methods, procedures, operational standards, safety standards or performance standards of a technical nature.

Incorporation as amended from time to time

(11) Documents may be incorporated by reference as amended from time to time.

For greater certainty

(12) Subsections (7) to (11) are for greater certainty and do not limit any authority to make regulations incorporating documents by reference that exists apart from those subsections.

2004, c. 15, s. 66

12. Subsections 30.1(3) and (4) of the Act are replaced by the following:

Exemption from *Statutory Instruments Act*

(4) An interim order is exempt from the application of sections 3 and 9 of the *Statutory Instruments Act*.

13. (1) Subsection 30.2(1) of the Act, as enacted by section 3 of chapter 42 of the Statutes of Canada, 2005, is replaced by the following:

Source: Bill C-51

Interim marketing authorization

30.2 (1) The Minister may issue an interim marketing authorization for a food that provides for any matter referred to in subsection (2), and may, by order, exempt the food from the application, in whole or in part, of sections 5, 6 and 6.1 and the applicable requirements of the regulations, if the Minister determines that the food would not be harmful to the health of the purchaser or consumer.

(2) Subsections 30.2(5) and (6) of the Act, as enacted by section 3 of chapter 42 of the Statutes of Canada, 2005, are replaced by the following:

Exemption from *Statutory Instruments Act*

(5) An authorization, a notice cancelling an authorization and an order exempting a food are exempt from the application of sections 3 and 9 of the *Statutory Instruments Act*.

When effective

(6) An authorization, a notice cancelling an authorization and an order exempting a food have effect from the time that they are made. An authorization ceases to have effect on the earliest of

(*a*) the day on which a notice cancelling the authorization is made,

(*b*) the day on which a regulation made under this Act, that has the same effect as the authorization, comes into force, and

(*c*) two years after the day on which the authorization is made.

Deeming

(7) For the purpose of a provision of this Act other than this section, a reference to regulations made under this Act is deemed to include authorizations and a reference to a regulation made under a specified provision of this Act is deemed to include a reference to the portion of an authorization containing a provision that may be contained in a regulation made under the specified provision.

1997, c. 6, ss. 66(1) and 91

14. The heading before section 31 and sections 31 to 32 of the Act are replaced by the following:

Source: Bill C-51

OFFENCES

Contravention

31. (1) A person who contravenes a provision of this Act or the regulations, does not do something that the Minister or an inspector directs them to do under this Act or does something that the Minister or an inspector directs them not to do under this Act is guilty of an offence and liable

(*a*) on conviction on indictment, to a fine of not more than $5,000,000 or to imprisonment for a term of not more than two years or to both; or

(*b*) on summary conviction, for a first offence to a fine of not more than $250,000 or to imprisonment for a term of not more than six months or to both and, for a subsequent offence, to a fine of not more than $500,000 or to imprisonment for a term of not more than 18 months or to both.

Due diligence

(2) Due diligence is a defence in a prosecution for an offence under subsection (1).

Contravention — wilfully or recklessly

(3) A person who, wilfully or recklessly, contravenes a provision of this Act or the regulations, does not do something that the Minister or an inspector directs them to do under this Act or does something that the Minister or an inspector directs them not to do under this Act is guilty of an offence and is liable

(*a*) on conviction on indictment, to a fine the amount of which is at the discretion of the court or to imprisonment for a term of not more than five years or to both; or

(*b*) on summary conviction, for a first offence to a fine of not more than $500,000 or to imprisonment for a term of not more than 18 months or to both and, for a subsequent offence, to a fine of not more than $1,000,000 or to imprisonment for a term of not more than two years or to both.

Sentencing considerations

(4) A court that imposes a sentence shall take into account, in addition to other principles that it is required to consider, the following factors:

(*a*) the harm or risk of harm caused by the commission of the offence; and

Source: Bill C-51

(*b*) the vulnerability of consumers of the food, therapeutic product or cosmetic.

Parties to offence

(5) If a person other than an individual commits an offence under this Act, any of the person's directors, officers, agents or mandataries who directs, authorizes, assents to, acquiesces in or participates in the commission of the offence is a party to the offence and is liable on conviction to the punishment provided for by this Act, even if the person is not prosecuted for the offence.

Proof of offence

(6) In a prosecution for an offence under this Act, it is sufficient proof of the offence to establish that it was committed by an employee, agent or mandatary of the accused, even if the employee, agent or mandatary is not identified or prosecuted for the offence.

Continuing offence

31.1 If an offence under this Act is committed or continued on more than one day, it constitutes a separate offence for each day on which it is committed or continued.

Limitation period

32. (1) A prosecution for a summary conviction offence under this Act may be instituted at any time within two years after the time the subject-matter of the prosecution becomes known to the Minister.

Minister's certificate

(2) A document purporting to be issued by the Minister, certifying the day on which the subject-matter of the prosecution became known to the Minister, is admissible in evidence without proof of the signature or official character of the person appearing to have signed it and is, in the absence of evidence to the contrary, proof of the matters asserted in it.

15. The portion of subsection 34(1) of the Act before paragraph (*a*) is replaced by the following:

Want of knowledge

34. (1) Subject to subsection (2), in a prosecution for the sale of an article in contravention of this Act or the regulations if the accused proves to the satisfaction of the court or judge that

Source: Bill C-51

1993, c. 34, s. 73; 1996, c. 19, s. 79; 2004, c. 23, s. 3

16. Sections 36 and 37 of the Act are replaced by the following:

Proof as to manufacturer or packager

36. (1) In a prosecution for an offence under this Act, proof that a package containing an article to which this Act or the regulations apply bears a name or address purporting to be the name or address of the person by whom it was manufactured or packaged is, in the absence of evidence to the contrary, proof that the article to which this Act or the regulations apply was manufactured or packaged by the person whose name or address appears on the package.

Certified copies

(2) In a prosecution for an offence under this Act, a copy of a document, or of an extract that was taken from a document, that is certified to be a true copy by the inspector who made it under paragraph 23(2)(*c*) is admissible in evidence and is, in the absence of evidence to the contrary, proof of its contents.

EXPORTS

Exemption — solely for export

37. (1) Subject to the regulations, this Act does not apply to a food, therapeutic product or cosmetic that is manufactured in Canada solely for the purpose of being exported.

No exemption

(2) Despite subsection (1), this Act applies in respect of a therapeutic product that is to be manufactured for the purpose of being exported in accordance with the General Council Decision, as defined in subsection 30(6), and the requirements of this Act and the regulations apply to the therapeutic product as though it were a therapeutic product that is to be manufactured and sold for consumption in Canada, unless the regulations provide otherwise.

ASSISTED HUMAN REPRODUCTION ACT

Non-application

38. (1) This Act does not apply to human reproductive material or *in vitro* embryos that are governed by the *Assisted Human Reproduction Act*.

Source: Bill C-51

Regulations continue to apply

(2) Despite subsection (1), regulations made under subsection 30(1) as it read before the coming into force of this section in respect of human reproductive material continue to apply, as amended from time to time, until they are repealed.

SOR/85-715; SOR/88-252; SOR/89-177 and 503; SOR/90-655; SOR/92-198; SOR/93-64; SOR/94-287; SOR/96-96; SOR/97-560; SOR/99-413 and 414; SOR/2007-120

17. Schedules A to F to the Act are repealed.

TRANSITIONAL PROVISIONS

Par. 23.5(1)(*a*) of the *Food and Drugs Act*

18. (1) If anything is seized before the coming into force of paragraph 23.5(1)(*a*) of the *Food and Drugs Act*, as enacted by section 10, the day on which it is seized is, for the purposes of that paragraph, deemed to be the day on which that paragraph comes into force.

Par. 23.5(1)(*b*) of the *Food and Drugs Act*

(2) If an owner or person who is entitled to possess a seized thing is, before the coming into force of paragraph 23.5(1)(*b*) of the *Food and Drugs Act*, as enacted by section 10, notified that the inspector released it, the day on which they are notified that the inspector released it is, for the purposes of that paragraph, deemed to be the day on which that paragraph comes into force.

Clinical trials

19. (1) A person who, before the coming into force of subsection 18.2(1) of the *Food and Drugs Act*, as enacted by section 8, is authorized under Division 5 of Part C of the *Food and Drug Regulations* to sell or import a drug — or to sell or import a natural health product under Part 4 of the *Natural Health Products Regulations* — for the purposes of a clinical trial is deemed to have been issued a clinical trial authorization in respect of that therapeutic product under that subsection.

Applications

(2) An application under Division 5 of Part C of the *Food and Drug Regulations* or Part 4 of the *Natural Health Products*

Source: Bill C-51

Regulations **that is pending or in progress immediately before the coming into force of subsection 18.2(1) of the *Food and Drugs Act*, as enacted by section 8, is deemed to be an application for a clinical trial authorization under that subsection.**

Clinical testing

20. (1) A person who, before the coming into force of subsection 18.2(1) of the *Food and Drugs Act*, as enacted by section 8, is authorized under Division 8 of Part C of the *Food and Drug Regulations* to sell, for the purposes of clinical testing, a drug for use in human beings or for use in animals that produce food, that are intended for consumption as food or in which the use of the drug could affect human health is deemed to have been issued a clinical trial authorization in respect of that therapeutic product under that subsection.

Applications

(2) An application under Division 8 of Part C of the *Food and Drug Regulations* that is pending or in progress immediately before the coming into force of subsection 18.2(1) of the *Food and Drugs Act*, as enacted by section 8, is deemed to be an application for a clinical trial authorization under that subsection.

Experimental studies

21. (1) A person who, before the coming into force of subsection 18.2(1) of the *Food and Drugs Act*, as enacted by section 8, is authorized under Division 8 of Part C of the *Food and Drug Regulations* to conduct an experimental study in respect of a drug for use in animals that produce food, that are intended for consumption as food or in which the use of the drug could affect human health is deemed to have been issued a clinical trial authorization in respect of that therapeutic product under that subsection.

Applications

(2) An application under Division 8 of Part C of the *Food and Drug Regulations* that is pending or in progress immediately before the coming into force of subsection 18.2(1) of

Source: Bill C-51

the *Food and Drugs Act*, as enacted by section 8, is deemed to be an application for a clinical trial authorization under that subsection.

Investigational testing

22. (1) A person who, before the coming into force of subsection 18.2(1) of the *Food and Drugs Act*, as enacted by section 8, is authorized under Part 3 of the *Medical Devices Regulations* to sell or import a medical device for the purpose of investigational testing is deemed to have been issued a clinical trial authorization in respect of that therapeutic product under that subsection.

Applications

(2) An application under Part 3 of the *Medical Devices Regulations* that is pending or in progress immediately before the coming into force of subsection 18.2(1) of the *Food and Drugs Act*, as enacted by section 8, is deemed to be an application for a clinical trial authorization under that subsection.

Drug identification numbers and notices of compliance

23. (1) A person who, before the coming into force of subsection 18.7(1) of the *Food and Drugs Act*, as enacted by section 8, is authorized under Division 1 of Part C of the *Food and Drug Regulations* to sell a drug in respect of which a drug identification number was assigned, or to sell or advertise a drug in respect of which a notice of compliance was issued under Division 8 of that Part C is deemed to have been issued a market authorization in respect of that therapeutic product under that subsection.

Applications

(2) An application under Division 1 or 8 of Part C of the *Food and Drug Regulations* that is pending or in progress immediately before the coming into force of subsection 18.7(1) of the *Food and Drugs Act*, as enacted by section 8, is deemed to be an application for a market authorization under that subsection.

Source: Bill C-51

Sales and imports — medical devices

24. (1) A person who, before the coming into force of subsection 18.7(1) of the *Food and Drugs Act*, as enacted by section 8, is authorized under Part 1 of the *Medical Devices Regulations* to sell or import a medical device is deemed to have been issued a market authorization in respect of that therapeutic product under that subsection.

Applications

(2) An application under Part 1 of the *Medical Devices Regulations* that is pending or in progress immediately before the coming into force of subsection 18.7(1) of the *Food and Drugs Act*, as enacted by section 8, is deemed to be an application for a market authorization under that subsection.

Sales — natural health products

25. (1) A person who, before the coming into force of subsection 18.7(1) of the *Food and Drugs Act*, as enacted by section 8, is authorized under Part 1 of the *Natural Health Products Regulations* to sell a natural health product is deemed to have been issued a market authorization in respect of that therapeutic product under that subsection.

Applications

(2) An application under Part 1 of the *Natural Health Products Regulations* that is pending or in progress immediately before the coming into force of subsection 18.7(1) of the *Food and Drugs Act*, as enacted by section 8, is deemed to be an application for a market authorization under that subsection.

Establishment licences

26. (1) A person who, before the coming into force of subsection 19.2(1) of the *Food and Drugs Act*, as enacted by section 8, is authorized under Division 1A of Part C of the *Food and Drug Regulations* to fabricate, package, label, distribute, import, wholesale or test a drug — or under Part 1 of the *Medical Devices Regulations* to sell or import a medical device — is deemed to have been issued an establishment licence in respect of that activity under that subsection.

Source: Bill C-51

Applications

(2) An application under Division 1A of Part C of the *Food and Drug Regulations* or Part 1 of the *Medical Devices Regulations* that is pending or in progress immediately before the coming into force of subsection 19.2(1) of the *Food and Drugs Act*, as enacted by section 8, is deemed to be an application for an establishment licence under that subsection.

Site licences

27. (1) A person who, before the coming into force of subsection 19.2(1) of the *Food and Drugs Act*, as enacted by section 8, is authorized under Part 2 of the *Natural Health Products Regulations* to manufacture, package, label or import for sale a natural health product is deemed to have been issued an establishment licence in respect of that activity under that subsection.

Applications

(2) An application under Part 2 of the *Natural Health Products Regulations* that is pending or in progress immediately before the coming into force of subsection 19.2(1) of the *Food and Drugs Act*, as enacted by section 8, is deemed to be an application for an establishment licence under that subsection.

Cells, tissues and organs

28. (1) A person who, before the coming into force of subsection 19.2(1) of the *Food and Drugs Act*, as enacted by section 8, is authorized under the *Safety of Human Cells, Tissues and Organs for Transplantation Regulations* to import, process, distribute or transplant a cell, tissue or organ is deemed to have been issued an establishment licence in respect of that activity under that subsection.

Applications

(2) An application for registration under the *Safety of Human Cells, Tissues and Organs for Transplantation Regulations* that is pending or in progress immediately before the coming into force of subsection 19.2(1) of

Source: Bill C-51

the *Food and Drugs Act*, as enacted by section 8, is deemed to be an application for an establishment licence under that subsection.

CONSEQUENTIAL AMENDMENTS

R.S., c. 20 (4th Supp.)

CANADA AGRICULTURAL PRODUCTS ACT

29. (1) Paragraph 21(1)(*c*) of the French version of the *Canada Agricultural Products Act* is replaced by the following:

c) exiger la communication, pour examen ou reproduction totale ou partielle, de tout document qui, à son avis, contient des renseignements utiles à l'exécution de la présente loi et des règlements.

(2) Subsection 21(3) of the French version of the Act is replaced by the following:

Assistance à l'inspecteur

(3) Le propriétaire ou le responsable du lieu visité, ainsi que quiconque s'y trouve, sont tenus de prêter à l'inspecteur toute l'assistance possible dans l'exercice de ses fonctions et de lui donner les renseignements qu'il peut valablement exiger quant à l'exécution de la présente loi et des règlements.

30. (1) Paragraph 22(2)(*b*) of the French version of the Act is replaced by the following:

b) la visite est nécessaire pour l'exécution de la présente loi ou des règlements;

(2) Subsection 22(4) of the French version of the Act is replaced by the following:

Assistance spéciale

(4) Tout agent de la paix est tenu de prêter à l'inspecteur, sur demande de celui-ci, l'assistance voulue pour le contrôle d'application de la présente loi et des règlements.

31. Paragraph 32(*p*) of the French version of the Act is replaced by the following:

p) fixer tous droits et redevances exigibles pour l'exécution de la présente loi et des règlements, ainsi que les intérêts afférents.

Source: Bill C-51

1997, c. 6 **CANADIAN FOOD INSPECTION AGENCY ACT**

32. Subsection 4(2) of the French version of the *Canadian Food Inspection Agency Act* is replaced by the following:

Délégation par le ministre

(2) Le ministre peut déléguer à toute personne les attributions qui lui sont conférées sous le régime de la présente loi ou de toute autre loi ou disposition dont l'Agence est chargée de l'exécution ou du contrôle d'application aux termes de l'article 11, sauf le pouvoir de prendre des règlements et le pouvoir de délégation prévu au présent paragraphe.

33. (1) Subsection 11(1) of the French version of the Act is replaced by the following:

Application de certaines lois

11. (1) L'Agence est chargée de l'exécution et du contrôle d'application des lois suivantes : la *Loi sur les sanctions administratives pécuniaires en matière d'agriculture et d'agroalimentaire*, la *Loi sur les produits agricoles au Canada*, la *Loi relative aux aliments du bétail*, la *Loi sur les engrais*, la *Loi sur l'inspection du poisson*, la *Loi sur la santé des animaux*, la *Loi sur l'inspection des viandes*, la *Loi sur la protection des obtentions végétales*, la *Loi sur la protection des végétaux* et la *Loi sur les semences*.

(2) Paragraphs 11(3)(*a*) and (*b*) of the French version of the Act are replaced by the following:

a) du contrôle d'application de la *Loi sur les aliments et drogues* en ce qui a trait aux aliments, au sens de l'article 2 de cette loi;

b) de l'exécution des dispositions de cette loi en ce qui a trait aux aliments, sauf si celles-ci portent sur la santé publique, la salubrité ou la nutrition.

34. Subsection 13(3) of the French version of the Act is replaced by the following:

Désignation à titre d'inspecteur

(3) Le président peut, aux fins qu'il précise, désigner, individuellement ou par catégorie, les inspecteurs — vétérinaires ou non —, analystes, classificateurs ou autres agents d'exécution pour

Source: Bill C-51

l'exécution ou le contrôle d'application des lois ou dispositions dont l'Agence est chargée aux termes de l'article 11.

35. Subsection 14(2) of the French version of the Act is replaced by the following:

Accords

(2) Dans le cadre de sa mission, l'Agence est l'autorité chargée de négocier et de conclure des accords en vue de l'application des exigences techniques pour les mouvements internationaux de produits ou d'autres choses régis par une loi ou disposition dont elle est chargée de l'exécution ou du contrôle d'application aux termes de l'article 11.

36. Sections 17 and 18 of the French version of the Act are replaced by the following:

Brevets, droits d'auteur, etc.

17. L'Agence peut rendre disponibles, notamment par vente ou attribution de licence, les brevets, droits d'auteur, dessins industriels, marques de commerce ou titres de propriété analogues dévolus à Sa Majesté du chef du Canada sous le régime des lois ou dispositions dont elle est chargée de l'exécution ou du contrôle d'application aux termes de l'article 11.

Injonction provisoire

18. L'Agence peut demander à un juge d'une juridiction compétente une ordonnance provisoire interdisant toute contravention à une loi ou disposition dont elle est chargée de l'exécution ou du contrôle d'application aux termes de l'article 11 — que des poursuites aient été engagées ou non sous le régime de celle-ci.

37. Subsection 19(1) of the French version of the Act is replaced by the following:

Rappel

19. (1) S'il a des motifs raisonnables de croire qu'un produit régi par une loi ou disposition dont l'Agence est chargée de l'exécution ou du contrôle d'application aux termes de l'article 11 présente un risque pour la santé publique ou celle des animaux ou des végétaux, le ministre peut, par avis signifié à la personne qui vend, met en marché ou distribue ce produit, en ordonner le rappel ou son envoi à l'endroit qu'il désigne.

38. Section 28 of the French version of the Act is replaced by the following:

Source: Bill C-51

Accord sur la perception des prix

28. L'Agence peut conclure avec une personne, un gouvernement provincial ou toute autre autorité un accord portant sur la perception des prix à payer sous le régime de la présente loi ou de toute autre loi dont elle est chargée de l'exécution ou du contrôle d'application aux termes du paragraphe 11(1) et autorisant, par dérogation aux paragraphes 17(1) et (4) de la *Loi sur la gestion des finances publiques*, la personne, le gouvernement provincial ou l'autorité à prélever des sommes d'argent sur le produit de ces prix.

39. Subsection 29(1) of the French version of the Act is replaced by the following:

Remise

29. (1) Le ministre peut faire remise du paiement des prix fixés dans le cadre des articles 24 ou 25 ou de toute loi dont l'Agence est chargée de l'exécution ou du contrôle d'application aux termes du paragraphe 11(1) ou des intérêts exigibles, ou en réduire le montant.

40. Section 36 of the French version of the Act is replaced by the following:

Nominations et désignations

36. Tous les inspecteurs — vétérinaires ou non —, analystes, classificateurs ou autres agents d'exécution nommés ou désignés conformément à une loi mentionnée à l'article 11 pour l'exécution ou le contrôle d'application d'un texte dont l'Agence est chargée aux termes de cet article sont réputés avoir été désignés par le président conformément au paragraphe 13(3) selon les conditions de leur nomination ou désignation originale.

R.S., c. C-38

CONSUMER PACKAGING AND LABELLING ACT

1999, c. 2, s. 44(2)

41. Subsection 2(2) of the French version of the *Consumer Packaging and Labelling Act* is replaced by the following:

Attributions du commissaire

(2) L'exécution de la présente loi, à l'exception du paragraphe 11(1), et le contrôle d'application de cette loi, à l'exception de ce qui a trait aux aliments, au sens de l'article 2 de la *Loi sur les aliments et drogues*, peuvent être assurés par le commissaire pour le compte du ministre de l'Industrie.

Source: Bill C-51

42. Subsection 3(2) of the Act is replaced by the following:

Exemption

(2) This Act does not apply to a therapeutic product within the meaning of the *Food and Drugs Act*.

R.S., c. 31 (4th Supp.), s. 6(2)

43. (1) Paragraph 13(2.2)(*b*) of the French version of the Act is replaced by the following:

b) il est nécessaire d'y pénétrer pour l'exécution et le contrôle d'application de la présente loi;

(2) Subsection 13(3) of the French version of the Act is replaced by the following:

Assistance à l'inspecteur

(3) Le propriétaire ou le responsable des lieux visités par l'inspecteur, ainsi que les personnes qui y travaillent, doivent lui prêter toute l'assistance possible dans l'exercice de ses fonctions et lui fournir, en ce qui concerne l'exécution de la présente loi et des règlements, les renseignements qu'il peut valablement exiger.

1996, c. 8

DEPARTMENT OF HEALTH ACT

44. Section 5 of the *Department of Health Act* is replaced by the following:

Inspectors and analysts

5. The Minister may designate an individual to be an inspector or an analyst for the purposes of any Act for which the Minister has responsibility and sections 22 to 24.2, 28, 29 and 35 of the *Food and Drugs Act* apply, with the modifications that the circumstances require, to the persons designated under this section.

R.S., c. E-15

EXCISE TAX ACT

R.S., c. 7 (2nd Supp.), s. 55(3)

45. Items 1 to 1.2 of Part VIII of Schedule III to the *Excise Tax Act* are replaced by the following:

1. A drug described in Schedule D to the *Food and Drugs Act* as that Schedule read before its repeal.

1.1 A prescription therapeutic product as defined in section 2 of the *Food and Drugs Act* that is a drug.

Source: Bill C-51

1993, c. 27, s. 179(1)

46. Paragraphs 2(*a*) and (*b*) of Part I of Schedule VI to the Act are replaced by the following:

(*a*) a drug included in Schedule C or D to the *Food and Drugs Act* as that Schedule read before its repeal,

(*b*) a prescription therapeutic product as defined in section 2 of the *Food and Drugs Act* that is a drug,

R.S., c. F-9

FEEDS ACT

1997, c. 6, s. 46

47. Subsection 6(1) of the French version of the *Feeds Act* is replaced by the following:

Désignation

6. (1) Les inspecteurs et les analystes chargés de l'exécution et du contrôle d'application de la présente loi sont désignés par le président de l'Agence canadienne d'inspection des aliments conformément à l'article 13 de la *Loi sur l'Agence canadienne d'inspection des aliments*.

48. (1) Paragraph 7(1)(*d*) of the French version of the Act is replaced by the following:

d) exiger la communication, pour examen, ou reproduction totale ou partielle, de tout livre, bordereau d'expédition, lettre de voiture, connaissement, document renfermant des indications sur la façon de faire les mélanges ou autre document relatif à l'exécution de la présente loi ou des règlements.

R.S., c. 31 (1st Supp.), s. 8(2)

(2) Paragraph 7(1.2)(*b*) of the French version of the Act is replaced by the following:

b) il est nécessaire d'y pénétrer pour l'exécution et le contrôle d'application de la présente loi;

(3) Subsection 7(2) of the French version of the Act is replaced by the following:

Assistance à l'inspecteur

(2) Le propriétaire ou le responsable du lieu visité, ainsi que quiconque s'y trouve, sont tenus de prêter à l'inspecteur toute l'assistance possible dans l'exercice de ses fonctions et de

Source: Bill C-51

lui donner les renseignements qu'il peut valablement exiger quant à l'exécution de la présente loi et des règlements.

R.S., c. F-10

FERTILIZERS ACT

1997, c. 6, s. 49

49. Subsection 6(1) of the French version of the *Fertilizers Act* is replaced by the following:

Désignation

6. (1) Les inspecteurs et les analystes chargés de l'exécution et du contrôle d'application de la présente loi sont désignés par le président de l'Agence canadienne d'inspection des aliments conformément à l'article 13 de la *Loi sur l'Agence canadienne d'inspection des aliments*.

R.S., c. 31 (1st Supp.), s. 9(2)

50. (1) Paragraph 7(1.2)(*b*) of the French version of the Act is replaced by the following:

b) il est nécessaire d'y pénétrer pour l'exécution et le contrôle d'application de la présente loi;

(2) Subsection 7(2) of the French version of the Act is replaced by the following:

Assistance à l'inspecteur

(2) Le propriétaire ou le responsable du lieu visité, ainsi que quiconque s'y trouve, sont tenus de prêter à l'inspecteur toute l'assistance possible dans l'exercice de ses fonctions et de lui donner les renseignements qu'il peut valablement exiger quant à l'exécution de la présente loi et des règlements.

R.S., c. F-12

FISH INSPECTION ACT

R.S., c. 31 (1st Supp.), s. 10(2)

51. Paragraph 4(1.2)(*b*) of the French version of the *Fish Inspection Act* is replaced by the following:

b) il est nécessaire d'y pénétrer pour l'exécution et le contrôle d'application de la présente loi;

1997, c. 6, s. 60

52. Subsection 17(1) of the French version of the Act is replaced by the following:

Inspecteurs

17. (1) Les inspecteurs chargés de l'exécution et du contrôle d'application de la présente loi sont désignés par le président de l'Agence

Source: Bill C-51

canadienne d'inspection des aliments conformément à l'article 13 de la *Loi sur l'Agence canadienne d'inspection des aliments*.

R.S., c. H-3

HAZARDOUS PRODUCTS ACT

R.S., c. 24 (3rd Supp.), s. 1

53. Paragraph 3(1)(*b*) of the *Hazardous Products Act* is replaced by the following:

(*b*) food, therapeutic product or cosmetic within the meaning of the *Food and Drugs Act*;

R.S., c. 24 (3rd Supp.), s. 1

54. Paragraph 12(*b*) of the Act is replaced by the following:

(*b*) food, therapeutic product or cosmetic within the meaning of the *Food and Drugs Act*;

1990, c. 21

HEALTH OF ANIMALS ACT

55. Section 30 of the French version of the *Health of Animals Act* is replaced by the following:

Désignation et affectation

30. Le ministre peut désigner une région ou affecter des locaux, laboratoires ou autres installations — au Canada ou à l'étranger — soit à une fin particulière, soit à l'exécution de la présente loi ou des règlements de façon générale et peut modifier, annuler ou rétablir cette désignation ou affectation.

56. (1) Subsection 31(2) of the French version of the Act is replaced by the following:

Mise à disposition de terrains ou de locaux

(2) Sur demande écrite du ministre, le propriétaire ou l'exploitant d'une installation de transport international fournit les terrains, locaux, laboratoires ou autres installations — matériel, ameublement et accessoires compris — appropriés pour les inspections ou l'exécution de la présente loi ou des règlements; il en assure par la suite l'entretien.

(2) Paragraphs 31(3)(*b*) and (*c*) of the French version of the Act are replaced by the following:

Source: Bill C-51

b) y mettre en place, y compris dans leurs environs, la signalisation qu'il juge utile pour leur exploitation ou en vue de la sécurité de leur usage, ou encore pour l'exécution de la présente loi ou des règlements;

c) les utiliser aussi longtemps qu'il l'exige pour l'exécution de la présente loi ou des règlements.

57. Subsections 35(2) and (3) of the French version of the Act are replaced by the following:

Assistance

(2) Le propriétaire ou le responsable du lieu visité en application de l'article 38, ainsi que quiconque s'y trouve, sont tenus de prêter à l'inspecteur ou à l'agent d'exécution toute l'assistance possible dans l'exercice de ses fonctions et de lui fournir les renseignements qui concernent l'exécution de la présente loi ou des règlements et dont il peut valablement exiger la communication.

Agent de la paix

(3) L'agent de la paix prête à l'inspecteur ou à l'agent d'exécution, sur demande, l'assistance nécessaire au contrôle d'application de la présente loi ou des règlements.

58. Paragraph 38(1)(*e*) of the French version of the Act is replaced by the following:

e) exiger la communication, pour examen ou reproduction totale ou partielle, de tout registre ou autre document renfermant, à son avis, des renseignements utiles à l'exécution de la présente loi ou des règlements;

59. Paragraph 39(2)(*b*) of the French version of the Act is replaced by the following:

b) la visite est nécessaire pour l'exécution de la présente loi ou des règlements;

R.S., c. 25 (1st Supp.)

MEAT INSPECTION ACT

60. (1) Paragraph 13(1)(*c*) of the French version of the *Meat Inspection Act* is replaced by the following:

c) exiger la communication, pour examen ou reproduction totale ou partielle, de tout livre, bordereau d'expédition, connaissement ou

Source: Bill C-51

autre document ou dossier qui, à son avis, contiennent des renseignements utiles à l'exécution et au contrôle d'application de la présente loi et des règlements.

(2) Subsection 13(2) of the French version of the Act is replaced by the following:

Assistance à l'inspecteur

(2) Le propriétaire ou le responsable du lieu ou véhicule visité, ainsi que quiconque s'y trouve, sont tenus de prêter à l'inspecteur toute l'assistance possible dans l'exercice de ses fonctions et de lui donner les renseignements qu'il peut valablement exiger quant à l'exécution et au contrôle d'application de la présente loi et des règlements.

(3) Paragraph 13(4)(*b*) of the French version of the Act is replaced by the following:

b) la visite est nécessaire pour l'exécution et le contrôle d'application de la présente loi;

1990, c. 20

PLANT BREEDERS' RIGHTS ACT

61. Subsection 43(1) of the French version of the *Plant Breeders' Rights Act* is replaced by the following:

Compétence de la Cour fédérale

43. (1) La Cour fédérale a compétence pour connaître de toute action ou procédure liée au contrôle d'application de la présente loi, à l'exception des poursuites pour infraction à celle-ci.

62. The portion of subsection 53(3) of the French version of the Act before paragraph (*a*) is replaced by the following:

Infraction : renseignements faux

(3) Commet une infraction quiconque, dans le cadre de l'exécution de la présente loi et en connaissance de cause :

63. Subsection 66(2) of the French version of the Act is replaced by the following:

Restrictions

(2) Le directeur ne procède, de son propre chef ou sur demande écrite, à l'une des mesures visées au paragraphe (1) que si elle favorise la bonne exécution de la présente loi et ne porte pas atteinte à l'intérêt de la justice.

Source: Bill C-51

64. Subsection 77(1) of the French version of the Act is replaced by the following:

Rapport d'exécution

77. (1) À l'expiration de la dixième année suivant l'entrée en vigueur de la présente loi, le ministre établit dans les meilleurs délais un rapport sur l'exécution de celle-ci au cours de cette période et le fait déposer devant chaque chambre du Parlement dans les quinze premiers jours de séance de celle-ci suivant son achèvement.

65. Section 78 of the French version of the Act is replaced by the following:

Rapport annuel

78. Le ministre établit chaque année un rapport sur l'exécution de la présente loi au cours de la précédente année civile et le dépose devant le Parlement dans les quinze premiers jours de séance de l'une ou l'autre chambre suivant son achèvement.

1990, c. 22

PLANT PROTECTION ACT

66. Section 19 of the French version of the *Plant Protection Act* and the headings before it are replaced by the following:

EXÉCUTION

INSTALLATIONS

Désignation et affectation

19. Le ministre peut désigner une région ou affecter des locaux, laboratoires ou autres installations — au Canada ou à l'étranger — soit à une fin particulière, soit pour l'exécution de la présente loi ou des règlements de façon générale; il peut modifier, annuler ou rétablir cette désignation ou affectation.

67. (1) Subsection 20(2) of the French version of the Act is replaced by the following:

Mise à disposition des installations

(2) Sur demande écrite du ministre, le propriétaire ou l'exploitant d'une installation de transport international fournit les terrains, locaux, laboratoires ou autres installations — matériel, ameublement et accessoires compris — appropriés pour les inspections ou l'exécution de la présente loi ou des règlements; il en assure par la suite l'entretien.

Source: Bill C-51

(2) Paragraphs 20(3)(*b*) and (*c*) of the French version of the Act are replaced by the following:

b) y mettre en place, y compris dans leurs environs, la signalisation qu'il juge utile pour leur exploitation ou en vue de la sécurité de leur usage, ou encore pour l'exécution de la présente loi ou des règlements;

c) les utiliser aussi longtemps qu'il l'exige pour l'exécution de la présente loi ou des règlements.

68. Subsections 23(2) and (3) of the French version of the Act are replaced by the following:

Assistance

(2) Le propriétaire ou le responsable du lieu visité en application de l'article 25, ainsi que quiconque s'y trouve, sont tenus de prêter à l'inspecteur toute l'assistance possible dans l'exercice de ses fonctions et de lui fournir les renseignements utiles à l'exécution de la présente loi ou des règlements et dont il peut valablement exiger la communication.

Agent de la paix

(3) L'agent de la paix prête à l'inspecteur, sur demande de celui-ci, l'assistance nécessaire au contrôle d'application de la présente loi ou des règlements.

69. Paragraph 25(1)(*d*) of the French version of the Act is replaced by the following:

d) exiger la communication, pour examen ou reproduction totale ou partielle, de tout document renfermant, à son avis, des renseignements utiles à l'exécution de la présente loi ou des règlements;

70. Paragraph 26(2)(*b*) of the French version of the Act is replaced by the following:

b) la visite est nécessaire pour l'exécution de la présente loi ou des règlements;

R.S., c. S-8

SEEDS ACT

71. (1) Paragraph 6(1)(*d*) of the French version of the *Seeds Act* is replaced by the following:

Source: Bill C-51

d) exiger la communication, pour examen, ou reproduction totale ou partielle, de tout livre, bordereau d'expédition, lettre de voiture, connaissement ou autre document relatif à l'exécution de la présente loi ou des règlements.

R.S., c. 31 (1st Supp.), s. 21(2)

(2) Paragraph 6(1.2)(*b*) of the French version of the Act is replaced by the following:

b) il est nécessaire d'y pénétrer pour l'exécution et le contrôle d'application de la présente loi;

(3) Subsection 6(2) of the French version of the Act is replaced by the following:

Assistance à l'inspecteur

(2) Le propriétaire ou le responsable du lieu visité, ainsi que quiconque s'y trouve, sont tenus de prêter à l'inspecteur toute l'assistance possible dans l'exercice de ses fonctions et de lui donner les renseignements qu'il peut valablement exiger quant à l'exécution de la présente loi et des règlements.

1997, c. 13

TOBACCO ACT

72. The definition "tobacco product" in section 2 of the *Tobacco Act* is replaced by the following:

"tobacco product" «*produit du tabac*»

"tobacco product" means a product composed in whole or in part of tobacco, including tobacco leaves and any extract of tobacco leaves. It includes cigarette papers, tubes and filters but does not include any food or therapeutic product that contains nicotine to which the *Food and Drugs Act* applies.

COORDINATING AMENDMENTS

2005, c. 42

73. (1) In this section, "other Act" means *An Act to amend the Food and Drugs Act*, chapter 42 of the Statutes of Canada, 2005.

(2) If section 1 of the other Act comes into force before section 4 of this Act, then, on the day on which that section 4 comes into force, section 4 of the *Food and Drugs Act* is renumbered as subsection 4(1) and is amended by adding the following:

Source: Bill C-51

Exemptions

(2) A food is not adulterated for the purposes of paragraph (1)(*d*)

(*a*) by an agricultural chemical or its components or derivatives, if the sale of the food is subject to an interim marketing authorization issued under subsection 30.2(1) and the amount of the agricultural chemical and the components or derivatives, singly or in any combination, in or on the food does not exceed the maximum residue limit that is set out in the authorization;

(*b*) by a veterinary drug or its metabolites, if the sale of the food is subject to an interim marketing authorization issued under subsection 30.2(1) and the amount of the veterinary drug and the metabolites, singly or in any combination, in the food does not exceed the maximum residue limit that is set out in the authorization; and

(*c*) by a pest control product as defined in subsection 2(1) of the *Pest Control Products Act* or its components or derivatives, if the amount of the pest control product or the components or derivatives in or on the food being sold does not exceed the maximum residue limit specified under section 9 or 10 of that Act.

(3) If section 1 of the other Act comes into force on the same day as section 4 of this Act, then that section 4 is deemed to have come into force before that section 1.

(4) If section 2 of the other Act comes into force before subsection 11(1) of this Act, then, on the day on which that subsection 11(1) comes into force, subsection 30(1) of the *Food and Drugs Act* is amended by striking out "and" at the end of paragraph (*z.16*) and by adding the following after paragraph (*z.17*):

(*z.18*) defining "agricultural chemical", "food additive", "mineral nutrient", "veterinary drug" and "vitamin" for the purposes of this Act; and

(*z.19*) respecting interim marketing authorizations, including applications for authorizations.

Source: Bill C-51

(5) If subsection 11(1) of this Act comes into force before section 2 of the other Act, then that section 2 is replaced by the following:

2. Subsection 30(1) of the Act is amended by striking out "and" at the end of paragraph (*z.16*) and by adding the following after paragraph (*z.17*):

(*z.18*) defining "agricultural chemical", "food additive", "mineral nutrient", "veterinary drug" and "vitamin" for the purposes of this Act; and

(*z.19*) respecting interim marketing authorizations, including applications for authorizations.

(6) If section 2 of the other Act comes into force on the same day as subsection 11(1) of this Act, then that section 2 is deemed to have come into force before that subsection 11(1) and subsection (4) applies as a consequence.

Canada Consumer Product Safety Act

74. (1) If a Bill entitled the *Canada Consumer Product Safety Act* (the "other Act") is introduced in the 2nd session of the 39th Parliament and receives royal assent, then subsections (2) and (3) apply.

(2) If section 73 of the other Act comes into force before section 53 of this Act, then that section 53 is repealed.

(3) If section 53 of this Act comes into force on the same day as section 73 of the other Act, then that section 53 is deemed to come into force before that section 73.

COMING INTO FORCE

Order in council

75. The provisions of this Act, other than sections 73 and 74, come into force on a day or days to be fixed by order of the Governor in Council.

Source: Bill C-51

C-52

Second Session, Thirty-ninth Parliament,
56-57 Elizabeth II, 2007-2008

HOUSE OF COMMONS OF CANADA

BILL C-52

An Act respecting the safety of consumer products

FIRST READING, APRIL 8, 2008

Source: Bill C-52

RECOMMENDATION

Her Excellency the Governor General recommends to the House of Commons the appropriation of public revenue under the circumstances, in the manner and for the purposes set out in a measure entitled "*An Act respecting the safety of consumer products*".

SUMMARY

This enactment modernizes the regulatory regime for consumer products in Canada. It creates prohibitions with respect to the manufacturing, importing, selling, advertising, packaging and labelling of consumer products, including those that are a danger to human health or safety. In addition, it establishes certain measures that will make it easier to identify whether a consumer product is a danger to human health or safety and, if so, to more effectively prevent or address the danger. It also creates application and enforcement mechanisms. The enactment makes consequential amendments to certain Acts.

Source: Bill C-52

TABLE OF PROVISIONS

AN ACT RESPECTING THE SAFETY OF CONSUMER PRODUCTS

Preamble

SHORT TITLE

1. *Canada Consumer Product Safety Act*

INTERPRETATION

2. Definitions

PURPOSE

3. Purpose

APPLICATION

4. Consumer products

PROHIBITIONS

5. Consumer products in Schedule 2
6. Products that do not meet the regulatory requirements
7. Manufacturer and importer
8. Other persons
9. Misleading claim — package and label
10. Misleading claim — advertise and sell
11. False or misleading information

TESTS, STUDIES AND COMPILATION OF INFORMATION

12. Tests, studies and information

PREPARING AND MAINTAINING DOCUMENTS

13. Requirement

DUTIES IN THE EVENT OF AN INCIDENT

14. Definition of "incident"

DISCLOSURE OF INFORMATION BY THE MINISTER

15. Personal information
16. Confidential business information — agreement

Source: Bill C-52

17.	Confidential business information — serious and imminent danger
18.	Disclosure to the public
	INSPECTORS
19.	Designation
20.	Obstruction and false statements
	INSPECTION
21.	Authority to enter a place
22.	Warrant or consent required to enter dwelling-house
23.	Restriction on movement
	PROCEDURES FOLLOWING SEIZURE
24.	Interference
25.	Storage of things seized
26.	Release of things seized
27.	Forfeiture — thing unclaimed
28.	Forfeiture — conviction for offence
29.	Forfeiture — on consent
	ANALYSIS
30.	Analysts
31.	Analysis and examination
	INSPECTORS' ORDERS
32.	Recall
33.	Taking measures
34.	Measures taken by the inspector
	REVIEW OF INSPECTORS' ORDERS
35.	Review officer
36.	Request for review
	INJUNCTION
37.	Court
	REGULATIONS
38.	Governor in Council
	INTERIM ORDERS
39.	Regulations

Source: Bill C-52

OFFENCES

40.	General
41.	Offences by corporate officers, etc.
42.	Offences by employees, agents or mandataries
43.	Continuing offence
44.	Venue
45.	Limitation period
46.	Admissibility of evidence
47.	Self-incrimination

ADMINISTRATIVE MONETARY PENALTIES

VIOLATION

48	Commission of violation

POWERS OF THE GOVERNOR IN COUNCIL AND MINISTER

49.	Regulations
50.	Notices of violation

PROCEEDINGS

51.	Issuance of notice of violation

PENALTIES

52.	Payment

COMPLIANCE AGREEMENTS

53.	Compliance agreements
54.	Refusal to enter into compliance agreement

REVIEW BY THE MINISTER

55.	Review under paragraph 52(2)(*b*)

ENFORCEMENT

56.	Debts to Her Majesty
57.	Certificate of default

RULES OF LAW ABOUT VIOLATIONS

58.	Violations not offences
59.	Certain defences not available
60.	Burden of proof
61.	Offences by corporate officers, etc.
62.	Vicarious liability — acts of employees and agents

Source: Bill C-52

iv

Source: Bill C-52

2nd Session, 39th Parliament,
56-57 Elizabeth II, 2007-2008

HOUSE OF COMMONS OF CANADA

BILL C-52

An Act respecting the safety of consumer products

Preamble

Whereas the Parliament of Canada recognizes the objective of protecting the public by addressing dangers to human health or safety that are posed by consumer products;

Whereas the Parliament of Canada recognizes that the growing number of consumer products that flow across the borders of an increasingly global marketplace make the realization of that objective a challenge;

Whereas the Parliament of Canada recognizes that along with the Government of Canada, individuals and suppliers of consumer products have an important role to play in addressing dangers to human health or safety that are posed by consumer products;

Whereas the Parliament of Canada wishes to foster cooperation within the Government of Canada, between the governments in this country and with foreign governments and international organizations, in particular by sharing information, in order to effectively address those dangers;

Whereas the Parliament of Canada recognizes that, given the impact activities with respect to consumer products may have on the environment, there is a need to create a regulatory system regarding consumer products that is complementary to the regulatory system regarding the environment;

Source: Bill C-52

Whereas the Parliament of Canada recognizes that a lack of full scientific certainty is not to be used as a reason for postponing measures that prevent adverse effects on human health if those effects could be serious or irreversible;

And whereas the Parliament of Canada recognizes that the application of effective measures to encourage compliance with the federal regulatory system for consumer products is key to addressing the dangers to human health or safety posed by those products;

Now, therefore, Her Majesty, by and with the advice and consent of the Senate and House of Commons of Canada, enacts as follows:

SHORT TITLE

Short title

1. This Act may be cited as the *Canada Consumer Product Safety Act*.

INTERPRETATION

Definitions

2. The following definitions apply in this Act.

"advertisement" «*publicité*»

"advertisement" includes a representation by any means for the purpose of promoting directly or indirectly the sale of a consumer product.

"analyst" «*analyste*»

"analyst" means an individual designated as an analyst under section 30 or under section 28 of the *Food and Drugs Act*.

"article to which this Act or the regulations apply" «*article visé par la présente loi ou les règlements*»

"article to which this Act or the regulations apply" means

(*a*) a consumer product;

(*b*) anything used in the manufacturing, importation, packaging, storing, advertising, selling, labelling, testing or transportation of a consumer product; and

(*c*) a document that is related to any of those activities or a consumer product.

Source: Bill C-52

"confidential business information" «*renseignements commerciaux confidentiels*»

"confidential business information" — in respect of a person to whose business or affairs the information relates — means business information

(*a*) that is not publicly available;

(*b*) in respect of which the person has taken measures that are reasonable in the circumstances to ensure that it remains not publicly available; and

(*c*) that has actual or potential economic value to the person or their competitors because it is not publicly available and its disclosure would result in a material financial loss to the person or a material financial gain to their competitors.

"consumer product" «*produit de consommation*»

"consumer product" means a product, including its components, parts or accessories, that can reasonably be expected to be obtained by an individual to be used for non-commercial purposes, including for domestic, recreational and sports purposes, and includes its packaging.

"danger to human health or safety" «*danger pour la santé ou la sécurité humaines*»

"danger to human health or safety" means any existing or potential hazard that is posed by a consumer product during or as a result of its normal or foreseeable use and that may reasonably be expected to cause the death of an individual exposed to it or have an adverse effect on that individual's health — including an injury — whether or not the death or adverse effect occurs immediately after the exposure to the hazard, and includes any exposure to a consumer product that is likely to have a chronic adverse effect on human health.

"document" «*document*»

"document" means anything on which information is recorded or marked and that is capable of being understood by a person or read by a computer or other device.

"government" «*administration*»

"government" means any of the following or their institutions:

(*a*) the federal government;

(*b*) a corporation named in Schedule III to the *Financial Administration Act*;

(*c*) a provincial government or a public body established under an Act of the legislature of a province;

Source: Bill C-52

(*d*) an aboriginal government as defined in subsection 13(3) of the *Access to Information Act*;

(*e*) a government of a foreign state or of a subdivision of a foreign state; or

(*f*) an international organization of states.

"import" « *importer* »

"import" means to import into Canada.

"inspector" « *inspecteur* »

"inspector" means an individual designated as an inspector under subsection 19(1).

"manufacture" « *fabrication* »

"manufacture" includes produce, formulate, repackage and prepare, as well as recondition for sale.

"Minister" « *ministre* »

"Minister" means the Minister of Health.

"person" « *personne* »

"person" means an individual or an organization as defined in section 2 of the *Criminal Code*.

"personal information" « *renseignements personnels* »

"personal information" has the same meaning as in section 3 of the *Privacy Act*.

"prescribed" *Version anglaise seulement*

"prescribed" means prescribed by regulation.

"review officer" « *réviseur* »

"review officer" means an individual designated as a review officer under section 35.

"sell" « *vente* »

"sell" includes offer for sale, expose for sale or have in possession for sale — or distribute to one or more persons, whether or not the distribution is made for consideration — and includes lease, offer for lease, expose for lease or have in possession for lease.

PURPOSE

Purpose

3. The purpose of this Act is to protect the public by addressing or preventing dangers to human health or safety that are posed by consumer products in Canada, including those that circulate within Canada and those that are imported.

Source: Bill C-52

APPLICATION

Consumer products

4. (1) This Act applies to consumer products with the exception of those listed in Schedule 1.

Tobacco products

(2) This Act applies to tobacco products as defined in section 2 of the *Tobacco Act* but only in respect of their ignition propensity.

Lighters and matches

(3) This Act applies to lighters and matches that display a tobacco product-related brand element within the meaning of section 2 of the *Tobacco Act* other than in respect of their advertisement.

PROHIBITIONS

Consumer products in Schedule 2

5. No person shall manufacture, import, advertise or sell a consumer product listed in Schedule 2.

Products that do not meet the regulatory requirements

6. No person shall manufacture, import, advertise or sell a consumer product that does not meet the requirements set out in the regulations.

Manufacturer and importer

7. No manufacturer or importer shall manufacture, import, advertise or sell a consumer product that

(*a*) is a danger to human health or safety;

(*b*) is the subject of a recall order made under section 32 or reviewed under section 36 or is the subject of a voluntary recall in Canada because the product is a danger to human health or safety; or

(*c*) is the subject of a measure that the manufacturer or importer has not carried out but is required to carry out under an order made under section 33 or such an order if it is reviewed under section 36.

Other persons

8. No person, other than a manufacturer or importer, shall advertise or sell a consumer product that they know or ought to know

(*a*) is a danger to human health or safety;

Source: Bill C-52

(*b*) is the subject of a recall order made under section 32 or reviewed under section 36 or is the subject of a voluntary recall in Canada because the product is a danger to human health or safety; or

(*c*) is the subject of a measure that has not been carried out but is required to be carried out under an order made under section 33 or such an order if it is reviewed under section 36.

Misleading claim — package and label

9. No person shall package or label a consumer product in a manner that is false, misleading or deceptive or that is likely to create an erroneous impression regarding the fact that it is not a danger to human health or safety, its certification related to its safety or its compliance with a safety standard or the regulations.

Misleading claim — advertise and sell

10. No person shall advertise or sell a consumer product that they know or ought to know is advertised, packaged or labelled in a manner that is false, misleading or deceptive or that is likely to create an erroneous impression regarding the fact that it is not a danger to human health or safety, its certification related to its safety or its compliance with a safety standard or the regulations.

False or misleading information

11. No person shall knowingly provide the Minister with false or misleading information in relation to a matter under this Act or the regulations.

TESTS, STUDIES AND COMPILATION OF INFORMATION

Tests, studies and information

12. The Minister may, by written notice, order any person who manufactures or imports a consumer product for commercial purposes to

(*a*) conduct tests or studies on the product in order to obtain the information that the Minister considers necessary to verify compliance with this Act or the regulations;

Source: Bill C-52

(*b*) compile any information that the Minister considers necessary to verify compliance with this Act or the regulations; and

(*c*) provide him or her with the documents that contain that information and the results of the tests or studies in the time and manner that the Minister specifies.

PREPARING AND MAINTAINING DOCUMENTS

Requirement

13. (1) Any person who manufactures, imports, advertises, sells or tests a consumer product for commercial purposes shall prepare and maintain

(*a*) documents that indicate

(i) in the case of a retailer, the name and address of the person from whom they obtained the product and the location where — and the period during which — they sold the product, and

(ii) in the case of any other person, the name and address of the person from whom they obtained the product and to whom they sold it, as the case may be; and

(*b*) prescribed documents.

Keeping and providing documents in Canada

(2) The person shall keep the documents at their place of business in Canada or at any other prescribed place in Canada and shall, on written request, provide the Minister with them.

Exemption — outside Canada

(3) The Minister may, subject to any terms and conditions that he or she may specify, exempt a person from the requirement to keep documents in Canada if the Minister considers it unnecessary or impractical for the person to keep them in Canada.

Importation

(4) A person who imports a consumer product for commercial purposes shall, no later than at the time of the product's importation, provide the Minister with those documents referred to in paragraph (1)(*b*) that are specified in the regulations.

DUTIES IN THE EVENT OF AN INCIDENT

Definition of "incident"

14. (1) In this section, "incident" means, with respect to a consumer product,

Source: Bill C-52

(*a*) an occurrence in Canada or elsewhere that results, or that could reasonably be expected to have resulted, in an individual's death or in serious adverse effects on their health, including a serious injury;

(*b*) a defect or characteristic that may reasonably be expected to result in an individual's death or in serious adverse effects on their health, including a serious injury;

(*c*) incorrect or insufficient information on a label or in instructions — or the lack of a label or instructions — that may reasonably be expected to result in an individual's death or in serious adverse effects on their health, including a serious injury; or

(*d*) a recall or measure that is initiated for human health or safety reasons by

(i) a foreign entity,

(ii) a provincial government,

(iii) a public body that is established under an Act of the legislature of a province,

(iv) an aboriginal government as defined in subsection 13(3) of the *Access to Information Act*, or

(v) an institution of an entity referred to in subparagraphs (ii) to (iv).

Requirement to provide information

(2) A person who manufactures, imports or sells a consumer product for commercial purposes shall provide the Minister and, if applicable, the person from whom they received the consumer product, with all the information in their control regarding any incident related to the product, within two days after they become aware of the incident.

Report

(3) The manufacturer of the consumer product or, if the manufacturer carries on business outside Canada, the importer, shall provide the Minister with a written report containing information about the incident, the product involved in the incident, any products that they manufacture or import, as the case may be, that to their knowledge could be involved in a similar incident and any measures they propose be taken with respect to those products, within

Source: Bill C-52

seven days after they become aware of the incident or within the time that, by written notice, the Minister specifies.

DISCLOSURE OF INFORMATION BY THE MINISTER

Personal information

15. The Minister may disclose personal information to a person or a government that carries out functions relating to the protection of human health or safety without the consent of the individual to whom the personal information relates if the disclosure is necessary to identify or address a serious danger to human health or safety. The exercise of the Minister's power is subject to the making of regulations respecting the disclosure of personal information.

Confidential business information — agreement

16. The Minister may disclose confidential business information to a person or a government that carries out functions relating to the protection of human health or safety or the environment — in relation to a consumer product — without the consent of the person to whose business or affairs the information relates and without notifying that person if they agree in writing to maintain the confidentiality of the information and to use it only for the purpose of carrying out those functions.

Confidential business information — serious and imminent danger

17. The Minister may, without the consent of the person to whose business or affairs the information relates and without notifying that person, disclose confidential business information about a consumer product that is a serious and imminent danger to human health or safety or the environment.

Disclosure to the public

18. The Minister may disclose to the public information regarding a danger to human health or safety that a consumer product poses.

Source: Bill C-52

INSPECTORS

Designation

19. (1) The Minister may designate an individual as an inspector for the purpose of the administration and enforcement of this Act and the regulations.

Certificate to be produced

(2) An inspector shall be given a certificate in a form established by the Minister attesting to the inspector's designation and, on entering a place pursuant to subsection 21(1), the inspector shall, if so required, produce the certificate to the person in charge of that place.

Obstruction and false statements

20. No person shall obstruct or hinder or knowingly make a false or misleading statement either orally or in writing to an inspector who is carrying out their functions.

INSPECTION

Authority to enter a place

21. (1) Subject to subsection 22(1), an inspector may, for the purpose of verifying compliance or preventing non-compliance with this Act or the regulations, at any reasonable time enter a place, including a conveyance, in which the inspector believes on reasonable grounds that a consumer product is manufactured, imported, packaged, stored, advertised, sold, labelled, tested or transported, or a document relating to the administration of this Act or the regulations is located.

Powers

(2) The inspector may

(*a*) examine or test anything — and take samples free of charge of an article to which this Act or the regulations apply — that is found in the place;

(*b*) open a receptacle or package that is found in the place;

(*c*) examine a document that is found in the place, make a copy of it or take an extract from it;

(*d*) seize and detain for any time that may be necessary

Source: Bill C-52

(i) an article to which this Act or the regulations apply that is found in the place, or

(ii) a conveyance;

(*e*) order the owner, or the person having possession, care or control, of a conveyance, to move it;

(*f*) use or cause to be used a computer or other device that is at the place to examine a document that is contained in or available to a computer system or reproduce it or cause it to be reproduced in the form of a printout or other intelligible output and remove the output for examination or copying;

(*g*) use or cause to be used copying equipment that is at the place and remove the copies for examination;

(*h*) take photographs and make recordings or sketches; and

(*i*) order the owner or person in charge of the place or a person who manufactures, imports, packages, stores, advertises, sells, labels, tests or transports a consumer product at the place to establish their identity to the inspector's satisfaction or to stop or start an activity.

Entering private property

(3) An inspector who is carrying out their functions may enter on or pass through or over private property without being liable for doing so and without the owner of the property having the right to object to that use of the property.

Assistance and information to be given to inspector

(4) The owner or person in charge of the place and every person found in the place shall give an inspector who is carrying out their functions all reasonable assistance and provide them with any information that they may reasonably require.

Warrant or consent required to enter dwelling-house

22. (1) If the place mentioned in subsection 21(1) is a dwelling-house, an inspector may not enter it without the consent of the occupant except under the authority of a warrant issued under subsection (2).

Source: Bill C-52

Authority to issue warrant

(2) A justice of the peace may, on *ex parte* application, issue a warrant authorizing, subject to the conditions specified in the warrant, the inspector who is named in it to enter a dwelling-house if the justice of the peace is satisfied by information on oath that

(*a*) the dwelling-house is a place described in subsection 21(1);

(*b*) entry to the dwelling-house is necessary for the purposes referred to in subsection 21(1); and

(*c*) entry to the dwelling-house was refused or there are reasonable grounds to believe that it will be refused.

Use of force

(3) In executing a warrant issued under subsection (2), the inspector may not use force unless they are accompanied by a peace officer and the use of force is authorized in the warrant.

Telewarrant

(4) If an inspector believes that it would not be practical to appear personally to make an application for a warrant under subsection (2), a warrant may be issued by telephone or other means of telecommunication on application submitted by telephone or other means of telecommunication and section 487.1 of the *Criminal Code* applies for that purpose with any necessary modifications.

Restriction on movement

23. An inspector may order the owner or person having possession, care or control of an article to which this Act or the regulations apply to not move it — or to restrict its movement — for as long as, in the opinion of the inspector, is necessary for the purposes referred to in subsection 21(1).

PROCEDURES FOLLOWING SEIZURE

Interference

24. Except with the authority of an inspector, no person shall remove, alter or interfere in any way with anything seized under this Act.

Storage of things seized

25. An inspector who seizes a thing under this Act may

(*a*) on notice to and at the expense of its owner or the person having possession, care or control of it at the time of its seizure, store it or move it to another place; or

Source: Bill C-52

(*b*) order its owner or the person having possession, care or control of it at the time of its seizure to store it or move it to another place at their expense.

Release of things seized

26. An inspector who seizes a thing under this Act shall release it if they are satisfied that the provisions of this Act and the regulations with respect to it have been complied with.

Forfeiture — thing unclaimed

27. (1) A seized thing is, at Her election, forfeited to Her Majesty in right of Canada if

(*a*) within 60 days after the seizure, no person is identified as its owner or as a person who is entitled to possess it; or

(*b*) the owner or person who is entitled to possess it, within 60 days after the day on which they are notified that the inspector has released the seized thing, does not claim it.

Proceedings instituted

(2) Subsection (1) does not apply if proceedings are instituted in respect of an offence that relates to the thing that was seized.

Disposal

(3) A seized thing that is forfeited may be disposed of at the expense of its owner or the person who was entitled to possess it at the time of its seizure.

Forfeiture — conviction for offence

28. (1) If a person is convicted of an offence under this Act, the court may order that a seized thing by means of or in relation to which the offence was committed be forfeited to Her Majesty in right of Canada.

Disposal

(2) A seized thing that is forfeited may be disposed of at the expense of its owner or the person who was entitled to possess it at the time of its seizure.

Forfeiture — on consent

29. If the owner of a seized thing consents to its forfeiture, the seized thing is forfeited to Her Majesty in right of Canada and may be disposed of at the expense of the owner.

Source: Bill C-52

ANALYSIS

Analysts

30. The Minister may designate an individual, or class of individuals, as an analyst for the administration and enforcement of this Act and the regulations.

Analysis and examination

31. (1) An inspector may submit to an analyst, for analysis or examination, anything seized by the inspector, or any sample of it, or any samples taken by the inspector.

Certificate or report

(2) An analyst who has made an analysis or examination may issue a certificate or report setting out the results of the analysis or examination.

INSPECTORS' ORDERS

Recall

32. (1) If an inspector believes on reasonable grounds that a consumer product is a danger to human health or safety, they may order a person who manufactures, imports or sells the product for commercial purposes to recall it.

Notice

(2) The order shall be provided in the form of a written notice and must include

(*a*) a statement of the reasons for the recall; and

(*b*) the time and manner in which the recall is to be carried out.

Taking measures

33. (1) An inspector may order a person who manufactures, imports, advertises or sells a consumer product to take any measure referred to in subsection (2) if

(*a*) that person does not comply with an order made under section 12 with respect to the product;

(*b*) the inspector has made an order under section 32 with respect to the product;

(*c*) the inspector believes on reasonable grounds that the product is the subject of a measure or recall undertaken voluntarily by the manufacturer or importer; or

Source: Bill C-52

(*d*) the inspector believes on reasonable grounds that there is a contravention of this Act or the regulations in relation to the product.

Measures

(2) The measures include

(*a*) stopping the manufacturing, importation, packaging, storing, advertising, selling, labelling, testing or transportation of the consumer product or causing any of those activities to be stopped; and

(*b*) any measure that the inspector considers necessary to remedy a non-compliance with this Act or the regulations, including any measure that relates to the product that the inspector considers necessary in order for the product to meet the requirements of the regulations or to address or prevent a danger to human health or safety that the product poses.

Notice

(3) The order shall be provided in the form of a written notice and must include

(*a*) a statement of the reasons for the measure; and

(*b*) the time and manner in which the measure is to be carried out.

Measures taken by the inspector

34. If a person does not comply with an order made under section 32 or 33 in the time specified, the inspector may, on their own initiative and at that person's expense, carry out the recall or measure required.

REVIEW OF INSPECTORS' ORDERS

Review officer

35. The Minister may designate any individual or class of individuals that are qualified as review officers for the purpose of reviewing inspectors' orders under section 36.

Request for review

36. (1) Subject to this section, an order that has been made under section 32 or 33 shall be reviewed, with respect to facts, by a review officer — other than the inspector who made the order — on the written request of the person to whom it was provided.

Source: Bill C-52

Contents of and time for making request

(2) The written request must state the grounds for the request, the evidence that supports those grounds and the decision that is sought and the Minister shall be provided with it within seven days after the day on which the order was provided or, in the event of a serious and imminent danger to human health or safety, any shorter period that may be specified in the order.

Refusal

(3) The review is to be refused if the request does not comply with subsection (2) or is frivolous, vexatious or not made in good faith.

Reasons for refusal

(4) If a request for a review is refused, the person who made the request shall be notified in writing with reasons for the refusal.

Review initiated by review officer

(5) A review officer — other than the inspector who made the order — may conduct the review, whether or not a request has been made under subsection (1).

Order in effect

(6) An order continues to apply during a review unless the review officer decides otherwise.

Decision on completion of review

(7) On completion of a review, the review officer shall confirm, amend, terminate or cancel the order.

Notice

(8) The person who made the request or, if there was no request, the person to whom the order was provided shall be notified in writing with reasons for the review officer's decision.

Effect of amendment

(9) An order that is amended is subject to review under this section.

INJUNCTION

Court

37. (1) If, on the application of the Minister, it appears to a court of competent jurisdiction that a person has done or is about to do or is likely to do an act or thing that constitutes or is directed toward the commission of an offence under this Act, the court may issue an injunction ordering the person who is named in the application to

(*a*) refrain from doing an act or thing that it appears to the court may constitute or be directed toward the commission of an offence under this Act; or

Source: Bill C-52

(*b*) do an act or thing that it appears to the court may prevent the commission of an offence under this Act.

Notice

(2) No injunction shall be issued under subsection (1) unless 48 hours' notice is served to the party or parties who are named in the application or the urgency of the situation is such that service of notice would not be in the public interest.

REGULATIONS

Governor in Council

38. (1) The Governor in Council may make regulations for carrying out the purposes and provisions of this Act into effect, including regulations

(*a*) exempting, from the application of this Act or the regulations or a provision of this Act or the regulations, a consumer product, or class of consumer products, including exempting products manufactured in Canada for export or imported solely for the purpose of export, and fixing the conditions of the exemption;

(*b*) exempting a class of persons from the application of this Act or the regulations or a provision of this Act or the regulations in relation to a consumer product or class of consumer products, and fixing the conditions of the exemption;

(*c*) amending Schedule 1 or 2 by adding or deleting a consumer product, or changing its description;

(*d*) respecting the preparation and maintenance of documents, including by specifying the documents or the class of documents to be prepared and maintained, where they may be kept and for how long;

(*e*) specifying the documents that an importer shall provide the Minister with under subsection 13(4);

(*f*) respecting the collection, use and disclosure of personal information or confidential business information by the Minister, including disclosure to the public;

Source: Bill C-52

(*g*) respecting the manufacturing, importation, packaging, storing, sale, advertising, labelling, testing or transportation of any consumer product or class of consumer products;

(*h*) prohibiting the manufacturing, importation, packaging, storing, sale, advertising, labelling, testing or transportation of any consumer product or class of consumer products;

(*i*) respecting the communication of health and safety information to the public by a person who manufactures, imports, advertises or sells a consumer product, including the communication of health and safety information by way of the product's label or instructions;

(*j*) respecting the time and manner in which information, notices and documents are to be provided or served under this Act;

(*k*) respecting the designation or recognition of persons who would be authorized to certify that a consumer product meets the applicable requirements and respecting their functions in relation to that certification;

(*l*) respecting the exercise of an inspector's, analyst's or review officer's functions and the circumstances in which an inspector may exercise their powers;

(*m*) respecting the taking of samples or the seizure, detention, forfeiture or disposal of anything under this Act;

(*n*) respecting the recall of a consumer product;

(*o*) respecting the measures referred to in section 33;

(*p*) respecting the review of inspectors' orders under section 36; and

(*q*) prescribing anything that by this Act is to be prescribed.

Source: Bill C-52

Externally produced material

(2) A regulation made under this Act may incorporate by reference documents produced by a person or body other than the Minister including by

(*a*) an organization established for the purpose of writing standards, including an organization accredited by the Standards Council of Canada;

(*b*) an industrial or trade organization; or

(*c*) a government.

Reproduced or translated material

(3) A regulation made under this Act may incorporate by reference documents that the Minister reproduces or translates from documents produced by a person or body other than the Minister

(*a*) with any adaptations of form and reference that will facilitate their incorporation into the regulation; or

(*b*) in a form that sets out only the parts of them that apply for the purposes of the regulation.

Jointly produced documents

(4) A regulation made under this Act may incorporate by reference documents that the Minister produces jointly with another government for the purpose of harmonizing the regulation with other laws.

Internally produced standards

(5) A regulation made under this Act may incorporate by reference technical or explanatory documents that the Minister produces, including

(*a*) specifications, classifications, illustrations, graphs or other information of a technical nature; and

(*b*) test methods, procedures, operational standards, safety standards or performance standards of a technical nature.

Incorporation as amended from time to time

(6) Documents may be incorporated by reference as amended from time to time.

For greater certainty

(7) Subsections (2) to (6) are for greater certainty and do not limit any authority to make regulations incorporating material by reference that exists apart from those subsections.

Source: Bill C-52

INTERIM ORDERS

Regulations

39. (1) The Minister may make an interim order that contains any provision that may be contained in a regulation made under this Act if he or she believes that immediate action is required to deal with a significant danger — direct or indirect — to human health or safety.

Cessation of effect

(2) An interim order has effect from the time that it is made but ceases to have effect on the earliest of

(*a*) 14 days after it is made, unless it is approved by the Governor in Council,

(*b*) the day on which it is repealed,

(*c*) the day on which a regulation made under this Act that has the same effect as the interim order comes into force, and

(*d*) one year after the interim order is made or any shorter period that may be specified in the interim order.

Exemption from *Statutory Instruments Act*

(3) An interim order is exempt from the application of sections 3 and 9 of the *Statutory Instruments Act*.

Deeming

(4) For the purpose of any provision of this Act other than this section, any reference to regulations made under this Act is deemed to include interim orders, and any reference to a regulation made under a specified provision of this Act is deemed to include a reference to the portion of an interim order containing any provision that may be contained in a regulation made under the specified provision.

Tabling of order

(5) A copy of each interim order must be tabled in each House of Parliament within 15 days after it is made.

House not sitting

(6) In order to comply with subsection (5), the interim order may be sent to the Clerk of the House if the House is not sitting.

Source: Bill C-52

OFFENCES

General

40. (1) A person who contravenes a provision of this Act or the regulations or an order made under this Act is guilty of an offence and is liable

(*a*) on conviction on indictment, to a fine of not more than $5,000,000 or to imprisonment for a term of not more than two years or to both; or

(*b*) on summary conviction, for a first offence to a fine of not more than $250,000 or to imprisonment for a term of not more than six months or to both and, for a subsequent offence, to a fine of not more than $500,000 or to imprisonment for a term of not more than 18 months or to both.

Due diligence available

(2) Due diligence is a defence in a prosecution for an offence under subsection (1).

Wilfully or recklessly

(3) A person who wilfully or recklessly contravenes a provision of this Act or the regulations or an order made under this Act is guilty of an offence and is liable

(*a*) on conviction on indictment, to a fine the amount of which is at the discretion of the court or to imprisonment for a term of not more than five years or to both; or

(*b*) on summary conviction, for a first offence to a fine of not more than $500,000 or to imprisonment for a term of not more than 18 months or to both and, for a subsequent offence, to a fine of not more than $1,000,000 or to imprisonment for a term of not more than two years or to both.

Sentencing considerations

(4) A court that imposes a sentence shall take into account, in addition to any other principles that it is required to consider, the following factors:

(*a*) the harm or risk of harm caused by the commission of the offence; and

(*b*) the vulnerability of individuals who use the consumer product.

Source: Bill C-52

Offences by corporate officers, etc.

41. If a person other than an individual commits an offence under this Act, any of the person's directors, officers, agents or mandataries who directs, authorizes, assents to, acquiesces in or participates in the commission of the offence is a party to the offence and is liable on conviction to the punishment provided for by this Act, even if the person is not prosecuted for the offence.

Offences by employees, agents or mandataries

42. In a prosecution for an offence under this Act, it is sufficient proof of the offence to establish that it was committed by any employee, agent or mandatary of the accused, even if the employee, agent or mandatary is not identified or is not prosecuted for the offence.

Continuing offence

43. If an offence under this Act is committed or continued on more than one day, it constitutes a separate offence for each day on which it is committed or continued.

Venue

44. A prosecution for an offence under this Act may be instituted, heard and determined

(*a*) in the place where the offence was committed or the subject-matter of the prosecution arose;

(*b*) where the accused was apprehended; or

(*c*) where the accused happens to be or is carrying on business.

Limitation period

45. Proceedings by way of summary conviction in respect of an offence under this Act may be instituted at any time within two years after the time the Minister becomes aware of the acts or omissions that constitute the alleged offence.

Admissibility of evidence

46. (1) In proceedings for an offence under this Act, a declaration, certificate, report or other document of the Minister or an inspector, analyst or review officer purporting to have been signed by that person is admissible in evidence without proof of the signature or official character of the person appearing to have signed it and, in the absence of evidence to the contrary, is proof of the matters asserted in it.

Copies and extracts

(2) In proceedings for an offence under this Act, a copy of or an extract from any document that is made by the Minister or an inspector, analyst or review officer that appears to have

Source: Bill C-52

been certified under the signature of that person as a true copy or extract is admissible in evidence without proof of the signature or official character of the person appearing to have signed it and, in the absence of evidence to the contrary, has the same probative force as the original would have if it were proved in the ordinary way.

Presumed date of issue

(3) A document referred to in this section is, in the absence of evidence to the contrary, presumed to have been issued on the date that it bears.

Notice

(4) No document referred to in this section may be received in evidence unless the party intending to produce it has provided reasonable notice of that intention on the party against whom it is intended to be produced together with a duplicate of the document.

Self-incrimination

47. The information and results contained in the documents that a person provides under an order made under section 12 may not be used or received to incriminate the person in any proceeding against them in respect of an offence under this Act.

ADMINISTRATIVE MONETARY PENALTIES

VIOLATION

Commission of violation

48. Every person who contravenes an order made under section 32 or 33 or reviewed under section 36 commits a violation and is liable to a penalty established in accordance with the regulations.

POWERS OF THE GOVERNOR IN COUNCIL AND MINISTER

Regulations

49. (1) The Governor in Council may make regulations

(*a*) fixing a penalty, or a range of penalties, in respect of each violation;

(*b*) classifying each violation as a minor violation, a serious violation or a very serious violation;

Source: Bill C-52

(*c*) respecting the circumstances under which, the criteria by which and the manner in which a penalty may be increased or reduced, including the reduction of a penalty pursuant to a compliance agreement; and

(*d*) respecting the determination of a lesser amount that may be paid as complete satisfaction of a penalty if paid within the prescribed time and manner.

Maximum penalties

(2) The maximum penalty for a violation is $5,000 in the case of a violation committed by a non-profit organization or by any other person for non-commercial purposes, and $25,000 in any other case.

Notices of violation

50. The Minister may

(*a*) designate individuals, or classes of individuals, who are authorized to issue notices of violation; and

(*b*) establish, in respect of each violation, a short-form description to be used in notices of violation.

PROCEEDINGS

Issuance of notice of violation

51. (1) If a person designated under paragraph 50(*a*) believes on reasonable grounds that a person has committed a violation, the designated person may issue, and shall provide the person with, a notice of violation that

(*a*) sets out the person's name;

(*b*) identifies the alleged violation;

(*c*) sets out the penalty for the violation that the person is liable to pay;

(*d*) sets out the particulars concerning the time and manner of payment; and

(*e*) subject to the regulations, sets out a lesser amount that may be paid as complete satisfaction of the penalty if paid within the prescribed time and manner.

Summary of rights

(2) A notice of violation must clearly summarize, in plain language, the rights and obligations under this section and sections 52 to 66 of the person to whom it is provided,

Source: Bill C-52

including the right to have the acts or omissions that constitute the alleged violation reviewed and the procedure for requesting that review.

PENALTIES

Payment

52. (1) If the person named in the notice pays, in the prescribed time and manner, the amount of the penalty or, subject to the regulations, the lesser amount set out in a notice of violation that may be paid in lieu of the penalty,

(*a*) they are deemed to have committed the violation in respect of which the amount is paid;

(*b*) the Minister shall accept that amount as complete satisfaction of the penalty; and

(*c*) the proceedings commenced in respect of the violation under section 51 are ended.

Alternatives to payment

(2) Instead of paying the penalty set out in a notice of violation or, where applicable, the lesser amount that may be paid in lieu of the penalty, the person named in the notice may, in the prescribed time and manner,

(*a*) if the penalty is $5,000 or more, request to enter into a compliance agreement with the Minister that ensures the person's compliance with the order to which the violation relates; or

(*b*) request a review by the Minister of the acts or omissions that constitute the alleged violation.

Deeming

(3) If a person who is provided with a notice of violation does not pay the penalty in the prescribed time and manner or, where applicable, the lesser amount that may be paid in lieu of the penalty, and does not exercise any right referred to in subsection (2) in the prescribed time and manner, the person is deemed to have committed the violation identified in the notice.

COMPLIANCE AGREEMENTS

Compliance agreements

53. (1) After considering a request under paragraph 52(2)(*a*), the Minister may enter into a compliance agreement, as described in that paragraph, with the person making the request on any terms and conditions that are satisfactory to the Minister, which terms and conditions may

Source: Bill C-52

(*a*) include a provision for the giving of reasonable security, in a form and in an amount satisfactory to the Minister, as a guarantee that the person will comply with the compliance agreement; and

(*b*) provide for the reduction, in whole or in part, of the penalty for the violation.

Deeming

(2) A person who enters into a compliance agreement with the Minister is, on doing so, deemed to have committed the violation in respect of which the compliance agreement was entered into.

Where compliance agreement complied with

(3) If the Minister is satisfied that a person who has entered into a compliance agreement has complied with it, the Minister shall cause a notice to that effect to be provided to the person, at which time

(*a*) the proceedings commenced in respect of the violation under section 51 are ended; and

(*b*) any security given by the person under the compliance agreement shall be returned to the person.

Where compliance agreement not complied with

(4) If the Minister is of the opinion that a person who has entered into a compliance agreement has not complied with it, the Minister shall cause a notice of default to be provided to the person to the effect that

(*a*) instead of the penalty set out in the notice of violation in respect of which the compliance agreement was entered into, the person is liable to pay, in the prescribed time and manner, twice the amount of that penalty and, for greater certainty, subsection 49(2) does not apply in respect of that amount; or

(*b*) the security, if any, given by the person under the compliance agreement shall be forfeited to Her Majesty in right of Canada.

Effect of notice of default

(5) Once provided with the notice of default, the person may not deduct from the amount set out in the notice any amount they spent under the compliance agreement and

(*a*) is liable to pay the amount set out in the notice; or

Source: Bill C-52

(*b*) if the notice provides for the forfeiture of the security given under the compliance agreement, that security is forfeited to Her Majesty in right of Canada and the proceedings commenced in respect of the violation under section 51 are ended.

Effect of payment

(6) If a person pays the amount set out in a notice of default under subsection (4) in the prescribed time and manner,

(*a*) the Minister shall accept the amount as complete satisfaction of the amount owing; and

(*b*) the proceedings commenced in respect of the violation under section 51 are ended.

Refusal to enter into compliance agreement

54. (1) If the Minister refuses to enter into a compliance agreement pursuant to a request under paragraph 52(2)(*a*), the person who made the request is liable to pay the amount of the penalty in the prescribed time and manner.

Effect of payment

(2) If a person pays the amount referred to in subsection (1),

(*a*) they are deemed to have committed the violation in respect of which the payment is made;

(*b*) the Minister shall accept the amount as complete satisfaction of the penalty; and

(*c*) the proceedings commenced in respect of the violation under section 51 are ended.

Deeming

(3) If a person does not pay the amount referred to in subsection (1) in the prescribed time and manner, they are deemed to have committed the violation identified in the notice of violation.

REVIEW BY THE MINISTER

Review under paragraph 52(2)(*b*)

55. (1) On completion of a review requested under paragraph 52(2)(*b*), the Minister shall determine whether the person requesting the review committed a violation and, if the Minister decides that the person committed a violation but considers that the amount of the penalty for the violation was not established in accordance with the regulations, the Minister shall correct the amount of the penalty, and the

Source: Bill C-52

Minister shall cause a notice of any decision under this subsection to be provided to the person who requested the review.

Payment

(2) If the Minister decides under subsection (1) that a person has committed a violation, the person is liable to pay the amount of the penalty confirmed or corrected in that decision in the prescribed time and manner.

Effect of payment

(3) If a person pays the amount referred to in subsection (2),

(*a*) the Minister shall accept the amount as complete satisfaction of the penalty; and

(*b*) the proceedings commenced in respect of the violation under section 51 are ended.

Review in writing

(4) A review by the Minister is to be in writing.

ENFORCEMENT

Debts to Her Majesty

56. (1) The following amounts constitute debts due to Her Majesty in right of Canada that may be recovered as such in the Federal Court:

(*a*) the amount of a penalty, from the time the notice of violation setting out the penalty is provided;

(*b*) every amount set out in a compliance agreement entered into with the Minister under subsection 53(1), from the time the compliance agreement is entered into;

(*c*) the amount set out in a notice of default referred to in subsection 53(4), from the time the notice is provided;

(*d*) the amount of a penalty as set out in a decision of the Minister under subsection 55(1), from the time the notice under that subsection is provided; and

(*e*) the amount of any reasonable expenses incurred pursuant to section 64, from the date they are incurred.

Time limit

(2) No proceedings to recover a debt referred to in subsection (1) may be commenced later than five years after the debt became payable.

Source: Bill C-52

Debt final

(3) A debt referred to in subsection (1) is final and not subject to review or to be restrained, prohibited, removed, set aside or otherwise dealt with except to the extent and in the manner provided by sections 52 to 55.

Certificate of default

57. (1) Any debt referred to in subsection 56(1) in respect of which there is a default of payment, or the part of any such debt that has not been paid, may be certified by the Minister.

Judgments

(2) On production to the Federal Court, the certificate shall be registered in that Court and, when registered, has the same force and effect, and all proceedings may be taken on the certificate, as if it were a judgment obtained in that Court for a debt of the amount specified in it and all reasonable costs and charges associated with the registration of the certificate.

RULES OF LAW ABOUT VIOLATIONS

Violations not offences

58. A violation is not an offence and, accordingly, section 126 of the *Criminal Code* does not apply.

Certain defences not available

59. (1) A person named in a notice of violation does not have a defence by reason that the person

(*a*) exercised due diligence to prevent the violation; or

(*b*) reasonably and honestly believed in the existence of facts that, if true, would exonerate the person.

Common law principles

(2) Every rule and principle of the common law that renders any circumstance a justification or excuse in relation to a charge for an offence under this Act applies in respect of a violation to the extent that it is not inconsistent with this Act.

Burden of proof

60. In every case where the facts of a violation are reviewed by the Minister, he or she must establish, on a balance of probabilities, that the person named in the notice of violation committed the violation identified in the notice.

Offences by corporate officers, etc.

61. If a person other than an individual commits a violation under this Act, any of the person's officers, directors, agents or mandataries who directs, authorizes, assents to,

Source: Bill C-52

acquiesces or participates in the commission of the violation is a party to and liable for the violation whether or not the person who actually committed the violation is proceeded against in accordance with this Act.

Vicarious liability — acts of employees and agents

62. A person is liable for a violation that is committed by any employee, agent or mandatary of the person acting in the course of the employee's employment or the scope of the agent or mandatary's authority, whether or not the employee, agent or mandatary who actually committed the violation is identified or proceeded against in accordance with this Act.

Continuing violation

63. A violation that is continued on more than one day constitutes a separate violation in respect of each day during which it is continued.

Forfeiture

64. Anything seized under this Act in relation to a violation is, at the election of Her Majesty in right of Canada, immediately forfeited to Her Majesty in right of Canada and may be disposed of, at the expense of its owner or the person entitled to possess it at the time of its seizure, if

(*a*) the person is deemed by this Act to have committed the violation; or

(*b*) the Minister, on the basis of a review under this Act, has determined that the person has committed a violation.

OTHER PROVISIONS

Evidence

65. In any proceeding for a violation or for a prosecution for an offence, a notice of violation purporting to be issued pursuant to this Act is admissible in evidence without proof of the signature or official character of the person appearing to have signed the notice of violation.

Time limit

66. No proceedings in respect of a violation may be commenced later than six months after the Minister becomes aware of the acts or omissions that constitute the alleged violation.

GENERAL PROVISIONS

Not a statutory instrument

67. For greater certainty, orders made under this Act, except section 39, are not statutory instruments within the meaning of the *Statutory Instruments Act*.

Source: Bill C-52

How act or omission may be proceeded with

68. If an act or omission can be proceeded with either as a violation or as an offence, proceeding in one manner precludes proceeding in the other.

Certification by Minister

69. A document appearing to have been issued by the Minister, certifying the day on which the acts or omissions that constitute the alleged offence or violation became known to the Minister, is admissible in evidence without proof of the signature or official character of the person appearing to have signed the document and, in the absence of evidence to the contrary, is proof that the Minister became aware of the acts or omissions on that day.

Publication of information about contraventions

70. The Minister may publish information about any contravention of this Act or the regulations, including a contravention referred to in section 48, for the purpose of encouraging compliance with this Act and the regulations.

CONSEQUENTIAL AMENDMENTS

R.S., c. E-14

EXCISE ACT

71. Section 248 of the *Excise Act* is replaced by the following:

Labels on containers of methyl-hydrate or denatured alcohol

248. All vessels containing wood alcohol or denatured alcohol, the labelling of which is not regulated by any regulations made under the *Hazardous Products Act* or the *Canada Consumer Product Safety Act*, shall be labelled in accordance with regulations prescribed under this Act for the purpose of ensuring that the contents of the vessels are clearly identified as a poison.

R.S., c. H-3

HAZARDOUS PRODUCTS ACT

R.S., c. 24 (3rd Supp.), s. 1

72. (1) The definitions "advertise", "controlled product", "hazardous product", "prohibited product" and "restricted product" in section 2 of the *Hazardous Products Act* are repealed.

(2) Section 2 of the Act is amended by adding the following in alphabetical order:

Source: Bill C-52

"controlled product" or "hazardous product" «*produit contrôlé*» ou «*produit dangereux*»

"controlled product" or "hazardous product" means any product, material or substance specified by the regulations made pursuant to paragraph 15(1)(*a*) to be included in any of the classes listed in Schedule II;

R.S., c. 24 (3rd Supp.), s. 1, c. 15 (4th Supp.), s. 9(2); 1996, c. 8, s. 26; 1997, c. 9, s. 104; 2002, c. 28, s. 85; 2004, c. 9, ss. 1 and 2, c. 15, s. 67

73. Part I of the Act is repealed.

R.S., c. 24 (3rd Supp.), s. 1

74. Paragraph 12(*f*) of the Act is replaced by the following:

(*f*) a consumer product as defined in section 2 of the *Canada Consumer Product Safety Act*;

SOR/85-378; SOR/86-943; R.S., c. 24 (3rd Supp.), s. 2(1); SOR/87-444; SOR/88-150 and 557; SOR/90-38 and 246; SOR/93-235; 1997, c. 13, s. 63; SOR/98-175; SOR/99-472; SOR/2001-270; SOR/2003-332; 2004, c. 9, s. 3; SOR/2004-46; SOR/2005-110, 133 and 343; SOR/2007-205 and 259

75. Schedule I to the Act is repealed.

COMING INTO FORCE

Order in council

76. The provisions of this Act come into force on a day or days to be fixed by order of the Governor in Council.

Source: Bill C-52

SCHEDULE 1
(Subsection 4(1) and paragraph 38(1)(c))

1. Explosives within the meaning of section 2 of the *Explosives Act.*
2. Cosmetics within the meaning of section 2 of the *Food and Drugs Act.*
3. Devices within the meaning of section 2 of the *Food and Drugs Act.*
4. Drugs within the meaning of section 2 of the *Food and Drugs Act.*
5. Food within the meaning of section 2 of the *Food and Drugs Act.*
6. Pest control products within the meaning of subsection 2(1) of the *Pest Control Products Act.*
7. Vehicles within the meaning of section 2 of the *Motor Vehicle Safety Act.*
8. Equipment within the meaning of section 2 of the *Motor Vehicle Safety Act* and set out in item 1 of Schedule I to that Act.
9. Vessels within the meaning of section 2 of the *Canada Shipping Act, 2001.*
10. Firearms within the meaning of section 2 of the *Criminal Code.*
11. Ammunition within the meaning of subsection 84(1) of the *Criminal Code.*
12. Cartridge magazines within the meaning of subsection 84(1) of the *Criminal Code.*
13. Cross-bows within the meaning of subsection 84(1) of the *Criminal Code.*
14. Prohibited devices within the meaning of paragraphs (*a*) to (*d*) of the definition "prohibited device" in subsection 84(1) of the *Criminal Code.*
15. Plants within the meaning of section 3 of the *Plant Protection Act.*
16. Seeds within the meaning of section 2 of the *Seeds Act.*
17. Controlled substances within the meaning of subsection 2(1) of the *Controlled Drugs and Substances Act.*
18. Aeronautical products within the meaning of subsection 3(1) of the *Aeronautics Act.*

Source: Bill C-52

SCHEDULE 2
(Section 5 and paragraph 38(1)(c))

1. Jequirity beans (*abrus precatorius*) or any substance or article that is made from or that includes jequirity beans in whole or in part.
2. Spectacle frames that, in whole or in part, are made of or contain cellulose nitrate.
3. Baby walkers that are mounted on wheels or on any other device permitting movement of the walker and that have an enclosed area supporting the baby in a sitting or standing position so that their feet touch the floor, thereby enabling the horizontal movement of the walker.
4. Products for babies, including teethers, pacifiers and baby bottle nipples, that are put in the mouth when used and that contain a filling that has in it a viable micro-organism.
5. Structural devices that position feeding bottles to allow babies to feed themselves from the bottle while unattended.
6. Disposable metal containers that contain a pressurizing fluid composed in whole or in part of vinyl chloride and that are designed to release pressurized contents by the use of a manually operated valve that forms an integral part of the container.
7. Liquids that contain polychlorinated biphenyls for use in microscopy, including immersion oils but not including refractive index oils.
8. Kites any part of which is made of uninsulated metal that is separated from adjacent conductive areas by a non-conductive area of less than 50 mm and that either

    (*a*) has a maximum linear dimension in excess of 150 mm, or

    (*b*) is plated or otherwise coated with a conductive film whose maximum linear dimension exceeds 150 mm.
9. Kite strings made of a material that conducts electricity.
10. Products made in whole or in part of textile fibres, intended for use as wearing apparel, that are treated with or contain tris (2,3 dibromopropyl) phosphate as a single substance or as part of a chemical compound.
11. Any substance that is used to induce sneezing, whether or not called "sneezing powder", and that contains

    (*a*) 3,3′-dimethoxybenzidine (4,4′-diamino-3,3′-dimethoxybiphenyl) or any of its salts;

    (*b*) a plant product derived from the genera *Helleborus* (hellebore), *Veratrum album* (white hellebore) or *Quillaia* (Panama Wood);

    (*c*) protoveratrine or veratrine; or

    (*d*) any isomer of nitrobenzaldehyde.

Source: Bill C-52

12. Cutting oils and cutting fluids, that are for use in lubricating and cooling the cutting area in machining operations, and that contain more than 50 µg/g of any nitrite, when monoethanolamine, diethanolamine or triethanolamine is also present.
13. Urea formaldehyde-based thermal insulation, foamed in place, used to insulate buildings.
14. Lawn darts with elongated tips.

Source: Bill C-52

EXPLANATORY NOTES

Excise Act

Clause 71: Existing text of section 248:

248. All vessels containing wood alcohol or denatured alcohol, the labelling of which is not regulated by any regulations made under the *Hazardous Products Act*, shall be labelled in accordance with regulations prescribed under this Act for the purpose of ensuring that the contents of the vessels are clearly identified as a poison.

Hazardous Products Act

Clause 72: (1) Existing text of the definitions:

"advertise", in relation to a prohibited product or restricted product, includes any representation by any means whatever for the purpose of promoting directly or indirectly the sale or other disposition of the product;

"controlled product" means any product, material or substance specified by the regulations made pursuant to paragraph 15(1)(*a*) to be included in any of the classes listed in Schedule II;

"hazardous product" means any prohibited product, restricted product or controlled product;

"prohibited product" means any product, material or substance included in Part I of Schedule I;

"restricted product" means any product, material or substance included in Part II of Schedule I;

(2) New.

Clause 73: Existing text of Part I:

PART I

PROHIBITED AND RESTRICTED PRODUCTS

APPLICATION

3. (1) This Part does not apply in respect of the advertising, sale or importation of any

(*a*) explosive within the meaning of the *Explosives Act*;

(*b*) cosmetic, device, drug or food within the meaning of the *Food and Drugs Act*;

(*c*) pest control product as defined in subsection 2(1) of the *Pest Control Products Act*; or

(*d*) nuclear substance, within the meaning of the *Nuclear Safety and Control Act*, that is radioactive.

(2) This Part does not apply to the advertising, sale or importation of a tobacco product as defined in section 2 of the *Tobacco Act* or the advertising of lighters or matches that display a tobacco product-related brand element, except to the extent that a cigarette described in item 41 of Part I of Schedule I is a prohibited product.

(3) If the Governor in Council does not make a regulation under paragraph 5(*b.1*) on or before June 30, 2004,

(*a*) the Minister shall prepare a report;

Source: Bill C-52

(*b*) the Minister shall cause a copy of the report to be tabled in each House of Parliament on any of the first ten days on which that House is sitting after June 30, 2004; and

(*c*) each House shall refer the report to the appropriate Committee of that House.

(4) The report is to include

(*a*) an explanation as to why the regulation has not been made;

(*b*) a schedule for the making of the regulation;

(*c*) a list of the safe-cigarette legislation in force in North America; and

(*d*) summaries of any scientific studies that have been reviewed by the Minister during the process of establishing the flammability standards to be used to test cigarettes.

PROHIBITIONS

4. (1) No person shall advertise, sell or import a prohibited product.

(2) No person shall advertise, sell or import a restricted product except as authorized by the regulations made under section 5.

REGULATIONS

5. The Governor in Council may make regulations

(*a*) authorizing the advertising, sale or importation of any restricted product and prescribing the circumstances and conditions under which and the persons by whom the restricted product may be advertised, sold or imported;

(*b*) prescribing the procedures to be followed by a board of review established pursuant to section 9 in conducting an inquiry;

(*b.1*) prescribing the method and flammability standard to be used to test cigarettes; and

(*c*) generally for carrying out the purposes and provisions of this Part.

INTERIM ORDERS

5.1 (1) The Minister may make an interim order that contains any provision that may be contained in a regulation made under this Part if the Minister believes that immediate action is required to deal with a significant risk, direct or indirect, to health or safety.

(2) The Minister may make an interim order in which any power referred to in section 6 is deemed to be exercised, if the Minister believes that immediate action is required to deal with a significant risk, direct or indirect, to health or safety.

(3) An interim order has effect from the time that it is made but ceases to have effect on the earliest of

(*a*) 14 days after it is made, unless it is approved by the Governor in Council,

(*b*) the day on which it is repealed,

(*c*) in the case of an interim order made under subsection (1), the day on which a regulation made under this Part that has the same effect as the interim order comes into force and, in the case of an interim order made under subsection (2), the day on which an order made by the Governor in Council under this Part that has the same effect as the interim order comes into force, and

(*d*) one year after the interim order is made or any shorter period that may be specified in the interim order.

(4) No person shall be convicted of an offence consisting of a contravention of an interim order that, at the time of the alleged contravention, had not been published in the *Canada Gazette* unless it is proved that, at the time of the alleged contravention, the person had been notified of the interim order or reasonable steps had been taken to bring the purport of the interim order to the notice of those persons likely to be affected by it.

(5) An interim order

(*a*) is exempt from the application of sections 3, 5 and 11 of the *Statutory Instruments Act*; and

(*b*) shall be published in the *Canada Gazette* within 23 days after it is made.

(6) For the purpose of any provision of this Part other than this section, any reference to regulations made under this Act is deemed to include interim orders, and any reference to a regulation made under a specified provision of this Act is deemed to include a reference to the portion of an interim order containing any provision that may be contained in a regulation made under the specified provision.

(7) A copy of each interim order must be tabled in each House of Parliament within 15 days after it is made.

(8) In order to comply with subsection (7), the interim order may be sent to the Clerk of the House if the House is not sitting.

AMENDMENTS TO SCHEDULE I

6. (1) The Governor in Council may, by order, amend Part I or II of Schedule I by adding thereto

(*a*) any product, material or substance that is or contains a poisonous, toxic, flammable, explosive, corrosive, infectious, oxidizing or reactive product, material or substance or other product, material or substance of a similar nature that the Governor in Council is satisfied is or is likely to be a danger to the health or safety of the public; or

(*b*) any product designed for household, garden or personal use, for use in sports or recreational activities, as life-saving equipment or as a toy, plaything or equipment for use by children that the Governor in Council is satisfied is or is likely to be a danger to the health or safety of the public by reason of its design, construction or contents.

(2) The Governor in Council may, by order, amend Part I or II of Schedule I by deleting therefrom any product, material or substance if the Governor in Council is satisfied that the inclusion of the product, material or substance in that Part is no longer necessary.

(3) For greater certainty, an order made pursuant to subsection (1) may describe a product, material or substance added thereby to Part I or II of Schedule I by reference to any properties or characteristics of the product, material or substance or by reference to any other criteria and any product, material or substance that has those properties or characteristics or meets those criteria shall, for the purposes of this Act, be deemed to have been added by the order to Part I or II, as the case may be, of Schedule I.

(4) An order made pursuant to subsection (1) incorporating a law, standard or specification by reference may incorporate that law, standard or specification as amended from time to time.

(5) [Repealed, 1996, c. 8, s. 26]

7. (1) The Minister shall cause a copy of each order made pursuant to subsection 6(1) to be laid before each House of Parliament on any of the first fifteen days on which that House is sitting after the day the order is made.

(2) If both Houses of Parliament resolve that an order or any part of an order made pursuant to subsection 6(1) should be revoked, the order or that part thereof is thereupon revoked.

Source: Bill C-52

BOARD OF REVIEW

8. Where a product, material or substance is added to Part I or II of Schedule I by an order made pursuant to subsection 6(1), any manufacturer or distributor of that product, material or substance or any person having that product, material or substance in possession for sale may, within sixty days after the date of the making of the order, request the Minister to refer the order to a board of review.

9. (1) On receipt of a request described in section 8, the Minister shall establish a board of review, in this section referred to as the "Board", consisting of not more than three persons and shall refer the order in respect of which the request was made to the Board.

(2) The Board shall inquire into the nature and characteristics of any product, material or substance to which an order referred to it under subsection (1) applies and shall give the person making the request and any other person affected by the order a reasonable opportunity of appearing before the Board, presenting evidence and making representations to it.

(3) The Board has all the powers that are or may be conferred by or under sections 4, 5 and 11 of the *Inquiries Act* on commissioners appointed under Part I of that Act.

(4) The Board, as soon as possible after the conclusion of its inquiry, shall submit a report with its recommendations to the Minister, together with all evidence and other material that was before the Board.

(5) Any report of the Board shall, within thirty days after its receipt by the Minister, be made public by the Minister, unless the Board states in writing to the Minister that it believes the public interest would be better served by withholding publication, in which case the Minister may decide whether the report, either in whole or in part, shall be made public.

(6) The Minister may publish and supply copies of a report referred to in subsection (4) in such manner and on such terms as the Minister deems proper.

DISCLOSURE

10. (1) Where the Minister has reason to believe that a product, material or substance is a product, material or substance that may be added to Part I or II of Schedule I by an order made pursuant to subsection 6(1), the Minister may, by registered mail, send a written notice to any manufacturer of the product, material or substance requesting the disclosure of information relating to the formula, composition, chemical ingredients or hazardous properties of the product, material or substance and such other information as the Minister deems necessary for the purpose of determining whether the product, material or substance is or is likely to be a danger to the health or safety of the public.

(2) Every manufacturer to whom a notice referred to in subsection (1) is sent shall disclose to the Minister, in the manner and within the period specified in the notice, any information described in that subsection that is requested in the notice and is in the possession of the manufacturer.

(3) Information received by the Minister from a manufacturer pursuant to subsection (1) is privileged and shall not be disclosed to any other person except as may be necessary for the administration or enforcement of this section or for the purposes of section 6.

Clause 74: Relevant portion of section 12:

12. This Part does not apply in respect of the sale or importation of any

. . .

(*f*) product, material or substance included in Part II of Schedule I and packaged as a consumer product;

2

Health Canada's Abuse of Power

by Helke Ferrie

"So, if you were sent a document showing that people were dying because of what Health Canada was doing, you would just ignore that because it's policy or directive?"
"Yes."

Interchange between Truehope lawyer **Shawn Buckley** and Health Canada agent **Miles Brosseau** during cross examination in court, 2006, about the fact that 3,000 patients in the clinical trial were deprived of their treatments causing documented suicides.

"In the councils of government, we must guard against the acquisition of unwarranted influence, whether sought or unsought, by the military-industrial complex. The potential for the disastrous rise of misplaced power exists and will persist. We must never let the weight of this combination endanger our liberties or democratic processes. We should take nothing for granted."

—Dwight Eisenhower,
from his farewell address, January 17, 1961

That governments lie when they are at war, is accepted. Indeed, as has often been said, truth is the first casualty of war. What is historically rather new is the fact that governments lie when it comes to the business of medicine. That's because medicine wasn't a business—until fairly recently. Today it is Big Business.

Medicine betrayed its soul when drugs and medical devices became stock market commodities and thereby became sources of wealth and power, fuelled by the deception that it takes big bucks to make break-through wonder drugs. Similarly, what the food industry has done to the quality of our food absolutely beats the simple crimes of 19th century food adulteration; back then, we had frequent incidents of food poisoning that sometimes killed a lot of people, while today we have systemic disease on a vast scale caused by toxic additives and depleted nutrients. This transformation also occurred when food became publicly traded Big Business.

Both food and medicine can only generate wealth as long as they are protected by "intellectual property rights" granted through complicit governments. That arrangement is also the primary source of the hallmark characteristics of Big Business Medicine and Big Business Food, namely the presence of toxicity and the depletion or outright absence of essential nutrients. Government regulatory systems support this arrangement under the pretext of working for the public good.

Fortunately, good medicine does exists. Virtually all of it was developed by the best minds in mainstream medicine or was imported from very ancient, often empirically verified traditions. There is a parallel universe of medicine; with very little money it has produced and continues to produce the bulk of the greatest medical advances through genuine research of real benefit to sick people. That research is not enslaved to what Dr. Shiv Chopra calls "tobacco science," and its results and products can only very rarely be patented. We *can* get good food, too—uncompromised and nutrient-rich—if we are determined enough. However, it has now become an outright fight for the right of access to both decent food and medicine. In fact this fight has moved into centre stage of the current human rights debate.

Most disturbing of all is the fact that this fight has all the signs and symptoms of the long fight against slavery. During that century, too, it was the governments that needed to change fundamentally before any action against slavery succeeded; the US even had a law forbidding any discussion about slavery in Congress, and it took John Quincy Adams his whole professional life to turn that around. Bill C-51 comes pretty close to that craziness in several sections (e.g. Sections 3/6 and 18) which could prevent a researcher from pursuing a line of questioning that the Minister of Health doesn't approve of. As you saw in lawyer Shawn Buckley's analysis earlier, looking into how vitamin C cures scurvy may or may not be approved.

The Truth Shall Make Us Free— Not If Health Canada Can Help It

Medicines that cure and maintain, and food that nourishes are in fact a single human rights issue, because sickness and health are functions of nutrition first and last. If essential nutrients, especially minerals, are absent or reduced in food (as is the case with processed or genetically engineered food), chronic disease is inevitable for most people. Restoration of health or slowing down progression are only possible if the missing nutrients are restored in therapeutic (i.e. high) doses. Even genetically mediated, hereditary health problems are usually only triggered if prerequisite nutrients are missing in the diet or compromised through toxins from the environment. The Truehope case, which is the subject of this chapter, is currently *the* classic case in point. By far the vast majority of mental health conditions are nutrient-dependent conditions and treating them strictly with symptom-control therapies ought to be malpractice, seeing the alleged supporting science is now known to have been fraudulent. More on that later.

The gene-nutrient interaction could also be seen as the old nature-nurture problem. Genes only express themselves properly if the organism in which they unfold their activities is correctly nourished; they fail to express themselves or cause systemic malfunction if the organism is subjected to toxic trespass or starved by empty calories. This is now the point at which nutritional imperatives in medicine and high-tech pioneering are meeting. This fact implies big bucks, potentially big profits, and the promise of a whole new way of doing medicine.

A June 2008 report in the *Proceedings of the US National Academy of Sciences* (at press time available only on-line—Google PNAS), led by molecular and cell biologist Nicholas Marini and Jasper Rine of the University of California at Berkeley, inform us that vitamins and minerals can fix genetic flaws found within a person's genome, so they don't cause disease expression and are prevented from being passed on. These days, personal genome sequencing is rapidly moving into the range of what ordinary people can afford; the prediction is about $100 per person within a few years. They began to work with the known fact that different people's enzyme systems work at different rates of efficiency, and since enzyme production as well as effectiveness are entirely dependent on the presence of specific essential minerals and vitamins, they showed that "simple supplementation... can often restore some of these deficient enzymes to full working order." Well, there goes down the toilet a whole lot of stuff in Big Pharma's line of products: most of those symptom-control drugs most of which only work by interfering with enzymes, instead of restoring them.

Marini and Rine further noted, sounding like naturopaths and orthomolecular doctors, that they "wouldn't be surprised if everybody is going to require a different optimal dose of vitamins based on their genetic makeup, based upon the kind of variance they are harboring in vitamin-dependent enzymes." Nutritional medicine calls this "biochemical individuality," a term coined in 1956 by the University of Texas biochemist Dr. Roger Williams (1893–1988), the discoverer of the B vitamins pantothenic acid and folic acid. His work prompted Linus Pauling to coin the term "orthomolecular" medicine.

The significance of these latest findings is of great importance to medicine as Big Business. The paradigm shift from toxic drugs to manage symptoms temporarily to non-toxic essential nutrients that cure and can even fix the genome has already happened in basic science and some branches of medical practice. The pharmaceutical industry knows economic recovery is impossible unless drastic changes take place. As one of its weekly publications, the *Genetic Engineering & Biotechnology News*, reports in virtually every issue on the advances made with biosimilars, trials are underway that work with substances that use vitamins and minerals, and Merck is pinning its hopes for economic survival on Cordaptive, a "new" drug expected to be a blockbuster, whose chief ingredient is vitamin B_3 (niacin—the vitamin with which Dr. Abram Hofer changed psychiatry).

In an unfettered true market economy, in which whatever works best is supposedly guided encouragingly by Adam Smith's "invisible hand," it is clear which of the two systems would win out. But as Robert Kennedy Jr. always likes to point out, we don't have a free market economy, much as we would really like it. If we did, Health Canada would never have even dreamed of shutting down a successful clinical trial, as happened in the Truehope case, but instead would have supported this project and publicized it far and wide and put Canadian medical research on the map and shown it to be a landmark in medical history. Undoubtedly, the truth shall makes us free—but not if Health Canada can help it.

This is not a nasty aside but anchored in cold, hard fact: The Natural Health Product Directorate of Health Canada in their *Status of Submissions Report* of March 2008 informs on the current status of natural health products on the market. Apparently, only 11% of the total applications between 2004 and 2008 have been approved for marketing licenses. Drug companies would storm Health Canada's offices yelling and screaming, if their applications were treated like this.

Medicine That Works Is A Charter Right

Medicine and food affect so many aspects of life that their abuse by government and Big Business raises serious questions about possible violations against several sections in the Charter. For example, the right to participation in government (Section 3) appears to be meaningless when considering the way our Members of Parliament currently respond to their constituents who are alarmed about Bill C-51 and C-52. The MPs' responses from *both* the Conservatives and Liberal parties are virtually identical in their canned messages. One can't get a topic-specific response out of either group of MPs! Is there a functioning Official Opposition left? Without a functioning opposition it is impossible for citizens to participate in any policy process.

Furthermore, it seems to me that we need to include in the interpretation of the Charter's right "to life, liberty and security of the person" (Section 7) the right to be protected from the "cost-benefit" games and "risk management" calculations which arbitrarily accept the death and injury of many for the profit of the few.

The abuse of Section 7 rights is compounded by the way bill C-51 proceeds on assumptions about what constitutes safe medicines. These assumptions are not supported by the Canadian Medical Association which on May 6, 2008, published an article in the CMAJ expressing dismay about how this bill proposes to "lower the threshold for initial marketing authorization," even though it is clear from years of research, as reviewed this year in the *New England Journal of Medicine*, that "rapidly approved drugs are more likely to be recalled or have subsequent safety problems." (Translation: shoddy drugs rushed to market kill more people—faster.) The CMAJ article points out that this proposed move hardly matches the rhetoric about this bill's intent as expressed by Prime Minister Stephen Harper who announced that negligent firms which "cut corners and play fast and loose with safety" should "be warned. You will soon face severe punishment if you willfully expose Canadians to danger."

The Prime Minister, with all due respect, seems to be unaware that the current Food and Drugs Act already gives the government all those powers of recall, crack-down, and enforcement of safety standards, but Health Canada only uses them, if at all, when they cannot avoid it any longer, and then only with the gentlest possible touch. The Food and Drugs Act is anchored in the Criminal Code, and Health Canada could suspend marketing permission for all those harmful antidepressants, cholesterol-lowering drugs, various arthritis medications —in fact most of what is currently listed in the CPS—which came to market on the basis of fraudulent science and since have killed or injured tens of thousands.

Reports on governments putting their regulatory agencies to work on the task of spinning the most fantastic structures of lies, in an effort to rev up profits for the drug and medical devices industry, have become so commonplace that the surprise effect has quite worn off. In fact, the real surprise comes whenever government does something that is not spin, such as when Canada passed the new pesticide legislation in 2004, which is actually rather life-friendly. Its enforcement is unlikely to be conducted by this government; it will undoubtedly lie asleep like Briar Rose, until woken by a European Union prince armed with the true love of humanity. See the story on the new EU treaty on toxic substances called REACH in Chapter 5.

The tragedy in this vast deception is that hundreds of thousands of people die needlessly and often horribly for the sake of profit, and that at the same time very good people with totally pure intentions are duped—doctors, patients, nurses, administrators, technicians who often sincerely believe they are doing the best for people by providing them with expensive treatments that almost never have any lasting benefit but speed up misery and death (chemotherapy, radiation, antidepressants, cholesterol-lowering drugs, most anti-inflammatory drugs etc.); tests that almost never predict correctly and increase the risk of harm beyond the risk of the disease itself (mammography, CAT scans, PSA tests); drugs of which most are mere magician's tricks demonstrating a measurable effect on symptoms while systematically depriving the patient of the essential nutrients required for healing; and so a huge amount of what Medicare pays for has become the leading cause of death.

And then there is our great arsenal of modern vaccines—those venerable sacred cows of medicine that are riding on the coat-tails of the two truly great vaccines in medical history (small pox and polio). The rest of the current and aggressively marketed vaccines not only rarely protect against the diseases they claim to protect against, but can cause irreparable, life-long harm. Alan Cassels, pharmaceutical policy researcher at the University of British Columbia, put it perfectly in an article published in September 2007 in *Common Ground*; he wrote: "Lock up your daughters, Gardasil is on the loose!" Governments are pushing it like mad, even though it does nothing to protect against cervical cancer, being designed to protect against some strains of viraly-caused genital warts which are not known to promote cancer;

in addition, Gardasil now has a death toll and complication incidence greater than all vaccines currently on the market.

Undeniably, vaccines are wonderful as tools of deception to make a government appear earnestly devoted to the public good and lots of people in government are duped themselves. They have to be—how else is it possible that one frequently sees some pitiable, uninformed minister of health publicly taking a shot of some totally useless flu vaccine and thereby compromising his or her immune system?

The abuse of one of the few classes of drugs that really ought to be sacred, namely antibiotics, is equally shameful. For several decades now Health Canada has ignored all warnings from science, the World Health Organization, and even the preferences of international trade partners, but continues to support the prophylactic use of carcinogenic antibiotics in food producing animals. How Health Canada management and a whole series of health ministers even fought their own regulatory scientists on this issue is told in the utterly fascinating book by Dr. Shiv Chopra, one of Canada's great Public Guardians, in his new book, *Corrupt to the Core* (see Chapter 4 and information on it at the very end of this book).

Understanding Psychopathy

Our lives depend on knowing the truth, refusing to be lied to, and becoming propaganda-proof. Indeed, it would probably be more appropriate to say that in order to become propaganda-proof one must understand the nature of psychopathy; that is the disease that the corporations have infected our governments with. The way in which Health Canada treats Canadians is very much like what was so well developed in the 2004 documentary film *The Corporation* which also is available in a book by the same title. The arguments are based on the work of an expert on psychopathy, Dr. Robert Hare, who identified as the classic signs of a psychopathic personality an approach to chosen goals that puts "everybody else ... at risk." Psychopaths "manipulate everything, including public opinion," they are "grandiose, always insisting 'that we are number one, we're the best."

Psychopaths "lack empathy" and have "asocial tendencies"; they don't "concerns themselves with their victims," they "refuse to accept responsibility for their actions" and are "unable to feel remorse." (p. 56–57)

In this chapter you will find reproduced the documents that tell the perfectly unbelievable story ofTruehope.The way in which Health Canada related to the participants in this famous clinical trial, conducted by the University of Calgary and a Harvard University psychiatrist is the most perfect example I have yet come across of pure psychopathy as government policy.The Health Canada part of this material should be in psychiatry textbooks.

Today, Canadians feel and understand that something is totally not right at Health Canada. Long before bills C-51 and C-52 appeared on the political scene, the Conservative government of Brian Mulroney started the process, the Liberals continued it, and the current Conservative government of Stephen Harper is trying to put the finishing touch on the process of deregulating foods and drugs. Given that in this respect there appears to be no difference between the parties, it makes sense that in this current emergency involving bills C-51 and C-52, the MPs of both parties supply the same non-answers to Canadians writing to them in protest.

Looking back at the events of 2004, it is instructive and gratifying to see how quickly and wisely Canadians responded to that irresponsible effort to deregulate medicine and foods.

I also included material from articles I wrote on the parallel medical universes. This information provides context for the subsequent way in which Health Canada went into attack mode when a medical trial showed astoundingly good results, using natural products in therapeutic doses, to treat a disease that is defended by the drug industry as its exclusive turf, namely depression and bipolar disorder. Dr. David Healy, the world-renowned pharmacologist and psychiatrist who exposed the tactics used to bring antidepressants to market, recently told *The Guardian* (April 7, 2008) that about 2.5 million children in the US are on drugs like Risperdal and the diagnosis of bipolar now conveniently includes irritability or just plain "difficult behavior."

Health Canada's Tries To Sell Deregulation

The blizzard that descended on central Ontario on the night of January 27th caused zero visibility, and traveling on the 401 was guesswork. It took me over ten hours to make it to Ottawa, twice the usual time, to reach my destination—a symposium on Health Canada's proposed "modernization" changes to the Food and Drugs Act. The event was hosted by the Canadian Health Coalition and was attended by scientists, famous media personalities, and concerned citizens. The event ended with the presentation of an open letter to the Prime Minister protesting the proposed sell-out of Canada's most precious natural resource—people—to the pharmaceutical and biochemical industry. It was signed by hundreds of Canada's most famous people—from Margaret Atwood to David Suzuki as well as thousands of ordinary people and supported by letters of endorsement from 26 countries. Two days later, the roads were clear and the land resplendent in glittering winter garb. As I drove home and tried to digest what I had learned, it occurred to me, that instead of the familiar bumper sticker reading "It is as bad as you think, and they are out to get you," we need one that reads: "They are much worse than you think, and they have already got you."

The government's effort to modernize the Foods and Drugs Act was outlined in the 2003 "Report on Plans and Priorities" in which it is stated that the act has "too narrow a focus on safety ... and does not allow for taking into account considerations other than safety and efficacy in managing health risks." The new act is supposed to "unleash business energies" and "reduce the regulatory burden on business," especially on the biotechnology and drug industries. Under the title "Health and Safety First," the government published its plans to give us all "a higher level of protection" through a new act:

- Instead of the current "duty to care" for Canadians, the act would be focused on risk management, a business concept that *includes* potential damage or death and even plans for it in its legal cost projections in the same way as a general calculates how many troops are likely to be killed in a campaign. Even if a drug turns out to be carcinogenic (e.g. antidepressants), because not everybody gets cancer, enough money can be made from people who don't notice the connection or don't get cancer to make sales drug cost-effective. Risk management is literally the opposite of "duty to care," the latter does not permit conscious inclusion of dead bodies whose litigious costs can be financially managed from the drug's profits.

- Proof of harm would be transferred from the drug company to the patient. Health Canada washes its hands of the problem because all safety issues would be dealt with by the producer; no independent evaluation or human trials would be required.
- Health Canada would no longer be liable—for anything. Nice move, given the fact that they are currently facing $12 billion worth of liability suits for regulatory negligence, faulty medical devices, tainted blood, as well as civil suits for harassment of their own scientists for not bending to corporate demands for approval shortcuts.
- Direct to consumer advertising (DTCA) of drugs would also be permitted. According to Stephen Leacock, advertising "is the science of arresting human intelligence long enough to get money from it." All scientific information concerning its efficacy and safety would be the "proprietary information" of that company. In the US, the sales from the 50 most advertised drugs account for 48% of the $20.8 billion *increase* in retail spending since advertising began big time in 1999. (From www.yourlawyer.com, Jan. 19, 2004)

Health Canada was invited to send a representative. Two were expected. One made excuses in the last moment and didn't show, the other announced at the outset that he was "not permitted to take any questions." He hastily left after reading his prepared statement on why the law needed "modernizing" to supposedly provide for better safety. When he had left, Dr. Michelle Brill-Edwards took to the podium and very gently observed that what we had all heard didn't reflect what the Food and Drugs Act actually states. She proceeded to give us all a short course in what is really written in that Act.

The Human Cost of Big Pharma's Profit

So, what about the recommendations made by Justice Krever and the Romanow Report? They are gone with the wind that whistles around Parliament Hill, and thousands of Canadians died—not for nothing, oh no! They made some companies very rich before they died. Both Justice Krever and Roy Romanow made it clear that the government's role is to protect the health and safety of its citizens, not to further investment interests that carry risk to health and safety. Health Canada appears to treat us as if human sickness is an infinite resource and as if people, like the environment and natural resources, don't need the application of the concept of sustainability. Consider the fact that the cost of prescription drugs in Canada increased between 1985 and 2000 a whopping 344% and that drugs alone cost the state more than fees for doctors and hospital care combined. And why are chronic disease and antibiotic-resistant illness increasing constantly, even though the population is not?

FDA records show that drug mark-ups frequently are in the 800,000 % range, but unrelated to production costs. That is because "most drug companies have a pipeline problem" (J. Surowiecki, February 16th, *The New Yorker*). The number of available chemical molecules is limited. That leaves price increases and mergers. The joke in this industry is that "you know you are in the pharmaceutical business when you have worked for five companies in the past two years and you are still sitting at the same old desk." They buy each other up in frantic haste to milk one more block buster drug. Surowiecki observes, "When the going gets tough, the tough go shopping."

As for their safety, consider that the journal *Pharmacy Today* reported a couple of weeks ago that in their (super-conservative estimate) at least 200,000 American die annually from drug side effects. The prestigious Johns Hopkins Medical School pegged the number at 250,000 six years ago, and the estimate for Canada is at 100,000 annually—and almost all are avoidable. That's 959 people a day or 4.5 million people in 12 years (the Nazis killed 6 million in that period).

This event in Ottawa was graced by stellar medical experts and internationally famous whistleblowers such as Dr. David Healy (antidepressant expert), Dr. Nancy Olivieri (blood disease expert), Terrence Young (former MPP whose daughter died from Prepulsid), Professor Barbara Mintzes (researcher in the effect of drug ads) of the University of British Columbia, Professor Joel Lexchin (specializes on the drug approval system) of York University, and Dr. Michelle Brill-Edwards, formerly the senior doctor in human drug regulation at Health Canada.

Terrence Young told the heart-breaking story of his daughter's death from Prepulsid, now the subject of an international class action suit involving the families of hundreds of victims. During the inquest, the drug company's representative said "We see Health Canada as our best customer." In a meeting with Health Canada regulators, Young learned that Health Canada sees its job as "helping companies get their drugs to market faster." When he insisted that a report include a warning against "corrupt practices" at Health Canada, he later found those words changed to "management practices."

Dr. Olivieri told the story of her ongoing legal battle against a drug that causes liver damage or failure in many patients and irreversible arthritis in many more. Former Health Minister Allan Rock refused to meet with her because the manufacturer's headquarters are in his riding. The Olivieri story has made medical history because it prompted a response from all the medical journals in the world whose editors began the process of setting new standards in an attempt to free medical research of corporate control.

Dr. David Healy described the process by which drug experts like himself are systematically duped by the manufacturer, denied access to the actual data, and presented with reports containing mysterious language: thus a certain percentage of patients on antidepressants developed "emotional lability" which later turned out to mean suicide. Another percentage of patients became "hostile," which turned out to be homicidal. Some "scientific" reports came from authors "TBD," which means "to be determined," having been pre-authored by anonymous industry writers. About half of all medical research publications are ghost written by the industry.

Dr. Brill-Edwards related an event that sums it all up perfectly. When Dr. Olivieri tried to engage a Health Canada Deputy Minister in a discussion about drug safety, he said, "Well, tell us what's unsafe about it." Dr. Brill-Edwards interrupted and said, "No! You provide us the proof that it is safe. That is your duty under the act."

"Safety and duty to care do not go out of date," states the report by the event's hosts, the Canadian Health Coalition's *Safety Last*. There is no need to renovate or modernize the Food and Drugs Act—the only thing Canadians want and need is that it is followed and enacted. Its safety requirements are today even more appropriate than they were when the act was written. Terrence Young went further and asserted that we need *criminal accountability* for Health Canada in the spirit of the recently passed bill C-45, which makes corporations responsible for disasters such as the Westray Mine tragedy, and the recent Supreme Court decision making polluting companies responsible for clean-ups. We need court actions to stop government collusion with industry and condemn this lucrative mass murder. We need to turn to the courts to establish if we are dealing with mere crooks or the criminally insane.

The health coalition's director Mike McBane put it all together back in 2004 and his words are even more true now, in 2008: "If Health Canada's proposed evisceration of the Foods And Drugs Act is allowed, there will literally be no limit to what the corporations will put in our stomachs and our blood-streams"—and ignorance will not only cease to be bliss but will become death.

Note: The above article is a short version of one published in *Vitality Magazine* in March 2004.

The Orthomolecular Universe

"Orthomolecular" was coined in 1968 by the late, great, two-time Nobel laureate Linus Pauling who published it for the first time that year on April 19 in the prestigious journal *Science*. Ortho is Greek for "correct." Pauling defined orthomolecular medicine as using "the right molecule in the right concentration" for the purpose of "the preservation of health and the treatment of disease by varying the concentrations in the human body of substances that are normally present in the body and are required for health."

Orthomolecular medicine professionals provide the body with the requisite vitamins, minerals, amino acids, essential fatty acids, enzymes, phytonutrients, and more, to heal and prevent illness. The entire supplement industry was born in the '60s because of Pauling's work with vitamin C and Dr. Abram Hoffer's spectacularly successful application of B vitamins in psychiatry. In the 1970s, Pauling and Hoffer were joined by University of Chicago allergist and immunologist Dr. Theron Randolph who adapted orthomolecular modalities to treat petrochemical and pesticide induced illness. Unlike synthetic drugs, essential nutrients not only are capable of effectively controlling symptoms, but they do so because nutrients have four fundamental properties that no human-made substance can ever have:

1. when depleted, nutrients are diagnostic of disease;
2. they are therapeutic and curative when used in optimal doses;
3. they detoxify because they neutralize or chelate harmful substances;
4. and they are fundamentally preventive of disease by regulating and maintaining homeostasis.

In clinical application, orthomolecular medicine is like a language that permits doctors to dialogue with nature and find out what the patient needs for restoration of health.

As for the sheer waste of money involved in focusing only on development of patentable medicines, Dr. Frederic Calon of Laval

University observed in the *Canadian Medical Association Journal* on February 14, 2006, that the price modern medicine pays for its ignorance about nonpatentable drugs is simply unsustainable. Calon is a molecular endocrinologist and oncologist who criticized the hundreds of millions of dollars spent on researching patentable molecules for cancer and Alzheimer's when, in fact, "it is quite possible that suboptimal consumption of [essential] fatty acids [due to junk and processed food]... will soon translate into increasingly more patients with Alzheimer's disease."

Calon goes on to support what was once heresy: "Folic acid, mineral and vitamin supplements are good examples of low-cost non-patentable drugs commonly recommended by health professionals. Americans experience osteoporotic fractures each year, with an annual cost of US$14 billion in health care alone" while "a 400 UI vitamin D and a 1,000 mg calcium supplement reduces the risk of fracture by at least 15% [and] costs less than CN$200 per patient per year." [By 2008 we have the voluminous research collected by the International Vitamin D Council showing that the daily dose required must be at least 1,000 UI of D.]

Orthomolecular physicians base their diagnoses on testable biochemical and physiological reality in the patient and then tailor their therapies to that patient's bio-individual needs. Most importantly, orthomolecular doctors teach us how to eat correctly, how to avoid environmental and food-based poisons and, therefore, how to live in accordance with the laws of nature. This is truly scientific medicine. As such it presents a challenge to what Dr. Hoffer calls "the Chronically Ethically Sick Medical Industrial Complex, or CESMIC," whose immense profits and state-bankrupting potential are supported by patent law.

Orthomolecular medicine was born in the minds of leading mainstream scientists and is no longer a small voice crying in the wilderness; it has become a parallel universe of scientists working at the most prestigious mainstream institutions. The following brief survey of the presence of orthomolecular research in modern medicine will come as a delightful surprise to those of us who are refugees from the authoritarian world of allopathic medicine.

The Role Of Nutrients In Curing Disease

Insulin for diabetes, iodine for thyroid insufficiency, cod liver oil and vitamin D for rickets, and vitamin C for scurvy are old and well-known examples of orthomolecular treatments. One of the world's most famous nutritional researchers, Bruce Ames, described in the *American Journal of Clinical Nutrition* (April 2002) that there are no less than "50 human genetic diseases due to defective enzymes [which] can be remedied or ameliorated by the administration of high doses of the vitamin component of the corresponding coenzyme which at least partially restores" the patient.

It is not difficult to understand the critical role of nutrition when considering a recent report on birth defects commissioned by the March of Dimes. It showed that nearly 8 million babies are born annually worldwide with genetic defects—70% being preventable simply by adding sufficient amounts of folates (B vitamins) or by preventing nutrient loss caused by food processing methods (*Los Angeles Times* Jan 31, 2006 and *Environmental Health Perspectives*, October 2006). Supporting this is the latest US government report on the nutritional status of Americans: it showed that 93% of Americans are seriously deficient (below RDA levels) in vitamin E; 56% are deficient in magnesium, 44% in vitamin C. (NHANES Report on www.lef.org, Oct 1, 2005)

Current research from genetics shows that without adequate nutrients, chromosomes are damaged and our DNA program cannot build or repair. On April 16, 2003 the National Institutes of Health held a press conference announcing that the Human Genome Project had sequenced more than 200 "environmentally responsive genes" all dependent upon specific nutrients, without which they develop "links to vascular disease and leukemia." (www.apps.niehs. nih.gov)

A study published in the February 2006 issue of *Environmental Health Perspectives* showed that placing children on an organic diet for merely 5 days reduced the measurable amounts of pesticide metabolites in their urine to zero. Organic food not only provides the required nutrients, but rapidly detoxes pesticide residues in the body, all of which are known to interfere with DNA activity.

Apparently the news is getting through to some hospitals. Since 1999, the percentage of hospitals offering nutritional supplementation has increased from a mere 7.7% to 19%, and 2,000 hospitals in the US have started to serve only organic food (Organic Consumers Association, July 20, 2006, *Integrative Medicine* Oct/Nov2006). Of further interest is also that the British prison system showed in a pilot study that violence was reduced by 40% by switching to whole foods (*The Guardian* Oct 17, 2006).

Prescription Drug Toxicity

The world's premier science journal, *Nature*, reported on September 28, that according to the US Institute of Medicine, the Food and Drug Administration is "unsafe, outdated, weak, disorganized, underfunded" and lacking "the money and muscle to police the safety of drugs already on the market." Apparently, business as usual is more deadly than usual. Yet the safety of vitamins and other supplements is better than ever: a report from New Zealand shows that natural medicines carry less risk to health and survival than being hit by a meteor, while the most risky thing you can do is go to a hospital—apparently even bungee jumping is safer. (www.zeusinfoservice.com Oct 13, 2006)

Support for this finding came from the 2003 annual report of the American Association of Poison Control Centers: 106,000 deaths were caused by pharmaceutical drugs, but only 2 deaths were suspected from nutritional supplements of which 53 billion doses are taken by Americans annually. (*Orthomolecular Medicine News Service*, November 9, 2005) Most helpfully, the American Association of Pharmacists published a book detailing which pharmaceutical drugs deplete essential nutrients. It comes in two versions: one for patients in ordinary language available on amazon.com, and the other for doctors with all the scientific literature. I have successfully used this information with family members who temporarily needed to take toxic drugs and recommend it highly.

Exciting Research In Orthomolecular Medicine

There are too many studies to list here which show that natural substances work best. Two examples: the extreme toxicity of antidepressants is in most cases easily avoided by taking non-toxic St. John's Wort instead (*British Medical Journal* Feb. 11, 2005), and the terrors of statin drugs are avoidable by taking essential fatty acids, B vitamins and magnesium instead (*Journal of the American College of Nutrition*, Oct 23, 2004).

The effectiveness of the B vitamin, Niacin, to control high blood pressure and treat most cardiac conditions is well established. Even fetal alcohol syndrome can be prevented with B vitamin supplementation in alcoholic mothers. Together with Vitamin D, Multiple sclerosis responds to these vitamins, and selenium has been shown to effectively treat HIV-AIDS and prevent mother-to-child transmission in studies conducted by the European Union (*Prostaglandins*, August 1989, *Proceedings of the National Academy of Science*, no 103, 2006; *PloS Medicine* vol 3 issue 4, free on-line www.plosmedicine.org; *Brain Research* 2006 p. 1073-74:25f; *Journal of Neuroscience*, Sept 20, 2006; *Medical Hypothesis* volume 62: 549f, 2004; *Journal of Acquired Immune Deficiency Syndrome* volume 42:523f, 2006; bibliographies on www.alternative health.com)

Vitamin A has been shown to cure leukemia, as reported by the Anderson Cancer Centre in Texas (*Pharmaceutical News*, June 7, 2004). The B vitamins cut the risk of esophageal and colon cancer in half, and successfully treat migraine, bipolar disorder and schizophrenia, as reported by Harvard Medical School, Dalhousie University, Australia's Griffith University and in many journals. Recently, the *Canadian Medical Association Journal* published the excellent results achieved in cancer patients with intravenous vitamin C (March 28, 2006).

Vitamin D should be taken in amounts of at least 1,000 IU daily and only from wild fish, never from farmed ones, according to the American Society for Bone and Mineral Research and the revised views of the Institute of Medicine (*Medical Post* October 3, 2006). Vitamin E is now proven to slow the progression of cataracts (*Medical*

Post September 13, 2005). Big Pharma even knows that their toxic drugs do less damage if they add some essential nutrients like Co-enzyme Q_{10}, upon which the functioning of the heart depends (*Integrative Medicine* October/November 2006 p. 24 f).

Dr. Telford of the Royal Jubilee Hospital in Victoria, BC, reported recently that he cures skin cancer patients with creams consisting of vitamins A, C and E (*Medical Post*, August 23, 2005). As for longevity, McMaster University researchers showed that supplementing lab animals with vitamins B, C, E, Cod Liver Oil, various enzymes, Alpha-lipoic Acid and minerals makes them live a lot longer and stay healthy (Society for Experimental Biology and Medicine, 2003, or rollocd@mcmaster.ca).

In January of 2006, two UK-based consumer groups, the Mental Health Foundation and Sustain, published reports entitled *Changing Diets, Changing Minds: How Food Affects Mental Wellbeing and Behaviour* and *Feeding Minds* respectively (both free on-line at www.sustainweb.org). In these reports the scientific facts are assembled that show how food production methods, farming practices, advertising, and environmental policies may soon cause the cost of mental health services to rise to £100 billion (UK currency) annually, because the diet does not contain the necessary essential nutrients, such as folic acid, omega-3 fatty acids, selenium, vitamin C, minerals, and the amino acid tryptophan. A pilot program was carried out in Rotherham, South Yorkshire during which mental patients were not allowed to consume convenience foods, snacks, chocolate bars, colas, and refined sugar products. Instead, they were given whole foods and essential nutrient supplementation. Some totally recovered and everyone improved.

Even the ultimate sacred cow of standard psychiatry, the famous serotonin theory of depression, has finally expired. The new journal *PloS Medicine* (http://medicine.plosjournals.org) was founded by thousands of US medical students and medical Nobel laureate Harold Varmus. In 2004, it published an article in the December 2005 issue entitled *Serotonin and Depression: A Disconnect between the Advertisements and the Scientific Literature.* Reviewing research since the 1960s, when this hypothesis was first suggested, the authors conclude that the US $3 billion antidepressant market, claiming this hypothesis as scientific justification for its existence, is based on nothing at all; they observe that "contemporary neuroscience research has failed to confirm *any* serotonergic lesion in *any* mental disorder and has in fact provided significant counterevidence to the explanation of a simple neurotransmitter deficiency." They conclude: "The incongruence between the scientific literature and the claims made by FDA-regulated SSRI [anti-depressant drugs] advertisements is remarkable, and possibly unparalleled."

PloS was founded in protest against the corruption pervading medical publications; it accepts no advertising, only publishes research free from all connections to the pharmaceutical industry, and is cost-free available on-line. Its founding medical students regularly campaign against corporate contamination of medicine by asking doctors to return even free pens given to them by drug reps.

The insight that brain health depends on *real* food and the *right* foods began in the late 1940s in Canada at the University of Saskatchewan with Dr. Abram Hoffer. His life's work could justly be described as being an essential nutrient in its own right. His research, being based on the right questions, correct observations, and relevant assumptions, has functioned like a vitamin, mineral, or essential fatty acid for the growth of medical knowledge. This so because such research sustains and nourishes every branch of inquiry it comes in contact with. It was my privilege to publish his scientific memoirs, *Adventures in Psychiatry* (Kos 2005).

This book is a feast for the mind and the spirit. It tells the wonderful story of the rebirth of nutritional medicine in the 20th century and its placement on new foundations of rigorous scientific methodology, made possible through the parallel developments in biochemistry and other basic sciences.

Today, much of what is known about the biochemistry of addiction, depression, schizophrenia, attention deficit disorders, the nutritional role in cancer prevention and treatment, the connection between stress and mental health, the nutritional deficiencies acting in synergy with vaccine toxicity in autism, and the nutritional regimes to reverse this condition, as well as the nutritional treatment of cardiovascular/lipid disorders were either pioneered by Dr. Hoffer or co-developed alongside other giants in those fields, such as two-time Nobel laureate Linus Pauling, Theron Randolph (the father of environmental medicine), Humphrey Osmond, Roger Williams (discoverer of Pantothenic acid and many other B vitamins), Irwin Stone (vitamin C pioneer), Bernard Rimland (autism research pioneer), and many others.

Dr. Hoffer dedicated his memoirs to Tommy Douglas who was Premier of Saskatchewan when Dr. Hoffer was professor of psychiatry in Regina. Douglas energetically supported Dr. Hoffer's efforts to humanize the appalling conditions in the mental asylums of that time and encouraged the research begun into the nutritional deficiency connections to mental disease.

We follow the author from his Saskatchewan farm childhood, subsequent training in bio-chemistry and agricultural science, his early insights into the central importance of soil and plant food quality to human and animal health, to his specialization in psychiatry, professorship at the University of Saskatchewan, and above all his daily work with patients. We learn of his disillusionment with traditional methods of treating the mentally ill (e.g. lobotomies), and we share his excitement of discovery as we read the stories of some of his dramatic cases which unfold like detective-stories. One example is that of the first patient successfully rescued in the early 1950s from end-stage catatonic schizophrenia through vitamin therapy:

> "Ken ... lay on his bed unresponsive, not able to eat or drink. Catatonic deaths [among schizophrenic patients] were not uncommon many years ago. We decided to make him the first patient to receive massive doses of the two vitamins ... niacin and vitamin C. We were certain we could not do Ken any harm since he was so close to death. We inserted a tube into his stomach since he could not swallow. Then we poured in a mixture of five grams of nicotinic acid and 2.5 grams of ascorbic acid. We waited anxiously by his bedside .... he seemed to grow no worse as this regimen was continued. On the second day he was able to sit up and drink his solution of vitamins. One month later he was completely normal!"

Another patient story is that of a man who, while walking in the city of Regina, suddenly thought he heard God telling him to go and assault a woman walking in front of him. The patient was successfully restrained and brought to the hospital where he came into Dr. Hoffer's care. After a few weeks on therapeutic doses of vitamins and a diet rich in fish to provide essential fatty acids, the patient's personality completely changed and he felt like somebody awaking from a strange dream. This was George Porteous. He recovered completely —and became the Lieutenant Governor of Saskatchewan. His gratitude to Dr. Hoffer was so great, that he permitted him to tell this story anywhere and anytime to help similarly suffering people have faith in the possibility of total recovery.

Dr. Hoffer patiently handled the insufferable stupidity and arrogance of medical authorities in government and at universities, often hell-bent on preserving their pride and the status quo rather than focus on the suffering of patients. You will laugh and weep reading this book and regain faith in both medicine and humanity. Harold D. Foster, who teaches medical geography at the University of Victoria in BC, noted about this book that Dr. Hoffer's work with vitamins served to " undermine the reigning medical paradigms for psychiatry and cardiovascular disease. Fathering a new paradigm does not promote popularity. Fortunately, Dr Hoffer .... has consistently proven to be able to stand up for the truth, regardless of personal cost. Look around you, there are health food stores everywhere—now and thank Abram Hoffer for his courage." Indeed, the first vitamin B tablets were made at the suggestion of Dr. Hoffer, back in the early 1950's, by a compounding pharmacist.

In his closing reflections Dr. Hoffer writes that "if research is to have any value at all it must explore outside what is currently known." He muses also about the fact that "advice from enemies and friends presents a major challenge to those who think outside the box. The enemies are easy to identify and their advice is easily dismissed," Dr. Hoffer writes, but the advice of friends is harder to deal with: "The most common bad advice I received from friends was not to continue what we were doing because it made us unpopular. It took me some thought an effort to reject this advice; I feel vindicated in this decision as I see that I have been very popular with my patients … for the past 50 years."

Sources:

Hoffer, *Adventures in Psychiatry—Scientific Memoirs*, Kos 2005, available through www.isom.org

A. Hoffer, *Putting It All Together: The New World of Orthomolecular Nutrition*, Keats, 1996

Note: From articles published in *Vitality Magazine* in February and November 2006

Natural Health Products at Risk

But New Private Members Bill Aims to Restore Freedom of Choice in NHPs

by Dr. James Lunney, MP
Vitality Magazine September 2003

Dr. James Lunney, MP was a chiropractor for approximately 24 years (last nine on Vancouver Island) before entering federal politics. He is the federal Member of Parliament for riding of Nanaimo-Alberni, on central Vancouver Island, BC. He is a member of the Canadian Alliance.

Much confusion currently exists about the new natural health product (NHP) regulations scheduled to come into force in early 2004. They were crafted under the old Food and Drugs Act, without the legislative renewal that was promised. Canadians had been led to believe that NHP would be considered by law as a third category; not food, not drugs. The reality is that under the new regulations, all natural health products will now be considered a subclass of drugs. They will be managed as food if no health claim, drugs there is a health claim.

On March 20, 2003, I introduced Private Members' Bill C-420, which cuts right to the heart of the matter to restore freedom of choice in personal health care. Bill C-420 would place NHPs under the authority of a food directorate, and would release the scientific information to allow Canadians to make informed decisions about their personal health care.

History of the Controversy

In Canada, natural health products have historically been regulated as either food or drugs. Health Canada determines how these products are classified, and has the power to take products off the market. Unfortunately, Health Canada has treated every natural health product, no matter how benign or beneficial, as a drug as soon as a health claim is made. In 1997, then-Minister of Health, David Dingwall, proposed new rules for NHPs, in an attempt to bring them all under the authority of a drug directorate. He also proposed increased fees for manufacturers and retailers, and the requirement for products to carry a drug identification number (DIN).

Immediately, natural health product consumers, advocates, retailers and manufacturers across the country voiced their opposition, insisting that the new 'drug-style' rules were completely inappropriate for products with a long history of safe use. Such regulation would increase costs to the consumer and drive the smaller manufacturers out of business. Faced with a huge public outcry, newly appointed Minister of Health, Allan Rock, placed a moratorium on the new regulations and commissioned the Standing Committee on Health to report on NHPs. Their report, entitled "Natural Health Products: A New Vision" was delivered in 1998, and contained 53 recommendations, including that NHPs be adequately defined, that they be allowed to make health claims, and that Sections 3(1), 3(2) and Schedule A of the Food and Drugs Act be reviewed to determine if they were still relevant. The government accepted the committee's 53 recommendations, and responded by setting up the Office of Natural Health Products (ONHP), with a Transition Team of seventeen experts to clarify and expand on the committee's work.

The Canadian Regulatory Regime

Unfortunately, the government failed to heed much of the committee's and the Transition Team's advice on the regulation of natural health products. Canadians were led to believe that there would be a separate category in law for NHPs, neither food nor drugs, that would allow some degree of supervision and good manufacturing practices without the onerous, costly regime that applies to patentable drugs. However, Health Canada decided to forego this recommendation and offer only a regulatory definition, placing all natural health products as a subclass of drugs. There is no third category, and the antiquated clauses remain in the Food and Drugs Act which make it illegal to advertise or label that an NHP can influence any of a long list of diseases and disorders (Schedule A) remain.

As part of the government's regulatory policy, Health Canada was required to provide a Regulatory Impact Analysis Statement (RIAS), in order to show that the costs of regulation will not outweigh the benefits. When the new regulations were proposed (published in Canada Gazette, Part I, December 22, 2001), the RIAS was suspiciously lean on numbers. The Natural Health Products Directorate (NHPD) merely stated that it had performed a cost-benefit analysis, and used the results to formulate the regulations.

No numbers, no proof. They did make an interesting statement in regards to the industry; it was recognized that "those NHP manufacturers who also manufacture drugs (and, therefore, hold valid establishment licences) would not incur significant costs for any additional NHP specific requirements. Manufacturers of NHPs only would probably incur some substantial costs." The government also failed to take the advice of the ONHP Transition Team to eliminate Sections 3(1), 3(2) and Schedule A of the Food and Drugs Act.

The Team was unequivocal when they stated that these sections "are no longer relevant. They do not serve any purpose that cannot be accomplished adequately by other sections of the legislation or regulations. More importantly, the schedule does not reflect contemporary scientific thought. The weight of modern scientific evidence confirms the mitigation and prevention of many diseases and disorders listed in Schedule A through the judicious use of NHPs. It is time that the legislation and regulations reflect the prevailing science." Yet the necessary call from the Health Committee and the Transition Team for legislative renewal to accompany NHP regulations has been ignored. Instead Health Canada announced (June 9) a new consultation on possible changes for a whole range of health bills shackling the antiquated Food and Drugs Act to the Hazardous Products Act, the Quarantine Act, and the Radiation Emitting Devices Act.

Any guess on when real changes to the Food and Drugs Act might occur? Your lifetime or mine? Even more troubling, as long as a government Bill is before the House, no Private Members' Bill can be introduced that deals with any of the subject matter: Meaning if Bill C-420 is defeated, similar legislation could not be reintroduced as long as the government sits on a complicated consultation. Sections 3(1), 3(2) and Schedule A of the Food and Drugs Act have been used to keep low-risk, low-cost, high-benefit natural health products away from Canadians. As soon as a health claim is made it triggers a 3(1) violation, Health Canada declares this product a drug and requires a multi-million dollar drug approval. This is not only unreasonable, it is unscientific and continues to be used to remove effective natural therapies from the marketplace.

RCMP Raids Office of Supplement Manufacturer

Let me illustrate. Recently a vitamin and mineral formula was developed in Alberta. Early results show phenomenal success in alleviating Bipolar Disease, a severe mental health condition that costs individuals, their families and society dearly. Providing the right nutritional support has already released many Canadians from their nightmare experiences. The province initiated a scientific response and the Alberta Science and Research Authority approved and funded a $544,000 study. Preliminary results have already been published in at least four peer-reviewed psychiatric journals. Unbelievably, Health Canada interpreted news of such success as a 3(1) violation, stepped in and shut down the study. In July, accompanied by RCMP, Health Canada raided the company offices and is now obstructing all access to this product.

Sadly, Health Canada has all too often shown its adversarial attitude towards low-risk, low-cost natural remedies. The government assured Canadians that NHPs would be given their own category in law with regulations reflecting their higher margin of safety, that regulation of NHPs would respect freedom of choice, and that NHPs would be treated with fairness. What has emerged in the new regulations is a betrayal of trust. The Vancouver based Fraser Institute entitled its review of the proposed regulations "A Cure Worse than the Illness." The 50-page report authored by Cynthia Ramsay is a valuable resource for those wanting a digest of the new regulations.

Bill C-420 Aims to Restore Freedom of Choice

Private Members' Bill C-420 was introduced to put the brakes on a bureaucracy out of control, and to restore Canadians' freedom of choice in personal health care. It would change the law and put NHPs under an appropriate food-style directorate; there would still be good manufacturing practices and supervision. It would also amend the definition of 'drug' to exclude food. Appropriate advice about the confidence level of health claims can be assured and Canadians can have the opportunity to access safe, low-cost options for personal health care. Bill C-420 would also repeal Sections 3(1), 3(2) and Schedule A of the Food and Drugs Act, as recommended by the ONHP Transition Team that was assembled to steer the new NHP Directorate into being. Their recommendation has been ignored. Unless these antiquated, unscientific clauses are removed, Health Canada will continue to use them to classify any effective NHP as a drug. Canadians are being betrayed. Bill C-420 cuts to the heart of the issue. It's time to take the club out of the hand of hostile Health Canada bureaucrats who know nothing about health and care even less. I am asking all Canadians who are informed about the benefits of natural health products and who are outraged by yet another government betrayal to contact their Member of Parliament and voice their support for Bill C-420. Together with caucus colleagues we have already submitted petitions with over 120,000 signatures calling for the changes in C-420, but much more effort is needed. The battle is not over 'til it's over! It's about access for Canadians to the best health care, the best science and the best health outcomes. Canada should be leading the world in health care outcomes. Let's remove the unscientific barriers and give Canadians every opportunity to enjoy optimal health. We have a window of opportunity. Phone, fax, write. Engage others. Contact our office. Join the battle!

Sources and Resources:

The text of Bill C-420 can be found at http://www.parl.gc.ca/37/2/parlbus/chambus/house/bills/private/C-420/C-420_1/C-420_cover-E.html

For more information and press releases regarding Bill C-420, visit http://www.jameslunneymp.ca

To find your Member of Parliament by Postal Code, visit http://www.parl.gc.ca/information/about/people/house/

Standing Committee on Health (1998). Natural Health Products: A New Vision. Joe Volpe, Chair, Ottawa: Government of Canada. Available at http://www.parl.gc.ca/InfoComDoc/36/1/HEAL/Studies/Reports/healrp02-e.htm

Office of Natural Health Products Transition Team (2000). A Fresh Start: Final Report of the ONHP Transition Team. Ottawa: Government of Canada. Available at http://www.hc-sc.gc.ca/hpfb-dgpsa/nhpd-dpsn/ transition_team_final_report_cp_e.html

Cynthia Ramsay (2002). A Cure Worse than the Illness: Canada's Proposed Regulatory Framework for Natural Health Products in Light of International Evidence. Vancouver, BC: Fraser Institute. Available at http://www.fraserinstitute.ca/admin/books/files/CureWorsethantheIllness.pdf

Natural Health Products Directorate (2001). Natural Health Product Regulations. Canada Gazette, Part I (December 22, 2001). 4912-4971. Available at http://canadagazette.gc.ca/partI/2001/20011222/pdf/g1-13551.pdf

Natural Health Products Directorate (2003). Natural Health Product Regulations. *Canada Gazette*, Part II (June 18, 2003). 1532-1607. Available at http://canadagazette.gc.ca/partII/2003/20030618/pdf/g2-13713.pdf

In the Provincial Court of Alberta

Citation: R. v. Synergy Group of Canada Inc., 2006 ABPC 196

Date: 20060728
Docket: 040608200P10103, 0203
Registry: Calgary

Between:

Her Majesty The Queen

- and -

The Synergy Group of Canada Inc.
and
Truehope Nutritional Support Ltd.

Decision of the Honourable Judge G. M. Meagher

I. BACKGROUND

[1] Anthony Stefan and David Hardy are the principals of the Defendants - The Synergy Group of Canada Inc. and Truehope Nutritional Support Ltd. ("Synergy" and "Truehope"). Mr. Stefan had lost his wife to bi-polar disorder through her suicide and had two children apparently suffering from the same disorder and becoming more and more unmanageable. Conventional pharmaceutical treatments were unsatisfactory. Mr. Hardy, with twenty years experience in the livestock feed business, informed Mr. Stefan of a vitamin/mineral supplement that had been used successfully with pigs over the years to reduce their rage and aggressive behaviour. They prepared a similar vitamin/mineral supplement and administered it to one of Mr. Stefan's children. Within weeks, the child's behaviour had returned to normal, without the drastic side effects often associated with drugs used to treat depression or bi-polar disorder. Similar results were observed with regards to Mr. Stefan's daughter when she started taking the vitamin/mineral supplement. Similar results were observed in other subjects and in May 1996, Synergy was incorporated as a research company.

[2] Over the next several years the significant results of treating depression and bi-polar disorder with vitamin/mineral supplements rather than conventional pharmaceuticals attracted interest from potential patients and experts in the field of treatment of depression and bi-polar

Source: The *Truehope Decision* by Judge G. M. Maegher, July 2006

Page: 2

disorder in Canada and the United States. The vitamin/mineral supplement went through several refinements and became known as "Empower Plus".

[3] Because the treatment of depression or bi-polar disorder could have serious side effects when an individual was reducing dependence on drugs while commencing treatment with the vitamin/mineral supplement, it was necessary to establish a unique screening, monitoring and support program called the "Truehope program" operated by a non-profit organization, the Defendant, Truehope.

[4] By 2002 - 2003, Synergy, the research organization, was raising funds, and Truehope was running the support program required for Empower Plus for approximately 3,000 people across Canada. The Truehope program was administered on a twenty-four hour a day basis with a staff of 25 experienced call-takers to assist with the screening, monitoring and support for participants in the Truehope program taking the vitamin/mineral supplement. The business conducted by the Defendants took orders from individuals in Canada and imported the vitamin/mineral supplement from a United States' based manufacturer. Empower Plus was then re-distributed in Canada to the participants in the Truehope program.

[5] In 2002, the Defendants had attracted the attention of Health Canada. Since the Defendants made claims that Empower Plus was useful for the treatment of depression and bi-polar disorder, Health Canada took the position that this brought the supplement within the definition of a "drug" within the meaning of the *Food and Drugs Act,* even though the product was clearly a vitamin/mineral supplement. Health Canada advised the Defendants that they could not sell or distribute the supplement in Canada without a Drug Identification Number or "D.I.N.". However, in order to get a D.I.N., the product would be required to undergo extensive testing designed for drugs or pharmaceuticals through the Therapeutic Products Directorate of Health Canada. In the normal course this would typically involve the testing of one active ingredient over the course of several years and at considerable expense. Such a drug testing regime was not suited to a vitamin/mineral supplement, or other health food products, which typically could have numerous active ingredients. The vitamin/mineral supplement in Empower Plus, for example, has approximately 24 ingredients. It would not be possible for the Defendants to obtain a Notice of Compliance and then a D.I.N. for Empower Plus, and Health Canada was well aware of this fact.

[6] At the same time, Health Canada had been working for several years to develop a Natural Health Products Directorate to regulate health food products because it was well known that the testing of health food products was not compatible with Health Canada's drug testing regime. Legislation establishing the Natural Health Products Directorate had been prepared and was making its way through Parliament, and a transition team had been established by Health Canada to oversee the establishment of this new regime more suited to dealing with health food products.

[7] Even though approximately 90% of the health food products sold in Canada were not required to conform to Health Canada's legislative regime for drugs, Health Canada insisted that

Source: The *Truehope Decision* by Judge G. M. Maegher, July 2006

Page: 3

the Defendants obtain a D.I.N. or stop selling and distributing Empower Plus to the thousands of participants in the Truehope program in Canada.

[8] At this time, the users of Empower Plus were being monitored through the Truehope program. If an individual stopped taking the supplement, or was denied access to the supplement, that person would revert within a matter of days to an earlier state of depression or bi-polar behaviour characterized by aggressiveness, mood swings, and violence to one's self or to others with a very real risk of personal injury and, in some cases, death. Conventional treatment with various drugs or pharmaceuticals and regular attendances with psychiatrists was not considered to be a viable or desirable alternative because of the serious negative side-effects associated with such medications.

[9] In June 2002 the Defendants wrote to Health Canada expressing their concerns that Health Canada may require a D.I.N. for the supplement and seeking a resolution to the problem. The Defendants referred to the new legislation being developed for health food products and to the encouraging findings of medical professionals whose patients were using the supplement and were involved in the Truehope program. The Defendants provided testimonials and letters of support from over 200 supporters. Most importantly, the Defendants requested a dialogue with Health Canada to work with the Defendants for a resolution such as a Ministerial Exemption or an agreement to continue to the sale and distribution of the supplement and the operation of the Truehope program. The Defendants also repeated an earlier request for a meeting with the Minister of Health.

[10] Representatives of the Defendants initiated a meeting with representatives of Health Canada in mid-January 2003, in Burnaby, British Columbia, to plead their case to continue to sell and distribute their supplement as monitored through the Truehope program and specifically requested a Ministerial Exemption for the supplement. The Defendants claimed to have contacted Health Canada and the office of the Minister of Health on numerous instances but had not received any responses. According to the Defendants, who were seeking to remain in compliance with the requirements of Health Canada, the options available to the Defendants arising from this meeting with Health Canada officials were to stop selling the supplement until they obtained a D.I.N. (which Health Canada knew the Defendants could not obtain under the then current drug approval regime) or move their business to the United States.

[11] The Defendants continued to request meetings by correspondence and by telephone with the Minister of Health but none were forthcoming. In early March, 2003, the Defendants again wrote to Health Canada officials and the Minister of Health outlining their concerns and requesting a detailed response to their correspondence from June 2002. Representatives of the Defendants continued to approach Health Canada officials on numerous occasions in an effort to find a solution to the sale and distribute of the supplement and to continue the Truehope program. Participants in the Truehope program wrote to Health Canada and to the Minister of Health to find a way to continue the supply of the supplement and the operation of the support program. Representatives of the Defendants made several trips to Ottawa attempting to meet with the Minister of Health and Health Canada officials but to no avail. They met with various

Source: The *Truehope Decision* by Judge G. M. Maegher, July 2006

Page: 4

members of Parliament to discuss their concerns and supported Bill C-420, a private Member's bill, to amend the *Food and Drugs Act and Regulations* to permit the sale of the supplement as a food and not as a drug.

[12] However, by the end of March 2003, Health Canada had issued directions to Canada Customs to stop all shipments of the supplement from the United States at the Canadian border. Only such supplement that was strictly proven to fall within the "personal use" exemption would be permitted to enter Canada. There was confusion and inconsistency with the application of this direction. There was panic and confusion amongst the participants of the Truehope program. Health Canada's response was to set up a 1-800 crisis line on which callers were advised that since the vitamin/mineral supplement would no longer be available they should contact their psychiatrists and return to conventional pharmaceutical treatments.

[13] In April 2003, the Defendants wrote to Health Canada warning Health Canada of the serious risk of harm and possible deaths by suicide from Health Canada's action to stop the importation of the supplement by ordering seizures of the supplement by Canada Customs at the Canada/United States border. Numerous previous warnings had been expressed in writing to Health Canada, including correspondence in June 2002 and in March 2003, but these warnings were apparently disregarded by Health Canada. The only witnesses called by the Crown were three compliance officers, one of whom merely assisted in the execution of the search warrant in July 2003. The other two compliance officers testified that they were aware of the warnings of harm but that this was not their concern. They testified that they were simply following orders from their superiors to strictly enforce the D.I.N. regulation against the Defendants.

[14] The Minister of Health had accepted numerous recommendations in 1999 from the Standing Committee on Health, many of which referred to the health food industry. The federal government had been slow to act on any of these recommendations. There was a transition team in place at Health Canada to establish the new Natural Health Products Directorate but the legislation and implementation had been bogged down. However, the new legislation and regulatory regime for the Natural Health Products Directorate was scheduled to come into force in January 2004.

[15] In the meantime, Canadian citizens took to smuggling the supplement into Canada for their own health or for the health of family members. Fearing for the health, safety and well-being of their participants in the Truehope support program, the Defendants continued to take orders for the supplement, transmit the orders to their manufacturer in the United States, and distribute the supplement in Canada. The Defendants continued to operate the Truehope program which was vital to the safe and effective use of the supplement. This conduct by the Defendants was contrary to the direction from Health Canada that, since Health Canada had determined that the supplement was a drug, it was not to be sold without a D.I.N.

[16] Also, over this period of time, the Defendants brought an application in the Federal Court of Canada in May 2003 for judicial review of decisions made by Health Canada with respect to the supplement and the seizure actions by Health Canada and Canada Customs.

Source: The *Truehope Decision* by Judge G. M. Maegher, July 2006

Page: 5

[17] In June 2003, a group of women known as the "Red Umbrellas" gathered on Parliament Hill. The women were either members of the Truehope program or had family members associated with the Truehope program. They were protesting the lack of response from Health Canada to their concerns for their well-being and the well-being of their family members caused by the border seizures, and the lack of response to the numerous concerns raised about the availability of the supplement and the operation of the Truehope program. In July 2003, they also protested Health Canada's conduct at the constituency office of the Minister of Health in Edmonton. No direct response was forthcoming from the Minister of Health or representatives of Health Canada; however, in July 2003 Health Canada executed a search warrant and raided the business premises of the Defendants.

[18] In September 2003, the Defendants brought an application in the Court of Queen's Bench of Alberta in response to a search and seizure operation by Health Canada on their businesses, seeking an order quashing the search warrant and returning all goods that had been seized pursuant to the search warrant.

[19] Under the new legislative and regulatory regime for natural health products that came into force in January 2004, a similar product to Empower Plus was submitted and eventually received approval. More significantly, in March 2004 the new federal Minister of Health granted an exemption to the Defendants for the Empower Plus supplement pursuant to the terms of a ministerial agreement that remains in force today. The supplement continues to be sold, distributed and monitored in Canada by the Defendants, Synergy and Truehope, under this agreement.

[20] Regardless of the foregoing, in May 2004, Health Canada instituted six charges against the Defendants for breaches of the *Food and Drugs Act* and *Food and Drug Regulations* during the period of January 1, 2003 and December 31, 2003. At the commencement of this twelve day trial on March 13, 2006, the prosecution entered Stays of Proceedings on five out of six charges. This Health Canada prosecution has proceeded on count number 3 - that the Defendants, between January 1, 2003 and December 31, 2003, unlawfully sold a drug for which a Drug Identification Number (D.I.N.) had not been assigned contrary to the provisions of the *Food and Drugs Act and Regulations*. The charge carries a maximum penalty on summary conviction for a first offence of a fine not exceeding $500.00, or for a term of imprisonment not exceeding three months, or to both. The Crown conceded at the outset of the trial that, in the event of a conviction, the Crown was only seeking a fine.

[21] The offence charged is a strict liability offence and the Crown has proven the *actus reas* of the offence. On the evidence, the Defendants were selling a drug as defined in the *Food and Drugs Act and Regulations* without a Drug Identification Number. This finding is based on the documentary evidence admitted as part of the Crown's case, the evidence of the Crown's witnesses and the evidence and admissions of Mr. Stefan and Mr. Hardy on behalf of the Defendants. This case is one of whether or not one or more of the defences claimed by the

Source: The *Truehope Decision* by Judge G. M. Maegher, July 2006

Page: 6

Defendants is available to them. The Defendants have argued for the defence of necessity, the defence of due diligence and for a stay of proceedings based on abuse of process.

[22] The evidence presented by both Health Canada and the Defendants was credible, with no significant inconsistencies or contradictions, and has been accepted subject to the further comments in the analysis that follows. In particular, the expert evidence presented by the Defendants - - Dr. Charles Popper, psychiatrist at Harvard University, Dr. Bonnie Kaplan, psychologist at the University of Calgary, and Mr. Bruce Dales, consultant, on the drug approval process and the classification of substances under the *Food and Drugs Act and Regulations* - - was clear and persuasive in support of the Defendants and not significantly affected by cross-examination. Also, the evidence of numerous witnesses called by the Defendants on the effects of the supplement on their lives or on the lives of their family members, and the effects of the actions or lack of action by Health Canada, was compelling and persuasive.

II. ISSUES

[23] There are four issues in this case, generally described as follows:

(1) Are either or both of the Defendants a "manufacturer" within the meaning of the *Food and Drugs Act and Regulations*?
(2) Are the Defendants entitled to the defence of necessity?
(3) Are the Defendants entitled to the defence of due diligence?
(4) Was the conduct of Health Canada an abuse of process sufficient to justify a stay of proceedings?

III. ANALYSIS

(1) MEANING OF "MANUFACTURER"

[24] The definition of "manufacturer" in the regulations under the *Food and Drugs Act* is found in section A.01.010 of the *Regulations*[1] and states:

> 19-12-96 "manufacturer" or "distributor" means a person, including an association or partnership, who under their own name, or under a trade -, design or word mark, trade name or other name, word or mark controlled by them, sells a food or drug: *(fabricant or distributeur)*

[25] The Defendants argued that, for all of 2003, the trademark under which the supplement was sold was controlled by True Hope Institute Inc. and at no relevant time did the Defendants, Synergy or Truehope, have control of the trademark under which the supplement was sold. The

1 *Food and Drug Regulations*, p.29, April 10, 2003 - Part A, Administration - General; Interpretation - A.01.010

Source: The *Truehope Decision* by Judge G. M. Maegher, July 2006

Page: 7

Defendants argued that this evidence demonstrated that the "manufacturer" was True Hope Institute Inc. because of its control of the trademark and that the Crown had failed to prove beyond a reasonable doubt that the Defendants, or either of them, were manufacturers within the meaning of the *Act* or *Regulations*.

[26] This argument attempts to limit "manufacturer" to the person or persons controlling the trademark under which a food or drug is sold. While this describes one of the persons or persons in the definition in the *Regulations*, in the plain wording of the definition "manufacturer" also means a person who under their own name sells a food or drug. The plain meaning of the definition of "manufacturer" in the *Regulations* contemplates two different categories of persons - in one case, a person, including an association or partnership, who under their own name sells a food or drug; or, in the other case, a person who under a trade -, design or word mark, trademark or other name, word or mark controlled by them, sells a food or drug. On the evidence presented at trial, the Crown has proven beyond a reasonable doubt that the Defendants were manufacturers, who under their own names, sold the vitamin/mineral supplement known as Empower Plus.

(2) DEFENCE OF NECESSITY

A) Onus of Proof

[27] There is an evidentiary burden upon the Defendants to place sufficient evidence before the Court to raise the defence of necessity. However, once there is sufficient evidence before the Court, the defence of necessity is raised and the Crown has the burden to prove beyond a reasonable doubt that the Defendants were not acting out of necessity. In ***R. v. Perka et al***, [1984] 2 S.C.R. 232 at pp.257-258:

> Although necessity is spoken of as a defence, in the sense that it is raised by the accused, the Crown always bears the burden of proving a voluntary act. The prosecution must prove every element of the crime charged. One such element is the voluntariness of the act. Normally, voluntariness can be presumed, but if the accused places before the court, through his own witnesses or through cross-examination of Crown witnesses, evidence sufficient to raise an issue that the situation created by external forces was so emergent that failure to act could endanger life or health and upon any reasonable view of the facts, compliance with the law was impossible, then the Crown must be prepared to meet that issue. There is no onus of proof on the accused.

[28] Justice Dickson for the majority went on the summarize a number of conclusions regarding the defence of necessity in terms of its nature, basis and limitations at p.259. In particular, the Court spoke of "moral involuntariness" in the following terms:

Page: 8

(4) the criterion is the moral involuntariness of the wrongful action;
(5) this involuntariness is measured on the basis of society's expectation of appropriate and normal resistance to pressure;

[29] The Supreme Court of Canada in ***R. v. Perka**, supra,* at p.248 described the defence of necessity and moral involuntariness in the following words:

> Conceptualized as an "excuse", however, the residual defence of necessity is, in my view, much less open to criticism. It rests on a realistic assessment of human weakness, recognizing that a liberal and humane criminal law cannot hold people to the strict obedience of laws in emergency situations where normal human instincts, whether of self-preservation or of altruism, overwhelmingly impel disobedience. The objectivity of the criminal law is preserved; such acts are still wrongful, but in the circumstances they are excusable.

This statement was cited with approval by the Supreme Court of Canada in ***R. v. Latimer***, [2001] 1 S.C.R. 3 at para. 26. Furthermore, Dickson J. at para. 27 stated ". . .It is well established law that the defence of necessity must be of limited application."

[30] In this case, the Defendants had the choice of stopping selling the supplement and operating the Truehope program or of disregarding the regulation requiring a D.I.N. The Defendants maintain that they were in a situation of emergency and were compelled by normal human instincts to disobey the regulation in order to protect other persons from harm.

B) Elements of the Defence of Necessity

[31] The Supreme Court of Canada in ***R. v. Latimer**, supra,* described ***R. v. Perka**, supra,* as the leading case on the defence of necessity. The Court stated at para. 28:

> *Perka* outlined three elements that must be present for the defence of necessity. First, there is the requirement of imminent peril or danger. Second, the accused must have had no reasonable legal alternative to the course of action he or she undertook. Third, there must be proportionality between the harm inflicted and the harm avoided.

[32] The Supreme Court of Canada in ***R. v. Latimer**, supra,* at para. 32 stated that, before applying the three requirements of the defence of necessity to the facts of a particular case, it was necessary to determine what test or tests governed the elements of the defence of necessity. The Court concluded at para. 33 that:

Source: The *Truehope Decision* by Judge G. M. Maegher, July 2006

Page: 9

The first and second requirements – imminent peril and no reasonable legal alternative – must be evaluated on the modified objective standard described above. As expressed in *Perka*, necessity is rooted in an objective standard: "involuntariness is measured on the basis of society's expectation of appropriate and normal resistence to pressure" (p.259). We would add that it is appropriate, in evaluating the accused's conduct, to take into account personal characteristics that legitimately affect what may be expected of that person. The approach taken in *R. v. Hibbert,* [1995] 2 S.C.R. 973, is instructive. Speaking for the Court, Lamer C.J. held, at para.59, that

> it is appropriate to employ an objective standard that takes into account the particular circumstances of the accused, including his or her ability to perceive the existence of alternative courses of action.

[33] While stating that a modified objective test should be applied to the first two elements of the defence of necessity, the Court in ***R. v. Latimer,*** *supra,* at para. 34 went on to state:

> The third requirement for the defence of necessity, proportionality, must be measured on an objective standard, as it would violate fundamental principles of the criminal law to do otherwise. Evaluating the nature of an act is fundamentally a determination reflecting society's values as to what is appropriate and what represents a transgression. . . . The evaluation of the seriousness of the harms must be objective.

C) Analysis

[34] The Defendants have presented sufficient evidence to the Court on the three elements of the defence of necessity to establish an air of reality to the defence. The Crown must therefore prove beyond a reasonable doubt that one or more of these elements does not apply on the facts of this case. The Crown based its case on proving that the supplement was sold without a D.I.N. and relied on the evidence of the compliance officers from Health Canada. The Crown further relied on evidence of the witnesses for the Defendants, and the Crown's cross-examination of those witnesses, to attempt to satisfy the onus on the Crown to prove beyond a reasonable doubt that the Defendants were not acting out of necessity.

i) Imminent Peril or Danger

[35] The test applicable to this requirement is a modified objective test which involves an objective evaluation, but one that takes into account the situation and characteristics of the Defendants (***R. v. Latimer,*** *supra*, at para. 32).

Source: The *Truehope Decision* by Judge G. M. Maegher, July 2006

Page: 10

[36] The evidence presented by the Defendants was credible and compelling with regards to imminent peril or danger. Mr. Stefan testified that the individuals who came to the Defendants for assistance were often the most severe cases to whom Empower Plus and the Truehope program were the last resort. He had had first-hand, personal experience with the ravages of depression and bi-polar disorder having lost his wife to suicide and having two children suffering from the same mental illness. He also had personal experience with the dangers associated with removing the supplement from such individuals. When the supplement was removed an individual regressed very rapidly and within a matter of a few days aggressiveness, violent behaviour, mood swings and the possibility of suicide quickly returned.

[37] His evidence was supported by the evidence of Sabine Colson, Autumn Springham, Debra Oxby and Sheila Stanley based on their personal experiences or observations of close family members regarding how depression and bi-polar behaviour rapidly returned when the supplement was not taken. This effect was also observed by Dr. Bonnie Kaplan, a psychologist at the University of Calgary, who had conducted case studies on the use of the supplement before her work was shut down by Health Canada.

[38] Dr. Charles Popper, a psychiatrist at Harvard University, who also teaches psychiatry to other psychiatrists, testified that when treatment was withdrawn the symptoms returned. Dr. Popper has most impressive qualifications. Although he was initially extremely skeptical with regards to the supplement, by the time of trial approximately 100 to 150 of his patients were using the supplement. He testified that he would have difficulty managing his practice if his patients had to return to conventional treatment by frequent interviews and the use of medications which lack the stability experienced by patients on the supplement. In addition to his patients, Dr. Popper testified to having consulted on 300 to 500 hundred additional patients on the supplement. Dr. Popper's expert evidence was that if the supplement became unavailable, symptoms associated with depression and bi-polar disorder, which would include aggressive behaviour, assaults, hospitalizations and suicides, would return.

[39] Ron LaJeunesse, the Alberta head of the Canadian Mental Health Association, was very knowledgeable of the risks facing persons with mental illnesses. He expressed grave concern for the conduct of Health Canada in preventing the supplement from coming into this country. He testified that death was a consequence of bi-polar disorder and that he was concerned that there would be suicides if individuals could not get access to the supplement.

[40] The evidence presented by the Defendants establishes that the Defendants believed that the persons in the Truehope program were in imminent peril or danger if they no longer had access to the supplement or to the Truehope program. The Court finds that this was a reasonably held belief.

[41] The Crown argued that there was no imminent peril or danger in the sense that the harm was not immediate or unavoidable. However, the onus is on the Crown to prove beyond a reasonable doubt that this requirement has not been met. The return of symptoms of depression and bi-polar disorder within a matter of a few days, with the attendant behaviours of aggression,

Source: The *Truehope Decision* by Judge G. M. Maegher, July 2006

Page: 11

assaults, hospitalizations and suicides was, in the eyes of the Defendants, imminent peril or danger to the persons who relied upon the Defendants to supply the supplement and administer the Truehope program.

[42] The Crown argued ***R. v. Morgentaler et al*** (1986), 22 C.C.C. (3d) 353 (Ont. C.A.) with regard to voluntariness. The Crown maintained that this portion of the decision of the Ontario Court of Appeal was upheld in the Supreme Court of Canada. At p.428 of the decision, the Court referred to an ". . . uncalculating response essential to 'involuntary' conduct." The Crown argued that since the conduct in this case was deliberate and planned - - disregarding the direction of Health Canada to stop selling the supplement with out a D.I.N. - - the conduct was not involuntary.

[43] However, the grounding of a ship after mechanical problems and deteriorating weather was found to be imminent peril or danger, even though the time frame involved could not be said to be immediate as in ***R. v. Perka***, *supra.* Also, the act of smuggling heroin under threats of harm to a family member was not immediate yet the Supreme Court of Canada allowed the common law defence of duress in ***R. v. Ruzic,*** [2001] 1 S.C.R. 687. Likewise, this Court finds that the return of devastating, possibly life-threatening behaviours within a few days constituted imminent harm or danger that the Defendants reasonably believed was unavoidable if access was prevented to the supplement and the Truehope program. Regarding the argument that the Defendants' conduct was planned and deliberate, the actions of the accused persons in ***R. v. Perka***, *supra* and ***R. v. Ruzic***, *supra,* were also planned and deliberate yet the Supreme Court of Canada found that the accused persons in those cases were entitled to the defences of necessity and duress respectively. Involuntariness means moral involuntariness. The Court is satisfied that the Defendants have presented sufficient evidence, applying the modified objective test, to establish that their conduct in ignoring the D.I.N. regulation and continuing to supply the supplement and operate the Truehope program was, in this sense, involuntary. As stated by the Supreme Court of Canada in ***R. v. Perka,*** *supra,* at p.248:

> . . . a liberal and humane criminal law cannot hold people to the strict obedience of laws in emergency situations where normal human instincts, whether of self-preservation or of altruism, overwhelmingly impel disobedience.

[44] The Crown also argued the case of ***R. v. Kreiger***, [2000] ABQB 1012 and ***R. v. Kreiger***, [2005] ABCA 202 in which case the Courts found that there was no air of reality on the evidence presented in support of the defence of necessity. In the present case, there is an air of reality to the defence of necessity sufficient to require the Crown to prove beyond a reasonable doubt that one or more of the requirements of the defence was not satisfied.

[45] The Crown also argued that the Defendants themselves were not facing imminent peril or danger. However, in 2003 there were approximately 3,000 individuals in Canada taking the supplement and being monitored by the Truehope program who were being placed in imminent peril or danger and the defence of necessity does extend to the protection of others from harm (***R.***

Source: The *Truehope Decision* by Judge G. M. Maegher, July 2006

Page: 12

***v. Perka**, supra*, p.248). There was ample evidence presented by the Defendants that Health Canada was aware of the possible harm to the participants including hundreds of letters of support, numerous correspondence, faxes and telephone calls, protests on Parliament Hill, questions in the House of Commons and a rally at the Minister of Health's constituency office in Edmonton. Health Canada's own conduct in setting up a 1-800 crisis line once the seizures commenced at the Canada/United States border is evidence that Health Canada was aware of the possible harm or danger to the participants. Health Canada received over 1000 calls on the crisis line.

[46] The Defendants presented sufficient evidence on the requirement of imminent peril or danger to the persons using the supplement and the Truehope program. The Crown has failed to prove beyond a reasonable doubt that the Defendants' conduct, viewed through a modified objective standard, was not involuntary in the sense of moral involuntariness. The Defendants were overwhelmingly compelled to disobey the D.I.N. regulation in order to protect the health, safety and well-being of the users of the supplement and the support program.

ii) No Reasonable Legal Alternative

[47] The second requirement for the defence of necessity is that there must be no reasonable legal alternative to disobeying the law. The test for this element is also the modified objective test. While this involves an objective evaluation, it should also take into account the situation and characteristics of the Defendants. The test is whether there was a "reasonable" legal alternative considering the situation and characteristics of the Defendants, not whether there was "any" alternative.

[48] The Defendants argued that the alternative sought by Health Canada, that the Defendants stop selling the supplement in Canada in 2003, was not a reasonable legal alternative. The Defendants pointed out that the conduct of the Defendants was not merely selling a vitamin/mineral supplement but also maintaining an absolutely necessary support program for persons who were treating mental illness with the supplement. The evidence presented by the Defendants was that it was vital to the health, safety and well-being of the persons on the supplement to be managed through the support program. The Defendants presented evidence that up to 40% of the persons who applied for the program were not accepted and that the Defendants only took participants that could be effectively managed within the support program. The Defendants also established a fund to provide the supplement and support program to persons who could not otherwise afford it. In fact, two of the Crown witnesses who were compliance officers with Health Canada gave evidence as to the thoroughness of the screening process and the continuous monitoring within the support program when they were investigating the Defendants.

[49] Dr. Popper gave evidence on behalf of the Defendants supporting the Defendants' contention that this was the only program of its kind at the time and that only the Defendants had the expertise to effectively screen and monitor participants in the support program. Dr. Popper testified that he learned from the Defendants how to manage the transition for individuals on medications to the supplement. Only persons who were screened and accepted into the Truehope

Source: The *Truehope Decision* by Judge G. M. Maegher, July 2006

Page: 13

program were provided with the supplement. The supplement and the support program worked together, for the health, safety and well-being of the persons taking the supplement. There had to be a support program. Therefore any reasonable legal alternative would be required to include this support program.

[50] The Defendants argued that with approximately 3000 participants effectively using the supplement and the Truehope program in 2003, with the harm that these individuals faced if denied access to the supplement or the support program, and with the regulatory regime undergoing a transition to a new health products regime more suited to vitamin/mineral supplements, there was no reasonable legal alternative but to continue selling the supplement and maintaining the support program. A number of alternatives were examined.

[51] The Defendants argued that getting a D.I.N. was not an alternative. The Defendants presented credible and reliable evidence that it would have been impossible to obtain a D.I.N. for a vitamin/mineral supplement because the drug testing regime to which D.I.N.s applied was not suited to the testing of a vitamin/mineral supplement which was a health food product. The Defendants presented expert evidence in this regard through Mr. Dales, on the classification of substances and on applications for approvals under the *Food and Drugs Act and Regulations*. Also, Mr. Stefan understood from his dealings with representatives of Health Canada that the Defendants would not be able to get a Notice of Compliance (a pre-requisite to obtaining a D.I.N.) and that the Defendants should not bother applying for a D.I.N. In addition, Dr. Kaplan's experiences in dealing with Health Canada was that the Defendants would not get a D.I.N.

[52] Another alternative was negotiations with Health Canada. The Defendants made numerous efforts to met with Health Canada to work out a resolution to this developing problem. According to Mr. Stefan, the Therapeutic Products Directorate of Health Canada was not prepared to work towards a resolution with the Defendants. The only alternative suggested by representatives of Health Canada was to stop selling the supplement or leave the country and take the business to the United States. Despite numerous and various attempts to negotiate a solution with Health Canada, the Defendants were not successful in negotiating a resolution such as a Ministerial Exemption or an agreement with Health Canada. However, when Mr. LaJeunesse of the Canada Mental Health Association intervened with Health Canada on behalf of specific individuals to continue to obtain access to the supplement, his interventions were successful in every case.

[53] Health Canada's response to the public outcry was to establish a 1-800 crisis line that received over one thousand telephone calls. The callers were advised to go to a psychiatrist. By this action, Health Canada recognized that there could be serious consequences and harm for individuals no longer able to access the supplement or the Truehope program. Because of the harm associated with conventional psychiatric treatment with medications that had negative side effects and the fact that participants would refuse to undergo such treatments, the Defendants did not consider referring the 3000 participants in the Truehope to psychiatrists to be a reasonable legal alternative.

Source: The *Truehope Decision* by Judge G. M. Maegher, July 2006

Page: 14

[54] Another alternative explored by the Defendants was to obtain a Ministerial Exemption. The compliance officers from Health Canada called as witnesses by the Crown were not aware that such an exemption was possible. Mr. Stefan testified that he made numerous telephone calls and wrote several letters attempting to get a meeting with the Minister of Health but to no avail. Mr. Stefan made trips to Ottawa and supported protests in favour of the continued supply of the supplement and the maintenance of the Truehope program. He appeared before the Standing Committee on Health and supported Bill C-420 which was a private member's Bill intended to amend the definitions on the *Food and Drugs Act* to allow for the supplement to be sold in Canada as a food and not as a drug. Attempts were made to reach the Minister of Health at her Edmonton office but they were not successful. All of the efforts undertaken by the Defendants to meet with representatives of Health Canada and to meet with the Minister of Health to make their case for an agreement or for a Ministerial exemption were ignored.

[55] The only alternative proposed by Health Canada (besides to stop selling the supplement) was for the Defendants to leave the country and to move to the United States. The Defendants indicated that this alternative was seriously considered but that there were numerous problems. These problems included not knowing if the United States would permit them to immigrate or obtain working visas, and not having the finances to move their business and their families to the United States. The only evidence presented by the Crown was that at one time the supplement had been provided through a corporate agent in the United States but the circumstances regarding this relationship and its viability were not clearly established in evidence by the Crown.

[56] Another possible alternative suggested by the Crown in argument was to direct the users to prepare their own supplement with "off the shelf" products. This was not a reasonable alternative when dealing with 3,000 participants attempting to obtain the supplement and the maintenance of the Truehope program to assist these persons with their mental health issues.

[57] Another alternative attempted by the Defendants was to take legal proceedings. The Defendants also testified that they took legal proceedings in the Federal Court of Canada in May 2003 to challenge the order or direction by Health Canada to stop the importation of the supplement at the Canada/United States border. Legal proceedings were also taken in the Court of Queen's Bench of Alberta to challenge the search warrant under which Health Canada entered the business premises of the Defendants to seize computers and business records in July 2003.

[58] A further alternative was to employ the "personal use" exemption. There was insufficient evidence before the Court on the effectiveness of this exemption and whether or not the support program could have been maintained under such a scheme. There was evidence of inconsistent application of this exemption. There was evidence before the Court that attempts to use this exemption still resulted in the supplement being stopped at the Canada/United States border.

[59] Counsel for the Defendants also argued that the Defendants were under a duty or duties described in s.216 and 217 of the *Criminal Code of Canada* to continue to provide the vitamin/mineral supplement and to maintain the support program or possibly face the consequences of being charged with criminal negligence. The Defendants provided several cases

Source: The *Truehope Decision* by Judge G. M. Maegher, July 2006

Page: 15

in support of their argument, ***R. v. LeBlanc***, [1977] 1 S.C.R. 239; ***R. v. Nelson***, [1990] O.J. No. 139 (Ont. C. A.); ***R. v. Sullivan*** (1986), 31 C.C.C. (3d) 62 (B.C.S.C.); ***R. v. Rogers***, [1968] C.C.C. vol. 4 278 (B.C.C.A.); ***R. v. Homeberg*** (1921), C.C.C. Vol. XXXV 250 (Alta.S.C.A.D.). Further, the Defendants argued that it was established law that it was no defence to charges of criminal negligence to say that one had to cause harm because one had to comply with licensing requirement.

[60] Another alternative was to obtain an agreement with the Minister of Health to permit the supplement to be brought into Canada. Given the conduct of Health Canada officials and the Minister of Health in 2003, this was not a reasonable alternative at the time. It is noteworthy, however, that in March 2004 such an agreement was made with a new Minister of Health. This agreement is evidence that by early 2004 the Minister of Health thought that there was no other reasonable legal alternative for resolving the supply of the supplement and the operation of the support program. This agreement remains in effect today, permitting the sale of the supplement and the operation of the support program.

[61] The Defendants took numerous steps seeking a resolution to the problem. The Defendants considered or attempted numerous alternatives regarding how to continue to supply the supplement and to maintain the support program without running afoul of existing legislation and Health Canada.

[62] The Crown argued that there were reasonable legal alternatives to the conduct of the Defendants in continuing to sell the supplement and to maintain the support program. The Crown initially argued that it was not up to the Crown to suggest reasonable legal alternatives. However, once the Defendants presented sufficient evidence to raise the defence of necessity, then the onus was on the Crown to prove beyond a reasonable doubt that there were no reasonable legal alternatives, bearing in mind the modified objective test for this requirement.

[63] The Crown argued that economics was not a defence. However, evidence led by the Defendants established that the business of the Defendants was more than just selling the supplement but included a vital and essential support program. The Defendants also provided the financial means for persons who wished to take the supplement and be on the program but could not afford to do so. The Defendants' evidence was clear and credible that their business was never about earning a profit but in developing and delivering a vitamin/mineral supplement and support program that provided a viable alternative to the conventional treatment of depression and bi-polar disorder without the significant negative side effects of such treatment. The supplement and the support program were and are inextricably connected to each other.

[64] The Crown suggested the "off the shelf" alternative, that individual users of the supplement cobble together their own vitamin/mineral supplement from existing "off the shelf" products. The Crown suggested that the Defendants should have encouraged the participants to do so and somehow maintained the support program. This argument suggests that the Crown agreed that the vitamin/mineral supplement was not harmful and casts doubt on the Crown's

Source: The *Truehope Decision* by Judge G. M. Maegher, July 2006

Page: 16

assertion that Health Canada had concerns for the safety of the supplement. This argument also disregards the necessity of the Truehope program and disregards that the sale and distribution of the product must be controlled and managed through the support program. It is not a reasonable legal alternative to suggest that thousands of people make their own supplement and somehow maintain the support program.

[65] The Crown suggested that it was a reasonable alternative for the Defendants to remove the boron and or germanium from the supplement. However, this argument only goes so far as to state that these were Health Canada concerns. There was no evidence before the Court that the removal of either or both of these ingredients would have resulted in the Defendants obtaining a D.I.N. or would have prevented the enforcement actions being taken by Health Canada. In fact, the evidence before the Court was that regardless the Defendants were not going to get a D.I.N. for the supplement. Lastly, the supplement is still being sold today under the agreement with the Minister of Health containing the same ingredients that it contained in 2003.

[66] The Crown submitted that a further alternative was that the Defendants could have stopped making treatment claims. Again, there was no evidence that if the Defendants modified or stopped their treatment claims that this would have resulted in the Defendants obtaining a D.I.N. or would have resulted in the cessation of the enforcement proceedings by Health Canada. However, there was evidence that the Defendants sought to obtain advice and assistance from Health Canada regarding amendments or modifications to their website but that no such assistance was forthcoming.

[67] Another course of action suggested by the Crown as a reasonable legal alternative was that the Defendants could have sold their rights in the supplement to a company in the United States and negotiated a contractual relationship for a percentage of profits to continue the support program. The Crown pointed to the fact that a relationship had existed with a corporation called Evince in the United States until October 2002. However, there was not sufficient evidence before the Court of the details of the past relationship with Evince or why that relationship ended. There was also insufficient evidence before the Court to determine if it was indeed possible to sell the rights in the supplement to a company in the United States and to negotiate a contractual relationship for a financial percentage to continue the support program.

[68] Applying a modified objective test, the Court must consider whether or not reasonable legal alternatives existed, taking into account the perception, experiences and circumstances of the Defendants. The evidence presented by the Defendants established that the Defendants did not consider that stopping the sale and distribution of the supplement, because they had not or could not obtain a D.I.N., was a reasonable legal alternative. The evidence also established that the Defendants considered and attempted to find a number of alternatives. The Defendants believed that to protect the participants in the Truehope program from harm that there was no reasonable legal alternative but to disobey the D.I.N. regulation. This was a reasonably held belief. The Crown has failed to prove beyond a reasonable doubt, based on the modified objective test, that there were reasonable legal alternatives available to the Defendants.

Source: The *Truehope Decision* by Judge G. M. Maegher, July 2006

Page: 17

iii) Proportionality

[69] The third element of the defence of necessity is the requirement that there is proportionality between the harm inflicted and the harm avoided. The Supreme Court of Canada in ***R. v. Latimer,*** *supra,* at para. 34 stated:

> The third element for the defence of necessity, proportionality, must be measured on an objective standard, as it would violate fundamental principles of criminal law to do otherwise. Evaluating the nature of an act is fundamentally a determination reflecting society's values as to what is appropriate and what represents a transgression. . . . The evaluation of the seriousness of the harms must be objective. . . .

[70] The harm that the Defendants sought to avoid was the rapid return of the symptoms associated with depression and bi-polar disorder which could result in aggressive behaviour, assaults, hospitalizations and suicides. The alternative of being placed under psychiatric care with regular interviews and medications that had serious negative side-effects was also a harm that the Defendants sought to avoid. The Defendants in argument characterized the harm sought to be avoided as being the most serious harm of all, that is, severe incapacitation and possibly death due to mental illness.

[71] There was ample evidence presented from both ordinary and expert witnesses that the symptoms associated with depression and bi-polar disorder returned rapidly, within a matter of a few days. Mr. Stefan had observed this personally through his son and daughter, and on a broader scale with the thousands of Canadians who were participating in the Truehope program. Ms. Springham described her severe incapacitation prior to the supplement and was fearful and concerned that without the supplement she would not be able to care for her children and her family and that she could not go out in public for fear of her behaviour. She feared being medicated and consumed with drugs, and becoming suicidal and hospitalized. Ms. Oxby described the harm as having to hear her son beg her to kill him several times a day and watching her son deteriorate as he lost his mental health, his friends, his self-esteem, his dignity and his will to live. Ms. Stanley expressed similar concerns with regards to her daughter and her husband. Ms. Colson described self-inflicted injuries, being involuntarily committed, and becoming useless to the point where she had formulated a plan to kill herself before she lost her mental health again.

[72] The expert evidence before the Court with regards to the objective harm that could occur included the observations of Dr. Bonnie Kaplan, a psychologist from the University of Calgary, who observed the rapid return of symptoms once the supplement was discontinued and Dr. Charles Popper, a psychiatrist from Harvard University, who testified that if the supplement became unavailable there would be aggressive behaviour, assaults, hospitalizations, incarcerations and suicides. He testified that his patients would have to be returned to medications which lack stability and had negative side-effects. Overall, Dr. Popper testified that

Source: The *Truehope Decision* by Judge G. M. Maegher, July 2006

Page: 18

he would not be able to manage his practice at the level to which it had grown and he would have refer patients away from his practice.

[73] The Defendants argued that there was no harm in not having a D.I.N. since 90% of the natural health product industry was not in compliance. Also, there was an interim Drug Identification Number directive in place by Health Canada exempting products. There was a new regulatory regime or system being developed, *The Natural Health Products Regulations*, that were more suited to the natural health product industry and were to come into force on January 1st, 2004. Health Canada itself classified the product as Type ll, meaning that the risk of serious health consequences was remote, and Health Canada was prepared to allow the purchase of supplement under the "personal use exemption" in any event during this period. Ultimately, the Minister of Health agreed to the sale and distribution of the supplement and the operation of the support program and the Defendants continue to operate under this agreement today.

[74] On a purely objective basis, based on the evidence of ordinary witnesses and expert witnesses, the harm sought to be avoided to the thousands of participants in the Truehope program was significant and severe. The existence of this harm was not seriously questioned by the Crown and any possible harm from the use of the supplement appears to be of little concern to Health Canada today.

[75] The Crown argued that the Court should consider the bigger picture of the importance of regulatory schemes to the governance of the country and the potential harm if this method of governance was undermined. The Crown referred specifically to ***R. v. Wholesale Travel Group Inc.***, [1991] 3 S.C.R. 154 at pp.221-222. In particular at p.221 the Court stated:

> Statistics such as these make it obvious that government policy in Canada is pursued principally through regulation. It is through regulatory legislation that the community seeks to implement its larger objectives and to govern itself and the conduct of its members. The ability of the government effectively to regulate potentially harmful conduct must be maintained.

The Crown argued that this must be taken into consideration in determining the proportionality between the harm inflicted and the harm avoided. The Crown argued that the purpose of the D.I.N. was to protect the public from a company or companies that would develop a drug and place it on the market without going through the testing requirements of the appropriate regulatory body.

[76] In assessing the harm inflicted on the regulatory process it is important to note that a D.I.N. was a requirement relating to drugs under the Therapeutic Products Directorate and primary related to pharmaceuticals. The regulatory process itself was in a state of change and transition while the new Natural Health Products Directorate more suited to health food products like the supplement, was being established. The new regulatory scheme was scheduled to be brought into force on January 1st, 2004. Also, from March 2004 to the present the Defendants

Source: The *Truehope Decision* by Judge G. M. Maegher, July 2006

Page: 19

have continued to sell and distribute the supplement and to operate the support program under an agreement with the Minister of Health. Health Canada itself considered the product to be in its Type ll category which meant the risk of serious health consequences was remote. Health Canada made the product available under its "personal use exemption" provisions. The legislation and regulations provided that on a summary conviction proceeding for a first offence of selling a product without a D.I.N. a defendant is liable to a fine not exceeding $500.00 dollars or to imprisonment for a term not exceeding three months or both. In these circumstances, little harm would have been inflicted on a regulatory process that was not suited to health food products like the supplement and that was in the process of being replaced.

[77] The Crown argued that the Defendants were responsible for creating the risk and described their conduct as a complete failure to attempt to abide by the Regulations. However, the evidence established that the Defendants, from 1996 on, developed a vitamin/mineral supplement that was effective for the treatment of some mental illnesses without the negative side-effects of medications associated with conventional psychiatric treatments. The supplement served to reduce the risk to individuals taking the supplement, provided they participated in the Truehope program. The risk that arose was in preventing these individuals from having access to the supplement or, having access to the supplement, not having access to the Truehope program. Rather than a complete failure to abide by the Regulations, the Defendants undertook extensive efforts throughout the course of 2002 and 2003 to meet with the Minister of Health and to work with the representatives of Health Canada in order to find a resolution to the problem within the existing and pending legislative and regulatory framework.

[78] On a purely objective basis, the harm inflicted in the circumstances of this case was insignificant when compared to the harm avoided. The harm avoided was clearly and unquestionably greater than the harm inflicted. The onus was on the Crown throughout the trial to prove the case against the Defendants beyond a reasonable doubt. Since sufficient evidence was presented by the Defendants to raise the defence of necessity, the onus was on the Crown to disprove the defence of necessity beyond a reasonable doubt. To do so, the Crown had to establish beyond a reasonable doubt that one of the three elements or requirements of the defence of necessity had not been met. On the foregoing analysis, the Crown has failed to satisfy the burden of proof and the Defendants are entitled to the defence of necessity.

(3) THE DEFENCE OF DUE DILIGENCE

[79] The offence for which the Defendants stand charged under the *Food and Drugs Act and Regulations* is a strict liability offence. In the leading case of ***R. v. Sault Ste. Marie (City)***, [1978] 2 S.C.R. 1299, (1978) 40 C.C.C. (2d) 353 at p.374 the Supreme Court of Canada described a strict liability offence and the defence of due diligence in the following terms:

> 2. Offences in which there is no necessity for the prosecution to prove the existence of *mens rea*; the doing of the prohibited act *prima facie* imports the offence, leaving it open to the accused to avoid liability by proving that he took all reasonable care. This

Source: The *Truehope Decision* by Judge G. M. Maegher, July 2006

Page: 20

> involves consideration of what a reasonable man would have done in the circumstances.

The Supreme Court of Canada at p.373 stated that the onus of proof was on the defendant to establish the defence on a balance of probabilities when it stated:

> . . . While the prosecution must prove beyond a reasonable doubt that the defendant committed the prohibited act, the defendant must only establish on the balance of probabilities that he has a defence of reasonable care.

[80] The evidence presented by the Defendants established that the Defendants were not going to obtain a D.I.N. for the supplement. The expert evidence of Mr. Dales, consultant, with regards to the classification of substances and the approval process under the *Food and Drugs Act and Regulations* was that the process for the approval of a new drug through the Therapeutic Products Directorate of Health Canada, was a process which would take several years and cost millions of dollars. In the end, Mr. Dales evidence was that it would have been impossible to obtain a D.I.N. for this vitamin/mineral supplement because of the nature of the product as a health food product with multiple ingredients going through a therapeutic drug testing regime which typically tested products with only one or two ingredients.

[81] Other evidence presented by the Defendants also established that representatives of Health Canada knew that the Defendants would not obtain a D.I.N. for the supplement but did not clearly state this to the Defendants in meetings, in numerous telephone conversations, in e-mails and in correspondence with the Defendants. Nonetheless, the Defendants, understood they were not going to obtain a D.I.N. from the Therapeutics Products Directorate of Health Canada. It was also apparent from the discussions and e-mails between Dr. Kaplan and representatives of Health Canada that the Defendants would not be able to obtain a D.I.N. Health Canada would not give permission to Dr. Kaplan to continue to conduct clinical trials that Dr. Kaplan and the Defendants hoped would assist in the approval process.

[82] As a result, the Defendants focused their efforts to obtain approval from Health Canada for the continued sale and distribution of the supplement and the operation of the Truehope program by trying to obtain a Ministerial Exemption, which was provided for in the *Food and Drugs Act and Regulations,* and by trying to reach an agreement with Health Canada or the Minster of Health under which these activities could be continued. The Defendants were made numerous attempts to approach the Minister of Health directly and through representatives of Health Canada to plead their case for a Ministerial Exemption. In fact, the head of the transition team establishing the new Natural Health Products Directorate, had recommended this course of action. For whatever reasons, in 2003 the Defendants were unable to successfully pursue this alternative.

[83] Considerable efforts were made to bring attention to the plight of the participants and to obtain a meeting with the Minister of Health. A group of women called the "Red Umbrellas",

Source: The *Truehope Decision* by Judge G. M. Maegher, July 2006

Page: 21

who either personally or through members of their families had experienced the successful treatment of depression and bi-polar disorder with the vitamin/mineral supplement, protested on Parliament Hill. Questions were raised by Members of Parliament in the House of Commons. A private member's bill, Bill C-420 was presented to amended the *Food and Drugs Act and Regulations* to permit the sale and distribution of the supplement. Dr. Lunney, a Member of Parliament, attempted to intervene on behalf of the Defendants to obtain a meeting with the Minister. Supporters of the Defendants staged a rally at the constituency office of the Minister of Health. All of these efforts made by the Defendants during 2003 were unsuccessful in obtaining a meeting with the Minister of Health or a Ministerial Exemption or an agreement with the Health Canada to permit the sale of the supplement and the operation of the support program. However, the eventual solution that was available through the next Minister of Health by March 2004 was an agreement with the Defendants to permit the sale and distribution of the supplement and the operation of the Truehope program on certain conditions that today are largely ignored. The decision of this Minister is evidence that the Ministerial Exemption or agreement was the only reasonable legal alternative to resolve the problem against the background of the existing legislation. It is also noteworthy that the Defendants continue the sale of the supplement and the operation of the support program under the terms of this agreement to the present day. It is also evident that the Defendants took all reasonable care to comply with the law in the circumstances.

[84] The Defendants presented other evidence to establish that the Defendants took all reasonable care. The Defendants made numerous attempts to have Health Canada negotiate with the Defendants for a resolution of these matters. Numerous telephone calls, correspondence and e-mails were directed towards Health Canada to raise Health Canada's awareness of the problems that could be and were created by the stoppage of the supplement at the Canada/United States border. Significant actions were taken in Ottawa, in the House of Commons, and in Edmonton but the Defendants' pleas and requests were ignored.

[85] In their continuing efforts, the Defendants took legal proceedings in the Federal Court of Canada in May 2003 to prevent the stoppages of the supplement at the Canada/United States border. When Health Canada executed search warrants against the business of the Defendants in July 2003, the Defendants brought an action in the Court of Queen's Bench of Alberta challenging the validity of the search warrant.

[86] The Defendants had followed a course of conduct from 1996 to 2003 that involved the development and refinement of the supplement, the sale and distribution of the supplement, and the monitoring of its use through the Truehope program. This course of conduct had been accepted by Health Canada until March 2003. Counsel for the Defendants in argument referred to s.216 and 217 of the *Criminal Code* regarding the duty of persons undertaking acts. These provisions state as follows:

> **DUTY OF PERSONS UNDERTAKING ACTS DANGEROUS TO LIFE.**
> **216.** Every one who undertakes to administer surgical or medical treatment to another person or to do any other lawful act that may

Page: 22

endanger the life of another person is, except in cases of necessity, under a legal duty to have and to use reasonable knowledge, skill and care in so doing.

DUTY OF PERSONS UNDERTAKING ACTS.
217. Every one who undertakes to do an act is under a legal duty to do it if an omission to do the act is or may be dangerous to life.

[87] While the Defendants may not have been specifically aware that they may be subject to criminal prosecution for a breach of these sections of the *Criminal Code*, three points are relevant. Firstly, ignorance of the law would afford them no excuse or defence. Secondly, claiming compliance with the D.I.N. regulation would not have afforded them a defence. Thirdly, the evidence is overwhelming that the Defendants considered themselves under a duty to protect the health, safety and well-being of the thousands of persons taking the vitamin/mineral supplement, to distribute the supplement and to monitor those persons through the Truehope program.

[88] The only alternative suggested by Health Canada representatives, other than stopping selling the product, was that the Defendants move to the United States. The Defendants provided evidence that Mr. Stefan and Mr. Hardy gave serious consideration to this possibility but in the end determined it was not financially feasible and there were too many questions to be resolved with regards to re-locating their families and businesses to another country. In any event, the Defendants did not consider this to be a reasonable legal alternative in order to comply with a regulation that 90% of the natural health product industry was not required to comply with, and where the regulatory regime governing the supplement was scheduled to be changed January 1st, 2004.

[89] Other alternatives such as relying upon individuals through the "personal use exemption" or by purchasing the ingredients "off the shelf" to make the supplement themselves were not reasonable in the context of thousands of individuals who were successfully using the supplement that had been refined over several years and who required support through the Truehope program.

[90] The Crown argued that the Defendants did not take all reasonable steps to comply with the law. The Crown maintained that the Defendants could have stopped selling the supplement. Considering the duty of care that the Defendants considered that they were under, this was not what a reasonable person would have been expected to do in the circumstances. Another suggestion was that the Defendants could have waited for the new Natural Health Products Directorate to be established in 2004. This was not a reasonable course of action because thousands of people were already using the supplement and this would have had the same effect as stopping selling the supplement and operating the support program. Another suggestion was that the Defendants could have hired an expert such as Mr. Dales to go through the drug approval process. However, Mr. Dales' expert evidence was that the product would be considered a new

Source: The *Truehope Decision* by Judge G. M. Maegher, July 2006

Page: 23

drug, would be required to go through numerous steps in a process that would take a minimum of five years and at a cost of millions of dollars, and ultimately be unsuccessful because of the nature of the product and the requirements of the drug approval process. To expect the Defendants to embark on such a process in 2003, when the new Natural Health Products Directorate and a new regulatory regime was to come into force on January 1st, 2004, was not reasonable.

[91] Other suggestions by the Crown of reasonable steps that the Defendants failed to take were that the Defendants did not remove the treatment claims or the boron or germanium in the supplement. However, there was no evidence that taking these steps were measures that would lead to Health Canada to change its position that the Defendants required a D.I.N. It was also suggested that the Defendants could have made changes to their website to comply with the Regulations but there was no evidence that taking such a step would have been effective. In fact there was evidence that the Defendants sought assistance from Health Canada regarding suggestions and advice regarding changing the website but none was forthcoming.

[92] The Defendants took all reasonable care that could have been expected of a reasonable person in the circumstances to comply with the requirements of Health Canada under the *Food and Drugs Act and Regulations*. The backdrop of circumstances include that it was not possible for the Defendants to obtain a D.I.N. for the supplement, that a new Natural Health Products Directorate with an approval process suited to natural health food products was about to come into force on January 1st, 2004, that their numerous efforts to obtain a resolution to the concerns of Health Canada regarding the sale and distribution of their product were being largely ignored by Health Canada, and that the thousands of individuals who had found relief from mental illness through the supplement without the negative side effects of conventional medications were relying upon them to continue to sell and distribute their product and to maintain the Truehope = program. The fact that the Minister of Health in March 2004 made an agreement for the sale and distribution of the supplement and the operation of the Truehope program that continues to this day is evidence that the Defendants acted reasonably in 2003 and that there was no other reasonable legal alternative at the time. Therefore, the Defendants took all due care to comply with the *Act and the Regulations*. The Defendants have established on a balance of probabilities that the Defendants took all reasonable care to comply with the *Food and Drugs Act and Regulations* that would be expected of a reasonable person in these circumstances and are entitled to the defence of due diligence.

(4) ABUSE OF PROCESS

[93] It is established law that the Defendants, to obtain a stay of proceedings for an abuse of process, whether by common law doctrine or by *Charter* breach, must establish on a balance of probabilities that to allow the Crown to proceed against the Defendants would violate the community's sense of fair play or decency or that the proceedings would be oppressive. The Defendants in this case seek a stay of proceedings based upon the common law doctrine of abuse of process. The Defendants referred to the Supreme Court of Canada decision of ***R. v. Keyowski***, [1988] 1 S.C.R. 657 which summarized the test for abuse of process at pp.658-659 as follows:

Source: The *Truehope Decision* by Judge G. M. Maegher, July 2006

Page: 24

> The availability of a stay of proceedings to remedy an abuse of process was confirmed by this court in *R. v. Jewitt*, [1985] 2 S.C.R. 128. On that occasion the Court stated that the test for abuse of process was that initially formulated by the Ontario Court of Appeal in *R. v. Young* (1984), 40 C.R. (3d) 289. A stay should be granted where "compelling an accused to stand trial would violate those fundamental principles of justice which underlie the community's sense of fair play and decency", or where the proceedings are "oppressive or vexatious"([1985] 2 S.C.R. at pp. 136-137). The Court in *Jewitt* also adopted "the caveat added by the Court in *Young* that this is a power which can be exercised only in the 'clearest of cases'" (p.137).

[94] The Defendants further referred to the case of ***R. v. Young,*** *supra,* at p.290, that one case to which abuse of process applies is:

> . . . [W]here the executive action leading to the institution of proceedings is offensive to the principles upon which the administration of justice is conducted by the courts. . .

[95] The Defendants argued that in 2003 approximately 90% of the natural health food products industry was not in compliance with the *Food and Drugs Act and Regulations*. Evidence was presented that the D.I.N. regulation did not fit the natural health products industry and that the regulatory process itself was in a transitionary period with new regulations to govern the natural health products industry scheduled to come into force in January, 2004. The Defendants argued that since there was evidence that withdrawing the supplement would cause harm to the users of the supplement, the efforts of Health Canada to stop the sale of the supplement in 2003 were an abuse of process. This Court is not prepared to find that the efforts of Health Canada to stop the sale of the supplement in 2003 constitutes the "clearest of cases" in order to justify a stay of proceedings for abuse of process. Health Canada's efforts were directed at stopping the sale and distribution of a product that purported to treat mental illnesses. According to the *Food and Drugs Act and Regulations* in force at the time the supplement was therefore technically a drug which had not been tested and approved within the existing regulatory scheme for a drug product.

[96] The Defendants argued that this prosecution is an abuse of process because it is an attempt to make the Defendants stop selling the supplement where there is clear evidence that to stopping the sale of the supplement and/or the operations of the Truehope program could cause serious harm and possibly death. Since the charge before the Court was laid after the present agreement was made by the Minister of Health to permit the sale of this product and the operation of the Truehope program by the Defendants, this prosecution is clearly not an attempt to stop the sale of the supplement and a conviction for breach of the D.I.N. regulation will not

Source: The *Truehope Decision* by Judge G. M. Maegher, July 2006

Page: 25

result in stopping the sale of the supplement or the operation of the Truehope program today. Therefore this argument of abuse of process is rejected.

[97] A further argument advanced by the Defendants was that the commencement of this prosecution following the agreement that was reached with the Minister in March 2004 is an abuse of process. The Defendants referred to the case of ***R. v. Young,*** *supra,* where the Court found that it was an abuse of process to proceed with a prosecution on an issue that the Executive had already resolved. The Defendants argued that their case was even stronger because, firstly, the same branch of the Executive was involved, as opposed to different branches of government in ***Young,*** *supra,* and, secondly, in the present case an agreement had already been reached with the Minister of Health to resolve the issues which continues to the present day. While these matters were resolved by an agreement with the Minister in March 2004 which continues through to today, the fact remains that in 2003 the Defendants were in breach of the D.I.N. regulation and have admitted as much.

[98] Is this prosecution, commenced after the agreement in 2004, for conduct from 2003, an abuse of process amounting to the "clearest of cases"? The Supreme Court of Canada in ***R. v. Regan***, [2002] 1 S.C.R. 297 at para. 50 cited with approval the statement of L'Heureux-Dubé J. in ***R. v. O'Connor***, [1995] 4 S.C.R. 411 at para 73 as follows:

> This residual category does not relate to conduct affecting the fairness of the trial or impairing other procedural rights enumerated in the *Charter*, but instead addresses the panoply of diverse and sometimes unforeseeable circumstances in which a prosecution is conducted in such a manner as to connote unfairness or vexatiousness of such a degree that it contravenes fundamental notions of justice and thus undermines the integrity of the judicial process.

At para. 52 the Supreme Court of Canada referred to ***Blencoe v. British Columbia (Human Rights Commission),*** [2000] 2 S.C.R. 307, 2000 SCC 44 at para. 133 where Bastarache J., stated that the abuse "must have cause actual prejudice of such magnitude that the public's sense of decency and fairness is affected." The Court went on to discuss, at paras. 53 and 54 that a stay of proceedings for abuse of process has a very high threshold which has been frequently described as the "clearest of cases". The Court stated at para. 54 that two criteria must be met:

> (1) the prejudice caused by the abuse in question will be manifested, perpetuated or aggravated through the conduct of the trial, or by its outcome; and
>
> (2) that no other remedy is reasonably capable of removing that prejudice. [*O'Connor,* at para. 75]

Source: The *Truehope Decision* by Judge G. M. Maegher, July 2006

Page: 26

[99] In particular, at para. 55 of ***Regan,*** *supra,* the Court stated:

> . . . When dealing with an abuse which falls into the residual category, generally speaking, a stay of proceedings is only appropriate when the abuse is likely to continue or be carried forward.

That is not the case with the prosecution that is before this Court. The actual prejudice is not of such a magnitude nor is it likely to be continued or carried forward. The onus is on the Defendants in advancing this argument to satisfy the Court on a balance of probabilities, not only that this is an abuse of process, but that it is the "clearest of cases".

[100] The Crown relied upon ***R. v. Regan,*** *supra,* and ***R. v. Power***, [1994] 1 S.C.R. 601 decisions of the Supreme Court of Canada to demonstrate that the conduct of Health Canada was not an abuse of process, and even if such conduct was found to be an abuse of process, this was not the "clearest of cases" for the Court to direct a stay of proceedings. The Crown referred to ***R. v. Powers,*** *supra,* at p.615:

> . . . [C]ourts have a residual discretion to remedy an abuse of the court's process but only in the "clearest of cases", which, in my view, amounts to conduct which shocks the conscience of the community and is so detrimental to the proper administration of justice that it warrants judicial intervention.

The Court went on at p.616 to state:

> To conclude that the situation "is tainted to such a degree" and that it amounts to one of the "clearest of cases", as the abuse of process has been characterized by the jurisprudence, requires overwhelming evidence that the proceedings under scrutiny are unfair to the point that they are contrary to the interests of justice. . . . Where there is conspicuous evidence of improper motives or of bad faith or of an act so wrong that it violates the conscience of the community, such that it would genuinely be unfair and indecent to proceed, then, and only then, should courts intervene to prevent an abuse of process which could bring the administration of justice into disrepute. Cases of this nature will be extremely rare.

[101] While the prosecution of the Defendants was commenced in 2004 after an agreement had been entered into with the Minister to provide for the sale and distribution of the supplement and the operation of the Truehope program may amount to an abuse of process, this Court is not prepared to find that the commencement of this prosecution after the agreement by the Minister is the "clearest of cases" which would entitle the Defendants to a stay of proceedings. The onus is on the Defendants on a balance of probabilities to satisfy the Court that this is the "clearest of

Source: The *Truehope Decision* by Judge G. M. Maegher, July 2006

Page: 27

cases" of an abuse of process to warrant the remedy of a stay of proceedings and the Defendants have not satisfied this onus.

[102] The Defendants argued that there were other instances of conduct by representatives of Health Canada that should be considered as contributing to an abuse of process. One such argument was that the Court was being asked to endorse the blind following of policy in the face of evidence that following such policy would cause harm. The Crown witnesses were compliance officers who were not concerned with the consequences the seizure of the supplement on the thousands of persons using the supplement and involved in the Truehope program. They steadfastly maintained that the product was a drug that did not have a D.I.N., that the Defendants were in breach of the D.I.N. regulation, and that Health Canada was entitled to take enforcement proceedings against them to stop the sale and distribution of the supplement in Canada contrary to the *Food and Drugs Act and Regulations*. They were aware of the letter of March 6th, 2003 from the Defendants to Health Canada voicing concerns that denial of the supplement would jeopardize the health of the participants in the program and the April 29th, 2003 letter warning that the seizures were putting such people at risk. The Crown witnesses maintained that they were just taking orders and following the policies and directives of their superiors. The Crown witnesses were unaware of any mechanism to deal with circumstances where an enforcement action could be harmful to health nor did they investigate this matter further. Unfortunately, none their superiors testified at the trial.

[103] Another example of the conduct of Health Canada that contributed to an abuse of process was that representatives of Health Canada were not forthcoming with the Defendants by failing to tell them that it was not possible for the Defendants to obtain a D.I.N. for the supplement under the existing drug approval regime, even though this belief was known at different levels of Health Canada. Health Canada had this knowledge as demonstrated in various emails and other dealings with Dr. Kaplan. Furthermore, when the Defendants attempted to obtain information under the *Access to Information Act*, information demonstrating this knowledge was edited from the communications with Dr. Kaplan. Then, only edited copies were provided to the Crown for purposes of disclosure to the Defendants. The Court directed that unedited copies be provided. Also, Health Canada had collected materials with regards to calls to the 1-800 crisis line that had been established by Health Canada but failed to disclose this information in the disclosure provided to the Defendants before trial. When the Defendants requested these materials they were still not disclosed. The materials were ultimately found and provided to the Defendants within two hours of this Court ordering the production of the materials mid-way through this trial.

[104] Another example of the conduct of Health Canada that the Defendants argued amounted to an abuse of process was the double standard that applied to people seeking the release of the supplement through Ron LaJeunesse of the Canadian Mental Health Association. The evidence established that in every case where Mr. LaJeunesse intervened to obtain the release of the supplement that had been seized at the Canada/United States border he was successful. This was not the case for the Defendants or other persons seeking release of the supplement seized in the same circumstances.

Source: The *Truehope Decision* by Judge G. M. Maegher, July 2006

Page: 28

[105] Another example of the conduct of Health Canada alleged to contribute to abuse of process was that Health Canada did not provide the Defendants with an opportunity to contribute information to the Health Hazard Evaluation and Health Canada's assessment of risk of the supplement. The Defendants argued that Health Canada even resisted meeting with the Defendants for the purpose of sharing information for the evaluation. Even without the participation of the Defendants, the Health Hazard Evaluation of Health Canada for the supplement was that the risk of harm from the use of the supplement was remote. The Defendants argued that the conduct of Health Canada, in the face of their own findings and with the knowledge that the withdrawal of the supplement and the termination of the support program could have serious health consequences to the participants, amounted to an abuse of process.

[106] A further argument advanced by the Defendants was that it was an abuse of process for Health Canada to attempt to enforce a regulation that did not fit the natural health product industry and that by its conduct Health Canada was forcing law-abiding citizens to break the law by smuggling the supplement into Canada for their own health, safety and well-being or for the health, safety and well-being of family members.

[107] A further argument advanced by the Defendants was that the Defendants could have been subject to criminal prosecution for criminal negligence if they had stopped the sale and distribution of the supplement and the operation of the support program. The Defendants argued it would be no defence for the Defendants to argue that they were merely complying with the D.I.N. regulation.

[108] Overall, the Defendants argued that the foregoing conduct of Health Canada taken together should be seen to offend the community's sense of fair play and decency and that this prosecution should be seen as oppressive and vexatious thereby amounting to an abuse of process by Health Canada.

[109] In reply, the Crown argued that neither the conduct of Health Canada throughout 2003 nor this prosecution should be seen as an abuse of process. The Crown argued that there was an interim D.I.N. directive in place to assist with transitional matters. There was a policy that provided a "personal use exemption" for individuals who wished to obtain this supplement. The fact that 90% of the natural health product industry was not in compliance did not justify the Defendants' lack of compliance where the Defendants were making treatment claims associated with the product. Furthermore, Health Canada had expressed some concerns with the existence of boron and germanium in the product. The Court has noted that the Defendants were in breach of the D.I.N. regulation. Also the Minister of Health and Health Canada were not required by law to provide a Ministerial Exemption or to enter into any agreement with the Defendants. While the seizures of the supplements at the Canada/United States border have been challenged in the Federal Court of Canada and the search warrant for the business premises of the Defendants was challenged in the Court of Queen's Bench of Alberta, there have been no findings to date that these actions by Health Canada were not taken within the law.

Source: The *Truehope Decision* by Judge G. M. Maegher, July 2006

Page: 29

[110] While this Court is not prepared to find that the various instances of the conduct of the representatives of Health Canada amount to the "clearest of cases" of an abuse of process to warrant a stay of proceedings, this Court does find that some of this conduct would have influenced the Defendants' beliefs that there was no reasonable legal alternative other than to disobey the D.I.N. regulation and that they had taken all reasonable care in the circumstances to comply with the law.

IV. CONCLUSION

[111] The Defendants are not guilty of Count #3 in the Information. The Defendants are entitled to rely upon the defence of necessity, which once raised was not disproved beyond a reasonable doubt by the Crown. Furthermore, this being a strict liability offence the Defendants are entitled to the defence of due diligence. On a balance of probabilities the Court is satisfied that the Defendants took all reasonable care that would be expected of a reasonable person in the circumstances to comply with the *Food and Drugs Act and Regulations* as evidenced by their considerable efforts to obtain a Ministerial Exemption or agreement during 2003. The findings that the Defendants had no reasonable legal alternative and took all reasonable care to comply with the law in the circumstances are supported, in part, by the fact that by March 2004 the new Minister of Health entered into an agreement to permit the sale and distribution of the supplement and the operation of the Truehope program, which agreement continues to the present day.

Heard on the 13th day of March, 2006 to the 24th day of March, 2006 and the 28th day of March, 2006 to the 29th day of March, 2006.

Dated at the City of Calgary, Alberta this 28th day of July, 2006.

G. M. Meagher
A Judge of the Provincial Court of Alberta

Appearances:

K. Brown
for the Crown

S. Buckley
for the Defence

Source: The *Truehope Decision* by Judge G. M. Maegher, July 2006

Buckley & Company

Law Office

600 - 235 First Avenue, Kamloops, B.C. V2C 3J4 Phone: 372-1404 Fax: 374-5800

8 August 2006

Our File: 19 0035 003

The Honourable Tony Clement
Minister of Health
Minister's Office - Health Canada
Brooke Claxton Blg., Tunney's Pasture
Postal Locator: 0906C
Ottawa, Ontario
K1A 0K9

Public Letter

Dear: Mr. Clement

Re: Public Letter Calling for a Public Inquiry into Health Canada

This is a public letter.

I am writing this letter on behalf of the Synergy Group of Canada Inc. ("Synergy") and Truehope Nutritional Support Ltd. ("Truehope"). The purpose of this letter is to seek:

1. a meeting with you to discuss the issues raised in this letter, and

2. a public inquiry into the actions of Health Canada.

Synergy and Truehope were charged on May 24, 2004, with selling their product, EMPower Plus without a Drug Identification Number ("DIN"). On July 28, 2006, following a lengthy trial, both Synergy and Truehope were acquitted. In essence, the Judge found that Synergy and Truehope were morally obligated to continue selling EMPower Plus without a DIN. I am enclosing copies of the transcript of the judgement and of the reasons for judgement. Some of the highlights of the judgment include findings of fact by the Trial Judge that:

- following the discovery that bi-polar disorder could be effectively treated with a vitamin/mineral supplement, Synergy was incorporated as a research company to promote research into this finding;

- because the treatment of depression or bi-polar could have serious side effects when an individual was reducing dependence on drugs while commencing treatment with EMPower Plus, it was necessary to establish a unique screening, monitoring and support program called the Truehope program. This program is operated by Truehope which is a non-profit organization;

Source: *Buckley Demanding Inquiry 2006*

- 2 -

- by 2002-2003 approximately 3,000 Canadians were taking EMPower Plus through the Truehope program;

- although Health Canada was demanding that Synergy and Truehope get a DIN for EMPower Plus, it was not possible for them to get a DIN. Further, Health Canada knew that it was impossible for them to get a DIN;

- at the time the Natural Health Products Directorate was being set up by Health Canada to regulate products such as EMPower Plus because the drug testing regime required to get a DIN was not compatible with natural health products such as EMPower Plus;

- at the time Synergy and Truehope were being told to stop selling EMPower Plus without a DIN, a full 90% of the natural health products in Canada did not have DINs. Despite this EMPower Plus was singled out for enforcement action;

- Synergy and Truehope took many efforts to communicate with Health Canada that stopping the sale of EMPower Plus would put the health of thousands of Canadians at risk. These efforts included:

    - letters to Health Canada and the Minister of Health;

    - letters from Truehope program participants and medical professionals;

    - providing copies of peer-reviewed journal publications on EMPower Plus showing tremendous efficacy and safety;

    - meetings with Health Canada officials;

    - requests for meetings with the Minister of Health;

- despite all of the communications, Health Canada issued directions to Canada Customs in March of 2003, to stop shipments of EMPower Plus from crossing the border from the United States unless the shipment was proven to fall within the "personal use" exemption;

- the stoppage of shipments at the border caused panic and confusion amongst the participants of the Truehope program. In response Health Canada set up a 1-800 crisis line. The notes taken by Health Canada employees of calls to this line were entered as Exhibit 65 in the trial;

- Synergy and Truehope warned Health Canada that the stoppage of shipments at the border created a serious risk of harm including possible deaths by suicide. These warnings were expressed in writing and verbally;

- two of the Health Canada employees who testified at trial said they were aware of the warnings of harm, but that this was not their concern. They were simply following orders to enforce the DIN regulation;

Source: *Buckley Demanding Inquiry 2006*

- 3 -

- in response to Health Canada's action to stop shipments at the border, Canadian citizens took to smuggling the supplement into Canada for their own health or for the health of family members;

- in June 2003, a group of women known as the "Red Umbrellas" gathered on Parliament Hill to protest against Health Canada's actions. In July 2003, they also protested at the Minister of Health's office in Edmonton;

- on January 1, 2004, the Natural Health Products Regulations came into force. The DIN regulation no longer applied to Synergy and Truehope;

- in March 2004, the new Minister of Health, Pierre Pettigrew, granted an exemption to Synergy and Truehope allowing EMPower Plus to be sold under the ministerial agreement. Dr. James Lunney, Member of Parliament, negotiated the agreement with the Minister. This agreement remains in force;

- despite all of the above Health Canada laid the DIN charge in May of 2004;

- there was clear evidence corroborating the warning by Synergy and Truehope that taking EMPower Plus off of the market was dangerous. For example:

    - Dr. Bonnie Kaplan, a psychologist from the University of Calgary, had observed the rapid return of the symptoms of bi-polar if EMPower Plus is withdrawn;

    - several lay witnesses testified of the return of bi-polar symptoms to themselves or to family members if EMPower Plus is not taken;

    - Dr. Charles Popper, a psychiatrist at Harvard University, testified that if EMPower Plus became unavailable, symptoms associated with depression and bi-polar disorder would return including aggressive behaviour, assaults, hospitalizations and suicides;

- Ron LaJeunesse, the Alberta head of the Canadian Mental Health Association in 2003, expressed grave concern for the conduct of Health Canada in preventing EMPower Plus from coming into Canada. He was concerned that there would be suicides if individuals could not get access to the supplement;

- Synergy and Truehope were overwhelmingly compelled to disobey the DIN regulation in order to protect the health, safety and well-being of the users of EMPower Plus;

- Synergy and Truehope would have been liable under the Criminal Code for criminal negligence if they had stopped selling EMPower Plus in accordance with Health Canada's direction.

All of these actions by Health Canada took place before you became the Minister of Health. In fact, the Conservative Party was extremely critical of the then Liberal Government for Health

Source: *Buckley Demanding Inquiry 2006*

- 4 -

Canada's actions. For example:

- on June 2, 2003, the Honourable James Lunney addressed the House of Commons stating:

  "Mr. Speaker, one in five Canadians experiences mental illness at some point in their lives. The cost to family and society is enormous.

  Bipolar disease results in manic-depressive swings, and people in the depressive phase of the illness are at high risk of suicide. Recently, a natural health product was developed in Alberta that has brought hope to thousands of sufferers. Researchers at the University of Calgary, led by Dr. Bonnie Kaplan, have documented the phenomenal results. The findings have been published in peer-reviewed psychiatric journals and repeated by Harvard researcher Dr. Charles Popper.

  Unbelievably, Health Canada has ordered the study stopped and is withholding product at the border because of an antiquated clause in the Food and Drugs Act that prevents claims about natural health products.

  I was in Edmonton last week to meet with concerned citizens who feel their personal health and security are threatened by these actions of Health Canada. The minister and her department are being sued for obstructing the well-being of people affected by the seizure of their nutritional products.

  Why does the minister defend antiquated and unscientific clauses in the Food and Drugs Act to obstruct freedom of choice in health care?"

- On June 12, 2003, the Honourable James Lunney addressed the House:

  "Mr. Speaker, visiting Parliament today is a courageous group of women, the women with the red umbrellas. They came from across the country to share their stories of recovery from the debilitating disease of bipolar depression.

  These women lived through tragedy until they discovered a simple vitamin and mineral supplement which helped them to recover their lives and restore them to their families. Over the past year Health Canada has initiated progressive restrictions on their supplement. The simple vitamin and mineral formula has been turned back at the border and people calling Health Canada are being told the product has been banned.

  Clinical studies have been published in peer-reviewed journals like the Journal of Clinical Psychiatry, and the Journal of Child and Adolescent Psychopharmacology. Unbelievably, research at the University of Calgary which was funded by the Alberta Science and Research Authority was shut down by Health Canada, even though there is no evidence of harm to anyone taking this product. These people are here representing thousands across the country who

Source: *Buckley Demanding Inquiry 2006*

- 5 -

feel their health and security are being threatened by this Health Canada embargo.

Will the minister ensure access to this product is not impeded and that the right to freedom of choice in personal health care by Canadians is respected?"

- on October 20, 2003, while debating Bill C-420, the Honourable James Lunney said:

"A mineral supplement, which was developed in Alberta, called EMPower+, has been helping Canadians with a mental illness known as bipolar disease or manic depression. There is a tremendous cost to the individuals and there is a high risk of suicide.

We actually have people in the House today who are here because they are concerned. They are watching the debate and many are watching across the country because they are concerned. They feel their lives are being threatened because Health Canada is taking the products off the market simply because people begin to tell others that this could help them with their mental illness. There are over 3,000 Canadians receiving help from this product and yet Health Canada would move to take it off the market. They want to know, why would Health Canada do this when there is evidence of benefit?

I would like to give an example. There was a lady from Ontario who had been on psychiatric drugs for 18 years. Her husband had been on suicide watch for many years. She has been taking this vitamin and mineral product for about two and a half years and she is off her psychiatric drugs. She is not trying to kill herself or her husband any more. She is holding down a job, paying taxes and she is volunteering. She wants to know, why would Health Canada take this away from her? Frankly, so do I...

In times when health costs are spiralling, Canadians would expect Health Canada to have an interest in a product that might lower the cost, lower the morbidity of a serious disease, and improve clinical outcomes. That was the approach of the Province of Alberta when it heard about the effect that EMPower+ was having on Albertans, it asked to look into this. There are huge costs associated with it. A $544,000 study was set up at the University of Calgary under the leadership of Dr. Bonnie Kaplan. Canadians feel betrayed and certainly the people taking the product who have their lives back feel betrayed when Health Canada hears about this and moves in to shut down the study...

This is made even worse if Health Canada is complicit in maintaining that which is contrary to the public interest. It seems to me that Health Canada ought to be on the forefront of advancing opportunities to advance health care in Canada. If a natural health product can do that, Canadians have a right to know and have a right to access low risk products."

Source: *Buckley Demanding Inquiry 2006*

- 6 -

- on November 20, 2004, while debating Bill C-420, the Honourable Colin Carrie said:

> "Let us take, for example, a product developed in Alberta; Empower Plus. This product has been helping patients with bipolar disease and manic depression. People with these problems are at a high risk of suicide and are sometimes not very productive in their lives. There are over 3,000 Canadians finding a benefit from this product.
>
> The Province of Alberta initiated a scientific response to this product and the Alberta Science and Research Authority approved and funded a $544,000 study. Preliminary results have already been published in at least four peer-reviewed psychiatric journals. Amazingly, Health Canada interpreted news of this success as a subsection 3(1) violation and shut down the study. Last July, Health Canada, while accompanied by the RCMP raided the company's offices and began obstructing access to the product. This makes no sense at all."

Later in that debate the Honourable James Lunney said:

> "A couple of members mentioned Empower Plus. We had principally women come here who had been impacted by bipolar disease, as well as many men. An 11 year old boy was here. He came with his mother from Nova Scotia. He had only been able to go to school for a year and a half because prior to that he was trying to hurt himself all the time. This product has had a phenomenal effect on people with bipolar disease in particular.
>
> Why is it that Health Canada would send in the police to raid this little company, with no evidence of harming anybody and tremendous evidence of benefit, steal its computers, and contact 3,000 Canadians to tell them to get back on their psychiatric drugs and off this natural vitamin and mineral based compound?"

- on May 16, 2005, at the Standing Committee of Health, the Honourable Colin Carrie said to Mr. Stephan and Mr. Hardy from Truehope:

> "I think everybody who's heard your story sees how the status quo right now is just an absurd enforcement of these regulations...
>
> I think, if you talk to the members here, we'd all be totally offended - we are offended - that you went through what you did here. We'd like to see that not happen to anybody else."

The Honourable Rob Merrifield said:

> "Actually, you don't have to convince me at all of your product, and it's not that I've used it, but I've certainly talked to enough individuals who have testified to me the value of your product. We fought hard over the last number of years as you've gone through your difficulty to try to add some sanity into Health Canada in the way they've applied that law..."

Source: *Buckley Demanding Inquiry 2006*

- 7 -

It is clear, that the Conservative Party has been consistent in viewing Health Canada's treatment of Synergy and Truehope which culminated in the Court proceedings as abusive and wrong. At the same time, I understand that with the Court process under way when you became Minister, it may have looked inappropriate to intervene regardless of the position of the current Government.

Now that this matter is no longer before the Court, we feel it is appropriate to at this time request an inquiry.. It is now time to answer questions such as that posed by the Honourable James Lunney above, namely:

> Why is it that Health Canada would send in the police to raid this little company, with no evidence of harming anybody and tremendous evidence of benefit, steal its computers, and contact 3,000 Canadians to tell them to get back on their psychiatric drugs and off this natural vitamin and mineral based compound?

Indeed, considering that Conservative Party's criticism of Health Canada's actions in this matter have been completely validated by the Court decision, it would be inappropriate not to have an inquiry.

The question of whether Health Canada caused deaths in this matter.

One of the witnesses at the trial was Ron LaJeunesse. Mr. LaJeunesse was the head of the Canadian Mental Health Association in Alberta. He has an impressive history of working with the mentally ill. This included being in charge of all of the mental health programs run by the Province of Alberta.

Mr. LaJeunesse testified that the Canadian Mental Health Association investigated EMPower Plus and determined that it was beneficial. When Health Canada started stopping shipments of EMPower Plus at the border, the Canadian Mental Health Association was active in intervening on behalf of its members to ensure the product could cross the border.

As the stoppages continued, Mr. LaJeunesse **publicly blamed Health Canada for two suicides caused by Health Canada's stoppage of the product at the border**. He publicly blamed Health Canada for the two suicides in his capacity as the head of the Alberta Branch of the Canadian Mental Health Association.

It is important to note that neither Mr. LaJeunesse nor the Canadian Mental Health Association had any connection with either Synergy or Truehope. Their involvement was motivated by their mandate to protect persons with mental health issues.

I was counsel for Synergy and Truehope at the trial. As their counsel, I did not try to prove to the Court that these suicides happened. That was not necessary to the defence case. Also, in speaking with Mr. LaJeunesse, I was advised that the families of the two victims did not want to be identified or to testify. I was not going to force the families to be identified or to testify at the trial where this was not necessary. Different considerations apply, however, to a public inquiry into whether Health Canada actually caused deaths in this matter.

Source: *Buckley Demanding Inquiry 2006*

- 8 -

I think it would be fantastic to suggest that Mr. LaJeunesse and the Canadian Mental Health Association were lying when they publicly blamed Health Canada for two suicides. I do not believe for a moment that either would make the allegations unless they believed them to be true.

I am also mindful based on all of the testimony at the trial, that suicides would be expected if EMPower Plus became unavailable. It became unavailable to some due to Health Canada's action of stopping shipments at the border. Dr. Charles Popper, psychiatrist at Harvard Medical School, made it abundantly clear that there would be suicides if the product became unavailable.

We also know from the absolutely bone-chilling notes of the 1-800 crisis line calls, that the participants pleading to Health Canada for their lives were worried of suicide.

Finally, we have the testimony of some of the participants at trial that they would have killed themselves rather than to go back to the despair of mental illness.

In light of the foregoing, it is very likely that the actions of Health Canada in this matter caused suicides. It is also possible that these suicides may not be limited to the ones that Mr. LaJeunesse blamed on Health Canada.

Honourable Minister, we are calling on you to hold a public inquiry to:

A. determine if Health Canada's actions led to suicides in this matter as has been publicly alleged by the former head of the Alberta Branch of the Canadian Mental Health Association.

Was Health Canada and/or employees of Health Canada acting criminally?

It is clear from the Trial Judge's decision that Synergy and Truehope had a duty under the *Criminal Code* to ignore Health Canada's direction to stop selling. If Synergy and Truehope had taken EMPower Plus off of the market, they would have been liable under the criminal negligence provisions of the *Criminal Code*.

It is clear from the trial evidence and judgement, that taking EMPower Plus off of the Canadian market would have caused deaths and hospitalizations. Synergy and Truehope would have been criminally liable if they had done so. At the same time Health Canada, despite numerous warnings and in the face of evidence that taking the product off of the market would cause harm, pressed ahead.

The trust Canadians have in Health Canada to protect them from harm has been shaken. If in this case Health Canada deliberately or recklessly caused harm, the public's confidence can only be restored by holding Health Canada to account.

Honourable Minister, it cannot be that Health Canada and Health Canada employees are

Source: *Buckley Demanding Inquiry 2006*

- 9 -

immune from the law. We are calling on you to hold a public inquiry to determine:

B. whether Health Canada and/or any employees of Health Canada were acting criminally when taking action to remove EMPower Plus from the market.

How can it be that Health Canada does not consider suicides by Canadians as relevant?

At least two Health Canada Inspectors were involved in stopping shipments at the border. These were Sandra Jarvis and Miles Brosseau. Both made it clear they did not consider evidence that their actions were causing harm was relevant.

When Sandra Jarvis learned of the news stories in which Mr. LaJeuness of the Canadian Mental Health Association was publicly blaming Health Canada for two suicides, she did nothing. She continued to stop shipments. She testified that she took no steps because **she did not believe the news of suicides was relevant to the investigation of the prosecutions**. This can be found at page 130 of the Court Transcript.

Similarly, on September 18, 2003, both Ms. Jarvis and Mr. Brosseau had a telephone call with their supervisor Dennis Shelley and Tony Stephan of Truehope. Mr. Stephan spoke of two families who had suicides because of their inability to get the product. Amazingly there was no response by Health Canada to look into these allegations of suicide. Indeed, Ms. Jarvis testified that her role was to gather evidence for the case. **There was no evidentiary value in looking into allegations of suicide**. This is found at page 128 of the Court Transcript.

When Ms. Jarvis read the testimonies of the Ladies with Red Umbrellas, she ignored it. She testified:

> "I was under the understanding that they were taking that action because they believed in the -- the -- you know, the effectiveness of the product. It did not have an impact on - I didn't believe it had any support to the evidence of selling a product that was unapproved which was essentially my role." (Transcript page 119).

When learning of a similarly impassioned plea for access to the product from another participant Ms. Jarvis said:

> "You know, I -- I thought of it personally, it concerned me personally. I didn't feel it was really relevant to the fact that this drug does not have DIN number. Whether or not it, you know, did amazing things or not, the fact of the matter is, it was in violation of the law." (Transcript page 44).

The evidence of Mr. Brosseau was equally frightening. Mr. Brosseau seemed to go out of his way to avoid looking into evidence that Health Canada's actions were causing harm. He was questioned about a June 17, 2002 letter that had been sent warning of harm and attaching 200 letters from participants and medical professionals pleading for continued access to the product. Mr. Brosseau explained that he did not read it in depth because it was not a directive to take action. It had no bearing on how Health Canada acted. **If he had a document indicating people were dying he would ignore it because it is not a policy or a directive** (Transcript

Source: *Buckley Demanding Inquiry 2006*

- 10 -

page 250).

On September 18, 2003, Mr. Brosseau had a conference call with his supervisor Dennis Shelley, Ms. Jarvis, Tony Stephan and David Hardy. Mr. Stephan read a story from the Medical Post about severe angst about the product not being available. He also spoke of two suicides. Mr. Brosseau testified that he did not verify the Medical Post story as it would not have allowed him to make any changes to his enforcement action. Further, **it did not alarm him that his enforcement actions may be leading to deaths and hospitalizations. This is because he did not have first hand knowledge** (Transcript p. 263).

This is a small sample of the evidence of harm that these Health Canada Inspectors ignored.

It is clear on the evidence that Ms. Jarvis and Mr. Brosseau were taking orders from above. Other than Dennis Shelley, the supervisors actually responsible for this matter have not been identified. Some documents leave the impression that Joan Korol was involved in this matter.

Honourable Minister, how can it be that Health Canada Inspectors that are supposed to be protecting the health of Canadians, can consistently ignore evidence that their actions are causing harm and even death **because it is not relevant: because there is no evidentiary value in looking into allegations of suicide?**

Honourable Minister, ordinary Canadians who have no idea that Health Canada would not consider their deaths to be relevant, would be shocked at the revelations that came out at the trial.

We are calling on you to hold a public inquiry to determine:

C. how can it be that Health Canada does not consider harm and suicides caused by Health Canada's actions to be relevant to an investigation?

Why would Health Canada shut down the University of Calgary clinical trial when it was approved by three ethics committee boards and funded by the Alberta Science and Research Authority?

As you are aware, following the very successful case series trials at the University of Calgary,the University approached the Alberta Government seeking funding for a large clinical trial. The Alberta Science and Research Authority agreed that it was in the public interest to run the clinical trial and provided over $500,000 of funding.

The clinical trial was run by the Faculty of Medicine at the University of Calgary. For the trial to run, the Alberta Science and Research Authority, the University of Calgary, and the Faculty of Medicine had to satisfy themselves that the design of the trial was safe. The trial design also had to get the approval of multiple ethics committees. All of the groups involved were satisfied that the trial was safe and ethical.

The trial was progressing without any evidence of harm to the trial participants when Health Canada intervened to shut the trial down. Health Canada's reasons were that the University did

Source: *Buckley Demanding Inquiry 2006*

- 11 -

not seek prior Health Canada approval. There were three problems with Health Canada's approach:

> **First**, Health Canada was of the opinion that the University would not be able to get Health Canada approval for the clinical trial. This is because the approval process for clinical trials is similar to the approval process to obtain DINs. For the same reasons Synergy and Truehope could not get a DIN for the product, the University of Calgary would be unable to get approval from Health Canada to run a clinical trial. We know from documents and evidence that came out at trial that Health Canada believed the University would not be able to get approval. Despite this Health Canada had the University go through a long and involved process of trying to get approval. This ultimately proved unsuccessful and the clinical trial was stopped.
>
> The absurd outcome of this was that Universities could not run clinical trials on vitamin and mineral supplements containing ingredients ordinary Canadians could purchase in Health Food stores because such supplements did not fit the chemical drug testing model. If the University of Calgary had wanted to run a clinical trial on the effect oranges have on scurvy, they would not be able to get pre-approval as an orange would never pass the chemical drug testing model. This leads to the second problem;
>
> **Second**, it was not the practice of Universities to seek Health Canada approval for nutrition research. If a University wanted to study the effect of oranges on scurvy, they would not ordinarily seek Health Canada approval. In this case the University was studying a vitamin and mineral supplement with ingredients readily available in health food stores. In Health Canada's world the supplement was a new drug. In the real world it was a multi-vitamin;
>
> **Third**, although the clinical trial was sponsored and ran by the University of Calgary, Synergy and Truehope had made inquiries of Health Canada concerning whether pre-approval from Health Canada was necessary. At the time the Natural Health Products Directorate was in the process of being set up. They were told that pre-approval was not necessary.

If you inquire of the researchers at the University of Calgary as to the reasons Health Canada gave to shut down the study, you will find that the University has grave concerns about the low quality of Health Canada's science.

Health Canada's actions in shutting down a safe provincially funded clinical trial is inexcusable in light of the fact that Health Canada later gave permission for the clinical trial to proceed. Once the Natural Health Products Directorate was established, they granted the University of Calgary permission to proceed with the clinical trial. The clinical trial is currently running without evidence of harm.

We are calling on you to hold a public inquiry to determine:

> D. why Health Canada would shut down the University of Calgary study when there was no evidence of harm and when Health Canada could not realistically criticize the design of the trial or the quality of the doctors and researchers running the

Source: *Buckley Demanding Inquiry 2006*

- 12 -

trial;

E. why Health Canada would have the University of Calgary go through the exercise of trying to get approval for the clinical trial when Health Canada believed that the University could not meet Health Canada's chemical drug requirements for approval;

F. how the Alberta Science and Research Authority and the University of Calgary should be compensated for the hundreds of thousands of taxpayer dollars that were wasted when Health Canada wrongfully shut down the clinical trial.

How could Health Canada and the former Minister of Health ignore thousands of Canadians who begged and pleaded for their lives?

When Health Canada began stopping shipments of EMPower Plus at the border, the 1-800 crisis line was set up. It became clear through the evidence at trial that this line did not actually help Truehope participants. It was patronizing and demeaning. Fortunately, however, the Health Canada employees taking the calls made detailed notes of the conversations. These notes were entered as Exhibit 65 at the trial.

Although there are over 700 pages of notes, it is essential that you read them. I can tell you that you will be shocked and horrified. I could only read bits at a time because they are too troubling. They document scores of vulnerable Canadians who had finally found health pleading with Health Canada for their very lives and sanity. As a human being I find it inconceivable that these notes did not cause Health Canada to re-evaluate what it was doing.

In addition to the crisis line notes, there were hundreds of letters sent by Canadians pleading for access to the product. Ordinary Canadians who rely on a product for their health, can really only communicate with Health Canada by calls and letters. Yet these were systematically ignored. There seems to be no mechanism within Health Canada to take the views of Canadians seriously.

Honourable Minister, **I am calling on you to personally read the 1-800 crisis line notes** and to hold a public inquiry to determine:

G. how Health Canada and the former Minister of Health could ignore the input of vulnerable Canadians who called, wrote and protested on a life and death issue, and

H. how is it that ordinary Canadians are to have a voice in Health Canada decisions that affect their health?

Why is it that evidence was suppressed prior to trial?

We know from the Judgement of the Trial Judge that Health Canada knew that Synergy and Truehope could not get a DIN. We also know that 90% of the natural health product industry

Source: *Buckley Demanding Inquiry 2006*

- 13 -

did not have DINs and that there was no reason to single EMPower Plus out for enforcement action.

Health Canada ran a criminal trial calling evidence that Synergy and Truehope did not have a DIN. Health Canada never explained to the Court that it was impossible for Synergy and Truehope to get a DIN and that Health Canada knew this. This fact goes to the core of the most obvious defence available, that of due diligence, and yet it was suppressed.

We also know that when Health Canada shut down the clinical trial run by the Faculty of Medicine at the University of Calgary, that Health Canada knew that they were not going to grant approval to the University to run the clinical trial. However, documents showing this were not disclosed as they should have been as part of the criminal disclosure process. What is worse is that documents obtained by Synergy under the *Access to Information Act* were edited so that this information was deleted. It was only after the Trial Judge ordered disclosure during the trial that the truth became apparent. Copies of some of the edited and unedited versions of documents have become trial exhibits.

Finally there are the notes of the 1-800 crisis line calls. These should have been disclosed prior to trial as part of the disclosure process. They should also have been disclosed under the Access to Information Act request. We had specifically requested them prior to the trial. At a pre-trial conference the Judge made it clear they should be disclosed. On the third day of trial when they had still not been disclosed, we made an application to the Court for a disclosure order. Health Canada's lawyer explained to the Court that the documents were "undiscoverable". That Health Canada had searched and searched for them and they could not be found. The Judge made an order they be disclosed. The Judge also made it clear that if the documents were not disclosed by the end of the Crown's case that the Court would consider stopping the trial. Within half an hour of this order the "undiscoverable" documents were discovered.

I cannot say whether the 1-800 crisis line documents were being deliberately suppressed or whether it was just an amazing coincidence that after weeks of searching they happened to be discovered within minutes of the disclosure order. What is clear, however, is that there was a pattern whereby Health Canada withheld evidence from Synergy/Truehope, and the University of Calgary. We are calling on you to hold a public inquiry to determine:

I. whether Health Canada withheld evidence from Synergy, Truehope, the University of Calgary and the Court.

Why did Health Canada carry on a public charade that Synergy and Truehope should have obtained a DIN without telling the Court or the public that getting a DIN was impossible?

The Trial Judge found as a fact that Health Canada knew that Synergy and Truehope could not have obtained a DIN. Health Canada also knew that 90% of the natural health product industry did not have DINs when it singled Synergy and Truehope out.

In issuing public warnings and statements, and in charging Synergy and Truehope with selling without a DIN, Health Canada never communicated to the public or to the Court that it was impossible for Synergy and Truehope to get a DIN. Nor was it communicated that Synergy and

Source: *Buckley Demanding Inquiry 2006*

- 14 -

Truehope were in the company of 90% of the natural health product industry who also did not and could not get DINs. Synergy and Truehope were unfairly vilified by Health Canada's statements.

As discussed above, Health Canada ran a trial charging Synergy and Truehope of selling EMPower Plus without a DIN number and yet did not call evidence to explain to the Court that Health Canada believed it was impossible for them to get a DIN. This issue went straight to the primary defence for this type of offence, the defence of due diligence. It appears as if Health Canada was more concerned with getting a conviction at any cost, than with being fair to Synergy, Truehope, and the Court.

Considering that Health Canada knew that Synergy and Truehope could not get a DIN, Health Canada's directions to stop selling until they get a DIN can only be interpreted as veiled directions to stop selling forever. Why was Health Canada hiding that its real intention was to take EMPower Plus off of the market permanently?

We are calling on you to hold a public inquiry to determine:

J. why Health Canada would direct Synergy and Truehope to stop selling until they have a DIN when Health Canada knew they could not get a DIN. Why was Health Canada not upfront with its intention to have the product permanently withdrawn from the market?

Why was the charge laid to enforce a regulation that no longer applies?

The offence date was 2003. As of January 1, 2004, the DIN regulation no longer applied. The product EMPower Plus is a natural health product which became subject to the Natural Health Product Regulations on January 1, 2004 (the "NHP Regulations"). The NHP Regulations came into force because of the recognition that the drug regulations, such as the DIN regulation, did not suit the natural health product industry.

Despite the facts that:

- the DIN regulation no longer applied, and
- 90% of the industry did not comply with the DIN Regulation,

the charge was laid and proceeded with. This raises question as to why Health Canada would proceed. Does it not create disrespect for the legal system when that system is used to enforce a regulation that no longer applies because it could not be adhered to in the first place?

Synergy and Truehope are not the only examples of this bizarre approach. I am aware that Biomedica in Duncan, B.C., is also facing charges alleging offences in 2003 of the old drug regulations. Like Synergy and Truehope, Biomedica is now regulated under the NHP Regulations.

We are calling on you to hold a public inquiry to determine:

Source: *Buckley Demanding Inquiry 2006*

- 15 -

K. how the public interest is served by charging companies with violations of drug regulations that were inappropriate and which no longer apply because they were inappropriate?

How could the charge be laid after an agreement was reached with the Honourable Pierre Pettigrew permitting the sale of EMPower Plus?

In March 2004, the new Minister of Health, Pierre Pettigrew, granted an exemption to Synergy and Truehope allowing EMPower Plus to be sold under the ministerial agreement. A Minister of Health will only grant a ministerial exemption under the Act if it is in the public interest to do so.

A couple of months after the Minister of Health agreed that EMPower Plus could be sold without a DIN, Synergy and Truehope were charged with selling without a DIN.

We are calling on you to hold a public inquiry to determine:

L. how could the charge be laid after an agreement was reached with the Honourable Pierre Pettigrew permitting the sale of EMPower Plus?

When faced with evidence that EMPower Plus could be a breakthrough in treating bi-polar disorder, why didn't Health Canada contact the researchers involved?

This may be the largest Health Canada investigation ever. If it is not the largest ever, it is certainly one of the largest. The investigation went on for two years prior to the charge being laid. The raid of the Truehope call centre with Health Canada employees and the RCMP was a well organized and large undertaking. It may be that several man years of time were devoted to this file.

Despite the size and complexity of the investigation, it appears that no Health Canada inspector took the time to ever call researchers such as Dr. Charles Popper at Harvard University, or Dr. Bonnie Kaplan at the Faculty of Medicine at the University of Calgary to determine whether EMPower Plus was safe or effective. Health Canada had been given the journal publications of these doctors on EMPower Plus.

Honourable Minister, EMPower Plus may be the single biggest breakthrough in the treatment of mental illness in history. Rather than confirm that this was a breakthrough that needed to be supported by Health Canada, Health Canada took all means in its power to stop the breakthrough.

We are calling on you to hold a public inquiry to determine:

M. how it came about that Health Canada took all means in its power to stop what may be the most significant breakthrough in the treatment of mental illness ever;

N. how it can be that Health Canada can conduct such a large investigation without

Source: *Buckley Demanding Inquiry 2006*

- 16 -

ever contacting the researchers for information?

How could the former Minister of Health have practised a double standard in 2003?

Ron LaJeunesse testified at the trial that when Health Canada began stopping shipments of EMPower Plus at the border the Canadian Mental Health Association ("CMHA") intervened. When a client of the CMHA complained that a shipment was stopped, Mr. LaJeunesse would intervene. He was given a contact person in the Minister's Office to contact. Every single time he called to get a shipment released, the shipment was released. This meant that if you were a client of the CMHA who was lucky enough to ask the CMHA for help, you had access to EMPower Plus.

Contrasted against this were the hundreds of Canadians who pleaded with Health Canada as documented in the 1-800 crisis line notes, the hundreds of letters sent to Health Canada, or the press conferences following political protests. These Canadians were told the product was dangerous and were denied access.

This meant there were two groups of Canadians treated very differently. There was the CMHA group who was given access every time Mr. LaJeunesse intervened. There was the other group whose cries for help were ignored. If Health Canada actually believed that the product posed a real health risk, there would not have been an elite group of Canadians whose access to the product was protected.

We are calling on you to hold a public inquiry to determine:

O. how it was that a double standard was applied to who could access the product?

How can it be that Health Canada stood by while otherwise law abiding Canadians became smugglers to protect their health or to protect the health of family members?

When Health Canada began stopping shipments at the border, many Canadians who had found freedom from mental illness were not willing to return to being sick. Family members of persons being helped by EMPower Plus were not willing to allow their children or loved ones return to mental illness. Rather than allow this to happen, otherwise law abiding Canadians formed smuggling rings to protect their health or to protect the health of family members. Some of them testified at the trial that they felt degraded having to resort to smuggling.

These smuggling rings became necessary because Health Canada ignored their calls, letters and political protests.

We are calling on you to hold a public inquiry to determine:

P. how can it be that Health Canada stood by while otherwise law abiding Canadians became smugglers to protect their health or to protect the health of family members?

Source: *Buckley Demanding Inquiry 2006*

- 17 -

How can it be that Health Canada is still stopping shipments of EMPower Plus?

After a long trial in March in which it became obvious that there was a real and immediate danger to denying Canadians access to EMPower Plus, Health Canada appears to have stopped a shipment in July 2006. This was four days before the Court decision was set to be delivered.

At this time I cannot confirm that it was Health Canada that had the shipment stopped. All we know is that on July 24, 2006, there was a shipment of EMPower Plus stopped at the border. The shipment was then released on August 3, 2006. It seems that the shipment may have been released due to the timely intervention of your Office.

Honourable Minister, we are deeply troubled that in July 2006, when it is clear that thousands of Canadians rely upon EMPower Plus for their mental health, that Health Canada would be taking any action to stop shipments at the border.

We are calling on you to hold a public inquiry to determine:

Q. whether Health Canada is still taking action to stop shipments of EMPower Plus at the border, and

R. what safeguards can be put into place to ensure that the access of Canadians to EMPower Plus can be protected from Health Canada?

How can Health Canada be refusing to licence EMPower Plus with Boron?

Synergy and Truehope have applied to the Natural Health Product Directorate for a licence for EMPower Plus with boron. To date, a license has not been granted with boron because Health Canada is voicing concerns about boron.

All of the leading experts on boron state that not only is boron safe but it is an essential mineral for health. Indeed, not only is boron essential for health, but several studies have shown that boron dramatically reduces the incidence of prostate cancer. Prostate cancer is the leading cancer in men. Rather than restricting boron, Health Canada should be actively promoting boron. The world standard is to allow up to 20 mg of boron a day. The amount of boron in EMPower Plus is well below the world standard.

I would be willing to put you in touch with the leading experts on boron. It appears that Health Canada is once again ignoring science in the position it is adopting. Canadians are being denied access to a mineral that is essential for health.

We are calling on you to hold a public inquiry to determine:

S. why Health Canada is refusing to allow Canadians access to boron when the leading scientists have shown boron is an essential mineral, and

T. whether Health Canada's refusal to approve a licence for EMPower Plus with boron was motivated by Health Canada's unrelenting drive to try to convict

Source: *Buckley Demanding Inquiry 2006*

- 18 -

Synergy and Truehope of selling EMPower Plus without a DIN?

We are making this letter public, because although the Conservative Party has consistently criticized Health Canada's actions in this matter, there is still a large number of Canadians who are completely unaware of what has happened. We believe that it will strengthen the position of your colleagues who called for these questions to be answered while in opposition if the Canadian public is educated on what you were fighting for. Indeed many Canadians will be unaware that it was matters such as this that led the Conservative Party to put into its policy document a call for greater access to natural health products.

We are grateful that the Conservative Government is emphasizing openness and accountability. This is a welcome change from the Liberal Government of Jean Chretien and Anne McLellan who refused to hear pleas for help from vulnerable Canadians and from the Conservative Opposition.

I am inviting you to contact me so that we can set up a meeting to discuss the issues raised in this letter between yourself, David Hardy, Tony Stephan and myself. I would also look into seeing if the University of Calgary would send someone like Dr. Bonnie Kaplan to attend. Finally, I would contact Ron LaJeunesse to see if he could attend.

I look forward to hearing from you.

Yours truly,

Shawn P. Buckley
Law Corporation

cc. Prime Minister Stephan Harper
The Honourable James Lunney
The Honourable Colin Carrie
The Honourable Rob Merrifield

enclosures

Source: *Buckley Demanding Inquiry 2006*

Health Canada / Santé Canada

Health Products and Food Branch / Direction générale des produits de santé et des aliments

Health Products and Food Branch
Inspectorate
Graham Spry Building, 3rd Floor
250 Lanark Avenue
Address Locator # 2003D
OTTAWA, Ontario
K1A 0K9

December 21, 2007

07-130555-499

Mr. Anthony F. Stephan and Mr. David Hardy
Synergy Group of Canada Inc.
635-2 Avenue West
Cardston, Alberta
T0K 0K0

Truehope Nutritional Support Ltd.
635-2 Avenue West
Cardston, Alberta
T0K 0K0

Dear Messrs. Anthony F. Stephan and David Hardy:

Re: EMPowerplus

We are aware that you recently made representations to the North Peace Tribal Council concerning the alleged merits of EMPowerplus, including those relating to pregnant women.

As you are aware, Health Canada has communicated its concerns to you in the past regarding the use of the product by pregnant women. In assessing your product licence application (PLA) for EMPowerplus, the Natural Health Products Directorate (NHPD) advised you that the safety of this supplement in pregnancy and breast-feeding women has not been sufficiently demonstrated, in part because the ingredients boron and vanadium are potentially toxic at higher doses.

Health Canada also remains concerned with the advertising and sale of this product as a treatment and/or cure for serious medical conditions including bipolar disorder and clinical depression. The claim for which you have submitted evidence in support of your PLA is "Nutritional support for mental and physical well-being." In light of this, NHPD has required that the label for EMPowerplus include the following statements: "If you have any serious pre-existing health conditions consult a physician" and "This product should not be used as a replacement for prescribed medication for serious psychiatric conditions. Such illnesses should be treated only under the supervision of a physician." If you wish to obtain market authorization for claims for serious conditions such as depression and bi-polar disorder, we invite you to submit supporting evidence through a subsequent application.

.../2

Canada

Source: Health Canada replies to Truehope, 2007

- 2 -

We remind you that a Natural Health Product (NHP) can be legally sold only when Health Canada issues a licence for it or pursuant to the Special Access provision found in s. 103.1 of the *Natural Health Products Regulations* which, under certain conditions and following a review of an application, may permit the sale of an unlicenced NHP. Judge Meagher's decision of July 28, 2006 concluded that Synergy Group of Canada Inc. and Truehope Nutritional Support Ltd. were not guilty of the charge of selling a drug without market authorization between January 1, 2003 and December 31, 2003. The judgment did not absolve these companies from having to comply with current legal requirements. Consequently, the Court decision does not mean that EMPowerplus can be sold without market authorization in Canada. Therefore, your assertions that your companies have a legal obligation to sell EMPowerplus are not supported in the judgment and are incorrect. Furthermore, Judge Meagher's decision did not determine whether EMPowerplus is safe and effective. Such a determination is made by Health Canada for the purposes of the *Food and Drugs Act* and *Regulations* upon the submission of appropriate scientific evidence.

Finally, we have concerns with the provision of medical advice by Truehope Nutritional Support Ltd. staff. In particular, Health Canada has recently received two complaints, one of which indicates that medical advice is being provided with respect to children, while the other indicates that Truehope staff are providing medical diagnosis and treatment advice to consumers. It is also apparent from a complaint received subsequent to the Information Update (issued February 2007), that Truehope staff continued to advise patients to modify their intake of, or cease taking, medication prescribed by their physicians.

In light of the potential risks to health associated with EMPowerplus, including inappropriate recommendations regarding its conditions of use, we request that your advertising and sale of this product comply with the *Food and Drugs Act* and its *Regulations*. Please respond to the undersigned by Friday, January 4, 2008, indicating how you intend to comply with the *Food and Drugs Act* and *Regulations*.

Yours truly,

Diana Dowthwaite
Director General
HPFB Inspectorate

Philip Waddington
Director General
Natural Health Products Directorate

Source: Health Canada replies to Truehope, 2007

TRUEHOPE

Truehope Nutritional Support Ltd.
Box 1254
Cardston, Alberta, Canada.
T0K 0K0

Fax (403) 758-6073
Ph. 1-888-TRUEHOPE
truehope@telus.blackberry.net
www.truehope.com

Minister's Office - Health Canada
Brooke Claxton Building, Tunney's Pasture
Postal Locator: 0906C
Ottawa, Ontario, Canada
K1A 0K9

January 3, 2008

Without Prejudice

Re: Diana Dowthwaite, Director General HPFB Inspectorate letter dated December 21, 2007 requesting a response with regard to compliance with the Food and Drug Act and Regulations

Dear Diana Dowthwaite,

Once again, the Health Products and Food Branch Inspectorate have demonstrated what we consider, an unwillingness to serve their stewardships with integrity and fairness. Even your letter of December 21, 2007, which we received Christmas Eve, came at a time of national holiday with a response required in 11 days. In view of the deliberate timing during the Christmas and New Year holiday season, we have made every effort to respond within the time you have required. It is important to note that many of the issues stated within your letter could have been resolved much earlier had we not been prevented from meeting with you (refer to Phil Waddington's letter of June 27, 2007). We will answer your concerns on a line by line basis. In order to facilitate this, we have placed your original letter text in bolded italics and our response follows your letter text. We have sent this response letter to Minister Clement, Deputy Minister Rosenberg, Joy Smith MP Chair of HESA, Industry Stakeholders and all MP's.

1

Source: Truehope responds to Health Canada, 2006

Introduction

We declare the assertions within your letter to be false, and your presentation of information to be deceptive. We assert that Truehope has been, and continues to be, compliant with the Food and Drugs Act and the Regulations. It is now four years since Truehope initially filed an NPN PLA application for Truehope EMP/EMPowerplus with Boron. Even now, we are shocked that two weeks after a very productive meeting with Health Canada (NHPD), held on December 6th, 2007 in Ottawa, which was initiated by Truehope in good faith and at great expense, resulted in the inaccurate characterization of Truehope and the accusation of non-compliance.

To this point, Health Canada has acted unreasonably; delaying progress in taking EMPowerplus into the medical system, presenting shifting requirements and never-ending deficiency notices, and refusing to acknowledge worldwide accepted nutritional science. Their actions caused the injury, hospitalization and death of desperate Canadians who looked to their government for security. Health Canada has held no regard for constitutional law, the criminal code of Canada, and the required integrity in dealing with the courts. Its agents have attempted to withhold information vital to the lives of Canadians, deceiving the courts in filing false affidavits, denying Canadians their right of full disclosure, willfully working against the mind and will of Parliament and the people of Canada. These agents hold themselves out as a law unto themselves; generating policy and regulation without oversight. Health Canada continually exhibits, throughout our struggle, and in the struggle of other industry stakeholders, a cheating of the process for the obtaining of regulatory validation. Health Canada has displayed a disturbing attitude toward the value of Canadian lives. They have betrayed-as government agents, the trust of Canadians. Health Canada clearly serves an agenda outside of the expected service to Canadians.

Therefore, we have lost faith in the process and the integrity of their office. We continue to cooperate, with hope and seek the support of all Canadians in removing the unworkable agendas within Health Canada.

2

Source: Truehope responds to Health Canada, 2006

Response

HC- We are aware that you recently made representations to the North Peace Tribal Council concerning the alleged merits of EMPowerplus, including those relating to pregnant women.

TH-The merits of EMPowerplus have been determined by health professionals and experts alike. We are now entering into a phase where major research is taking place on a clinical basis throughout the world. These researchers are undertaking to complete clinical research to explain what they have observed in the lives and practices of patients and doctors. Medical Journal publications are now in process, indicating substantive change in the lives of those people who have benefited through nutrition (EMPowerplus). Truehope is sought out by health professional groups throughout the world to share the profound nature of our discovery and program. These health professionals speak highly of the merits of EMPowerplus. Throughout all of this, Truehope continues to function as a non-profit organization dedicated to helping the poorest, meekest and most humble of Canadians, the mentally ill. We now have over 42,000 in our unique database, many of whom no longer express any symptoms of their previously diagnosed CNS disorders.

> "There is expert and objective evidence from Dr. Charles Popper, psychiatrist at Harvard University, who also taught other psychiatrists. He testified that when the treatment was withdrawn the symptoms returned. His expert evidence was that if the supplement became unavailable, symptoms associated with depression and bi-polar disorder, which would include aggressive behavior, assaults, hospitalizations and suicides, would return". Judge Meagher (Regina vs Truehope, July 28, 2006)

HC-As you are aware, Health Canada has communicated its concerns to you in the past regarding the use of the product by pregnant women.

TH-Can we take any of Health Canada's concerns seriously or with credibility?

For example: In 2003 Health Canada placed on their website an advisory against EMPowerplus warning Canadians not to take EMPowerplus because it contains phenylalanine:

"In addition, Empowerplus contains dl-phenylalanine (DLPA). This compound can affect mood and the nervous system. Therefore, DLPA should be taken only under medical supervision."

ADVISORY - 2001-41 "Health Canada's actions against Empowerplus"

3

Source: Truehope responds to Health Canada, 2006

TH-The absurdity of this advisory is that Diet Coke, peas, turkey and many foods all contain higher amounts of phenylalanine than EMPowerplus on a daily basis. Should Canadians seek medical supervision for the consumption of everyday foods and beverages? When challenged on this basis, Health Canada withdrew discussion on this issue, but continues to post this advisory on the web.

TH-We are not aware of any Health Canada communication outlining concern for the use of EMPowerplus by pregnant women. We do note that part of the NPN negotiations have provided some discussion with regard to use by pregnant and nursing women. We respectfully request that you forward to us the said communication.

HC-In assessing your product licence application (PLA) for EMPowerplus, the Natural Health Products Directorate (NHPD) advised you that the safety of this supplement in pregnancy and breast-feeding women has not been sufficiently demonstrated...

Helpful Truehope Background

- In January 2004 the Natural Health Products Directorate-NHPD came into being.
- In February 2004 Truehope made application for Truehope EMP, the exact formulation as Truehope EMPowerplus. After numerous IRN submissions, at great expense to Truehope, we were granted market approval for EMP with only a required warning for Phenylketonurics because EMP contains Phenylalanine.
- On May 4th 2005, Truehope received NPN# 80000383 with Boron and Vanadium and the claim: "Support for Mental and Physical Wellbeing"
- Approximately one week after receiving the verbal confirmation of the NPN, Phil Waddington (NHPD) contacted us to advise that TPD had concerns with Boron, but that an addendum would be granted within 2-3 weeks to include Boron. We were assured that a refiling would not be necessary. Two years and eight months have now passed with numerous IRN submissions requested at great expense to Truehope. We fully complied with requests, hoping that Health Canada would act in good faith and keep their word. The above actions demonstrate a willingness on the part of Truehope to comply with the NHPD over the past four years of submissions and resubmissions.

4

Source: Truehope responds to Health Canada, 2006

TH-At no time has EMPowerplus for pregnant and breast-feeding women ever been demonstrated to be of harm. At the completion of our last meeting in Ottawa on December 6th, 2007, Health Canada (Phil Waddington, Don Boyer, Alison Ingham, Stephanie Collins), agreed with Truehope (David Hardy, Anthony Stephan, Ian Stewart, Drew Dahl, Shawn Buckley), to look into the safety for pregnant and breast feeding women further. There was also a possible solution discussed, with favourable response on both sides, to consider a label direction that: "Pregnant and breast-feeding women should consult with their health practitioner prior to taking EMPowerplus" **Why is there now a sudden change in posture away from the agreed cooperation to resolve label concerns?**

Why is the Director General of the HPFB Inspectorate inaccurately surmising on behalf of Phil Waddington, who was the lead representative for Health Canada at the said meeting?

The application for the product license is still active (NPN). The file is not closed. Therefore, how can judgement be passed on this file while all of the science is being actively reviewed by both sides, and with us exercising our right to challenge any and all data? Has the file been closed without our notification? Furthermore, any implication that Truehope has been uncooperative and non-compliant with the Natural Health Products Regulations is completely false and misleading.

HC-...in part because the ingredients boron and vanadium are potentially toxic at higher doses.

TH-The levels of Boron and Vanadium in EMPowerplus are well within Health Canada's evidence-based nutrition policies and standards guidelines as outlined in the Health Canada Food and Nutrition Dietary Reference Intake table. See Appendix 1

http://www.hc-sc.gc.ca/fn-an/nutrition/reference/table/ref_elements_tbl_e.html

5

Source: Truehope responds to Health Canada, 2006

Excerpts from Health Canada publications

Dietary Reference Intakes: *The Essential Guide to Nutrient Requirements* is the summary of the Dietary Reference Intakes series. It has been developed by the Institute of Medicine of the National Academies in partnership with Health Canada. This 541 pages book offers the most accurate, practical, up-to-date information for designing nutrition education programs, assessing and planning diets for individuals and groups, establishing standards for food assistance programs and nutrition labelling, the development of new products by the industry and evaluating the adequacy of food supplies in meeting national nutritional needs. This summary report is targeted to all stakeholders in the nutrition community, in both languages to replace Nutrition Recommendations; Report of the Scientific Review Committee (*Recommandations sur la nutrition; Rapport du Comité de révision scientifique*) published in 1990 in Canada and the 1989 10th edition of the Recommended Dietary Allowances summary in United States. (http://www.hc-sc.gc.ca/fn-an/nutrition/reference/reports-rapports/index_e.html)

Dietary Reference Intakes (DRIs) are nutrient values that guide decision-making on nutrition policies and programs. DRIs are based on the latest science about human nutrition needs for healthy individuals.

Comparison Between Truehope EMPowerplus and Health Canada's Dietary Reference Intake (DRI)

Nutrient	EMPowerplus (8 Caps/day)	Health Canada's DRI
Boron	1.28 mg/day 6.4% of UL	17-20 mg/day
Vanadium	.636 mg/day 35% of UL	1.8 mg/day*

*There is no UL listed for pregnant and breast-feeding women only for women 19 - 70+

The above table shows Health Canada promoting Boron and Vanadium at a level greater than provided by EMPowerplus. What then is the real concern or agenda within the HPFB Inspectorate with regard to EMPowerplus? It could be said that your comments in paragraph two of your letter intend to deceive readers into thinking the levels of Boron and Vanadium are at toxic levels in EMPowerplus, which Health Canada's standards demonstrate is not true.

See Appendix 1 to view a copy of the Health Canada DRI Table

HC -The claim for which you have submitted evidence in support of your PLA is "Nutritional support for mental and physical well-being." In light of this, NHPD has required that the label for EMPowerplus include the following statements: "If you have any serious pre-existing health conditions consult a physician" and "This product should not be used as a replacement for prescribed medication for serious psychiatric conditions.

6

Source: Truehope responds to Health Canada, 2006

TH-Health Canada's NHPD has not required us to include these label statements to date because we are still actively involved in the NPN PLA process of negotiation. We were advised at the last mentioned meeting that an IRN would be forthcoming outlining a request for further label changes. We have not received this IRN.

Furthermore, we take issue with the concern Health Canada has over claims made under section 3(1) of the Food and Drugs Act. Justice Canada has provided an opinion to Health Canada that indicates that section 3(1) would not withstand a Charter challenge under section 2(b) of the Canadian Charter of Rights and Freedoms. These documents support the understanding that Health Canada could not withstand a Charter challenge on this issue. Why then are you attempting to enforce a law that you clearly understand violates the constitution?

See Appendixes 2&3 which are copies of internal Health Canada documents provided to Truehope

On May 16, 2005, at the Standing Committee of Health, the Honorable Colin Carrie said to Mr. Stephan and Mr. Hardy from Truehope:

"I think everybody who's heard your story sees how the status quo right now is just an absurd enforcement of these regulations...
I think, if you talk to the members here, we'd all be totally offended - we are offended - that you went through what you did here. We'd like to see that not happen to anybody else."

*House of Commons

The Honorable Rob Merrifield past Chair of the Committee said:

"Actually, you don't have to convince me at all of your product, and it's not that I've used it, but I've certainly talked to enough individuals who have testified to me the value of your product. We fought hard over the last number of years as you've gone through your difficulty to try to add some **sanity into Health Canada** in the way they've applied that law..."

Section 52, *Constitution Act, 1982,* The Constitution of Canada is the supreme law of Canada, and any law that is inconsistent with the provisions of the Constitution is, to the extent of the inconsistency, of no force or effect.

HC-Judge Meagher's decision of July 28, 2006 concluded that Synergy Group of Canada Inc. and Truehope Nutritional Support Ltd. were not guilty of the charge of selling a drug without market authorization between January 1, 2003 and December 31, 2003.

TH-While the DIN charge spanned the period January 1, 2003 and December 31, 2003, the need to comply with the Criminal Code 217 in avoiding criminal negligence is as relevant today as it was in 2003. Once again, are you prepared to personally accept responsibility for the injury and possible death of Canadians?

7

Source: Truehope responds to Health Canada, 2006

HC-The judgment did not absolve these companies from having to comply with current legal requirements.

TH-Truehope has made every effort to comply with the NHPD since their inception of January 1st 2004. Our first filing for Truehope EMP with Boron and Vanadium was made February 14th, 2004. It has now been four years since we first demonstrated compliance with an application for a Natural Health Product Number. What evidence is there that Truehope is non-compliant?

During our Court Trial with Health Canada it became evident that Health Canada had assessed internally that Truehope was never going to be able to satisfy TPD with regard to DIN requirements, although Truehope was led to believe that they could.

> "First of all there was evidence before the Court that it would have been impossible, expert evidence before the Court that it would have been impossible to obtain a drug identification number. Not only was there expert evidence to this affect, but also that this was known to representatives of Health Canada, although they were not forthcoming in telling the defendants that they were not going to get a DIN. This is also supported by the experiences and dealings that Dr. Kaplan had with representatives of Health Canada when they stopped, when Health Canada stopped the clinical trials that she was attempting to conduct." Judge Meagher (Regina vs Truehope, July 28, 2006)

TH-Is this another attempt by Health Canada to cheat the process and mislead Truehope with NHPD promises, delays and shifting requirements with the intent not to award an NPN for EMPowerplus?

TH-A higher and more serious legal requirement which Judge Meagher stressed is the very real risk of Truehope facing criminal negligence charges if we do not provide EMPowerplus to participants.

8

Source: Truehope responds to Health Canada, 2006

HC-Furthermore, Judge Meagher's decision did not determine whether EMPowerplus is safe and effective. Such a determination is made by Health Canada

TH-During the Court Trial the safety of EMPowerplus was determined by Health Canada through a Health Hazard Evaluation to be a Class 2 Health Risk; a situation in which the use of, or exposure to, a product may cause temporary adverse health consequences or where the probability of serious adverse health consequences is remote. Risk of harm was not sufficient to prevent a Ministerial exemption for importing EMPowerplus into Canada under Personal Use Enforcement Directive.

> "Health Canada itself considered the product a type 2 category, which meant the risk of serious consequences was remote". Judge Meagher (Regina vs Truehope, July 28, 2006)

TH-The effectiveness of EMPowerplus was also determined by Health Canada to be significant enough to prompt Health Canada to set up a 1 800 Crisis Line for all those who had been relying on EMPowerplus but could not access this product because of Health Canada's actions. This is an absolute admission of the effectiveness of EMPowerplus.

> "Health Canada recognized that there could be serious consequences and harm for individuals no longer able to access the supplement or the Truehope program". Judge Meagher (Regina vs Truehope, July 28, 2006)
>
> "...thousands of individuals who had found relief from mental illness through the supplement without the negative side effects of conventional medications were relying upon them to continue to sell and distribute the product and to maintain the support program". Judge Meagher (Regina vs Truehope, July 28, 2006)

9

Source: Truehope responds to Health Canada, 2006

HC-Therefore, your assertions that your companies have a legal obligation to sell EMPowerplus are not supported in the judgment and are incorrect.

TH-Truehope is obligated under Section 217 of the Criminal Code of Canada to continue to act under legal duty as explained by Judge Meagher. Are we to assume, once again, that you are willing to accept personal liability with regard to Section 217 for the injury and possible loss of life through compliance to your demands?

"I will just briefly refer to Section 217, it says: Everyone who undertakes to do an act is under a legal duty to do it, if an omission to do the act may be dangerous to life. The defendants could have been at risk of criminal prosecution if they stopped providing the supplement and providing the support program. They had undertaken this course of conduct over the course of the past several years. Ignorance of the law would have afforded them no excuse. The Crown had raised the fact that it was not clear that they were even aware of this at the time. That is fine; ignorance of the law is no excuse. Secondly, claiming that they had to comply with a DIN regulation would not have provided them with any defense. And thirdly, the evidence is overwhelming that the defendants considered themselves under a duty to protect the health, safety and well being of the thousands of persons taking the supplement, that they had to continue distributing the supplement and monitoring the progress of those persons through the TrueHope Support Program." Judge Meagher (Regina vs Truehope, July 28, 2006)

"There is also evidence from Ron LaJeunesse of the Canadian Mental Health Association, of his grave concerns with the conduct of Health Canada in preventing the supplement would result in suicides. The defendants were overwhelmingly compelled to disobey the DIN regulation in order to protect the health, safety and well being of the users of the supplement and the support program. ...This Court finds that the return of devastating, possibly life threatening behaviours within a few days constituted imminent harm or danger that the defendants reasonably believed was unavoidable if access was prevented to the supplement and the program. ...There was ample evidence presented from both ordinary and expert witnesses that the symptoms associated with depression and bi-polar disorder returned rapidly, within the matter of a few days. There was expert evidence before the Court as well, from Dr. Kaplan, who observed the rapid return of symptoms once the supplement was discontinued. And Dr. Charles Popper, who I have referred to earlier, who testified that if the supplement was unavailable there would be aggressive behaviour, assaults, hospitalizations, incarcerations and death". Judge Meagher (Regina vs Truehope, July 28, 2006)

TH-One of our greatest concerns is the lack of remorse, and the cold-blooded calculated manner in which Health Canada injured and destroyed the lives of innocent citizens through their actions. Sufficient evidence was brought forward in the trial that demonstrated the lack of compassion and concern for human life by agents who continue under your direction.

10

Source: Truehope responds to Health Canada, 2006

The transcripts include the testimonies of two Health Canada agents who claim adherence to policy is paramount, even over lives. Agent Sandra Jarvis said,

> "Whether or not (EMPowerplus), you know, did amazing things or not, the fact of the matter is, it was in violation of law." She testified that in spite of her knowledge of direct harm to Canadians, she continued turning back the legally imported nutritional supplement from the USA because the product did not have a drug identification number. Agent Miles Brosseau was questioned by Truehope Lawyer, Shawn Buckley. "So if you were sent a document . . . showing that people were dying because of what Health Canada was doing . . . you would just ignore that because it's not a policy or directive?" Brosseau answered "Yes."

Inspectorate agents were aware that people were in crisis and dying because of their actions. The Canadian Mental Health Association went to the media, demanding that Health Canada stop the embargo. Agents ignored hundreds of letters and over one thousands phone calls from citizens crying and even begging on Parliament Hill. Does the inspectorate under your direction support this kind of wanton and reckless behavior? Are you now moving toward a similar position?

HC-Finally, we have concerns with the provision of medical advice by Truehope Nutritional Support Ltd. staff. In particular, Health Canada has recently received two complaints, one of which indicates that medical advice is being provided with respect to children, while the other indicates that Truehope staff are providing medical diagnosis and treatment advice to consumers. It is also apparent from a complaint received subsequent to the Information Update (issued February 2007), that Truehope staff continued to advise patients to modify their intake of, or cease taking, medication prescribed by their physicians.

TH-Truehope does not provide medical advice, diagnosis, or treatment advice and we invite Health Canada to present such evidence. We stress to all who come to Truehope that we are not medical practitioners and do not hold our selves out to be doctors. We do provide nutritional advice and direct callers to work with their health professionals.

At the time of your Truehope update (February 07) the Health Canada Adverse Reaction Database had over 17,000 adverse reactions on the most popular antidepressant medications. It should be curious to Canadians that two alleged complaints against Truehope would seem significant to Health Canada in light of the thousands of verifiable complaints associated with approved drugs.

11

Source: Truehope responds to Health Canada, 2006

HC-In light of the potential risks to health associated with EMPowerplus...

TH-Please outline the potential risks to health associated with EMPowerplus since your own Health Hazard Evaluation assesses EMPowerplus as a Class II risk, which presents a risk far less than consuming peanuts. Approximately 120 people die each year in the USA from peanut allergies. Truehope has over 42,000 people in our participant database from 50 countries with not a single serious reaction being reported to Truehope outside of drug complications listed on Health Canada's website and drug company monographs.

> "In these circumstances little harm would have been inflicted on the regulatory process. So on a purely objective basis the harm inflicted in the circumstances of this case was insignificant when compared to the harm avoided. The harm avoided was clearly and unquestionably greater than the harm inflicted". Judge Meagher (Regina vs Truehope, July 28, 2006)

As a final response with regard to your letter we request this case be debated before the non-partisan Standing Committee on Health. We think this will be an important venue for this landmark case as there will soon be hundreds of similar concerns coming forth from an industry-wide movement. Legislation and the 53 recommendations that came out of the Standing Committee on Health devolved into Health Canada's intended agenda to keep natural health products within the realm of TPD and the Drug Inspectorate. This was never the intent of the Canadian people or the Standing Committee on Health. Health Canada's bureaucracy hijacked the process, which was intended to satisfy the needs of Canadians and the Natural Health Products industry. A third category has not been achieved, except in name only.

As you are aware, we recently circulated a $20,000 reward letter for information that could expose serious corruption within Health Canada. We posted this letter on our website: www.healthcanadaexposed.com. As a result of this initiative within Health Canada and other sources, we now have in our possession information that exposes serious corruption within Health Canada. One example of the information soon to come forward identifies a manager within the Inspectorate and his subordinates conspiring to deceive a judge in swearing and filing a false affidavit. Truehope is now engaging a prosecuting attorney to prepare court action against these agents on the basis of this, and even more significant evidence.

12

Source: Truehope responds to Health Canada, 2006

We are going to continue to expose Health Canada agents in their wrong doings and position ourselves as an industry leader in bringing to light corruption. We will not rest until corrupt agents are forced to answer for their misdeeds publicly and are brought to justice. No longer will the status quo be acceptable to cover-up the illegal action within Health Canada.

We wish, at this time, to advise you that any attempt to hold hostage the innocent within Canada by detaining, retaining, or suspending shipments of EMPowerplus into Canada will be seen, by thousands of Canadians benefiting from this product, as an act of cruelty toward the mentally ill. Your actions at that point will only put these people in a position of self-defence.

Further copies of this document are available in PDF format on
www.healthcanadaexposed.com

Sincerely,

David L. Hardy	Anthony F. Stephan
Co-founder –Truehope	Co-Founder – Truehope

XC: www.healthcanadaexposed.com
Hon. Stephen Harper – Prime Minister
DM –Morris Rosenberg
All members of the Standing Committee on Health
All Members of Parliament
Industry Stakeholders
Phillip Waddington - NHPD
Diana Dowthwaite –Inspectorate

13

Source: Truehope responds to Health Canada, 2006

APPENDIX 1 Health Canada DIETARY REFERENCE INTAKE TABLE

http://www.hc-sc.gc.ca/fn-an/nutrition/reference/table/ref_elements_tbl_e.html

Health Canada Santé Canada — Canada

Français | Contact us | Help | Search | Canada Site
A-Z Index | Consultations | Media Room | It's Your Health | Home

Health Canada • Food & Nutrition •

Home > Food and Nutrition > Nutrition & Healthy Eating > Dietary Reference Intakes > DRI Tables

Dietary Reference Intakes

Reference Values for Elements

	Arsenic[1/]		Boron		Calcium		Chromium		Copper			Fluoride		Iodine		
Unit	N/A		mg/day		mg/day		µg/day		µg/day			mg/day		µg/day		
	AI	UL[2/]	AI	UL	AI	UL	AI	UL[2/]	EAR	RDA/AI	UL	AI	UL	EAR	RDA/AI	UL
Infants																
0-6 mo	ND	ND	ND	ND	210*	ND	0.2*	ND	ND	200*	ND	0.01*	0.7	ND	110*	ND
7-12 mo	ND	ND	ND	ND	270*	ND	5.5*	ND	ND	220*	ND	0.5*	0.9	ND	130*	ND
Children																
1-3 y	ND	ND	ND	3	500*	2500	11*	ND	260	340	1000	0.7*	1.3	65	90	200
4-8 y	ND	ND	ND	6	800*	2500	15*	ND	340	440	3000	1*	2.2	65	90	300
Males																
9-13 y	ND	ND	ND	11	1300*	2500	25*	ND	540	700	5000	2*	10	73	120	600
14-18 y	ND	ND	ND	17	1300*	2500	35*	ND	685	890	8000	3*	10	95	150	900
19-30 y	ND	ND	ND	20	1000*	2500	35*	ND	700	900	10000	4*	10	95	150	1100
31-50 y	ND	ND	ND	20	1000*	2500	35*	ND	700	900	10000	4*	10	95	150	1100
51-70 y	ND	ND	ND	20	1200*	2500	30*	ND	700	900	10000	4*	10	95	150	1100
>70 y	ND	ND	ND	20	1200*	2500	30*	ND	700	900	10000	4*	10	95	150	1100

Source: Truehope responds to Health Canada, 2006

Females																
9-13 y	ND	ND	ND	11	1300*	2500	21*	ND	*540*	**700**	5000	2*	10	*73*	**120**	600
14-18 y	ND	ND	ND	17	1300*	2500	24*	ND	*685*	**890**	8000	3*	10	*95*	**150**	900
19-30 y	ND	ND	ND	20	1000*	2500	25*	ND	*700*	**900**	10000	3*	10	*95*	**150**	1100
31-50 y	ND	ND	ND	20	1000*	2500	25*	ND	*700*	**900**	10000	3*	10	*95*	**150**	1100
51-70 y	ND	ND	ND	20	1200*	2500	20*	ND	*700*	**900**	10000	3*	10	*95*	**150**	1100
>70 y	ND	ND	ND	20	1200*	2500	20*	ND	*700*	**900**	10000	3*	10	*95*	**150**	1100
Pregnancy																
< 18 y	ND	ND	ND	17	1300*	2500	29*	ND	*785*	**1000**	8000	3*	10	*160*	**220**	900
19-30 y	ND	ND	ND	20	1000*	2500	30*	ND	*800*	**1000**	10000	3*	10	*160*	**220**	1100
31-50 y	ND	ND	ND	20	1000*	2500	30*	ND	*800*	**1000**	10000	3*	10	*160*	**220**	1100
Lactation																
< 18 y	ND	ND	ND	17	1300*	2500	44*	ND	*985*	**1300**	8000	3*	10	*209*	**290**	900
19-30 y	ND	ND	ND	20	1000*	2500	45*	ND	*1000*	**1300**	10000	3*	10	*209*	**290**	1100
31-50 y	ND	ND	ND	20	1000*	2500	45*	ND	*1000*	**1300**	10000	3*	10	*209*	**290**	1100

This table presents *Estimated Average Requirements (EARs) in italics*, **Recommended Dietary Allowances (RDAs) in bold type** and Adequate Intakes (AIs) in ordinary type followed by an asterisk (*). Tolerable Upper Intake Levels (ULs) are in shaded columns.

[16]Although a UL was not determined for arsenic, there is no justification for adding arsenic to food or supplements.

[17]Due to lack of suitable data, ULs could not be established for arsenic and chromium. This does not mean that there is no potential for adverse effects resulting from high intakes.

Note: These are reference values for normal, apparently healthy individuals eating a typical mixed North American diet. An individual may have physiological, health, or lifestyle characteristics that may require tailoring of specific nutrient values.

	Iron[18]			**Magnesium**			**Manganese**		**Molybdenum**			**Nickel**		**Phosphorus**		
Unit	**mg/day**			**mg/day**			**mg/day**		**µg/day**			**mg/day**		**mg/day**		
	EAR	RDA/AI	UL	EAR	RDA/AI	UL[19]	AI	UL	EAR	RDA/AI	UL	AI	UL	EAR	RDA/AI	UL
Infants																
0-6 mo	*ND*	0.27*	40	*ND*	30*	ND	0.003*	ND	*ND*	2*	ND	ND	ND	*ND*	100*	ND
7-12 mo	*6.9*	11	40	*ND*	75*	ND	0.6*	ND	*ND*	3*	ND	ND	ND	*ND*	275*	ND

Source: Truehope responds to Health Canada, 2006

Children																
1-3 y	*3.0*	**7**	40	*65*	**80**	65	1.2*	2	*13*	**17**	300	ND	0.2	*380*	**460**	3000
4-8 y	*4.1*	**10**	40	*110*	**130**	110	1.5*	3	*17*	**22**	600	ND	0.3	*405*	**500**	3000
Males																
9-13 y	*5.9*	**8**	40	*200*	**240**	350	1.9*	6	*26*	**34**	1100	ND	0.6	*1055*	**1250**	4000
14-18 y	*7.7*	**11**	45	*340*	**410**	350	2.2*	9	*33*	**43**	1700	ND	1.0	*1055*	**1250**	4000
19-30 y	*6*	**8**	45	*330*	**400**	350	2.3*	11	*34*	**45**	2000	ND	1.0	*580*	**700**	4000
31-50 y	*6*	**8**	45	*350*	**420**	350	2.3*	11	*34*	**45**	2000	ND	1.0	*580*	**700**	4000
51-70 y	*6*	**8**	45	*350*	**420**	350	2.3*	11	*34*	**45**	2000	ND	1.0	*580*	**700**	4000
>70 y	*6*	**8**	45	*350*	**420**	350	2.3*	11	*34*	**45**	2000	ND	1.0	*580*	**700**	3000
Females																
9-13 y	*5.7*[‡]	**8**[‡]	40	*200*	**240**	350	1.6*	6	*26*	**34**	1100	ND	0.6	*1055*	**1250**	4000
14-18 y	*7.9*[‡]	**15**[‡]	45	*300*	**360**	350	1.6*	9	*33*	**43**	1700	ND	1.0	*1055*	**1250**	4000
19-30 y	*8.1*[‡]	**18**[‡]	45	*255*	**310**	350	1.8*	11	*34*	**45**	2000	ND	1.0	*580*	**700**	4000
31-50 y	*8.1*[‡]	**18**[‡]	45	*265*	**320**	350	1.8*	11	*34*	**45**	2000	ND	1.0	*580*	**700**	4000
51-70 y	*5*[‡]	**8**[‡]	45	*265*	**320**	350	1.8*	11	*34*	**45**	2000	ND	1.0	*580*	**700**	4000
>70 y	*5*[‡]	**8**[‡]	45	*265*	**320**	350	1.8*	11	*34*	**45**	2000	ND	1.0	*580*	**700**	3000
Pregnancy																
< 18 y	*23*	**27**	45	*335*	**400**	350	2.0*	9	*40*	**50**	1700	ND	1.0	*1055*	**1250**	3500
19-30 y	*22*	**27**	45	*290*	**350**	350	2.0*	11	*40*	**50**	2000	ND	1.0	*580*	**700**	3500
31-50 y	*22*	**27**	45	*300*	**360**	350	2.0*	11	*40*	**50**	2000	ND	1.0	*580*	**700**	3500
Lactation																
< 18 y	*7*	**10**	45	*300*	**360**	350	2.6*	9	*35*	**50**	1700	ND	1.0	*1055*	**1250**	4000
19-30 y	*6.5*	**9**	45	*255*	**310**	350	2.6*	11	*36*	**50**	2000	ND	1.0	*580*	**700**	4000
31-50 y	*6.5*	**9**	45	*265*	**320**	350	2.6*	11	*36*	**50**	2000	ND	1.0	*580*	**700**	4000

This table presents *Estimated Average Requirements (EARs) in italics*, **Recommended Dietary Allowances (RDAs) in bold type** and Adequate Intakes (AIs) in ordinary type followed by an asterisk (*). Tolerable Upper Intake Levels (ULs) are in shaded columns.

[18]The requirement for iron is 1.8 times higher for vegetarians due to the lower bioavailability of iron from a vegetarian diet.

[19]The UL for magnesium represents intake from a pharmacological agent only and does not include intake from food and water.

[‡]For the EAR and RDA, it is assumed that girls younger than 14 years do not menstruate and that girls 14 years and older do menstruate. It is assumed that

Source: Truehope responds to Health Canada, 2006

women 51 years and older are post-menopausal.

Note: These are reference values for normal, apparently healthy individuals eating a typical mixed North American diet. An individual may have physiological, health, or lifestyle characteristics that may require tailoring of specific nutrient values.

	Selenium			Silicon		Vanadium		Zinc			Potassium		Sodium		Chloride		Sulfate	
Unit	µg/day			N/A		mg/day		mg/day			mg/day		mg/day		mg/day		N/A	
	EAR	RDA/AI	UL	AI	UL	AI	UL	EAR	RDA/AI	UL	AI	UL	AI	UL	AI	UL	AI	UL
Infants																		
0-6 mo	*ND*	15*	45	ND	ND	ND	ND	*ND*	2*	4	400*	ND	120*	ND	180*	ND	ND	ND
7-12 mo	*ND*	20*	60	ND	ND	ND	ND	*2.5*	**3**	5	700*	ND	370*	ND	570*	ND	ND	ND
Children																		
1-3 y	*17*	**20**	90	ND	ND	ND	ND	*2.5*	**3**	7	3000*	ND	1000*	1500	1500*	2300	ND	ND
4-8 y	*23*	**30**	150	ND	ND	ND	ND	*4.0*	**5**	12	3800*	ND	1200*	1900	1900*	2900	ND	ND
Males																		
9-13 y	*35*	**40**	280	ND	ND	ND	ND	*7.0*	**8**	23	4500*	ND	1500*	2200	2300*	3400	ND	ND
14-18 y	*45*	**55**	400	ND	ND	ND	ND	*8.5*	**11**	34	4700*	ND	1500*	2300	2300*	3600	ND	ND
19-30 y	*45*	**55**	400	ND	ND	ND	1.8	*9.4*	**11**	40	4700*	ND	1500*	2300	2300*	3600	ND	ND
31-50 y	*45*	**55**	400	ND	ND	ND	1.8	*9.4*	**11**	40	4700*	ND	1500*	2300	2300*	3600	ND	ND
51-70 y	*45*	**55**	400	ND	ND	ND	1.8	*9.4*	**11**	40	4700*	ND	1300*	2300	2000*	3600	ND	ND
>70 y	*45*	**55**	400	ND	ND	ND	1.8	*9.4*	**11**	40	4700*	ND	1200*	2300	1800*	3600	ND	ND
Females																		
9-13 y	*35*	**40**	280	ND	ND	ND	ND	*7.0*	**8**	23	4500*	ND	1500*	2200	2300*	3400	ND	ND
14-18 y	*45*	**55**	400	ND	ND	ND	ND	*7.3*	**9**	34	4700*	ND	1500*	2300	2300*	3600	ND	ND
19-30 y	*45*	**55**	400	ND	ND	ND	1.8	*6.8*	**8**	40	4700*	ND	1500*	2300	2300*	3600	ND	ND
31-50 y	*45*	**55**	400	ND	ND	ND	1.8	*6.8*	**8**	40	4700*	ND	1500*	2300	2300*	3600	ND	ND
51-70 y	*45*	**55**	400	ND	ND	ND	1.8	*6.8*	**8**	40	4700*	ND	1300*	2300	2000*	3600	ND	ND
>70 y	*45*	**55**	400	ND	ND	ND	1.8	*6.8*	**8**	40	4700*	ND	1200*	2300	1800*	3600	ND	ND
Pregnancy																		
< 18 y	*49*	**60**	400	ND	ND	ND	ND	*10.5*	**12**	34	4700*	ND	1500*	2300	2300*	3600	ND	ND
19-30 y	*49*	**60**	400	ND	ND	ND	ND	*9.5*	**11**	40	4700*	ND	1500*	2300	2300*	3600	ND	ND
31-50 y	*49*	**60**	400	ND	ND	ND	ND	*9.5*	**11**	40	4700*	ND	1500*	2300	2300*	3600	ND	ND

Source: Truehope responds to Health Canada, 2006

Lactation																		
< 18 y	*59*	**70**	400	ND	ND	ND	ND	*10.9*	**13**	34	5100*	ND	1500*	2300	2300*	3600	ND	ND
19-30 y	*59*	**70**	400	ND	ND	ND	ND	*10.4*	**12**	40	5100*	ND	1500*	2300	2300*	3600	ND	ND
31-50 y	*59*	**70**	400	ND	ND	ND	ND	*10.4*	**12**	40	5100*	ND	1500*	2300	2300*	3600	ND	ND

This table presents *Estimated Average Requirements (EARs) in italics*, **Recommended Dietary Allowances (RDAs) in bold type** and Adequate Intakes (AIs) in ordinary type followed by an asterisk (*). Tolerable Upper Intake Levels (ULs) are in shaded columns.

[20]Although silicon has not been shown to cause adverse effects in humans, there is no justification for adding silicon to supplements.

[21]Due to lack of suitable data, ULs could not be established for silicon, potassium, and sulfate . This does not mean that there is no potential for adverse effects resulting from high intakes.

[22]Although vanadium in food has not been shown to cause adverse effects in humans, there is no justification for adding vanadium to food and vanadium supplements should be used with caution. The UL is based on adverse effects in laboratory animals and this data could be used to set a UL for adults but not children and adolescents.

[23]The requirement for zinc may be as much as 50 percent greater for vegetarians, particularly for strict vegetarians whose major food staples are grains and legumes, due to the lower bioavailability of zinc from a vegetarian diet.

[24]The beneficial effects of potassium appear to be mainly from the forms of potassium found naturally in foods such as fruits and vegetables. Supplemental potassium should only be provided under medical supervision

[25]Grams of sodium x 2.53 = grams of salt.

[26]Sodium and chloride are normally found in foods together as sodium chloride (table salt). For this reason, the AI and UL for chloride are set at a level equivalent on a molar basis to those for sodium, since almost all dietary chloride comes with sodium added during processing or consumption of foods.

[27]An AI for sulfate was not established because sulfate requirements are met when dietary intakes contain recommended levels of sulfur amino acids (protein).

Note: These are reference values for normal, apparently healthy individuals eating a typical mixed North American diet. An individual may have physiological, health, or lifestyle characteristics that may require tailoring of specific nutrient values.

Date Modified: 2005-08-04 Important Notices

Source: Truehope responds to Health Canada, 2006

Appendix 2

Health Canada / Santé Canada
Deputy Minister / Sous-ministre
Ottawa, Canada K1A 0K9

Seen by MO

FOR DECISION

Your file / Votre référence
02-116416-386
Our file / Notre référence

OCT - 4 2002

MEMORANDUM TO THE MINISTER

SUBJECT: Proposed Schedule A Consultations and Direct to Consumer Advertising

SUMMARY:

A 1999 Standing Committee on Health made 53 recommendations regarding the regulation of natural health products. Some recommendations were general in nature and referred to the current Act or Regulations. Two of these were that Health Canada review the diseases listed in Schedule A of the *Food and Drugs Act*, and that Health Canada initiate a review to determine whether subsections 3(1) and (2) of the *Food and Drugs Act* or all of the diseases listed in Schedule A should be deleted.

Health Canada struck an internal working group that has initiated this work, and is ready to launch the consultation with the release of a Guidance Document (Phase I) and the formation of an external (with internal participation) working group (Phase II).

Direct to Consumer Advertising (DTCA) refers to advertising of prescription products to the general public. Pressure to act on DTCA before the long-term Legislative Renewal strategy occurs mounts from media and industry. Provincial and territorial governments, health professionals and associations, and patient and consumer advocacy groups advise caution.

Current regulations do not provide sufficient penalty to strongly encourage compliance while the Department of Justice considers that the current provisions would probably not withstand a Charter challenge. Forthcoming under separate cover is a legal opinion of a possible charter challenge on the grounds of freedom of speech.

We recommend that Health Canada implement Schedule A Consultations as soon as possible.

.../2

Canada

Source: Truehope responds to Health Canada, 2006

Appendix 3

David K Edwards
09/05/2002 03:37 PM

Document E

To: Christophe Roy/HC-SC/GC/CA@HWC
cc: Ann Sztuke-Fournier/HC-SC/GC/CA@HWC, Melanie Forget/HC-SC/GC/CA@HWC, Deborah Kryhul/HC-SC/GC/CA@HWC

Subject: Re: Request for a Legal Opinion

Constitutionality

I must further note that a legal opinion was obtained in February 1999 from the Human Rights Law Section of Justice on the subject of the application of the *Canadian Charter of Rights and Freedoms* to the prohibition of advertising found in section 3 of the Act. The opinion was asked for in the context of a proposed bill respecting food. In 1989, an Ontario Provincial Court decision in Thomas Lipton Inc. ((1989), 51 C.C.C. (3d) 104, affirmed on appeal to the General Division, unreported) had concluded that subsection 3(1) of the *Food and Drugs Act* infringes section 2(b) of the Charter. The opinion states that "Since the provision in question would ban certain types of advertising, there is no doubt that the courts would find that this provision infringes freedom of expression as guaranteed by section 2(b) of the Charter. (...) As such, it would be necessary to determine whether the infringement is justified under section 1 of the Charter which permits reasonable limits on Charter rights." The opinion reviews very thoroughly each element necessary for that justification. It comes to the conclusion that subsection 3(1) of the Act would undoubtedly be found to constitute an infringement of the freedom of expression guaranteed by section 2(b) of the Charter and that there is a serious risk that the courts would find that subsection 3(1) does not minimally impair the freedom of expression and therefore that the courts would not uphold subsection 3(1) as a reasonable limit under section 1 of the Charter.

While steps could be taken towards securing compliance with FDA ss. 3(1) – in the event that the representations in question can indeed be well characterized as contraventions of this subsection – ultimately launching a prosecution would may still not be advisable in light of the significant charter risks involved.

20

Source: Truehope responds to Health Canada, 2006

3

The Mockery of Informed Consent

"It is not the function of our Government to keep the citizen from falling into error; it is the function of the citizen to keep the Government from falling into error."

—Robert Houghwout Jackson
Chief Judge, War-Crimes Tribunal, Nuremberg, 1945

Informed consent is the basis of medical law. If bills C-51 and C-52 become law we will loose access to reliable information, the right to consent or refuse, and all Canadians will be redefined (by implication) as so mentally challenged as to require the government's supposedly noble-minded and protective guidance with regard to the quality of food, drugs, natural health products, cosmetics, and medical devices.

A state of perfect, benevolent control is awaiting us all.

Legally, consent implies that one is assumed to be able and at liberty to survey a range of options—in a word: choice. Consent also implies the possibility of refusal—again: choice. Informed consent is defined as *"a condition whereby a person can be said to have given consent based on appreciation and understanding of the facts."* That further implies that the "person" is smart enough to be capable of such understanding.

But the eighth paragraph of the preamble informs Canadians: "Only products that meet legislative requirements are [to be] available to the public." That, as it happens, is the nightmare from which we are all trying to awake. Over the past couple of decades those folks in Health Canada and their directing ministers have already been following the policy stated in that eighth preamble. That is why, in spite of 97% of us objecting to being force-fed genetically engineered foods and carcinogen and prion-laced animal products, we have been told by the government this stuff is good for us and quite safe. They recently told us so again by killing bill C-517; it would at least have allowed us to decide what we want to eat, through mandatory labeling. Now they want to make their science-challenged certainty, on these matters of quality, law.

C-51 transfers all meaningful choice *and* all the understanding, presumed necessary for a conscious choice, to the discretionary powers of the minister who "*may* establish committees for the purposes of seeking advice" [20.4 (1)]. When all information is censored, doctored, and not independently verifiable, understanding becomes impossible. Then choice becomes impossible and consent becomes a mockery. The Minister is free to pick committee members from anywhere he or she pleases, because there is no elaboration in this bill as to who should be picked. There is not even a hint at a guarantee of independence.

We have a fairly good idea whom the government has in mind; Sections 3 and 30 inform us they mean any old (helpfully undefined) "industrial and trade organizations [and] foreign governments," whose regulatory notions our Minister of Health may believe to be good for us; these can be made part of our own law—without even consulting Parliament. This is not especially mysterious: we know very well that the entire current alphabet soup of treaties—in force or still in the process of being forced on us—requires that all regulatory agencies be "harmonized," e.g. NAFTA (which Canadians rejected in a referendum, but Prime Minister Mulroney put into effect anyway, we kicked him out and the next PM went right on with it), CAFTA, the SPP (Security and Prosperity Partnership—wow! do they have a way with words), and of course the United Nations' Codex Alimentarius which is enforced by the WTO with its secret courts; we are one of the member countries.

Come to think of it, this sheds an eerie light on the fourth preamble to the proposed bill. It states: "Whereas the Parliament of Canada recognizes that **cooperation among regulators** of foods, therapeutic products and cosmetics contributes to the health and safety of the public." [Emphasis added.] What cooperation? Which regulators? Where are the regulators who have earned our trust? Those regulators who actually had the nerve to attempt acting in the public interest, because they understood the difference between "tobacco science" (like Dr. Shiv Chopra and Dr. Gerard Lambert), and the real thing, and because they were nit-pickingly careful (like Dr. Margaret Haydon)—those regulators always wound up fired or became so disgusted they had no option but to resign (like Dr. Michelle Brill-Edwards), or were removed out of harm's way (like Dr. David Graham of the FDA)—harm, that is, to the manufacturers of toxic drugs and medical devices that also can kill. Under the circumstances, it is interesting that Canada has had such surprisingly effective regulators—their defiance actually managed to get some of the Food and Drugs Act requirements honored. Maybe bill C-51 is aimed as much at neutralizing Canadians with brains, as it is at those regulators who might become pesky.

Actually, what we all really would like to see is that the government obeys the laws of the land and orders Health Canada to obey this act—which is already *all* about *all* the safety we sorely needed, but don't seem to get. We need bills C-51 and C-52 about as badly as we want cancer, heart disease, birth defects, and autoimmune disease all of which disobeying the current Food and Drugs Act has been promoting energetically. The current act guarantees safety—if followed. The proposed bills guarantee nothing except arbitrary exercise of power.

The Council of Canadians puts it all together perfectly on their website:

> *"The Harper government's new food and drug, and consumer safety legislation—bills C-51 and C-52—was developed with the aim of copying U.S.-style policies in Canada in response to corporate pressure—not public concerns.*

"Harper's Food and Drug Act amendments (Bill C-51) were drafted in cooperation with U.S. regulators based on a Security and Prosperity Partnership (SPP) promise last August to share 'best practices' and create common North American environmental and health policies. In February 2007, a corporate advisory group to the SPP called for 'a new North American Regulatory Cooperation Framework in 2007,' that would ensure 'consistent application of standards and regulatory requirements within each country.'

"The public was not consulted."

"Bill C-51 would introduce U.S.-style 'progressive licensing' for new pharmaceutical products in Canada. This means relying on ***corporate information*** *to fast-track the drug approval process, and then letting drug companies keep track of the impact on our health. Progressive licensing means the government will 'manage the damage after the fact, but they refuse to protect us from getting those problems in the first place,' according to Michael McBane of the Canadian Health Coalition. A recent study from* THE NEW ENGLAND JOURNAL OF MEDICINE *found that fast-tracking drugs to market in the United States has led to significantly more recalls for safety reasons. According to an* ENVIRONICS *Poll conducted in April, 2008, 87% of Canadians agree that Canada should maintain the ability to set its own independent environmental, health and safety standards, even if this might reduce cross-border trade opportunities with the United States.*

"With Bill C-51, Prime Minister Harper is obviously more concerned with corporate and U.S. priorities than the health and safety of Canadians." (www.canadians.org)

Infallibility Has Arrived In Ottawa

The wordsmiths who created C-51 are very good indeed and should, instead of working for the government, be doing Hollywood film scripts for the entertainment of us all.

If an unsuspecting Alien were to come upon this document without knowing the context, he or she or it would probably be in a state of mounting alarm after just a few pages. C-51 conveys a sense of frightful urgency, conjuring up images of extreme danger, to millions of helpless people, who must immediately be saved, at any cost, from some perfectly horrible foods, murderous drugs, and unspeakably dreadful medical devices—not to mention some cosmetics straight out of some mad scientist's laboratory. An extreme state of emergency has a big portion of this planet in its grip because untold numbers of criminals are lurking everywhere who specialize in secretly manufacturing food and medicines that are extremely harmful. Only through extreme measures of mind-boggling fines and jail terms is there any hope of survival for millions of humans.

The Alien would feel slightly reassured when realizing that a gloriously heroic effort is now commencing that will restore safety and security as soon as the old rules, that allowed all this criminality to proliferate, have been swept aside and this very important and astoundingly capable person, called The Minister, has been put in charge to clean this mess up all by himself with a firm hand and new, effective shock-and-awe measures.

If we then were to explain to our Alien, that actually this is "doublespeak," straight out of a novel called *1984*, meaning that the exact opposite is being proclaimed from what is being done, and that the old rules were perfect but nobody paid any attention to them, and yes—this place is pretty much awash in toxic foods and drugs, that lots of humans are being fooled into using those dangerous medical devices, but that all this is the very source of this planet's wealth—well, then our Alien would experience a panic attack and hasten to his spaceship to get the hell off this planet and enter the safety of hyperspace.

Sad to say, we can't go with the Alien. We have to stick it out right here and face down yet another government that has no idea what "public interest" actually means.

If C-51 were to become law, the first Minister of Health to implement it would also be the first Pope of Medicine—say, Pope Tony I—presumed to be infallible. Unlike the Pope in Rome, the medical pope would not even have an important old book to fall back on, because this pope is also allowed to change the book as he or his friends please.

In Sections 3 and 18 it is stated that the *"Minister may, on application, issue a clinical trial authorization to a person in respect of therapeutic products."* Now, a "person," in practice is more likely than not a corporation which legally have person status, but none of the responsibilities of a person. The Minister furthermore "*may, without having to give the holder of the authorization an opportunity to make representations, suspend a clinical trial authorization if the Minister is of the opinion that an immediate suspension is necessary to respond to a serious and imminent risk of injury to the health of a clinical trial subject or a person who is involved in the clinical trial.*"

What this means in practice, is that the Minister of Health overrides the already existing university-based ethics committees. The members of the Canadian Association of University Teachers (CAUT) who a few years ago so ably defended Dr. Nancy Olivieri against Health Canada's collusion with Big Pharma, should take note of this bill.

The reader has by now read the Truehope case material and will notice that this grab for total control appears to be the government's response to that judge who must have annoyed them very much indeed. Never again will Health Canada—come hell, high water, democracy, scientific independence, or desperately ill people—be told in a court of law that people are more important than arbitrary policy; that the public interest is protected when the existing Food and Drugs Act is actually obeyed. Be it the universities of Calgary, Harvard, or Hippocrates himself come-back-from-the-dead: no way will there be a medical trial done in this country unless the Minister likes it. He sure didn't like the Truehope trial and the fact that it was in accord with the letter and the spirit of the law—so, change the law and all is well! No wonder, that nowhere in this bill is the term "risk" defined. They messed around with the word "sell," despite its *Oxford English Dictionary* definition, but the work "risk" is—well, too risky to fiddle with.

I don't actually know with certainty if there are countries in which the government decides what medical research may take place. If there are, they sure aren't making headlines with the great science they are producing. The only cases of such breath-taking arrogance that immediately come to mind are from the classic tyrannies of the 20th century, such as Hitler's Germany and Stalin's Soviet Union. Fast forward to Canada in 2004 and we actually find our government shutting down a successful university-run clinical trial in which the participating patients were dramatically improving from the experimental therapy.

The trouble is, that even if one could succeed in changing "may" to "shall" in Section 20.4 (1) so "the Minister *shall* (instead of *may*) establish committees for the purpose of seeking advice," one would then still have to throw out at least two-thirds of this bill to bring it even a little in line with such universally respected notions as "academic freedom," "science in the public interest," and "research integrity"—all of which imply that political and money-driven interests not only must take the backseat, but stay out of the vehicle entirely.

Codex

What fascinates me is how close the intent and even often the wording of this bill is to the currently pending FDA Revitalization Act, Senate Bill S.1082. Since the US has laws protecting natural health products (DSHEA), the equivalent of which would have been MP James Lunney's C-420 you read all about in chapter 1. The US has also successfully established through federal court orders that health claims can be made for vitamins C, E, B as well as Co-enzyme Q_{10}. As the leading medical journals were becoming angrier at FDA mismanagement and the body count from pharmaceutical drugs rose with every year, while the body count from natural health products remained conspicuously absent, some people became worried. For the details got to www.iahf.com and read the analyses provided by Byron Richards. Hence it suddenly appears that the FDA needs revitalizing and Health Canada needs modernizing. If both had just obeyed the laws they have got already, as all those regulatory whistle blowers have testified, we would all be so much healthier.

S.1082 has all the same provisions as our proposed bills C-51 and C-52. Furthermore, these legislative efforts in the US and Canada are also almost entirely identical to the directives adopted by the international Codex Alimentarius whose heavy-handed ways were successfully challenged all the way up to the International Court of Justice in 2006.

This United Nations committee, charged with establishing international standards for both foods and drugs, decided in 2002 to place all natural health products into the same category as drugs—just like bill C-51 proposes to do by lumping everything into the term "therapeutic products." The US bill S.1082 also has those kinds of clauses that would undermine their current differentiation between drugs and natural health products. Again, just like bill C-51, Codex adopted the terms suggested by something called the 2002 *EU Directive* which ignored even the most basic medical body of science in nutrition and medicine. It stated in Article 6 (2) that no claims could be made to suggest that "food supplements [have] the property of preventing, treating, or curing a human disease, or refer to such properties."

Furthermore, since all the natural health products on European markets (many familiar to most households since Roman times) had never been subjected to clinical trials and toxicity tests, (as pharmaceutical drugs must undergo), Codex and the European Parliament decreed that all natural health products would have to go off European markets in August 2005—until proven "safe" in drug-trial terms, one by one.

The Alliance for Natural Health filed a case challenging this decision with the European Advocate, a court that deals with EU countries' trade issues. On April 5, 2005, the Advocate General for the EU ruled that this attempt to limit the availability of vitamins, minerals, herbs, and other essential nutrients was invalid. Justice Leendert A. Geelhoed found the *EU Directive* to be in violation of the EU Constitution, various trade laws, and international trade treaties as well.

He pointed out that the European Union's Constitution clearly forbids in its Article 152 (4c) any attempt by any one member country to "harmonize legislation on public health" with the other member countries. Secondly, citing a long list of case law and treaties, Justice Geelhoed ruled that EU trade law, as well as the applicable international trade treaties, do not allow the arbitrary "prohibition …

[of] substances ... which no one has ever doubted are essential for the diet and/or which have not been shown to represent a danger to health." He found that instead of "facilitating trade," as these laws and treaties require, this *Directive* and Codex policy create illegal obstacles to trade and erect illegal barriers to their availability.

I bet, if Canadian lawyers looked at the implications of C-51 from this angle, they would also find that trade laws are likely violated in the Americas as well as by both Canada's proposed bills and S.1082 in the US.

Justice Geelhoed further observed that the *Directive's* specifications, and thereby Codex's prejudices, "betray a preference for the inorganic forms ... which results in unjustifiable and disproportionate exclusion, of their natural forms, which are nevertheless common in the normal diet and generally better tolerated by the body." Having put his finger on the sore spot, namely the attempt to allow the marketing only of Big Pharma's synthetic products, he simultaneously showed that this trickery is a violation of trade laws, to which the term "disproportionate exclusion" refers (i.e. anti-monopoly principles of fair trade). He observed that this "significantly affects the freedom of market operators by impeding the continuation of activities previously regarded as permissible and safe."

The arbitrary powers the *Directive* granted were seen as being so outrageous that Justice Geelhoed found them to be "about as transparent as a black box" and in total contravention to all existing legal rights or "essential guarantees ... which are basic principles of law." Maybe, we should have a chat with this Justice Geelhoed and ask him what he thinks of our C-51!

Finally, Justice Geelhoed observed: "It would be odd to start the evaluation procedure [of all supplements according to risk assessment principles used for toxins and synthetic drugs] from zero again, when it is clear that the products concerned have already undergone [tests] establishing safety and bioavailability ... [which should be used] as the existing evaluations as a starting point."

A year later, a ruling came down from the International Court of Justice which stated that while natural health products could be regulated in various ways by EU member states, the notion of presumed toxicity was indeed absurd. The court stated that only synthetic substances could be presumed toxic until proven harmless, while natural substances must be assumed to be safe.

The Alliance for Natural Health then took this to the High Court of the UK in 2007 where in essence all this was once again affirmed, this time specifically for one of the EU member states, namely the UK.

The Alphabet Soup Takes Over

In June 2006 the FDA—and thereby Canada also—entered into a very scary agreement with the European Commission to the effect that the US and the EU would harmonize their policies on drugs and natural medicines (food supplements). More recently, Canada entered into this SPP "partnership" which, however, right from the start excluded all of us 30 million Canadians, seeing we weren't even asked if we would like to be "secure" and "prosper" along the lines of this treaty. Among the SPP's many provisions, is once again the need to "harmonize" the healthcare systems of the countries involved and streamline the regulatory agencies as well. We weren't asked if we thought this to be a good idea. Even though less than one third of us voted in Prime Minister Stephen Harper, he seems to think he knows best what we all need and want.

In fact, the *intentions* of Codex and the EU *Directive*, were adopted by Canada even though the European court and the International Court of Justice had ruled against that pernicious nonsense! On December 26, 2007, while all of us were attending to our Christmas turkeys, some unknown turkeys in Ottawa published Project 1539 in the *Canada Gazette,* the government's newspaper. It is reproduced in full in this chapter and follows the material taken from some of my recently published articles on issues of informed consent.

Project 1539 is important because it treacherously, by Order in Council, while everybody in the whole country was preoccupied, simply killed Project 1474 that had preceded it and which was the result of MP Dr. James Lunney's effort, namely bill C-420. You read his article in the first chapter earlier. Project 1474 was crafted after public consultations had taken place, the available and verifiable science had been presented, the known clinical evidence had been provided by practitioners, and this Project also allowed for health claims to be made for natural health products with regard to specific diseases listed in Schedule A of the Food and Drugs Act.

Allowing these scientifically grounded and empirically verified health claims would have opened up the way for our universities to teach these treatments. However, when everybody returned from their Christmas vacations, Project 1539 had mysterious emerged and was now the law.

The two Projects, 1474 and 1539, have almost nothing in common. The writers of the latter even assert that this is the result of extensive consultations with stakeholders, when in fact most of what they originally suggested is now ignored, or else 1474 would still be in force. On page 7 of 1539 the reader will find "acute psychotic conditions," "anxiety states" and "depression" put into the group of conditions natural health products may ***not*** claim to be able to treat. A perfectly aimed blow at Truehope and that offending legal judgment against Health Canada. So, for whose benefit is this?

The last item in this chapter is a superb analysis of the Truehope treatment protocol contrasting it to psychotropic drugs. I figured I better let it be known what good science looks like when it is allowed to do its thing without interference—before it is too late and the medical pope takes over and this type of information may no longer be readily available.

Recommended Sources:

S. Tipps, ed. *Codex Alimentarius—Global Food Imperialism: A Compendium of Articles on Codex*. Foundation for Health Research, 2007

B J. Richards. *Fight For Your Health*, www.TruthInWellness.com, 2007

C. Dean, Md. *Death by Modern Medicine*, Matrix Veritee, 2005. Dr. Dean has attended many Codex meetings as an observer and has devoted a whole section of this book to this: www.drcarolyndean.com.

www.alliance-natural-health.org for all Codex-related information in Europe as well as the court judgments mentioned above.

Sickness for Beginners

"The person who takes medicines must recover twice: once from the disease and once from the medicine."

—Sir William Osler (1849–1919)

Everyone will sooner or later consult a doctor. That encounter may save your life dramatically in emergency medicine, or lead you into a living hell for a very long time and probably kill you, if chronic disease and cancer are involved. For the latter, modern medicine offers drugs derived from synthetic chemistry designed to control symptoms and ensure loyal "consumers" until death—caused usually by the side effects, one of which is drug-induced nutritional deficiency. Package inserts clearly state "this drug does not cure." The word cure has become a four-letter word in modern medicine.

Human systems are essentially labyrinths; medicine is no exception. As in the Greek myth, when entering such a system one better have Ariadne's thread, as the hero Theseus did when seeking out the subterranean monster, the Minotaur, to find the way back out. The Minotaur in our lives is illness, a monster that paralyses through fear, and heroes are heroes because they conquer their fear—after that, slaying the monster is not necessarily a big deal. Being a hero isn't all that difficult. Anyone who employs critical thought in the face of authority already is a hero.

Your Doctor

The dramatic change that medicine has experienced over the past half century or so has to do with the fact that the old notion of one cause-one-effect has been proven virtually invalid; most sickness is a complex of one or many causes. Many disease states can be caused by one specific toxin found in a pesticide, for example, and one specific disease can be caused by many different toxins, organisms, or nutritional deficiencies.

Science has proven exhaustively that every disease is caused by some kind of identifiable challenge to the body's defenses, primarily the liver and the immune system (e.g. bacteria, viruses, parasites, radiation, systemic electro-magnetic interference, stress-induced hormonal imbalances with toxic consequences, environmental or pharmaceutical toxins causing organ damage or genetic interference which result in the malfunctioning of vital enzymes, nutritional deficiencies or excess nutrition of some specific kind, and more). Every disease state is in theory (and increasingly also in practice) curable by making the immune system and liver into the patient's allies. This is done by removing that harmful cause and fueling the body with those deficient nutrients.

Synthetic drugs are never nutrients and always increase toxicity, sometimes only temporarily and necessarily. All drugs stress the liver and the immune system. However, a disease is never a drug deficiency, and all illness is always accompanied by serious nutrient deficiencies, which most drugs make worse.

Furthermore, the descriptive labels known as diagnoses lead often to lethal "cognitive traps," as Dr. J. Groopman explains in his fascinating book *How Doctors Think*. At autopsy, he reports, at least 15% of diagnoses are proven to have been wrong, which is why the patient is dead. He cites research showing that 80% of serious harm can be explained by a "cascade of cognitive errors," all stemming from not having listened carefully to the patient and reflexively plugging the patient into handy diagnoses.

When showing my physician husband this book, he snorted, "Most *don't* think." His respect for standard medical practice got its first shock when a few weeks after completing his specialization exams, he ran into one of his smartest colleagues. When he asked his friend about his current reading, expecting to discuss new research, his friend answered: "I am only studying the fee schedule now."

Medicine's Shadow

Since the 1970s, money interests have steadily taken control over how governments run health care systems, how doctors practice, and how medical research is conducted. Last November, I attended an event at the University of Toronto; the guest speaker was Dr. Richard Smith, who until recently was for 20 years the editor of the *British Medical Journal*, one of the "Big Five." His brilliant, witty, and sad discussion of the phantom world that medical journals have become was as profoundly disturbing as was his admission that he had been unable to stop this corrupting process. He confirmed what the editors of the *New England Journal of Medicine*, Marcia Angell and Jerome Kassierer, had reported in their own recent books about their failed battles against the dominance of financial interests which ultimately are the source of drugs being the leading cause of death.

When asked if one could trust *any* leading medical journals, Dr. Smith laughed out loud and exclaimed: "No!" And how should patients protect themselves from doctors acting in good faith on this mostly fraudulent research? Dr. Smith replied, "Patients have to understand that they are actually in a bogus contract with the doctor. The patient thinks the doctor can fix my problem. That is a very powerful fantasy! Patients need to invest time and energy in researching [their problem] and be smarter than the doctor. Nowadays that is possible!" and he recommended the internet-based open-access medical journals which are free of advertising and Big Pharma interference.

Because of this relentless push to produce patentable, lucrative symptom-control drugs, researchers around the world have concluded, after combing through 9.4 million research papers at the US National Library of Medicine in 4,000 journals, that "the vast majority of published research… is false." (*Wall Street Journal*, Sept. 17, 2007). As for mandatory continuing medical education, *Nature* reported on September 22, 2007, these conferences are basically "re-allocated marketing events" controlled by the funding pharmaceutical and medical devices industries. Not surprisingly then, on January 7 and 8, CBC reported that the Health Canada warnings about adverse events associated with prescription drugs are generally ignored by doctors: "We cannot open the letter for them. We cannot make them read them," the HC spokesperson said.

Basic Survival Tips

It is charitable and proper to forgive those who sacrifice their profession and their patients to be drug-pushers, for they know not what they do. But it is vital that patients know, that only those doctors who determinedly think outside those boxes provided to them by the disease industry and their lackeys, our ministries of health, will dare to go for the "cure." Patients can't wait until medical schools and journals are reformed and profit ceases to dominate medicine. You need to take charge.

- Ask your doctor if he or she sees drug reps and point out that they are neither patients nor medically trained, so you—the patient—expect equal time.
- Never (except in genuine emergencies when broad-spectrum antibiotics are necessary to save time) accept an antibiotic unless the target bacteria has been identified through appropriate lab tests and it is certain your infection is not caused by a virus, which antibiotics can't kill. Antibiotic resistance is possibly the greatest health threat in the world today—caused mostly by careless prescribing and their prophylactic use in food-producing animals. Taking the wrong antibiotic may also cause serious harm to your immune system.
- Always demand that pain, chronic or acute, is treated to the fullest extent, as it is now internationally recognized as the 5th vital sign and must be treated with the drugs that work best for you and in the individually necessary dosage.
- Always demand a full explanation (about diagnosis, treatment, drugs prescribed, dangers of that drug etc.) because informed consent is the law governing medical practice, and if necessary remind your doctor of that fact.
- Always ask if the drug prescribed is still under patent protection. If it is, ask to see the current CPS (*Compendium of Pharmaceuticals and Specialties*) to check for Health Canada warnings (the older the drug, the safer it generally is, especially if it is off patent). If available, insist on a generic equivalent or substitute if

available, as the Canadian Medical Association guidelines expects doctors to do. New and improved is almost always a potentially fatal illusion.

Advanced Survival Tips

While discussing this article with my husband, he suggested that it is vital, when consulting a doctor, "never to use a conventional diagnostic term." If you say "I am so depressed," sixty seconds later you will have a prescription and be headed for Antidepressant Hell, because you have just pushed a well-worn button. To find out what awaits you on those drugs, spend a couple of hours surfing the net by typing in search words such as "SSRIs + adverse events" or "+ legal actions."

Should you ever be tempted to take a drug you see advertised on American television, unavoidable since Direct to Consumer Advertising (DTCA) of drugs is permitted in the US, clear your brains as fast as possible by surfing the net for information on DTCA. Google the names of Barbara Mintzes and Alan Cassels whose work is the most trustworthy and comprehensive in this area. Any drug that *needs* heavy, glitzy advertising is a big seller and more often than not a big killer. Those are also the drugs created for the diseases invented by the pharmaceutical industry to create a new market niche. Really good drugs are never advertised, e.g. penicillin.

Should your doctor offer you enrollment in a drug trial, remember that doctors get paid big bucks for such recruitments. Guy Faguet, author of *The War On Cancer*, spent his life as a leading researcher with the US National Institutes of Health and the American Cancer Society. He describes drug trials as nothing less than "human toxicity tests." (As an aside, note that he disapproves of mammography and PSA tests for prostate check-ups because of their unacceptably high false positives!) On September 27 last year, the *New York Times* published the salient details of the US Department of Health report on drug trials. The Inspector General concluded that "in many ways, rats and mice get better protection as research subjects than do humans."

If you are taking a drug and can't just simply stop doing so, consult the nutrient depletion handbook by the American Association of Pharmacists. It spells out which essential nutrients are depleted by every prescription drug. Supplementing with those nutrients is the logical thing to do and is guaranteed to reduce harmful side effects and may even get you off the drug altogether.

How do you know what is a bad drug? Any drug that stresses the liver should be avoided if at all possible. If it is not on the World Health Organization's Essential Drugs List, one should hesitate; not a single patented drug is on that list. It does not include cholesterol-lowering drugs, antidepressants and the like. The best source for all information on a drug is the excellent newsletter *Best Pills Worst Pills* (worstpills.org) published monthly by Ralph Nader's organization Public Citizen which has successfully challenged the FDA on many dangerous drugs and got them off the market. A quick internet survey on the number of law suits filed against a drug provides the most informative warning.

For every standard toxic treatment there exists a non-toxic alternative—every one of which was developed by mainstream medical research. Your doctor is not trained to look for alternatives and drug reps don't discuss them. Dr. Sherry Roger's *Total Health* newsletter is in my experience the best source for this information. In fact, never before in the history of medicine have we had this much choice.

Descartes (1590–1650) started us on the path of scientific thinking, which is both a habit and a method of anti-authoritarianism. Descartes taught that "systematic doubt" should be "the guiding principle for action"—a matter of life and death for patients. Uncritically accepting external authority of any kind is always the beginning of suffering, because then you have "squandered [your] resistance for a pocket-full of mumbles," as Simon and Garfunkle famously put it.

If anybody wonders if this article comes close to practicing medicine without a license, I better make it clear that my aim was to warn you against those who practice medicine *with* a license.

Indoctrinated Doctors

"Great is the power of steady misrepresentation."

—Charles Darwin (1809–1882)

Becoming a doctor takes many years. They learn an awful lot. But just exactly what do they learn and who decides what they are supposed to know? Any discussion of medical education starts with Dr. William Osler, who set the standard. In fact, McGill University is now trying to re-introduce an Osler-based program "to make doctors more humane" (*Medical Post*, Oct. 18, 2005). Dr. Osler's 1892 textbook, *Principles and Practice of Medicine*, was the first comprehensive medical textbook in history. It trained doctors throughout the world until 1950, at which time *Harrison's Principles of Internal Medicine*, now in it's 17th edition, replaced it.

A few years ago, my husband, who specializes in Post Traumatic Stress Disorder, discussed with a local colleague the possibility of having a workshop on PTSD for local physicians. "Sure!" was the reply. "Contact a drug rep and have him set it up. All you need to do is mention a couple of drugs and they'll pay for the event." My husband, who is in his 39th year of practice and who never allowed a drug rep into his office, said: "What?!" to which his colleague replied, "That's the way we get our continuing medical education now. They always give us a nice dinner."

His proposed presentation on how to treat PTSD successfully would have gone over like a lead balloon with Big Pharma, as it would have included the recent research results which show why it is best to *never* prescribe SSRI antidepressants because the documented risks include increased rates of suicide, murder, cancer, heart disease, sexual dysfunction, weight gain, diabetes, birth defects, and babies born with a full-blown addiction syndrome. Instead, his work focuses on truly effective treatment for PTSD, which always includes getting the patient off drugs safely.

Consider that the German Institute for Evidence-Based Medicine found that 94% of the information in the manufacturers' brochures sent to doctors on the 520 most commonly used drugs had "no basis in scientific evidence." (*Arznei Telegram*, March 2004). Dr. Osler had clear advice on drugs already in the late 1900s: "One of the duties of the physician is to educate the masses not to take medicines. Consider what surprising reactions may occur in the laboratory from the careless mixing of unknown substances. Be as considerate of your patient as you are of the test tube. To modern pharmacy we owe much, but the profession has no more insidious foe than the large hinterland pharmaceutical houses who have become a huge parasite. We all know too well the bastard literature which floods the mail, every page of which illustrates the truth of the axiom: the greater the ignorance the greater the dogmatism."

In Dr. Osler's days, people usually died from tuberculosis and pneumonia. Today, according to research from Johns Hopkins Medical School, which he co-founded, the leading cause of death is prescription drugs and inappropriate surgery, annually killing about 800,000 people in North America. (Sources in Dean 2004.)

The *British Medical Journal* reported on June 10, 2000, that death rates in Israel dropped by close to half when physicians went on a three-months strike. Funeral homes complained to the government, asking to have the contractual dispute settled. The same decrease had occurred during the 1983 strike. Only in the city of Netanya did death rates remain "normal"; doctors there have a "no-strike" clause in their contracts.

Medical Schools Financed by Big Pharma

Given these startling facts, we are entitled to ask some hard questions about current medical education. One answer comes from Dr. Drummond Rennie, one of the editors of the *Journal of the American Medical Association*, who said that "medical education is down the toilet" because research cannot be trusted anymore; its data are "doctored" to satisfy the drug companies, which pay for about 60%

of all medical research, as well as for most continuing medical education programs. In the year 2000, there were 314,022 pharmaceutical industry-sponsored conferences, but only a few hundred independent events took place. The medical schools themselves are largely financed by Big Pharma as well, and about 70 to 80% of the committee members generating practice guidelines have direct financial ties to the drug companies whose products they recommend.

JAMA's Dr. Rennie observed: "This practice stinks." According to Drs. Marcia Angell and Jerome Kassier, both editors at the prestigious *New England Journal of Medicine* for many years, medical education relies completely on Big Pharma. Most universities have even eliminated courses in pharmacology, so "doctors aren't even taught basic principles of drug action and use." In fact, medical school administrators refer to "students as consumers" and "to education and research as products" (Washburn). In the US, the free hand-outs and perks cost Big Pharma about $30,000 per year, per doctor. This is very disturbing, especially when the evidence suggests that for Big Pharma, "human life is just road-kill on the highway to profit," as former Health Canada drug safety expert, Dr. Michelle Brill-Edwards, puts it.

The Shifting Agendas Of Harrison's

I compared some key items in several (randomly picked) of the 16 editions of *Harrison's Principles of Internal Medicine* from the 1950s to today, being guided by Dr. Osler's observation that "the history of progress is a history of a struggle with one's own delusions." Here is some of what I found:

- **The 7th edition from 1972 weighed 5 lbs.** It has 37 entries on nutrition, 67 on vitamins and minerals and their essential functions are well discussed. The information is still true. Two interesting examples of treatment are with regard to Crohn's Disease and migraine. Back then, doctors were taught that corticosteroid therapy in Crohn's disease didn't work well at all, but dietary approaches, as successfully pioneered in the

1940s by Dr. Crohn himself, were recommended as having the best results. That is still true, but not in fashion anymore. Migraine was treated with dietary modifications and magnesium supplementation, and heavy-duty painkillers as needed. The preferred current pharmaceuticals are dangerous and very expensive. Asthma was already then seen as an environmentally-mediated disease and treated as such. We are slowly returning to that now.

- **The 9th edition of 1980 also weighs 5 lbs** and shows expanded sections on nutrition, including candidiasis; all that information is also still true. It has extensive new information on environmental and chemical toxins, advising the doctor always to inquire into a patient's workplace and home environments. Hypersensitivities to environmental toxins are well discussed, and the list of chemical poisons given is as relevant today as it was 26 years ago. The index has 110 poisons, including pesticides.
- **The 12th edition in 1991 weighs 9½ pounds.** In-depth discussions on pharmacology, adverse reactions, and a fabulous section on how diets affect a whole range of diseases appears now. The adverse drug events information is very good. The Recommended Daily Allowance (RDA) is handled with excellent criticism and correctly dismisses a one-size-fits-all approach because supplement needs differ when pregnant, aging, following surgery etc. Gluten-free, lactose-free, low-fiber diets are recommended for various conditions including Crohn's, along with cautious use of steroids. Then, most curiously the rot sets in and makes one sit up: many pages are devoted to supporting formula milk complete with the names of all the manufacturers! Harrison's turned advertorial! It gets worse: we find astounding nonsense such as too much Vitamin C supposedly causing kidney stones—not one reference! Even weirder is the fact that the list of poisons is down to 45, while all over the world chemical toxins have *increased* since the '70s by the thousands.

Amazingly, however, mercury dental amalgams are considered a bad idea—for all the right reasons (systemic disease). It took till June 2008 before the FDA finally admitted that this is so; by then various countries had already outlawed its use.

- **The 15th edition of 2001 weighs in at 9½ lbs.** The new sections include a fairly friendly discussion of alternative medicine, limited to Chinese medicine, Aryuveda, massage etc. Also new are sections on medical ethics, conflicts of interest and a fabulous section on the "Influence of Environmental and Occupational Hazards on Disease." Virtually all the diseases featured in the rest of this huge book are now also discussed in terms of potential environmental toxicity as causes. Wow! Science-based medicine must have been trying to really assert itself against Big Pharma spin. In the adverse drug events section the great range of individual reactions to drugs are discussed. Even the myth that vitamin C may cause kidney stone is debunked authoritatively—this time with references. However, some serious BS managed to get in after all: in another section we read that all orally consumed vitamins are absorbed 100%—again, without references. Wouldn't that be nice if it were true! Looks like somebody wants to keep vitamin consumption down, as well as draw attention away from bio-individuality. However, an excellent discussion on homocysteine made it through the censors: this marker for inflammation is far more important than cholesterol for cardiovascular disease (as Big Pharma kept making money on dangerous cholesterol-lowering drugs, research plodded on, thank God, and by June 2008 MIT researchers even proved that inflammation is the most reliable marker for cancer as well.) Very strange to behold, a few hundred pages later we have very nasty comments about health food stores, rather embarrassing for a venerable textbook. Somebody is now on the warpath against natural medicine. Yet, most encouragingly, the adverse drug reaction section is astounding in its exhaustive detail; obviously, pharmacists are insisting on getting a word or two in edgewise. The index on poisons includes more *drugs* than before, but for Crohn's disease the treatment is now only steroids and surgery. Dr. Crohn is moaning in his grave. Funny—did all those patients in the past, who were helped by diet, suddenly evaporate? Thankfully, the reader is told the RDA is a *guide* and not a law cast in stone, which is progress for sure.

- **The 16th edition of 2005 weighs 10¼ lbs.** What it took on in sheer physical bulk it sure lost in qualitative content, and what has increased in verbiage parallels the increase in disease incidence. Most disturbing is the fact that gone are discussions on ethics, conflicts of interest, economics; complementary medicine is dismissed with a nasty diatribe—again without any evidentiary support. Yet, the discussions on vitamins and minerals later on are factually not too bad: even St. John's Wort, Echinacea and Saw Palmetto are treated with a little respect. But suddenly the RDA is supposed to be "overly generous" (in fact it is mostly nutritional nonsense and totally out of synch with the published research); also, supplements supposedly carry "potential risks" (no sources given), and it is hammered in to doctors over and over again that the amount of each vitamin (e.g. something silly like 80 mg of C per day, no matter what the circumstances) must be the *total* derived from food *and* supplements. I suppose Codex committee members wrote this section! We supposedly get all we need from our diets. Undoubtedly somebody from the fast-food industry helped that Codex fellow as he fantasized away. Crohn's disease has become part of Irritable Bowel Syndrome (a symptom, not a disease)—an industry invention according to Moynihan and Cassels. However, Chronic Fatigue made it into text as a reality—obviously after a long and hard battle waged by patients and doctors. Yet, despite the international furor about the toxicity and ineffectiveness of antidepressants and the strong warnings published by the FDA, and eventually also Health Canada,

> this 2005 edition mentions just minor little problems with SSRIs: e.g. sleep disturbance, sexual dysfunction, jitters, and none of the deadly stuff. Oh dear.

Harrison's over time is a very mixed bag and rather than reflecting linear progress, the textbook reveals the up's and down's of genuine new discoveries and the creeping rot of outright corruption as it unfolds over the decades. If I was teaching at a medical school (I indulge in little fantasies sometimes), I would teach a whole year's course—compulsory—devoted to a minute comparison of this classic textbook's progress through time, starting with Osler's own work, written before any modern drugs were available. Only through careful comparison does one learn to think critically and develop awareness of how medicine can become abused and co-opted for purposes that have nothing to do with treating sick people and relieving suffering. Medical students should be fool-proofed against the myth of "new and improved."

Change is often a function of politics, not progress. Dr. Jozef Krop, an environmental medicine expert, told me that in 1964, when he started medical school in Poland, the textbooks were suddenly and completely changed from one year to the next. The textbooks used by the students of the previous year were filled with botanical medicine, while his texts only discussed drugs; only four herbal medicines were retained.

What *Harrison's* 17th edition will contain I don't know yet. But this is certain: Those trying to control the minds of young doctors best remember Proverbs 11:29: "He who troubles his own house shall inherit the wind."

Understanding Drugs

"Just say No!"

—NANCY REAGAN

Drug companies know that most drugs are unacceptably toxic and are re-focusing on "biologicals," which contain natural peptides, helpful bacteria, biologically engineered drugs (most new cancer drugs), and even drugs that deliver minerals, vitamins, and natural autocoids like histamine. The more bio-identical a drug can be made, the less toxic it will be to the liver, and the liver is boss in the body's biochemistry. Merck is hoping for financial recovery with its new cholesterol-lowering "drug," Cordaptive, whose active ingredient is Niacin (vitamin B_3), long known to be nature's prescription for cardiovascular disease. Drug companies have spent $76 billion since 2005 buying biotech companies because synthetic drug development, which earned them about $1 million per hour, is exhausted. Last December, Sidney Taurel, the chairman of Eli Lilly said: "I think the industry is doomed if we don't change."

Pharmaceuticals, like street drugs, are both intended to get addicts and patients hooked; many drugs are addictive and some, like Ritalin, work through the same cellular receptor sites used by crack cocaine. At a marketing conference for the managers of the world's largest pharmaceutical companies in March 2004 one of the first overheads read: "As a Marketer: which is better for business? Steady continuous use of your drug, or occasional use of your drug?"

There is one way in which street drugs differ from prescription drugs: drug pushers *without* an MD know exactly what their product does, while drug pushers *with* an MD don't know they are drug pushers and are pretty clueless about pharmacology. Last November, the Health Council of Canada published a report stating that "people are going out into practice without a comprehensive understanding either of how drugs work or how to use them rationally." Only 4 of Canada's 17 medical schools require just a short course on clinical pharmacology. Yet, doctors have sole prescription power over some 20,000 pharmaceutical drugs, which generate 400 million prescriptions annually, costing our healthcare system $24 billion. Even if doctors do sometimes read the Health Canada warnings on a drug, they don't seem to understand them. How else can one explain what Ontario's Auditor General found in 2007: that year over 18,000 alerts on known drug toxicity were provided by pharmacy computers for the prescriptions issued for the residents of 421 long-term care homes—yet, the prescribing doctors ignored these warnings 91% of the time.

The Royal College of Physicians and Surgeons of Canada was so shocked by these reports, they changed medical training requirements, starting 2008. Once medical students enter into specialization training they must study pharmacology for two years. This is undoubtedly very good news for Canadians, and will turn out to be bad news for undertakers and certainly for Big Pharma, because our doctors will understand drugs and not just believe what a drug rep tells them over wine and roses. Even with this new breed of doctors soon appearing, you might want some help in understanding drugs.

Every class of drugs currently used to treat the symptoms of cancer, diabetes, heart and autoimmune diseases, depression, psychiatric disorders etc is under some kind of regulatory investigation or the subject of class actions involving tens of thousands of people. They continue to be sold with advisories required by the FDA and Health Canada which inform that antidepressants may increase the risk of suicide and that they do increase the risk of cancer, diabetes, and osteoporosis; that non-steroidal anti-inflammatory drugs, the NSAIDs, and diabetes drugs like Avandia increase the risk of heart attacks; that all synthetic estrogenic drugs increase the risk of stroke because of the formation of blood clots; that cholesterol-lowering drugs increase the risk of most of the above and interfere with sleep; that certain cancer drugs can kill you from heart attacks and brain inflammation. Most of this information is freely available at your local drug store, in every doctor's office, and online in the annually updated CPS, the *Compendium of Pharmaceuticals and Specialties*.

Over the past decade, Big Pharma's "science engine has stalled," observed the *Wall Street Journal* on December 6, 2007. Computer-assisted "rational drug design" can no longer find new applications to known cellular targets in humans. The main reason being the discoveries made through the Human Genome Project. It was believed that about 10,000 useful targets would be available on human cells for drugs to act upon; in fact there are at most 1,000.

Furthermore, almost all blockbuster drugs are under increasingly successful legal attack for deaths and injury. Merck paid more than $ 4 billion (about one year's earnings) for the human disaster it created with the NSAID Vioxx, which killed about 150,000 since coming to market. The French government has charged GlaxoSmithKline and Sanofi Pasteur with "manslaughter" for the deaths caused by the Hepatitis B vaccine. Eli Lilly paid $1 billion in legal settlements to thousands of patients injured or killed by the antidepressant Zyprexa and now faces angry shareholders suing for "recklessly disregarding risks" and "illegal marketing tactics."

Investors are demanding to know why they are losing money. Wall Street evaluations were grim. Moody's assessed pharmaceuticals as "negative," i.e. don't invest. The FTSE Global Pharmaceutical Index fell by 19%, even though the price of drugs rose by 63% since 2002.

How Drugs Work

A current pharmacology textbook states: "The symptoms of a disease arise from a deficiency or excess of a specific metabolite in the body, from an infestation by a foreign organism, or from an aberrant cell growth." The "metabolite" might be the result of inflammation such as in arthritis, the "infestation" could be a bacterium, and "aberrant cell growth" would be cancer. "These problems can be addressed through enzyme inhibition," the textbook asserts, so these symptoms are simply stopped in their tracks. This is a bombshell of a statement. The entire textbook is guided by one aim: the biochemistry of symptom-control. The causes (infestation, aberrant cell growth etc) are dismissed right off the bat: drugs don't cure; they are not designed to cure. What follows over the next many hundred pages is indeed real and very clever biochemistry—devoted to one end only: symptom control.

Almost all drugs are *inherently* toxic and may cause a universal allergic response, such as ACE inhibitors, aspirin and antibiotics, or they deplete essential nutrients if they are enzyme inhibitors—and that is most of them. Drugs interfere with essential chemical pathways when they are "inhibitors" or "blockers." This interference is always potentially dangerous because it is a natural process which is being messed with for a purpose not its own. Enzymes are proteins that cause all the chemical reactions that keep us alive. Enzymes depend on essential minerals. Drugs are never as specific as their designers intended, so they go after the intended and many unintended targets. At first, symptom relief may occur, but then new symptoms start—the infamous side-effects, and so now more drugs are needed. The battlefield becomes larger and larger as greater numbers of enzyme populations are attacked, until finally even the drugs themselves fall victim to "friendly fire," and we have a regular world war going on in all bodily systems. This is why synthetic drugs are Killer No. 1.

When a drug is beneficial, it performs the way the Americans had hoped to in Vietnam, namely by specific "search and destroy" missions. Many antibiotics, medications used in acute heart failure, and some anticonvulsants are examples. (none are blockbuster drugs under patent protection.) These drugs can act fast, accurately and don't mess up the surrounding areas much, if at all, if they are used short-term.

According to the 16th edition of *Harrison's Principles of Internal Medicine*, the following are the drugs that cause 90% of the death and destruction (not just transient constipation, nausea, drowsiness, or temporary candidiasis): all the NSAIDs, digoxin, anticoagulants, diuretics, new-generation antibiotics (like Cipro), all cancer drugs, and hypoglycemics (for diabetes). Among the pain killers acetaminophen (Tylenol) is the most dangerous; most liver transplants are due to its long-term use.

The liver detoxifies natural and synthetic toxins. It does this through many enzymes which are divided into various families all of which arise out of one super-family called Cytochrome P450. If a drug rouses this super-family into action, the liver will quite literally fight to the death to protect you.

Various racial groups have over time evolved differences in Cytochrome P450. People of African and Afro-American origin react differently to many drugs than whites and Hispanics do: some people are "extensive metabolizers," and others are "slow metabolizers." Some people lack specific cell receptors for which a drug was originally designed: the cancer drug Herceptin, for example, becomes acutely toxic if the patient lacks those receptors. The new science of "genotyping" tries to deal with this.

Finally, age and sex are important. Men metabolize drugs differently than women. Antidepressants are less quickly and less seriously toxic (at first) in men, but tend to have side effects faster in women because their livers are in bodies with more female sex hormones which create a different environment for drugs. As we age, we are less able to metabolize drugs, hence side effects, especially when more than one drug is involved, are more severe.

Harrison's advises that old people should always be given minimum doses, and the use of more than one drug should be avoided. (Given the current norm of polypharmacy, especially in old age homes, one must wonder if doctors read *Harrison's* at all). When 5 drugs are given, a 5% chance exists of adverse events. However, drug action is "nonlinear," i.e. more than one target is hit and unpredictable interactions will occur. So, if 15 drugs are given simultaneously, the chance of serious adverse events is not just three times as much, i.e. 15%, but 40%—and we have that world war referred to above which ultimately is due to the depletion of essential nutrients, especially minerals.

A quick survey of the drugs responsible for 90% of adverse events and deaths, as listed in *Harrison's*, showed that they deplete: potassium (responsible for cell-to-cell communication), calcium (bones, central nervous system), all the B vitamins (all bodily systems require these, the liver stores them all), iron (oxygen transport in blood), vitamin D (DNA repair, cancer prevention), zinc and selenium (immune system), Co-Q_{10} (heart function), and magnesium (essential to everything, being the Queen of the Minerals). Some drugs also inhibit melatonin, such as most statins and antidepressants (the immune system does most of its work while you sleep). Antidepressants often wipe out the sex drive; severely reduced sex hormones then cause genital an aesthesia and impair memory and learning.

Learning To Protect Yourself

Symptoms are the urgent demand our bodies make on us for intelligent dialogue. The vast majority of synthetic drugs are designed to prevent such a dialogue. So, always ask: Does this drug cure or make me into a customer indefinitely? And: What is my body likely to do if I take this drug? The answer to the first protects your purse, to the second your liver. It is naïve in the extreme to take any drug on trust and not check it out in the CPS at the very least. Big Pharma does not deserve any trust; its products are the leading cause of death. Since those deaths were initiated by the prescriptions from well-meaning but often pharmacologically ignorant doctors, it is a health hazard to assume "the doctor knows best." Doctors need to be treated with polite doubt—like politicians. Their assertions must be verified carefully, mainly because they themselves have usually been duped.

1. If media reports tell of a drug's withdrawal or serious side effects, that *entire* class of drugs is bad news. All SSRI antidepressants were designed to act on the same targets. If one NSAID, like Vioxx, killed a lot of people, all the others in that drug family are likely dangerous.
2. If the CPS informs you that a drug is metabolized by Cytochrome P450, you know it will be liver-toxic. In situations when such a drug cannot be avoided (e.g. certain antibiotics for Lyme Disease, systemic infections from bacteria or fungi, pain control, etc) we may rely on guidance again from the 16th edition of *Harrison's*, which suggests taking glutathione supplements, or Alpha Lipoic Acid, or N'Acetyl L-Cysteine to assist the liver and thereby avoid the drug's known toxicity.
3. If you develop side effects, or if the drug doesn't work, *do not* increase the dose or add another such drug to "boost" the

first one. Rapid side effects suggests the patient is a slow metabolizer and must stop the drug, probably immediately; no effect suggest you may be a fast metabolizer and will get serious side effects if you increase the dose.

4. If you are currently on drugs, check Pelton and LaValle's books to see what essential nutrients this drug depletes and take those, as recommended in each case, for as long as it takes to either wean yourself off, or until you can substitute safer drugs and recover from side effects, or as a supplement while you need it.
5. To find reliable information on drugs, consult *Best Pills Worst Pills*.
6. Drug-drug interactions, as well as interactions between synthetic drugs and many foods, must be assumed (e.g. grapefruit juice); known interactions are listed in the blue pages of the annually updated CPS.

Sources and Resources:

Books mentioned in these articles are included in the Suggested Reading section at the end of this book. The following list is of the sources for the article on drugs in this chapter.

Alliance for Human Research Protection website reported in January 2007 various studies showing that SSRIs (a class of antidepressant drugs that include Prozac, Zoloft, Paxil etc.) increase risk of bone fractures. The publications cited came from the *Archives of Internal Medicine*, the McGill Centre for Bone and Periodontal Research, and the US National Institutes of Health: http://ahrp.blogspot.com

D. Armstrong. "Pfizer Is Sued Over Lipitor Marketing," on Bill Sardi's website December 20, 2007: Bsardi@aol.com

Associated Press, November 7, 2007. "Report: Merck Discloses 4 Tax Disputes"

B. Bartali et al. "Serum Micronutrient Concentrations and Decline in Physical Function Among Older Persons," JAMA, January 23, 2008

A. Berenson. "Cholesterol has No Benefit in Trial, Makers Say," *New York Times*, January 14, 2008

P. Biron MD et al. "Pharma-co-dependence exposed: Would it be time to say No thanks?," *Canadian Family Physician*, October 10, 2007

Y. Caraco MD. "Genes and the Response to Drugs," *New England Journal of Medicine,* December 30, 2004

Dr. H. Cass. *Supplement Your Prescription: What Your Doctor Doesn't Know About Nutrition*, Basic Health, 2007

Center for Disease Control, MMWR Weekly, February 9, 2007: "Unintentional Poisoning Deaths—United States 1999–2004" www.cdc.gov.mmwr

M. Eichenbaum & O. Burk. "CYP3A genetics in drug metabolism," *Nature Medicine*, Issue 7, p. 285-287, 2001

A. Elixhauser & P. Owens. "Adverse Drug Events in US Hospitals 2004," *Agency for Healthcare Research and Quality*, Statistical Brief # 29, April 2007

M.-A. Gagnon MD & J. Lexchin MD. "The Cost of Pushing Pills: A New Estimate of Pharmaceutical Promotion Expenditures in the United States, *PloS Medicine*, January 3, 2008

Compendium of Pharmaceuticals and Specialties, 2007 edition

Genetic Engineering News, February 1, 2008, "Annual Wall Street Analyst Roundup"

K. Giacomini et al. "When good drugs go bad." *Nature*, April 26, 2007

M. Goozner, *The $800 Million Pill*, University of California Press, 2004

Harrison's Principles of Internal Medicine, (current) 16th edition

CNNMoney.com, January 7, 2008. "Pharma Forecast Calls For More Of The Same"

G.F. Van Hare MD. "Antiarrhythmic Drug Dosages and Preparations for Children," 6th edition, posted on internet by the Pediatric

Arrhythmia Center at UCSF and Standford: http://pediep.stanford.edu/Drug_guide-2000.html

A. Harris. "FDA approves natural ingredients in new non-toxic cancer drug." Posted on www.thiskillscancer.com, June 7, 2007

S. Hasselberger. "Polypill—miracle cure or insanity?" on his website June 30, 2003; www.mediaexplorer.org/sepp

Healy MD. *Let Them Eat Prozac*, Lorimer 2003

T. Higgins MD. "Oral Hypoglycemic Drugs," website of *Boulder Medical Center*: www.bouldermedicalcenter.com/articles

D. Hodges. "More evidence links use of proton pump inhibitors to C. difficile," *Medical Post*, October 6, 2006 (his sources are in the CMAJ September 26, 2006 and JAMA December 21, 2005)

W. Kondro, "Health Canada proposes new regulatory regime for drugs," CMAJ, April 24, 2007

D. Lednicer. *New Drug Discovery & Development*, Wiley, 2007

A. Lepage-Monette. "Some statins linked to poor sleep," *Medical Post*, January 22, 2008

T. Leveque & J. Mackenzie. "Vaccine Companies Investigated for Manslaughter," *Reuters New Service*, February 1, 2008

B. Martinez & J. Goldstein. "Big Pharma Faces Grim Prognosis," *Wall Street Journal* December 6, 2007

T.J. Moore et al. "Serious adverse drug events reported to the FDA 1998–2005," *Archives of Internal Medicine,* 2007 volume 167: 1752-1759

MedicineNet.com, February 10, 2008. "beta Blockers," "Definition of ACE Inhibitors"

P.K. Myint et al. "Plasma vitamin C concentrations predict risk of incident stroke over 10 years...," *American Journal of Medicine*, January 2008

P. Moynihan & A. Cassels. *Selling Sickness: How The World's Largest Pharmaceutical Companies Are Turning us All Into Patients*, Nation, 2005

Murphy, T. "Shareholders Sue Lilly Over Zyprexa Woes," *Associated Press*, February 1, 2008

NEWSInferno.com January 23, 2008. "Big Pharma Prime for Attacks, Thanks to Defective, Ineffective Drugs"

S.J. Padayatty et al. "Intraveneously administered vitamin C as cancer therapy," CMAJ, March 28, 2006

R. Pelton & J. LaValle. *The Nutritional Cost of Prescription Drugs*, Morton, 2004 (for patients); *Drug-Induced Nutrient Depletion Handbook*, Lexi-Comp (for doctors: fully referenced and cross-referenced with essential nutrients information)

Press Release from Northwestern University (marla-paul@northwestern.edu) "Researchers find deadly prescription drug effects 6 years before FDA," May 28, 2007

Qi Chen et al. "Pharmacological asorbic acid concentrations selectively kill cancer cells." The National Academy of Sciences, *PNAS* September 20, 2005

L. Richwine. US FDA says reviewing Vyotrin cholesterol drug," *Reuters News Service* January 25, 2008

A. Rivkin. "Admissions to a medical intensive care unit related to adverse drug reactions," *American Journal of Health-System Pharmacy*, 2007, vol. 64 issue 17

H. Schneider MD. "Mood Disorders: Cognitive Behavioral Therapy and Pharmacotherapy," *GP Psychotherapist*, Spring 2008

Science Daily. "Why Anticancer Drug Avastin Causes Potentially Fatal Brain Inflammation in Certain Patients, Study Suggests," posted February 16, 2008

Science Daily. "Celecoxib Can Adversely Affect Heart Rhythm, Study Suggests" posted January 17, 2008

R. B. Silverman. *The Organic Chemistry of Drug Design and Drug Action*, 2nd ed, Elsevier, 2004

K.E. Stine & T.M. Brown. *Principles of Toxicology*, 2nd ed., CRC, 2006

E. Turner et al. "Selective Publication of antidepressant trials and its influence on apparent efficacy," *New England Journal of Medicine*, January 17, 2008

H. Young, "lack of pharmacological training causes overuse and misuse of drugs," CMAJ, January 29, 2008

Note: The revelations about the research fraud, on the basis of which especially many blockbuster drug treatments came to market, and the death toll associated with them, began to become public starting approximately 1998 when a University of Toronto professor, B. Pomeranz, began investigating iatrogenic (medically caused and unintended) deaths. Since then, investigations have increased and a veritable avalanche of sleaze has been and continues to be reported in mainstream publications, often the cause of legal action. Much of this information clusters around mental health therapies, which is the central case in this book. Below is a short bibliography of some of the most important information on mental health drugs everyone should know. Research this before filling a prescription of any kind, especially something that claims to treat depression, bi-polar disorder, hyperactivity, and so on. This list also includes references to mainstream research showing that natural health products not only work better than those drugs, but are far superior as therapies. This bibliography also updates and supports the research Truehope submitted to court, as reproduced at the end of this chapter.

BBC News (2008/02/26), *New generation antidepressants have little clinical benefit for most patients, research suggests.* news.bbc.co.uk/go/pr/fr. *[In this posting it is reported that Alan Johnson, the Health Secretary, has announced that 3,600 non-drug using therapists are to be trained, which the minister sees as a better alternative to drugs. Funding is to be discontinued for SSRIs in Britain.]*

DeAngelis, C.D., Fortanarosa, P.B. (2008) Impugning the integrity of medical science: The adverse effects of industry influence, *JAMA*, 299(15):1833-1835 [When interviewed about this article she said "We have given away our profession and we have got to get it back."]

Ellison. S, (2005). *Health Myths Exposed*, Author House

Ferrie, R.K., (2004) Problems with SSRIs in the treatment of traumatic syndromes. EMDR International Association Conference, Montreal.

Ferris, L.E. (2002). Industry-sponsored pharmaceutical trials and research ethics boards: Are they cloaked in too much secrecy?, *CMAJ,* 166.10

Freeman, M.P., Hibbelin, J.R., Stoll, A.L. et al. (2006) Omega-3 fatty acids: evidence basis for treatment and future research in psychiatry.

J.Clin Psychiatry; 67(12): 1954-67

Healy, D., (2004) Paxil and Prozac Can Make People Homicidal.

Guardian Sept 24, [He reports seeing trials using normal volunteers who became unaccountably aggressive, also presented to the US Congressional Committee on Safety and Efficacy concerns in antidepressants use in children September 23, 2004]

House of Commons UK Government (2004-05). *The Influence of the Pharmaceutical Industry,* Fourth Report of Session, Volume 1

Ioannidis, J.P.A., (2005) Why most published research findings are false.

PloS Medicine, 2(8) "There is increasing concern that most current published research findings are false," an epidemiologist looks at how the data can be spun.

Katz, L.Y., et al. (2008) Effect of regulatory warnings on antidepressant prescription rates, use of health services and outcomes among children, adolescents and young adults. *CMAJ*, 178(8): 1005-11

Kirsch, I., et al, 2008. Initial severity and antidepressant benefits: a meta-Analysis of data submitted to the FDA. *PloS Medicine* 5(2) e45

Lacasse, J.R. et al (2005) Serotonin and depression: A disconnect between advertisements and the scientific literature. *PloS Medicine* 2(12) e392 [Reported association of violent suicide attempts with low CSF serotonin concentrations likely represent studies with flaws in their methodology.]

Larson, J.,(1999) *Depression Free Naturally,* Ballantine Books. *[Here are found the protocols for weaning patients off antidepressants and other addictive drugs safely to ensure no sudden violent side-effects occur; it also provides the information on the brain chemistry involved and how to use nutritional medicine in depression and related conditions. These protocols were developed by Larson together with Dr. A. Hoffer and other orthomolecular medicine experts.]*

Levine,J., (1997) *Controlled trials of inositol in psychiatry.* Eur Neuropsychopharmacol. *7(2):147-55*

Palatnik,A., et al., (2001) *Double-blind, controlled, crossover trial of Inositol versus fluovoxamine for treatment of panic disorder.*

J. Clin Psychopharmacol *21(3):335-9 [Inositol was twice as effective for panic and had no side effects, it was equally effective for depression.]*

Peet, M., Glen, I., Horrobin, eds (1999), D., *Phospholipid Spectrum*

Disorder in Psychiatry, Marius Press [This is the source book for the information on essential fatty acids—EFAs—how they work and how they become depleted from various stressors]

Prowsky, J.E., (2005) Supplemental niacinamide mitigates anxiety symptoms: three case reports. *J. Molecular Medicine* 20(3):167-78

Ross, J., (2004) *The Mood Cure*, Penguin

Taylor,M.J., Wilder,H., Bhagwagar,Z., Geddes,J., (2004) Inositol for depressive disorders. *Cochrane Database Syst Rev.* 2004;(2): CD004049

Tracy, A.B. (1991) *Prozac—Panacea or Pandora's Box?*

Turner, E.H. et al, (2008) Selective publication of antidepressant trials and Its influence on apparent efficacy. *N Engl J Med* 17;358(3): 252-60

Smith, R.. (2006) *The Trouble With Medical Journals*, Royal Society of Medicine Press Ltd.

van der Kolk, B.A. et al. (2007) A randomized clinical trial of EMDR, fluoxetine, and pill placebo in the treatment of PTSD: treatment effects and long term maintenance. *J. Clin Psychiatry* 10(4)118 [see text for summary]

Wild, J.,(2005) Adult suicides linked to popular antidepressant, *Nature,* Aug, 486: 1073

To Find A Good Doctor:

American Academy for Environmental Medicine (Canada and US)

Canadian College for Naturopathy

Ontario College of Family Physicians (request nutritional/ environmental practitioners)

OMA Section for Complimentary Medicine

Gerson Institute

International Academy for Oral and Medical Toxicology

International Society for Orthomolecular Medicine

Important Website: www.ssristories.com
Provides the information on the incidents of random shootings and violence as well as suicides involving patients on SSRIs and similar antidepressant drugs as well as when they are taken off them without proper supportive protocols. This website was started and is updated monthly by A.B. Tracy, author of *Prozac—Panacea or Pandora's Box*? 1991.

Government of Canada Gouvernement du Canada Canada

Français Contact us Help Search Canada Site
Home About us History FAQ Site Map

Canada Gazette

Welcome to the official newspaper of the Government of Canada published since 1841

- News and announcements
- Mandate
- Consultation
- Recent *Canada Gazette* publications
  - Part I: Notices and proposed regulations
  - Part II: Official regulations
  - Part III: Acts of Parliament
- Learn more about the *Canada Gazette*
- Publishing information
  - Publishing requirements
  - Deadline schedule
  - Insertion rates
  - Request for insertion forms
  - Subscription information
- Useful links
- Archives (1998-2007)
- RSS news feeds

Notice

Vol. 141, No. 26 — December 26, 2007

Registration
SOR/2007-288 December 13, 2007

FOOD AND DRUGS ACT

Regulations Amending Certain Regulations Made under the Food and Drugs Act (Project 1539)

P.C. 2007-1916 December 13, 2007

Her Excellency the Governor General in Council, on the recommendation of the Minister of Health, pursuant to subsection 30(1) (see footnote a) of the *Food and Drugs Act*, hereby makes the annexed *Regulations Amending Certain Regulations Made under the Food and Drugs Act (Project 1539)*.

REGULATIONS AMENDING CERTAIN REGULATIONS MADE UNDER THE FOOD AND DRUGS ACT (PROJECT 1539)

FOOD AND DRUG REGULATIONS

1. The *Food and Drug Regulations* (see footnote 1) are amended by adding the following after section A.01.065:

EXEMPTIONS

Application

A.01.066. Sections A.01.067 and A.01.068 do not apply to

(*a*) a drug included in Schedule I, II, III, IV or V to the *Controlled Drugs and Substances Act*; or

(*b*) a drug that is listed or described in Schedule F, other than a drug that is listed or described in Part II of that Schedule and that is

(i) in a form not suitable for human use, or

(ii) labelled in the manner prescribed by paragraph C.01.046(*b*).

Advertising

A.01.067. A drug is exempt from subsection 3(1) of the Act with respect to its advertisement to the general public as a preventative, but not as a treatment or cure, for any of the diseases, disorders or abnormal physical states referred to in Schedule A to the Act.

Sale

A.01.068. A drug is exempt from subsection 3(2) of the Act with respect to its sale by a person where the drug is represented by label or is advertised by that

Source: Project 1539, *Canada Gazette*, 2007

person to the general public as a preventative, but not as a treatment or cure, for any of the diseases, disorders or abnormal physical states referred to in Schedule A to the Act.

NATURAL HEALTH PRODUCTS REGULATIONS

2. The *Natural Health Products Regulations* (see footnote 2) **are amended by adding the following after section 103.1:**

EXEMPTIONS

Advertising

103.2 A natural health product is exempt from subsection 3(1) of the Act with respect to its advertisement to the general public as a preventative, but not as a treatment or cure, for any of the diseases, disorders or abnormal physical states referred to in Schedule A to the Act.

Sale

103.3 A natural health product is exempt from subsection 3(2) of the Act with respect to its sale by a person where the natural health product is represented by label or is advertised by that person to the general public as a preventative, but not as a treatment or cure, for any of the diseases, disorders or abnormal physical states referred to in Schedule A to the Act.

COMING INTO FORCE

3. These Regulations come into force on June 1, 2008.

REGULATORY IMPACT ANALYSIS STATEMENT

(*This statement is not part of the Regulations.*)

Description

I. Overview of the regulatory proposal

This regulatory amendment amends the *Food and Drug Regulations* (FDR), the *Natural Health Products Regulations* (NHPR), and the *Medical Devices Regulations* (MDR). The amendment

(1) revises the list of Schedule A diseases;

(2) exempts natural health products (NHPs) and certain drugs from the prohibition of preventative claims for the diseases listed in Schedule A; and

(3) revises section 24(1) to replace the term "venereal disease" with "sexually transmitted diseases."

All other provisions of the *Food and Drugs Act* (FDA), the *Controlled Drugs and Substances Act* (CDSA), and their regulations continue to apply.

(1) Revising the list of Schedule A diseases

Schedule A to the FDA is a list of diseases, disorders or abnormal physical states (hereafter referred to as diseases) for which preventative, treatment, and cure claims are prohibited by subsections 3(1) and 3(2) of the FDA (hereafter referred to as section 3) in the labelling and advertising to the general public of any food, drug, cosmetic or medical device.

The broad terms "preventative" and "treatment" that are used in the FDA have always been interpreted by Health Canada to include "risk reduction" and "symptomatic treatment, respectively. Therefore, preventative, risk reduction, treatment, symptomatic treatment, and cure claims are prohibited in the labelling

Source: Project 1539, *Canada Gazette,* 2007

and advertising to the general public for diseases listed in Schedule A.

Examples of Schedule A diseases are cancer, appendicitis, gout, and heart disease. No comprehensive list of criteria with which to add or remove diseases from the Schedule A list was ever established until March 2006. At that time, a Scientific Advisory Panel (SAP) was convened to recommend the list of criteria. This panel was composed of experts from a range of healthcare specialities, including homeopathy, naturopathy, medicine, pharmacy, nutrition, advertising, and patient advocacy.

These Regulations revise Schedule A in accordance with the criteria identified by the SAP. This criteria is now used to populate the Schedule A list and is outlined in policy as it is done with the criteria used to populate the Schedule F list in the FDR. Criteria are a transparent mechanism to help ensure consistency in decisions with respect to inclusion and exclusion of diseases in Schedule A. If a disease does not meet any of the criteria, it will be removed from the Schedule A list. When a disease is removed from Schedule A, all products covered by section 3 (food, drugs, cosmetics, and medical devices) would no longer be subject to the preventative, treatment, and cure prohibitions for that disease. All these products continue to be subject to all other provisions in the FDA, the CDSA, and their regulations; therefore, any other restrictions on the labelling and advertising of claims or any conditions for market authorization of these products remain in place.

(2) Exempting NHPs and certain drugs from the preventative prohibition for diseases remaining in Schedule A

Section 3 of the FDA contains the labelling and advertising prohibitions for Schedule A diseases. Section 3 prohibits the advertising of any food, drug, cosmetic or medical device to the general public as a preventative, treatment or cure for any of the diseases referred to in Schedule A. Section 3 also prohibits the sale of any food, drug, cosmetic or medical device that is labelled or advertised to the general public as a preventative, treatment or cure for any of the diseases referred to in Schedule A.

The regulatory amendment exempts NHPs and certain drugs from the section 3 preventative prohibition for Schedule A diseases (preventative prohibition).

Drugs not included in the exemption are

. those listed or described in Part I or II of Schedule F to the FDR (prescription drugs), with the exception of veterinary-use drugs listed in Part II to Schedule F, so long as the drug is in a form not suitable for human use or is labelled for veterinary use only; and

. drugs included in any of Schedules I through V to the CDSA.

Both categories of drugs exempted from the scope of this regulatory exemption are already subject to a high degree of regulatory rigour, including extensive restrictions on sale and advertising to the general public. Section C.01.044 of the FDR restricts the advertising to the general public of Schedule F drugs (with the exception of veterinary-use drugs listed in Part II to Schedule F, so long as the drug is in a form not suitable for human use or is labelled for veterinary use only) to only brand name, proper name, common name, price, and quantity of the drug. The advertising to the general public of controlled drugs is prohibited by section 70 of the *Narcotic Control Regulations*, section G.01.007 of the FDR, and section 3 of the *Benzodiazepines and Other Targeted Substances Regulations*.

NHPs and drugs that are subject to these Regulations are permitted to carry preventative claims in the labelling and advertising to the general public for diseases that remain in Schedule A. For these NHPs and drugs, prevention of a Schedule A disease generally does not require practitioner intervention, but treatment or cure of a Schedule A disease would. It should be noted that these products are subject to all other provisions in the FDA, the CDSA, and their regulations, therefore, any other restrictions on the labelling and advertising of claims or any conditions for the market authorization of these products remain in

Source: Project 1539, *Canada Gazette,* 2007

place.

The Regulatory impact analysis statement (RIAS) uses the term "certain drugs" instead of using the term "non-prescription drugs" because some drugs that are regulated under the FDA and the FDR as non-prescription drugs are also regulated as Class A precursors under the *Precursor Control Regulations* of the CDSA. These drugs require a prescription when sold or provided in a quantity, per transaction, exceeding the maximum quantity, expressed as an absolute quantity or per package, specified for the precursor in the *Precursor Control Regulations*. Precursors are frequently used in the clandestine production of illicit drugs. The concept of "prescription" in this context is different than in the context of a Schedule F prescription drug because the requirement for a prescription for a Class A precursor is to monitor and control substances frequently used in the clandestine production of illicit drugs. In the case of a precursor that requires a prescription, there is no Pr or other symbol indicating "prescription" on the label of the precursor.

II. Reason for the regulatory proposal

Schedule A and its accompanying prohibition section 6A, the predecessor of section 3, were added to the FDA in 1934. Section 6A stated that

"No person shall import, offer for sale or sell any remedy represented by label or by advertisement to the general public as a treatment for any of the diseases, disorders or abnormal physical states named or included in Schedule A to this Act or in any amendment to such Schedule."

In 1946, section 6A was revised to state

"No person shall import, offer for sale or sell any food or drug represented by label or by advertisement to the general public as a treatment for any of the diseases, disorders or abnormal physical states named or included in Schedule A to this Act or in any amendment to such Schedule."

In 1952, section 6A was renumbered to section 7. In 1953, section 7 was replaced by section 3, which stated

"3(1) No person shall advertise any food, drug, cosmetic or device to the general public as a treatment, preventative or cure for any of the diseases, disorders or abnormal physical states mentioned in Schedule A.

3(2) No person shall sell any food, drug, cosmetic or device

(*a*) that is represented by label, or

(*b*) that he advertises to the general public

as a treatment, preventative or cure for any of the diseases, disorders or abnormal physical states mentioned in Schedule A."

In 1934, the Canadian public needed the health protection provisions of Schedule A and section 6A. The purposes of section 6A were

(1) to discourage self-treatment by the general public, which would delay or replace medical treatment for diseases listed in Schedule A;

(2) to encourage the general public to seek the advice of a doctor, or some other qualified health professional, prior to obtaining treatment and medication for serious diseases and/or conditions; and

(3) to make unnecessary the proof in each case that a food or a drug is either unsafe or valueless for the treatment of one of the serious diseases or conditions listed in Schedule A.

In 1953, section 7 was replaced by section 3 because, while section 7 had been useful and effective, it had been subject to arguments as to whether or not

Source: Project 1539, *Canada Gazette*, 2007

certain practices were clearly within its intent and were within its current language. One of the practices considered to have been within the intent of the 1953 FDA was the prohibition against the advertising of a food or a drug to the general public as a treatment for any of the Schedule A diseases. Subsection 3(1) was therefore added as a separate prohibition that did not tie the advertising of a product to its sale. The prohibitions against sale to the general public were strengthened by further restricting the kinds of representations that could be made regarding efficacy. Whereas previously only the labelling and advertising of a specific product as a treatment was prohibited, the labelling and advertising of a specific product as a preventative or cure was also prohibited. Section 3 clarified the type of products that could not be advertised to the general public, nor sold to the general public if so labelled or advertised. Whereas previously the FDA had referred to remedies and then to food and drugs, section 3 referred to "any food, drug, cosmetic or device" represented by label or advertised to the general public as a treatment, preventative or cure for one of the Schedule A diseases.

In 2007, the health care environment has changed substantially from when Schedule A and section 3 were added to the FDA. Medical science has advanced, pre-market review of drugs and NHPs is required, a prescription drug regime exists, and publicly funded health care is available. In addition, and as will be discussed in greater detail below, some of the original health protections afforded by Schedule A and section 3 are now addressed in regulations. As well, information about diseases where self-help is appropriate is increasingly available to the Canadian public who thus have the opportunity to make more informed decisions about their health. The public's desire for this approach is reflected in an increasing emphasis on alternative health care and a greater involvement of patients in their choice of treatment.

While some stakeholders oppose the restrictions of Schedule A and section 3, others feel that they serve a useful purpose but need to be modernized to reflect scientific and medical advances, and to reflect the contemporary health care environment. From 2003 to 2004, Health Canada convened a Schedule A External Working Group (EWG) composed of external stakeholders to examine Schedule A and section 3. In 2004, the EWG completed a majority report and minority report. In February 2005, Health Canada made two commitments to the EWG.

Health Canada's first commitment to the EWG was to propose a regulatory amendment to remove some section 3 prohibitions for Schedule A diseases. Health Canada fulfilled this commitment in November 2005 by prepublishing in the *Canada Gazette*, Part I (CG I), Project 1474, the proposed regulatory amendment to exempt non-prescription drugs and NHPs from the preventative and treatment prohibitions of section 3. Because both majority and minority reports recommended that experts review the diseases listed in Schedule A, Health Canada's second commitment to the EWG was to convene an expert scientific panel to develop criteria and review Schedule A diseases in order to reflect current scientific and medical knowledge. Health Canada fulfilled this commitment by convening a SAP in September 2005. The SAP was tasked (1) to recommend criteria by which diseases could be added to or removed from Schedule A, and (2) to recommend revisions of Schedule A using those criteria. The final recommendations of the SAP were completed and posted on the Health Canada Web site in March 2006.

In considering the recommendations made by the SAP to revise Schedule A, it became evident that such revisions should take place before or at the same time that any section 3 prohibitions were lifted. Therefore, Health Canada modified its approach with these Regulations (Project 1539) that achieve the original intent of Project 1474 by revising the list of Schedule A diseases and by removing the preventative prohibitions with respect to NHPs and certain drugs for diseases remaining in Schedule A.

Project 1474 was withdrawn in CG I at the same time that these Regulations were prepublished in CG I.

These Regulations are a one-step regulatory approach and maintain Health Canada's long held policy position that direct-to-consumer advertising should not

Source: Project 1539, *Canada Gazette,* 2007

be allowed for prescription drugs, nor drugs that treat or cure serious diseases as prohibited by section 3.

III. Details about the regulatory amendment

A. The criteria to revise Schedule A

The following are the criteria used to revise Schedule A:

1. The condition or disease results in serious risks to individuals and generally requires diagnosis, treatment, and management by a health professional.

2. The disease is likely to be spread within the population and may be a risk to public health without appropriate treatment.

3. There is an emergency situation where self-care is inappropriate or not possible.

4. The severity of the disease limits the person's ability to make health decisions.

5. The disease state has only recently been recognized by medical science and it is unclear whether or not self-treatment is appropriate.

6. The disease or condition is one which renders individuals especially vulnerable to harm (e.g. pregnancy).

B. The revision of the Schedule A list using the criteria

The SAP used the above criteria to recommend the following revisions to Schedule A:

1. Delete the following 17 diseases, disorders, and abnormal physical states:

. Alopecia (except hereditary androgenetic alopecia)

. Bladder disease

. Disease of the prostate

. Disorder of menstrual flow

. Dysentery

. Edematous state

. Epilepsy

. Gall bladder disease

. Gout

. Hypotension

. Impetigo

. Kidney disease

. Leukemia

. Liver disease (except hepatitis)

. Pleurisy

. Sexual impotence

. Tumor

Source: Project 1539, *Canada Gazette,* 2007

2. Add the following 6 diseases, disorders and abnormal physical states:

. Acute infectious respiratory syndromes

. Acute psychotic conditions

. Addiction, except nicotine addiction

. Dementia

. Haematologic bleeding disorders

. Hepatitis

3. Make the following 6 replacements:

Replace the reference to

. Alcoholism

with

. Acute alcoholism

Replace the reference to

. Anxiety state

with

. Acute anxiety state

Replace the reference to

. Arthritis

with

. Acute, inflammatory and debilitating arthritis

Replace the reference to

. Heart disease

with

. Congestive heart failure

Replace the reference to

. Hernia

with

. Strangulated hernia

Replace the reference to

. Venereal disease

with

. Sexually transmitted diseases

Each criterion used by the SAP to rationalize each disease listing is indicated after the disease name in the following revised list. The numbers 1 to 6 refer to

Source: Project 1539, *Canada Gazette,* 2007

the six criteria listed earlier under section "*A. The proposed criteria to revise Schedule A.*" This information is posted on the Health Canada Web site.

Acute alcoholism (1, 3)

Acute anxiety state (3)

Acute infectious respiratory syndromes (2, 5)

Acute psychotic conditions (3, 4)

Acute, inflammatory and debilitating arthritis (1)

Addiction, except nicotine addiction (1)

Appendicitis (3)

Arteriosclerosis (1)

Asthma (1, 3)

Cancer (1, 3)

Congestive heart failure (1, 3)

Convulsions (3)

Dementia (4)

Depression (1)

Diabetes (1)

Gangrene (3)

Glaucoma (1)

Haematologic bleeding disorders (1)

Hepatitis (1, 2, 3)

Hypertension (1)

Nausea and vomiting of pregnancy (6)

Obesity (1)

Rheumatic fever (3)

Septicaemia (3)

Sexually transmitted diseases (2)

Strangulated hernia (3)

Thrombotic and embolic disorders (1, 3)

Thyroid disease (1)

Ulcer of the gastro-intestinal tract (1, 3)

The qualifier, "except nicotine addiction," was not inserted following the listing "addiction" in Schedule A of the proposed regulatory amendment which was prepublished in the CG I, on June 16, 2007.

Nicotine addiction, if not exempted from the modified Schedule A, would be captured by the listing of "addiction" in Schedule A. Section 3 of the FDA

Source: Project 1539, *Canada Gazette,* 2007

prohibits the labelling and advertising of any food, drug, cosmetic or medical device to the general public for the prevention, treatment and cure for diseases listed on Schedule A. This omission would result in an inconsistency with the Schedule F (prescription drugs) listing for nicotine, which allows nicotine replacement therapies (NRTs) that have been approved by Health Canada for use in smoking cessation therapy to be labelled and sold without prescription, provided that the NRTs meet the form and concentration requirements listed in Schedule F. These products which have been approved by Health Canada have been on the market for some time.

This omission has been corrected, and the words "except nicotine addiction" have been added to qualify the listing of "addiction" in Schedule A.

C. The effect of the Schedule A revision on all products referred to in section 3 of the FDA

1. For a disease removed from Schedule A, the prohibitions in section 3 for labelling and advertising to the general public no longer apply to food, drugs, cosmetics, and medical devices. However, all other provisions of the FDA, the CDSA, and their regulations that already apply to these products continue to apply. For example, as explained earlier, section C.01.044 of the FDR continues to place advertising restrictions on Schedule F prescription drugs regardless of the disease for which the drug is claimed to prevent, treat or cure.

2. For a disease added to Schedule A, the prohibitions in section 3 for labelling and advertising to the general public apply to food, drugs, cosmetics, and medical devices. As well, all other relevant labelling and advertising provisions of the FDA, the CDSA, and their regulations continue to apply.

D. Food, medical devices, and cosmetics also continue to be prohibited from carrying preventative claims in the labelling and advertising to the general public for diseases remaining in Schedule A (unless otherwise permitted in other provisions in the FDA or its regulations)

1. Food

Food is not included in the preventative exemption for several reasons. First, the representation of a food for the "prevention, treatment or cure" of a disease, disorder or abnormal physical state brings it into the definition of a drug and this would then make it subject to the drug regulations. Second, section B.01.601 of the FDR already provides that a food with a label or advertisement that carries a statement or claim set out in the table following section B.01.603 is exempt from the provisions of the FDA, including section 3, and the FDR with respect to drugs. Finally, in order to help inform the Canadian public about the role that certain foods may play in reducing the risk of certain diseases, Health Canada announced in the fall 2005 *Smart Regulation Report on Actions and Plans* (RAP) that it intends to develop new regulations for the use of food labels and advertising as a means of delivering this health information to the public. It is anticipated that Health Canada will engage in stakeholder consultation regarding these new regulations in 2007.

2. Medical devices

Medical devices are not included in the preventative exemption since Class I and II medical devices do not undergo pre-market review, nor are their claims approved by Health Canada. Class I medical devices do not have a licence requirement and are not subject to pre-market review. Class II medical devices do have a licence requirement, but are licensed by attestation of safety and effectiveness by the manufacturer. Class III and IV medical devices undergo pre-market review, but generally require the intervention of a practitioner. Some in-vitro diagnostic devices are designated Class III for home use but, since their use is as a diagnostic (not as a preventative, treatment, nor cure), they were never subject to the section 3 prohibition.

Condoms are exempt from section 3 pursuant to subsection 24(1) of the *Medical Devices Regulations* (MDR) and may be advertised and sold to the general public

Source: Project 1539, *Canada Gazette,* 2007

for the purpose of preventing the transmission of sexually transmitted diseases if the advertisement and the label of the condom claim only that the condom reduces the risk of transmitting sexually transmitted diseases.

3. Cosmetics

Cosmetics are defined in the FDA as "any substance or mixture of substances manufactured, sold or represented for use in cleansing, improving or altering the complexion, skin, hair or teeth, and includes deodorants and perfumes." Cosmetics are not permitted to carry drug claims; therefore, cosmetics are not included in the preventative exemption. If they carry drug claims, the product is either regulated as a drug or an NHP, as explained in sections 2.1 and 2.2 of the *Guidelines for Cosmetic Advertising and Labelling Claims* posted on the Health Canada Web site, and as explained in the *Guidelines for Cosmetics Manufacturers, Importers and Distributors* also posted on the Health Canada Web site.

IV. Important components to the health protection afforded by legislation other than Schedule A and section 3

1. Section 9 of the FDA

Section 9 of the FDA prohibits false, misleading or deceptive labelling and advertising of drugs. Furthermore, this section mandates that a drug be labelled as required by the Regulations.

2. Section C.01.044 of the FDR

Section C.01.044 of the FDR restricts advertising to the general public of Schedule F prescription drugs to only brand name, proper name, common name, price, and quantity of the drug. The provision is in part intended to encourage patients to seek medical attention for serious diseases.

The determination of drug status is made by Health Canada's Drug Schedule Status Committee subsequent to the filing of an appropriate submission and at the recommendation of the clinical review bureau. This assessment is made on the basis of established and publicly available factors which include, but are not limited to, concerns related to the pharmacodynamic, pharmacokinetic and/or toxicological profile of the drug and the nature of the proposed therapeutic uses.

The following are the factors used by Health Canada to determine the drug schedule status for a particular drug. Drugs will be listed in Schedule F if any of the following apply (posted on the Health Canada Web site):

(*a*) individualized instructions and/or direct practitioner supervision, adjunctive therapy with scheduled drugs or routine laboratory monitoring are required;

(*b*) there is a narrow margin of safety between the therapeutic and toxic doses, especially in populations such as geriatrics, children and pregnant or nursing mothers;

(*c*) there are potential or known undesirable or severe side effects at normal therapeutic dosage levels;

(*d*) they are known by experimental data to induce toxicity in animals but have not been in clinical use long enough to establish the pattern or frequency of long-term toxic effects in humans;

(*e*) they are used in the treatment of a serious disease easily misdiagnosed by the public;

(*f*) their use may mask other ailments;

(*g*) they have contributed to, or are likely to contribute to, the development of resistant strains of micro-organisms in humans;

Source: Project 1539, *Canada Gazette,* 2007

(*h*) they possess a dependence or abuse potential that is likely to lead to harmful non-medical use;

(*i*) they possess a high level of risk relative to expected benefits; or

(*j*) they have a therapeutic effect based on recently elucidated pharmacological concepts, the consequences of which have not been established.

Exceptions will be considered for drugs if any of the following apply:

(*a*) are required to be readily available under emergency circumstances where it is not practical to obtain a prescription (such as adrenalin in insect bite kits);

(*b*) are rarely used without a practitioner's supervision, and where the need for free availability outweighs the need for protection under Schedule F (such as insulin and nitroglycerin); or

(*c*) have potential to produce dangerous interactions with other drugs or food constituents but effective labelling can minimize the risk.

In its review of veterinary-use drugs, the Department also considers if any one of the above-mentioned factors or any one of the following factors are present. If so, drugs used in animals will be listed on Part I of Schedule F:

. there exists a narrow margin of safety between the therapeutic and toxic dosages when used in animals;

. they are known by experimental data to induce toxicity in animals but have not been in clinical use for a sufficient period of time to establish the pattern or the frequency of long-term toxic effects in humans;

. they are known to be liable to be diverted to humans;

. it is not possible to write directions for use that could be easily followed by a layperson;

. they may be hazardous to the handler or administrator;

. they have contributed to or may contribute to the development of resistant strains of micro-organisms in humans and to dissemination of antimicrobial resistance genes;

. they are new antibiotics for veterinary use that may be used in human medicine or that may lead to cross-resistance to antibiotics used in human medicine;

. they possess the potential for an adverse impact on the environment as it relates to public health at therapeutic dosage rates; or

. their misuse may lead to potential "moderate to high levels" of risk from residues in food of animal origin.

3. *Controlled Drugs and Substances Act*

Section 70 of the *Narcotic Control Regulations*, section G.01.007 of the FDR, and section 3 of the *Benzodiazepines and Other Targeted Substances Regulations* prohibit the advertising of controlled drugs to the general public.

A substance that can alter mental processes and that may produce harm to health and to society when distributed or used without supervision may be added to a schedule to the CDSA. When determining in which schedule to the CDSA a substance should be listed, Health Canada considers several factors, including international requirements, the dependence potential and likelihood of abuse of the substance, the extent of its abuse in Canada, the danger it represents to the safety of the public, and the usefulness of the substance as a therapeutic agent.

Source: Project 1539, *Canada Gazette,* 2007

4. Pre-market review

To help protect the Canadian public from unsafe and/or ineffective health products, the FDR and the NHPR require that all drugs and NHPs undergo a submission review by Health Canada prior to being granted market authorization. The review is based on all the scientific data available to Health Canada on the safety of the product, its efficacy according to scientific and other types of evidence, as appropriate for the recommended use (e.g. evidence from references to traditional use or homeopathic pharmacopoeias, as permitted by the NHPR and guidance documents), and evidence that the product is of high quality. This evidence for safety, efficacy, and quality must be included in a submission to Health Canada for market authorization. Furthermore, claims or indications made on the label must be supported by the scientific evidence provided in the submission. The pre-market review requirements are found in sections C.01.014, C.08.002, C.08.002.1, and C.08.003 of the FDR, for drugs and, in sections 4 and 5 of the NHPR, for NHPs.

With respect to the pre-market review of submissions with Schedule A claims, the standard of evidence applied will depend upon the level of risk associated with the inherent safety of the product and the nature of the Schedule A claim being made. As Schedule A is generally characterized as a list of serious diseases, Health Canada will expect evidence beyond references to "traditional use" for NHPs, meaning the use of a medicinal ingredient within a cultural belief system or healing paradigm for at least 50 consecutive years, or evidence beyond references to claims from other healing paradigms not based on conventional pharmacology (such as homeopathy). These on their own are not a sufficient standard of evidence for Schedule A or other serious disease preventative claims, thus supporting human clinical evidence of efficacy and safety would be required.

If, in the review of a submission for either a Drug Identification Number (DIN), a Natural Product Number (NPN) or a Homeopathic Medicine Number (DIN-HM), it appears that any of the factors for Schedule F designation could apply and that any health risk thus identified cannot be mitigated (e.g. through appropriate cautionary labelling), then the product would be reviewed as a potential Schedule F prescription drug under Division 8 of the FDR or the submission applicant may withdraw the submission. In the case of the former, where the drug is added to Schedule F but is not a veterinary-use drug listed in Part II of Schedule F, the advertising restrictions of section C.01.044 of the FDR apply.

However, if there is conclusive scientific evidence to support a preventative claim for a Schedule A disease, then Health Canada may issue a market authorization for the product. Only after the issuance of a DIN, an NPN or a DIN-HM are manufacturers then permitted to label for and advertise to the general public the authorized preventative claims about Schedule A diseases for NHPs and drugs subject to these Regulations.

5. *Natural Health Products Regulations*

Although NHPs fall within the definition of drug in the FDA, it was recognized that these products would benefit from a regulatory framework more suitable to their generally relatively low risk. On January 1, 2004, the NHPR came into force. The NHPR are a comprehensive framework and include site licensing, good manufacturing practices, and product licensing (i.e. an NPN or a DIN-HM is issued). Provisions for clinical trials, adverse reaction reporting, labelling, and packaging are also included.

Although the NHPR came into force in 2004, transition provisions were developed in consultation with stakeholders to provide for the staged implementation of these NHPR. This allows time for training, education, and public awareness to help stakeholders comply with the NHPR.

The provisions set out a two-year transition period for site licensing, from January 1, 2004, to December 31, 2005, for manufacturers, packagers, labellers, and importers of NHPs conducting activities in Canada under the FDR.

Source: Project 1539, *Canada Gazette,* 2007

There is a six-year transition period for product licensing, from January 1, 2004, to December 31, 2009, for NHPs with DINs issued under the FDR. The applicable provisions of the FDR continue to apply for products with a DIN until they are licensed under the NHPR, or until the application is withdrawn. From January 1, 2004, all products not previously on the market that fit the NHP definition must comply with the NHPR immediately and must be subject to the full licence application process in order to be sold in Canada.

The *Compliance Policy for Natural Health Products*, posted on the Health Canada Web site, explains the compliance approach with respect to NHPs which have not received market authorization by way of a DIN, an NPN or a DIN-HM.

6. Advertising and terms of market authorization

Health Canada is the national regulatory authority for health product advertisement and bears the responsibility for enforcing the FDA, the FDR, the NHPR, and the CDSA and its regulations. More specifically, Health Canada

. develops guidance documents and policies for the interpretation of the regulatory framework for marketed health products; and

. oversees regulated advertising activities.

When permitted, advertising for drugs, including those subject to these Regulations, and NHPs should always be consistent with the terms of the product's market authorization or the authorized labelling material. Any changes in the terms of market authorization may have an impact on what is permitted to be advertised. Section A.5 of the *Consumer Advertising Guidelines for Marketed Health Products (for Nonprescription Drugs including Natural Health Products)*, which is posted on the Health Canada Web site, states that advertising must respect subsection 9(1) of the FDA and that advertising should clearly communicate the intended use of the product in a manner that is consistent with the terms of market authorization. Section 1.1 of this guideline further states that therapeutic claims for NHPs must be consistent with their terms of market authorization, which is the product licence, and that therapeutic claims for non-prescription drugs must be consistent with their terms of market authorization, which are the Labelling Standards, Category IV Monographs, Product Monographs or Authorized Labelling. Furthermore, section 1.4.1 of the *Guidance for Industry: Product Monograph*, also posted on the Health Canada Web site, states that the product monograph serves as a standard against which all promotional material, or advertising distributed or sponsored by the sponsor about a non-prescription drug which falls under Division 8 of the FDR can be compared. The product monograph establishes the parameters for all advertising, representations, and promotional or information material distributed or otherwise sponsored by the sponsor. It contains all the representations to be made in respect of the new drug, as set out in paragraphs C.08.002(2)(*k*) and C.08.003(2)(*h*) of the FDR.

With respect to drugs for human use, advertising preclearance agencies review and preclear advertising material in order to help industry ensure compliance with the regulatory provisions of the FDA, the FDR, the NHPR, and the CDSA and its regulations, and to help industry ensure consistency with the various Health Canada guidance documents and codes of advertising. The agencies also offer independent mechanisms to resolve complaints on advertising for authorized health products. This voluntary system of preclearance is carried out in conjunction with the compliance and enforcement powers of Health Canada.

7. Post-market surveillance

Finally, post-market surveillance is another mechanism to protect the health of the Canadian public by monitoring the safety, efficacy, and quality of health products after they have reached the marketplace. Health Canada undertakes compliance and enforcement activities to ensure that claims carried by marketed products are consistent with the market authorization granted under the FDA, the FDR, and the NHPR. Health Canada is prepared for the implementation of these

Source: Project 1539, *Canada Gazette,* 2007

amendments to the Regulations by increasing the number of inspectors and by providing the inspectors with access to databases that carry the exact wording of authorized Schedule A claims for use in compliance and enforcement activities. NHPs and drugs subject to these Regulations carrying claims which have not been reviewed by Health Canada, and NHPs and drugs subject to these Regulations carrying claims which differ from those which were approved are in violation of the FDA and the FDR or the NHPR, respectively.

V. The future of Schedule A and section 3 — Health Protection Legislative Renewal

Health Canada is currently reviewing its health protection legislation, with a view to preparing new legislation and regulations, that will address the needs of the Canadian public today and in the future.

Alternatives

Six options were considered in the development of these Regulations. The following summary table (Table A) indicates the mechanisms used in each option to permit claims currently prohibited by the FDA. Both mechanisms are described after the table. Option 6 is the chosen option.

Table A

		Mechanism to permit claims	
Option — General description		Revision to Schedule A	Exemption from section 3
1	Maintain the status quo	no	no
2	Permit risk reduction and symptomatic treatment claims	no	yes
3	Permit preventative and treatment claims	no	yes
4	Revise Schedule A with criteria in regulations	yes	no
5	Revise Schedule A with criteria in policy	yes	no
6	Revise Schedule A with criteria in policy and permit preventative claims	yes	yes

In reference to Table A — Explanation for how claims are permitted using the mechanism "Revision to Schedule A"

When the criteria are applied to Schedule A and a disease does not meet any of the criteria, that disease is removed from the list. The labelling and advertising prohibitions in section 3 no longer apply to the claims for that disease. This means that preventative, treatment or cure claims are permitted in labelling and advertising to the general public. Products continue to be subject to all other provisions in the FDA, the CDSA, and their regulations, therefore any other restrictions on the labelling and advertising of claims or any conditions for market authorization remain in place.

In reference to Table A — Explanation for how claims are permitted using the mechanism "Exemption from section 3"

NHPs and drugs subject to these Regulations are exempt from the preventative prohibition, which means that they are permitted to carry preventative claims in labelling and advertising to the general public. These products continue to be subject to all other provisions in the FDA, the CDSA, and their regulations, therefore any other restrictions on the labelling and advertising of claims or any conditions for market authorization of these products remain in place.

Option 1: Maintain the status quo

Mechanism used to permit claims: none

Source: Project 1539, *Canada Gazette,* 2007

With the exception of section B.01.601 of the FDR, as explained earlier in the RIAS, section 3 of the FDA continues to prohibit preventative, treatment, and cure claims in the labelling and advertising to the general public for the diseases currently listed in Schedule A.

Pros

. No regulatory changes are required, therefore no resources would be spent in implementing a regulatory amendment.

Cons

. The Schedule A list currently contains some diseases which no longer require the high level of regulatory rigour provided by section 3.

. Manufacturers who provide Health Canada with adequate evidence of the safety, quality and efficacy of their products are prohibited from labelling and advertising that their products prevent, treat or cure a Schedule A disease, even if they receive market authorization for such.

. The ability of the Canadian public to make informed decisions about their health is limited because products available to the general public are not permitted to be labelled as a preventative, treatment or cure for any Schedule A disease when there is evidence for such.

Conclusion: Option 1 is rejected.

<u>Option 2: Exempt drugs from the section 3 prohibitions on risk reduction and symptomatic treatment claims for Schedule A diseases</u>

Mechanism used to permit claims: Exemption from section 3

Option 2 would permit risk reduction and symptomatic treatment claims to be made about Schedule A diseases in the labelling and advertising to the general public for all drugs and all NHPs that have undergone pre-market review and have been granted market authorization for those claims, unless otherwise restricted in regulation, such as in the case of Schedule F prescription drugs and controlled substances scheduled under the CDSA.

Pros

. Manufacturers would no longer be prohibited from labelling and advertising to the general public when there is evidence for risk reduction and symptomatic treatment claims about Schedule A diseases for NHPs and certain drugs.

. The ability of the Canadian public to make informed decisions about their health is increased because products available to the general public are permitted to be labelled for risk reduction or symptomatic treatment for any Schedule A disease when there is evidence for such.

Cons

. The terms "risk reduction" and "symptomatic treatment" are not defined in the FDA, the FDR, nor the NHPR. They are difficult to define in regulation.

. The Schedule A list contains some diseases which no longer require the high level of regulatory rigour provided by section 3. It limits the Canadian public's access to labelling information that could serve to maintain or improve their health.

Conclusion: Option 2 is rejected.

<u>Option 3: Exempt non-prescription drugs and NHPs from the section 3 prohibitions on preventative and treatment claims for Schedule A diseases</u>

Source: Project 1539, *Canada Gazette,* 2007

Mechanism used to permit claims: Exemption from section 3

Option 3 would permit preventative, risk reduction, treatment, and symptomatic treatment claims to be made for Schedule A diseases in the labelling and advertising to the general public for non-prescription drugs and NHPs that have undergone pre-market review and have been granted market authorization for those claims.

Pros

. The broad terms "preventative" and "treatment" are terms used in the FDA and have been interpreted by Health Canada to encompass "risk reduction" and "symptomatic treatment," respectively.

. The broad exemptions of preventative and treatment would permit the the labelling and advertising to the general public of preventative, risk reduction, treatment or symptomatic treatment claims for non-prescription drugs and NHPs.

. The ability of the Canadian public to make informed decisions about their health is increased because NHPs and certain drugs would be permitted to be labelled to the general public for preventative, risk reduction, treatment or symptomatic treatment for any Schedule A disease when there is evidence for such because the claims would no longer be prohibited in labelling and advertising to the general public.

Cons

. The Schedule A list contains some diseases which no longer require the high level of regulatory rigour provided by section 3. It limits the Canadian public's access to labelling information that could serve to maintain or improve their health.

Conclusion: Option 3 is rejected.

Option 4: Amend Schedule A and include Schedule A criteria in regulation

Mechanism used to permit claims: Revision to Schedule A

Pros

. The revised Schedule A list contains diseases which require the high level of regulatory rigour provided by section 3.

. Criteria will improve predictability and consistency in Schedule A listings and enhance Health Canada's accountability, openness and transparency to stakeholders and the public.

Cons

. With Schedule A criteria in regulation, it is more difficult to keep the criteria responsive to current medical needs in the ever-changing health products and food environment because amending regulations in order to modify criteria takes a relatively longer time than revising a policy in order to modify criteria.

. There are preventative claims for diseases remaining in Schedule A which are appropriate for NHPs and certain drugs to carry in labelling and advertising, but which are prohibited by section 3.

Conclusion: Option 4 is rejected.

Option 5: Amend Schedule A and include Schedule A criteria in policy

Mechanism used to permit claims: Revision to Schedule A

Pros

Source: Project 1539, *Canada Gazette,* 2007

. The revised Schedule A list contains diseases which require the high level of regulatory rigour provided by section 3.

. With Schedule A criteria in policy, it is easier to keep the criteria responsive to current medical needs in the ever-changing health products and food environment. Revising a policy in order to modify criteria takes less time than amending regulations in order to modify criteria.

. Criteria will improve predictability and consistency in Schedule A listings and enhance Health Canada's accountability, openness and transparency to stakeholders and the public.

Cons

. There are preventative claims for diseases remaining in Schedule A which are appropriate for NHPs and certain drugs to carry in labelling and advertising, but which are prohibited by section 3.

Conclusion: Option 5 is rejected.

Option 6: Amend Schedule A by including criteria in policy and exempt NHPs and certain drugs from the preventative prohibition for Schedule A diseases

Mechanism used to permit claims: Revision to Schedule A and exemption to section 3

Option 6 was chosen because

. The revised Schedule A list contains diseases which require the high level of regulatory rigour provided by section 3.

. With Schedule A criteria in policy, it is easier to keep the criteria responsive to current medical needs in the ever-changing health products and food environment. Revising a policy in order to modify criteria takes less time than amending regulations in order to modify criteria.

. Criteria will improve predictability and consistency in Schedule A listings and enhance Health Canada's accountability, openness and transparency to stakeholders and the public.

. There are preventative claims for diseases remaining in Schedule A which are appropriate for NHPs and certain drugs to carry in labelling and advertising, and which are no longer prohibited by the preventative exemption to section 3.

Option 6 reflects the current health care context of a comprehensive regulatory system and a publicly funded health care system, and allows consumers to be made aware of substantiated, evidence-based labelling that previously was inaccessible due to the section 3 prohibition.

Benefits and costs

The following benefits and costs are associated with these Regulations.

Public

Benefits

. Consumers would have greater access to evidence-based information in labelling for NHPs and drugs subject to these Regulations. Authorized claims for marketed products are shared with the Canadian public through labelling. This increases the ability of consumers to make informed choices about their health, which satisfies the Canadian public's desire to participate in their health care.

. These Regulations are consistent with the following guiding principles outlined in the EWG's majority report on Schedule A and section 3, as posted on the

Source: Project 1539, *Canada Gazette,* 2007

Health Canada Web site: optimize health outcomes, improve access to validated health information and facilitate responsible self-care.

. These Regulations are consistent with a position of the EWG's minority report on Schedule A and section 3, as posted on the Health Canada Web site. The report supported labelling of products that is consistent with authorized product information.

. These Regulations are consistent with both majority and minority reports, which recommend that experts review the diseases listed in Schedule A.

. A Canadian public, better informed about NHPs and drugs subject to these Regulations, may have less need to use the health care system.

Costs

. There may be an increase in non-compliant labelling and advertising of Schedule A diseases for NHPs and drugs subject to these Regulations, which is disadvantageous to the consumer.

Government

Benefits

. These Regulations may result in less strain being placed on provincial health care plans because the Canadian public may be more aware of the benefits of NHPs and drugs subject to these Regulations.

Costs

The start-up costs to Government for implementation of these Regulations proposal are anticipated to be approximately $500,000 (plus departmental overhead). Annual ongoing costs to Government for implementation of these Regulations are anticipated to be $3,000,000 (plus departmental overhead). Government costs are anticipated to be

. an increase in the number of reviewers (6.5 persons) at Health Canada to address the projected increase in submissions;

. an increase in the number of inspectors (9 persons) at Health Canada to monitor compliance and adherence to guidelines, and to address the potential increase in investigations of whether manufacturers' claims exceed what is permitted by the terms of market authorization;

. an increase in the number of regulatory advertising officers (1.5 person) at Health Canada to deal with the potential increase in advertising complaints;

. the updating of databases holding authorized Schedule A claims, used by the inspectors and regulatory advertising officers;

. the revisions of existing consumer advertising guidance documents, revisions of standard operating procedures (SOPs), revisions of forms, and training required for inspectors to implement the change in regulations; and

. the evaluation of the impact of these Regulations.

Industry

Benefits

. Industry may benefit from a potential increase in sales of authorized NHPs and drugs subject to these Regulations due to an increase in claims in labelling and advertising.

Costs

Source: Project 1539, *Canada Gazette,* 2007

. There may be a cost to manufacturers of promoting a product in a market environment which is made more competitive by the partial lifting of an advertising prohibition.

In summary, the benefits that would be derived from these Regulations outweigh their costs.

Consultation

2002–2003: In 2002, Health Canada convened an internal working group on Schedule A. In February 2003, the group produced the *Schedule A and Section 3: Guidance Document* in order to clarify to stakeholders the intent and Health Canada's interpretation of the statute. This Guidance Document was posted on the Health Canada Web site.

2003–2004: In 2003, Health Canada convened an EWG on Schedule A, comprised of representatives from government and regulatory groups, professional associations, consumer/advocacy groups, advertising/media organizations, and food, health products and medical devices industries. The EWG was mandated (1) to develop criteria for determining Schedule A diseases; (2) to review Schedule A diseases; and (3) to recommend modifications to or elimination of Schedule A and section 3. The EWG submitted a majority report and a minority report in January 2004, and both were posted on the Health Canada Web site. The recommendations of the two EWG reports were considered when drafting these Regulations.

In February 2005, Health Canada met with the EWG and committed to convening a SAP to develop criteria for revising Schedule A and to propose revisions to Schedule A using these criteria. At the same time, Health Canada committed to proposing a regulatory amendment to permit risk reduction and symptomatic treatment claims for diseases listed in Schedule A, as per Option 2 explained earlier.

On September 21, 2005, the SAP was convened. It was composed of experts from a range of health care specialities, including homeopathy, naturopathy, medicine, pharmacy, nutrition, advertising and patient advocacy. In addition to the work outlined above, it was also tasked with examining the reasons for subsections 3(1) and 3(2) and Schedule A to determine what other options were now available in regulations to fulfill the intent behind the legislation.

On November 19, 2005, Project 1474 was pre-published in the CG I, for a 75-day comment period. During this time, 25 representations were received. Sixteen representations were in support of the proposal, eight representations were against the proposal, and one representation was neutral, meaning that no position was taken when providing comments.

Those stakeholders in support of Project 1474 were drug manufacturers, NHP manufacturers, medical devices manufacturers, media organizations, consultants and academics. Stakeholders against the proposal consisted of government ministries, health care associations, advocacy groups, and individuals.

Project 1474 and these Regulations both permit NPHs and certain drugs claims which are currently prohibited by section 3 in the labelling and advertising to the general public. However, the mechanism used in Project 1474 and these Regulations to achieve this objective is different. In Project 1474, exemptions to section 3 were used without any revisions to the list of Schedule A diseases. These Regulations achieve the original intent of Project 1474 by revising the list of Schedule A diseases and by permitting preventative claims for diseases remaining in Schedule A.

The following relationships can be drawn between Project 1474's CG I comments and these Regulations.

The following comments were received during the comment period for Project 1474. They were included in this RIAS as they are relevant to these Regulations

Source: Project 1539, *Canada Gazette,* 2007

(Project 1539):

Comments in support of Project 1474: Both projects 1474 and these Regulations (Project 1539) address that the Schedule A and section 3 provisions are out of date. Both acknowledge that there are NHPs and certain drugs which have scientific evidence for Schedule A claims. Both allow manufacturers to promote approved claims which would be currently prohibited in labelling and advertising to the general public.

Comments expressing concerns about Project 1474: The following stakeholder comments and the Department's responses are also applicable to these Regulations (Project 1539).

— *Comment*: Stakeholders stated that consumers would be confused that there are different rules for the labelling and advertising for prescription drugs versus NHPs/non-prescription drugs.

— *Response:* There are currently different rules for the labelling and advertising of prescription drugs and NHPs/non-prescription drugs. This is due to the difference between the higher-risk profile of prescription drugs and the lower-risk profile of NHPs/non-prescription drugs, and due to the difference in how the consumer accesses these products — the former are mediated through a physician and a pharmacist, and the latter are not.

— *Comment:* Stakeholders stated that NHPs should not carry Schedule A claims because the standards of evidence for the review of NHPs are inferior to those used for non-prescription and prescription drugs; therefore NHPs carrying Schedule A claims may increase the health risk to the Canadian public. Furthermore, stakeholders stated that the backlog of NHP submissions would result in non-compliant NHPs being on the market with Schedule A claims for years.

— *Response:* The standards of evidence for NHPs provide for a range of evidence appropriate to the safety risk inherent in the NHPs and the claim being made. Higher standards of evidence are required for higher-risk products; therefore, traditional references would not be considered a sufficient standard of evidence on their own for claims to prevent Schedule A or other serious diseases. There is no intent to accept different standards of evidence for NHPs as opposed to pharmaceuticals when accessing prevention claims of Schedule A diseases. For example, human clinical evidence will be required for NHPs advertising and labelling prevention claims for Schedule A diseases. Finally, products that present a significant risk to consumer health, including products that make unauthorized claims with respect to serious diseases, are targeted for compliance actions. Any backlog in assessment of NHP product licence applications is outside the scope of the risk-based approach to compliance.

The following is different between projects 1474 and these Regulations (Project 1539)

— *Comment:* In the Project 1474 consultation period, stakeholders stated that the Record of Proceedings (RoP) from the SAP should be available for consultation.

— *Response:* The recommendations of the SAP, which are in the RoP, were open for comment during these Regulations' (Project 1539) 75-day CG I consultation period.

— *Comment:* In the Project 1474 consultation period, stakeholders stated that the principle behind Schedule A is relevant today, therefore, changes should be made to Schedule A itself.

— *Response:* Revisions to Schedule A are included in these Regulations (Project 1539).

— *Comment:* In the Project 1474 consultation period, stakeholders stated that issues raised by the EWG should be addressed.

Source: Project 1539, *Canada Gazette,* 2007

— *Response:* The EWG recommended that revisions be made to Schedule A, these Regulations (Project 1539) respond to this recommendation.

On March 29, 2006, the recommendations by the SAP were finalized in a RoP and were posted on the Health Canada Web site.

Comments received during these Regulations' (Project 1539) comment period for Canada Gazette, Part I

On June 16, 2007, Project 1539 was prepublished in the CG I with a 75-day comment period. Twenty-six representations were received.

Fourteen of the twenty-six representations commented on the Schedule A amendment.Ten representations were in support and four expressed concerns. Twelve stakeholders did not comment on this aspect of the amendment.

Twenty-four of the twenty-six representations commented on the section 3 amendment. Twenty-two representations were in support and two expressed concerns. Two stakeholders did not comment on this aspect of the amendment.

Those stakeholders in support of the amendments included members of the following: professional health care associations, industry associations, NHP and drug manufacturers, public health/patient interest groups, advertising and marketing groups and individuals. Stakeholders who raised concerns about the amendments included members of the following: food industry consultants, consumer advocacy associations, NHP manufacturers and associations, and naturopathic health care associations.

Various issues were raised during the CG I comment period. Those issues that pertain to this amendment are addressed below. Some expressed concerns related to the NHP standards of evidence and are explained in previous sections of this RIAS. Issues that are broader than this amendment, such as these Regulations' implementation, are not addressed in the RIAS but have been forwarded to the affected areas in Health Canada.

Schedule A Revision

The four stakeholders who raised concerns about the revisions to Schedule A commented as follows:

Comment 1:

Why were certain diseases deleted from Schedule A?

Response 1:

Schedule A is populated with diseases that meet one or more Schedule A criteria outlined in Part III of this RIAS. This modernization generally includes life-threatening diseases and acute forms of specific diseases. Alopecia, dysentery, gout, hypotension, impetigo, pleurisy, and sexual impotence were not considered to be an acutely serious condition, nor did they meet any other Schedule A criteria, and were therefore removed from Schedule A.

All-encompassing listings were also removed from Schedule A and replaced with more specific forms of the disease that are most serious. Therefore, heart disease was replaced with congestive heart failure, anxiety state was replaced with acute anxiety state, hernia was replaced with strangulated hernia, liver disease was replaced with hepatitis, and arthritis was replaced with acute, inflammatory, debilitating arthritis.

Schedule A was revised to include specific diseases, thus general diseases of the major organs such as bladder disease, disease of the prostate, gall bladder disease, and kidney disease were removed.

Schedule A was additionally revised to remove symptomatic illnesses such as

Source: Project 1539, *Canada Gazette,* 2007

disorder of menstrual flow and edematous state.

Lastly, repetitive listings were removed in order to streamline Schedule A. Epilepsy, leukemia, and malignant tumors now fall under "convulsions," "cancer," and "cancer," respectively. Benign tumors were removed as they do not meet any Schedule A criteria. Alcoholism was removed since it now falls under "addiction;" "acute alcoholism" does not refer to the degree/stage of alcohol addiction and remains on the list as it refers to the state of inebriation.

Furthermore, Schedule A will undergo periodic updates to reflect the evolving scientific opinion/research and any rising issues stemming from these amendments. An updated Guidance Document will also clarify the amendments to Schedule A and section 3 (i.e., updated definitions and synonyms).

Comment 2:

There was concern as to how the revised Schedule A diseases would be interpreted by Health Canada during the review of a submission.

Response 2:

Health Canada will assess whether the applicant has provided sufficient evidence to support the product's quality, safety, and efficacy on a case-by-case basis. Health Canada will also ensure that interpretations for the diseases remaining in Schedule A are consistent throughout the Department in order to determine whether or not specific claims are in violation of section 3 of the FDA.

A monograph is a written description of particular elements on an identified topic. The NHPD allows applicants to reference a NHPD monograph in support of the safety and efficacy of the NHP as part of their product licence application. This process is efficient for both applicants and Health Canada, since there is no need to evaluate the safety and efficacy of NHP ingredients that are already known to be safe and efficacious when used under the conditions specified in the NHPD monograph. It should be noted that some monographic claims may now be considered to be a Schedule A claim. All licensees using that claim would be contacted in order to make a label change and to update the monograph.

An updated synonym list and definitions for Schedule A diseases will be provided in the revised *"Schedule A and Section 3: Guidance Document."*

Comment 3:

Schedule A is not reduced enough and should be eliminated entirely.

Response 3:

Revision of Schedule A was guided by the Schedule A criteria, outlined earlier in the RIAS. Schedule A will undergo periodic revisions to reflect evolving scientific research and any issues which stem from these regulations.

Section 3 Amendment

The two stakeholders who raised concerns about the section 3 amendment commented as follows:

Comment 1:

These Regulations should exempt treatment as well as prevention claims from the prohibition contained in section 3.

Response 1:

Schedule A has been revised to include diseases which meet one or more Schedule A criteria. The exemption for treatment claims is no longer required since the diseases which have been removed from Schedule A are no longer subject to the prohibition in section 3. Consequently, products for these diseases

Source: Project 1539, *Canada Gazette,* 2007

would be permitted to carry approved treatment, prevention and cure claims.

Comment 2:

It will be difficult to distinguish between prevention claims and treatment claims since the terms are difficult to define and would therefore result in consumer confusion.

Response 2:

Health Canada currently makes the distinction between treatment and prevention claims during pre-market review for health products. Health Canada reviews the content of the label during the review process to ensure that the label clearly reflects the approved conditions of use.

Comment 3:

There is concern that non-prescription drugs and NHPs will be labelled and advertised for the purpose of preventing, treating and curing the diseases that were removed from Schedule A.

Response 3:

This amendment to remove restrictions to labelling and advertising does not in any way remove any other requirements contained in the FDA, the CDSA, and their regulations. All products that make claims for diseases removed from Schedule A must undergo pre-market review, and only approved claims will be permitted to be labelled and advertised on non-prescription drugs and NHPs. All non-prescription drugs and NHPs continue to be subject to all other provisions in the FDA, the CDSA, and their regulations, including any other restrictions on labelling and advertising of claims or any conditions for market authorization for these products.

If during pre-market review it appears that any of the factors for Schedule F designation could apply, then the product would be reviewed as a potential Schedule F prescription drug under Division 8 of the FDR, or the applicant may withdraw the submission.

Comment 4:

It is premature to further limit the regulatory oversight of NHPs while the vast majority now on the market are unlicensed and while NHPD is conducting the first formal review of its regulatory approach.

Response 4:

Products that present a significant risk to consumer health, including products that make unauthorized Schedule A claims with respect to serious diseases, are targeted for compliance actions. Nine new inspectors have been allocated to address any compliance and enforcement issues with respect to Schedule A.

General Comment

There was one general comment regarding the wording in the RIAS:

Comment:

What does "certain drugs" mean in the RIAS?

Response:

The RIAS uses the term "certain drugs" instead of using the term "non-prescription drugs" because some drugs that are regulated under the FDA and the FDR as non-prescription drugs are also regulated as Class A precursors under the *Precursor Control Regulations* of the CDSA. These drugs require a prescription when sold or provided in a quantity, per transaction, exceeding the

Source: Project 1539, *Canada Gazette,* 2007

maximum quantity, expressed as an absolute quantity or per package, specified for the precursor in the *Precursor Control Regulations*. Precursors are frequently used in the clandestine production of illicit drugs. The concept of "prescription" in this context is different than in the context of a Schedule F prescription drug because the requirement for a prescription for a Class A precursor is to monitor and control substances frequently used in the clandestine production of illicit drugs. In the case of a precursor that requires a prescription, there is no Pr or other symbol indicating "prescription" on the label of the precursor.

Conclusion

As noted earlier, the only change made to the proposed Regulations that were prepublished in the CG I is that "addiction" was changed to "addiction, except for nicotine addiction." This change removes any inconsistency with the Schedule F listing for nicotine, which allows nicotine replacement therapies (NRTs) that have been approved by Health Canada for use in smoking cessation therapy to be labelled and sold without prescription, provided that the NRTs meet the form and concentration requirements listed in Schedule F.

Compliance and enforcement

These Regulations do not alter existing compliance authorities under the FDA and its Regulations enforced by the Health Products and Food Branch Inspectorate (HPFBI). It should be noted that compliance and enforcement resources are being enhanced for the implementation of this amendment.

Contact

Project 1539
Policy Division
Bureau of Policy, Science, and International Programs
Therapeutic Products Directorate
Holland Cross
Tower B, 2nd Floor
Address Locator 3102C5
1600 Scott Street
Ottawa, Ontario
K1A 0K9
Telephone: 613-948-4623 (please refer to Project 1539)
Fax: 613-941-6458 (please refer to Project 1539)
Email: regaff-affreg@hc-sc.gc.ca

Footnote a

S.C. 1999, c. 33, s. 347

Footnote 1

C.R.C., c. 870

Footnote 2

SOR/2003-196

NOTICE:
The format of the electronic version of this issue of the *Canada Gazette* was modified in order to be compatible with hypertext language (HTML). Its content is very similar except for the footnotes, the symbols and the tables.

Top of page

Important notices

Updated: 2007-12-28

Source: Project 1539, *Canada Gazette,* 2007

A REPORT ON THE USE OF PSYCHIATRIC MEDICATIONS THEIR SAFETY AND EFFICACY

Providing a Detailed Meta-Analysis

TRUEHOPE

A NON-PROFIT SUPPORT FOR THE MENTALLY ILL

Source: A Report on the use of Psychiatric Medications—Their Safety and Efficacy: Providing a Detailed Meta-Analysis" by *Truehope*, 2003

A REPORT ON THE USE OF PSYCHIATRIC MEDICATIONS AND THEIR EFFECTS

EXECUTIVE SUMMARY

- Research into the use of medications in the U.S. demonstrates that over 200,000 deaths are created within the hospital setting annually. Additionally over 2.1 million serious injuries take place. These occur from properly prescribed medications. Adverse Drug Reactions (ADRs) make these reactions between the fourth and sixth leading cause of death. In the year 2000 medication ADRs, drug related morbidity and mortality exceeded $177.4 billion in the ambulatory setting in the United States. The largest component of this total cost was associated with drug related hospitalizations. Since 1995, the cost of drug related problems have more than doubled.

- Data from numerous studies are demonstrating that clinical efficacy is not sufficient to warrant the risk of prescribing some of the most commonly used psychiatric medications.

- Extensive research shows that psychiatric medications are actually producing serious patient illness and hospitalizations.

- Relapse into hospital for a psychiatric patient is a common event in spite of continual medication maintenance treatment. Data shows a ***5-year relapse rate to be well over 70%*** in spite of optimal pharmacological treatment.

- Of great concern is the growing evidence that many psychiatric medications raise the risk of cancer, addiction, and suicide. For instance, a woman taking certain psychiatric medications ***more than doubles her risk of ovarian cancer.*** Indeed, the use of one antidepressant Paxil (Paroxetine) is a ***greater risk factor for cancer than is smoking***.

DETAILED ANALYSIS

ADVERSE DRUG REACTIONS (ADRs)

In 1998 researchers at the University of Toronto reviewed adverse drug reactions (ADRs) in U.S. hospitals. Estimations using 1994 data showed that there were 106,000 fatalities and over 2.1 million serious complications requiring hospitalization due to ADRs. "The study excluded errors in drug administration, noncompliance, overdose, drug abuse, therapeutic failures, and possible ADRs." These deaths or injuries resulted from properly prescribed medications. The researchers stated, "The incidence of serious and fatal ADRs in U.S. hospitals was found to be extremely high." 106,000 people had fatal ADRs while hospitalized, "making these reactions between the **fourth and sixth leading cause of death**."[1]

In 1995 Johnson and Bootman published a study in the *Archives of Internal Medicine* in which they stated, "drug related morbidity and mortality was estimated to cost $76.6 billion in the ambulatory setting in the United States."

Based on 1992 figures, these same investigators stated that "the number of admissions that was estimated from the model suggested that **28.8% of all hospital admissions were a result of drug – related morbidity and mortality…** Our results indicate that drug – related morbidity and mortality should be considered one of the leading diseases in terms of resources consumed…The estimated number of deaths owing to ADRs (drug related problems) ranged from **79,159 to 198,815 deaths**." [2]

A 2001 update to the 1995 Johnson – Bootman study completed by Ernst and Grizzle at the

  Phone: 1-888-TRUEHOPE July 23, 2003

Source: A Report on the use of Psychiatric Medications—Their Safety and Efficacy: Providing a Detailed Meta-Analysis" by *Truehope*, 2003

University of Arizona, concluded that overall, the cost of U.S. drug related morbidity and mortality exceed $177.4 billion in the year 2000 with over **200,000 deaths** created annually. The largest component of this total cost was associated with drug related hospitalizations. Since 1995, the cost of drug related problems have more than doubled "Strategies for preventing drug-related morbidity and mortality are urgently needed." [3]

Table 1. Direct Costs of Medical Conditions United States [4]

Condition	Source	$-billion
Non-Insulin – Dependent Diabetes	Wolf et al. 1994	15.5
Obesity (1990)		45.8
Diabetes (1990)	Amer.Diabetes Assoc. 1993	45.2
Cardiovascular Disease (1992)	American Heart Association 1993	117.0
Drug-Related Morbidity and Mortality (1994)	**Johnson & Bootman**	**76.6**
Drug Related Morbidity and Mortality (2000) [3]	**Ernst & Grizzle**	**177.4**

The Institute of Medicine, a section of the prestigious National Academy of Sciences, reported in 1999 that as many as 98,000 people die every year in U.S. hospitals from medical errors. Many deaths are attributable to the use of medications. The report stimulated a swift response from Congress when the US President ordered congressional hearings into the matter.[5 6]

Applying the above data to Canada, based on U.S. – Canadian population figures, approximately 20,000 deaths per annum occur from ADR's at a cost of 17.7 billion dollars.

IS CLINICAL EFFICACY A REALITY?

In the past two years there have been a number of media stories on the extreme side effects of certain psychiatric medications.[7 8 9 10 11]

The FDA (US food and Drug Administration) has issued numerous warnings on their website[12] to advise consumers and physicians of the dangers that are posed by using some psychotropic medications. Numerous medical journals are publishing studies questioning the efficacy and or safety of some of these medications.[13 14 15 16 17]

The February 13, 2002 edition of the British Society Guardian published an article entitled "Psychiatrists Shift the Mood on Antidepressants." The Royal College of Psychiatrists, which represents about 10,000 psychiatrists, has taken a more cautious approach conceding that antidepressants such as Prozac may have only a 50% success rate in treating depression.[18]

Providing a question as to efficacy is the 1998 report published in the APA Journal entitled "Listening to Prozac but Hearing Placebo", the article details the meta-analysis of 19 drug studies. In short, the research showed that 75% of the "beneficial effect" of anti-depressant medication can be attributed to placebo effect. [19]

A July 5, 2002 study[20] also published in the APA Journal by Kirsch et al. analyzed all of the data submitted to the U.S. Food and Drug Administration (FDA) for approval of the six most widely prescribed antidepressants between 1987 and 1999. More than half of the 47 studies found that patients on antidepressants improved no more than those on placebos, Kirsch says. "They should have told the American public about this. The drugs have been touted as much more effective than they are." Celexa, Prozac, Paxil, Zoloft, Effexor and Serzone were part of this evaluation.[21] "They believe the difference between the patient's response to medication and response to placebo was small enough to be considered clinically meaningless." [22]

Research is showing that a significant number of serious side effects creating hospitalization admissions and even death (e.g. depression, cardiac arrest, serotonin syndrome, fatal poisoning etc.) are produced by the medications themselves. Many studies have supported these findings. [23 24 25 26 27 28 29 30 31 32 33 34 35 36 37 38 39 40 41 42 43 44 45 46 47 48 49 50 51 52]

  Phone: 1-888-TRUEHOPE July 23, 2003

Source: A Report on the use of Psychiatric Medications—Their Safety and Efficacy: Providing a Detailed Meta-Analysis" by *Truehope*, 2003

The New England Journal of Medicine, released on April 17, 2003, indicated that **1 in 4 patients receiving a medication prescription would be injured by that prescription.** The study presented by Gandhi et al.[53] revealed that the greatest source of injury was produced by the SSRI antidepressant type medications. "It is a problem that is common, in many cases the impact could be prevented or reduced, and it has a large impact on patients", said Tejal Gandhi an internist at Brigham and Women's Hospital in Boston, a Harvard University Facility.[54]

More than 200,000 Canadian school children take Ritalin (methylphenidate), yet the *Canadian Medical Association Journal* says the clinical trials of this drug have often been biased and poorly constructed. [12 55] The Canadian article reviewed 62 randomized trials that involved a total of 2897 participants with a primary diagnosis of ADHD. The article stated, "However, these apparent beneficial effects are tempered by a strong indication of publication bias and the lack of robustness of the findings, especially those involving ADD features. **Methylphenidate also has an adverse event profile that requires consideration.**" In other words, these researchers believed that studies have tended to minimize the negative side effects of Ritalin.

Brain research carried out at John Hopkins University has shown that methamphetamine is toxic and damaging to both dopamine and serotonin brain neurons. In studies with laboratory rats, methamphetamine fed at 4 mg/day for only 3 days caused nerve fiber degeneration. Brain cells were permanently damaged by methamphetamine.[56 57] Much more research is needed on the possible adverse effects of psychiatric medications on brain cells, especially in developing brains.

RELAPSE IN SPITE OF MEDICATION

Relapsing into a psychotic, depressive or bipolar episode while on medications is a common occurrence that leaves the patient crippled and despairing. Career, family, education etc. are put on hold while the patient works through the episode. Often, medication changes are initiated at this point, sometimes exacerbating the episode while the physicians attempt to bring a state of chemical balance into the patient's life. For the safety of the patient, hospitalization often occurs at this point, creating an even greater burden for the already overtaxed medical system. In spite of the best of medications, this revolving door phenomenon occurs all too often.

Gitlin et. al. reported in bipolar patients that despite continual medication maintenance treatment, data "indicated a 5-year risk of relapse into mania or depression of **73%**." Of those who relapsed, two-thirds had multiple relapses. Relapse could not be attributed to inadequate medication. Even for those who did not relapse, the presence of significant mood symptoms was observed. "Even aggressive pharmacological maintenance treatment does not prevent relatively poor outcome in a significant number of bipolar patients."[58]

Licht et al. reported significant relapse in 148 patients using only lithium as a mood stabilizer, thirty-two (21.6%) patients were readmitted within two years with a new affective disorder episode.[59]

In another relapse study, 15 patients with bipolar I disorder, who relapsed while on lithium despite positive initial response and adequate compliance, were treated by cognitive-behavioral methods in an open trial.[60] In follow-up ranging from 2-9 years, 5 of the 15 patients (33%) experienced a new affective episode.

A study involving two groups of patients taking either risperidone or haloperidol showed that the risk of relapse of schizophrenia was 34% for the former and 60% for the latter.[61] Many mentally disordered individuals travel a "revolving door". Their episodes of relapse can be devastating, destroying their hopes for wellness, as well as their careers and family stability.

Summary:
Psychiatric medications do not overcome the risk for relapse which is very high for both affective disorders and psychosis. [62 63 64 65]

Page 3 of 14 Copyright © Truehope Nutritional Support Ltd Phone: 1-888-TRUEHOPE July 23, 2003

Source: A Report on the use of Psychiatric Medications—Their Safety and Efficacy: Providing a Detailed Meta-Analysis" by *Truehope*, 2003

SIDE EFFECTS - THE UNTOLD DANGER

Table 2 Below shows the top ten most commonly prescribed psychiatric medications in the U.S.[66] for the year 2000. We will now review each one individually for side effects. The information in the following is somewhat limited. In other words the side effects presented by these medications are more extensive than indicated.

#	BRAND NAME	GENERIC NAME	MED. CLASS
1	Xanax	Alprazolam	Benzodiazapine
2	Zoloft	Sertraline	SSRI
3	Prozac	Fluoxetine	SSRI
4	Paxil	Paroxetine	SSRI
5	Ativan	Lorazepam	Benzodiazapine
6	Elavil	Amitriptyline	Antidepressant
7	Ambien	Zolpidem	Sleep Aid Hypnotic
8	Desyrel	Trazodone	Sleep Aid Hypnotic
9	Valium	Diazepam	Benzodiazapine
10	Klonopin	Clonazepam	Benzodiazapine

Benzodiazepine Class of Medications
1. Xanex (Alprazolam), 5. Ativan (Lorazepam), 9. Valium (Diazepam), 10. Klonopin (Clonazepam)

Benzodiazepine Addiction & Withdrawal:
In Canada the benzodiazepines are considered to be a controlled medication. The Canadian Compendium of Pharmaceuticals and Specialties (CPS) quotes the following side effects for the benzodiazepines:

"**WARNINGS:** Benzodiazepines are not recommended for use in patients with a major depressive disorder or psychosis in which anxiety is not a prominent feature. **PRECAUTIONS:** Benzodiazepines may cause psychologic or physical dependence... Abrupt (or gradual reduction) of benzodiazepines may lead to symptoms such as anxiety, insomnia, irritability, gastrointestinal discomfort, anorexia, diaphoresis, photophobia, or increased sensitivity to noise. More severe symptoms may occur such as confusion, depersonalization, myoclonus, delirium, psychosis,[67 68] or seizures."[69]

Health Canada made the following statements in their report entitled "The Effects of Tranquillization: Benzodiazepine Use in Canada."[70]

- ✓ "The major indication of dependence is the development of withdrawal symptoms, which have been now clearly established at therapeutic dose levels." [71 72 73 74 75 76 77]
- ✓ "The high incidence of withdrawal symptoms suggests that a substantial minority of patients taking benzodiazepines chronically are pharmacologically dependent."[78]
- ✓ "One such carefully controlled study of withdrawal symptoms in patients who had been on ***low doses of benzodiazepines*** for a mean of 3.6 years, found between 27 and 45 percent evidencing clear withdrawal symptoms."[79]
- ✓ Babies have been born in an addicted state to mothers using benzodiazepines: "neonates born to drug-dependent women have shown withdrawal symptoms."

Addiction of unborn and newly born children is a major phenomenon. Medication withdrawal syndromes have been observed increasingly in children with mothers using psychotropic medications.[80] Research into babies suffering with Neonatal Withdrawal Syndrome report the following symptoms: continuous high-pitched cry, frantic sucking of fists, tremors, poor sucking response, sweating, and in some cases convulsions.[81 82]

Cancer Risk from Benzodiazepine and Antidepressant Usage
Two studies have reported a positive association between antidepressant and benzodiazepine use and the development of cancer. Harlow and Cramer [83] carried out a case control study of ovarian cancer incidence and obtained an adjusted risk ratio of **2.1,** indicating that use of these medications for

  Phone: 1-888-TRUEHOPE July 23, 2003

Source: A Report on the use of Psychiatric Medications—Their Safety and Efficacy: Providing a Detailed Meta-Analysis" by *Truehope*, 2003

more than 1-6 months resulted in more than doubling a woman's risk of ovarian cancer. Among women who first used these drugs before age 50 years the odds ratio was **3.5**. Among those who used them more than 10 years, the risk increased to **9.7**.

Dalton and colleagues[84] recently conducted a population-based study that followed for 7 years a total of 30,807 adult antidepressant users. They found an increased risk of non-Hodgkin's lymphoma among subjects who received greater than 5 prescriptions.

Indiscriminate and Irresponsible Prescribing of Benzodiazepines by Medical Practitioners

Treatment guidelines in the U.K. recommend the use of benzodiazepines for a maximum of 4 weeks. In Canada and the U.S. it is common practice to prescribe these medications for years.

Health Canada guidelines recommend prescribing only for short term use: "continuous use should not exceed two weeks".[85]

"The costs of continued use of benzodiazepines require careful consideration. The concern with payment must extend beyond the price of prescriptions to the total cost to the health care system. Inappropriate prescribing may well keep individuals visiting physicians…for considerably longer than necessary." [86] Many studies have supported this position. [87]

Summary

Benzodiazepines are medications that can be very dangerous when not used prudently. Cancer research shows that patients using benzodiazepines for over 10 years exhibit a 970% increase in risk of developing ovarian cancer. Addiction and withdrawal symptoms have been well established in scientific literature. Health Canada has issued warnings about prescribing of benzodiazepines in excess of two weeks. However, many physicians in North America prescribe them in an indiscriminate manner, as demonstrated by the fact that Xanex is the most frequently prescribed psychotropic medication.

SSRI Class of Medications

2. Zoloft (Sertraline), 3. Prozac (Fluoxetine), 4. Paxil (Paroxetine)

Cancer Risks Associated With Paxil Usage

The *American Journal of Epidemiology* published two studies in 2000 by Cotterchio and colleagues which demonstrated that Paxil presented a **720%** increase in risk of breast cancer in females. [14, 88] The Canadian Cancer Society website indicates that for heavy smokers there is a **400%** increase in risk for cancer. In other words, Paxil use creates a greater risk factor for breast cancer than heavy smoking. With over **3,000,000** Canadian prescriptions for Paxil in the year 2000 this is major cause for concern.[89]

SSRI's and Withdrawal Symptoms

On Februray 2, 2002 the British Medical Journal published an article entitled "Withdrawal from paroxetine can be severe, warns FDA". The article outlined in detail how paroxetine (Paxil) creates dependence and withdrawal in a significant percentage of patients. "This drug has been promoted as safe and easy to discontinue," said Charles Medawar, head of Social Audit. "The fact that it can cause intolerable withdrawal symptoms of this kind and lead to dependence is enormously important…" Dr. Peter Haddad, consultant psychiatrist for Salfords Mental Health Service NHS Trust, welcomed the FDA's safety warning. He said, "Withdrawal side effects from antidepressants are far more common than many people realize."[90]

The FDA issued a warning about Paxil on December 14, 2001. "During *Paxil* marketing, there have been spontaneous reports of similar adverse events… upon the discontinuation of *Paxil* (particularly when abrupt), including the following: dizziness, sensory disturbances (e.g., paresthesias such as electric shock sensations), agitation, anxiety, nausea, and sweating. These events are generally self-limiting. **Similar events have been reported for other selective serotonin reuptake inhibitors**." [91]

The above FDA statement describes some of

Page 5 of 14 Copyright © Truehope Nutritional Support Ltd Phone: 1-888-TRUEHOPE July 23, 2003

Source: A Report on the use of Psychiatric Medications—Their Safety and Efficacy: Providing a Detailed Meta-Analysis" by *Truehope*, 2003

the symptoms of protracted withdrawal. In some cases these symptoms can persist for a number of years.

Studies involving other SSRI's including Luvox showed negative results in drug withdrawal.[92] A group of French researchers reported severe withdrawal syndromes in 6 patients prescribed Effexor (Venlafaxine).[93] There have been hundreds of studies published in the medical literature which demonstrate the significant symptoms that are produced when withdrawing from SSRI drug treatment.[94 95 96 97 98 99 100 101 102 103 104 105 106 107 108 109 110 111 112 113 114 115 116 117 118 119 120 121 122 123 124 125 126 127 128 129 130 131 132 133 134 135 136 137 138 139 140 141 142 143 144 145 146 147 148 149 150]

ABC News reported on May 24, 2001 that "up to 85% of patients who take these kinds of drugs (SSRIs) may have some type of symptom when they stop, studies say. According to recent research in the *Journal of Clinical Psychiatry,* as many as 70% of General Practitioners and 30% of psychiatrists do not know about the side effects of ending serotonin boosting drugs. Getting off these drugs properly is an issue that is underappreciated," says Dr. Alexander Bodkin, director of the clinical psychopharmacology research program at Mclean Hospital. **"These drugs are being prescribed without the full knowledge of how they should be monitored."**[151]

As with the benzodiazepines, babies have been born in an addicted or toxic state to mothers using SSRIs.[152 153 154 155 156 157]

Akathisia from SSRIs

Akathisia is a medication-induced disorder consisting of extreme restlessness, irritability and agitation.[158 159 160 161 162] It is often associated with the withdrawal symptoms of insomnia, headaches, nervousness, anxiety, anorexia, tremors, weight loss, nausea, diarrhea and can be coupled with **suicidal ideation, homicidal thoughts and or acts.**[163]

The number of people using psychotropic medication who suffer with Akathisia is significant. A study on Prozac reported in the *Journal of Clinical Psychiatry* estimated that the number of Prozac users who experience Akathisia is between 10 and 25%.[164] There are numerous studies relating psychotropic medication-induced Akathisia with suicidal, homicidal, and violent behavior.[165 166 167 168 169 170 171] As reported in a two-year study, Akathisia may create an inability to control impulses.

SSRIs and Suicide

Other researchers found that patients suffering Prozac-induced Akathisia became preoccupied with thoughts of suicide.[172 173 174 175 176 177] Symptoms of agitation, panic, anxiety, mania and Akathisia can prompt suicidal or violent acts.[178 179 180] Akathisia and associated extreme acts of violence have been reported with other categories of psychiatric medication. For instance, Haldol-induced Akathisia was reported in three patients who attacked other people or committed murder.

Paxil (Seroxat) has been found to increase suicidal ideation and suicide in youth. "New expert advice recommends that the drug Seroxat (paroxetine) is not used to treat children and teenagers under the age of 18 years", said Professor Alasdair Breckenridge, Chairman of the U.K. Medicines and Healthcare Products Regulatory Agency. "It has become clear that the benefits of Seroxat in children for the treatment of depressive illness do not outweigh these risks."[181] The British government has now prohibited sales of Paxil (Seroxat) for youth under the age of 18.[182]

There have been a number of lawsuits involving medication and Akathisia. The following is an Associated Press release:

CHEYENNE, Wyo. (AP) June 6, 2001: *"The manufacturer of the nation's second-best-selling anti-depressant must pay $8 million to the relatives of a man who killed himself and three others after taking the drug Paxil, jurors said.*

Jurors in U.S. District Court considering the wrongful death civil suit returned a verdict against SmithKline Beecham today. They received the case Tuesday afternoon. Relatives of Donald Schell, 60, claim the man, originally from Gillette, Wyo., took two Paxil tablets

Source: A Report on the use of Psychiatric Medications—Their Safety and Efficacy: Providing a Detailed Meta-Analysis" by *Truehope*, 2003

before shooting his wife, their daughter, his granddaughter and himself to death on Feb. 13, 1998."

Research published in the *American Journal of Psychiatry* supports the possibility that SSRI medications may induce suicidal ideation in some patients. The study, by Teicher and colleagues at Harvard Medical School, reported on six patients who were depressed but *not* suicidal before they started taking SSRI medication. Within a few weeks of taking the drug, the patients experienced "intense, violent suicidal preoccupation." [183]

Another important study involving children and adolescents and the use of Prozac demonstrated self destructive phenomena created by Akathisia.[184]

Psychiatric medications in other categories:

6. Amitriptyline (Elavil)

Amitriptyline is a tricyclic antidepressant with many side effects, as demonstrated by the following:

"Depressed patients, particularly those with known manic-depressive illness, may experience a shift to mania or hypomania. Schizophrenic patients may develop increased symptoms of psychosis; patients with paranoid symptomatology may have an exaggeration of such symptoms. Tricyclic antidepressant drugs, including amitriptyline HCl, particularly when given in high doses, have been reported to produce arrhythmias, sinus tachycardia, and prolongation of the conduction time. Myocardial infarction and stroke have been reported with drugs of this class. After prolonged administration, abrupt cessation of treatment may produce nausea, headache, and malaise. Gradual dosage reduction has been reported to produce, within two weeks, transient symptoms including irritability, restlessness, and dream and sleep disturbance." [185]

In a recently published study on "The effects of tricyclic antidepressants on breast cancer risk" published in the *British Journal of Cancer*, a number of the tricyclics were implicated in raising the risk of breast cancer. Amitriptyline was an exception, and was not shown to increase cancer risk rate, while some of the other TCA's (tricyclic antidepressants) did.[13 84]

A number of studies have shown that tricyclic medications have induced manic episodes in patients suffering with various mental disorders. [186 187 188]

7. Ambien (Zolpidem)

Ambien is commonly used as a sleep aid. Like the other top ten medications, it has a number of negative side effects. The following adverse events included in DSM-III-R criteria for uncomplicated sedative/hypnotic withdrawal were reported during U.S. clinical trials following placebo substitution occurring within 48 hours following last Zolpidem treatment: fatigue, nausea, flushing, lightheadedness, uncontrolled crying, emesis, stomach cramps, panic attack, nervousness, and abdominal discomfort.[189 190] There have been adverse events reported such as delirium, nightmares and or mania being induced in patients using Zolpidem. Research is also showing that Zolpidem may create dependence in some patients.[191 192 193 194]

8. Desyrel (Trazodone)

Trazodone is also used as a common sleep aid. Research has shown numerous negative events associated with Desyrel usage. [195 196 197 198 199 200]

Summary

Hundreds of studies suggest that further research is needed on the safety of psychiatric medications. ADRs are a major cause of illness and death. **The top ten most prescribed psychotropic medications exhibit serious and dangerous side effects**. Addiction and withdrawal have become huge problems for many patients using psychotropic medications. The efficacy of these medications is also being questioned by many psychiatrists and especially by the patients using them.

Page 7 of 14 Phone: 1-888-TRUEHOPE July 23, 2003

Source: A Report on the use of Psychiatric Medications—Their Safety and Efficacy: Providing a Detailed Meta-Analysis" by *Truehope*, 2003

FOOTNOTE REFERENCES:

[1] Lazarou J et al. (1998). Incidence of adverse drug reactions in hospitalized patients. *JAMA, 279,* 1200-5

[2] Johnson J, Bootman L (1995). Drug related morbidity and mortality, *Arch Intern Med 155*, 1949-1956

[3] Ernst F.R., Grizzle A.J., Drug Related Morbidity and Mortality: Updating the Cost-of-Illness Model, J Am Pharm Assoc. 2001;41:192-9

[4] Johnson J, Bootman L (1995). Drug related morbidity and mortality, *Arch Intern Med 155*, Page 1954 (Table 4)

[5] Kohn LT et al., To err is human: Building a safer health system. Washington D.C. Institute of Medicine 1999

[6] Leape L (2000). Institute of Medicine medical error figures are not exaggerated. *JAMA, 284,* 95-97

[7] Reuters: "Company Strengthens Warning on Schizophrenia Drug – Clozaril", February 21, 2002.

[8] ABC News: "Antidepressants – Suicide Link: Harvard Psychiatrist calls for studies", May 15, 2001

[9] ABC News: "Falling Off Prozac" May 24, 2001.

[10] National Post: "Little Scientific Proof Ritalin Effective, Researchers Discover" Nov 27, 2001.

[11] The Globe and Mail: "Prozac May Trigger Suicide", April 14, 2001

[12] FDA WEBSITE http://www.fda.gov/medwatch/safety.htm

[13] Sharpe CR et al. (2002). The effects of tricyclic antidepressants on breast cancer. *British Journal of Cancer, 86,* 92-97

[14] Cotterchio M et al. (2000). Antidepressant medication use and breast cancer risk. *Am J Epidemiol, 152,* 951-957

[15] Venning G (2000). Antidepressant drugs have previously been shown to be ineffective in mild depression, *Brit Med J, 320,* 311

[16] Van Praag H (1996). Psychiatry and the march of folly? interview with D. Healy in *The Psychopharmacologists*, London: Chapman & Hall (Altman), 367.

[17] Moncrieff J, Are antidepressants overrated? A review of methodological problems in antidepressant trials. *J Nervous & Mental Disease*, 2001, 189, 288-295.

[18] Society Guardian February 13, 2002 http://society.guardian.co.uk/mentalhealth/story/0,8150,649503,00.html

[19] Kirsch I, et al., "Listening to Prozac but Hearing Placebo" APA, Prevention and Treatment, Vol 1,Article 0002a, June 26, 1998

[20] Kirsch I, et al., "The Emperor's New Drugs" APA Prevention and Treatment, Vol 5, Article 23, July 15, 2002

[21] USA Today July 7, 2002 – Study: Antidepressants Barely Better Than Placebo.

[22]APA Press Release July 5, 2002 http://www.apa.org/releases/antidepressants.html.

[23] Fluvoxamine (Faverin): Adverse reaction profile. *Current Problems in Pharmacovigilance*, No 22, May 1988, 1-2. www.socialaudit.org/REFS.html

[24] Palmer JL (2000). Postoperative delirium indicating an adverse drug interaction involving the SSRI, paroxetine, *J Psychopharmacol, 14,* 186-188

[25] Pirmohamed M, Breckenridge AM, Kitteringham NR, Park BK (1998). Adverse drug reactions, *Brit Med J, 316,* 1295-1298.

[26] Preda A. et al., Antidepressant – associated mania and psychosis resulting in psychiatric admissions. J Clin Psychiatry 2001 Jan;62(1):30-3

[27] Warren M. et al., Two case reports of trazodone – induced mania. Am J Psychiatry 1984 Sep;141(9): 1103-4

[28] Sandyk R, Hurwitz MD "Toxic irreversible encephalopathy induced by lithium carbonate and haloperidol. A report of 2 cases.

[29] Hoehn J. et al., "Sudden cardiac death with clozapine and sertraline combination". Ann Pharmacother 2001 Jul-Aug:35(7-8):862-6

[30]Steiner W. et al., Neuroleptic – induced supersensitivity psychosis in patients with bipolar affective disorder. Acta Psychiatr Scand 1990 May;81(5):437-40

[31] Go F.S., Malley E.E., et al., Manic Behaviors associated with fluoxetine in three 12 -18 year – olds with obsessive – compulsive disorder J Child Adolesc Psychopharmacol 1998;8(1):73-80

[32] Yuvarajan R., et al., Mania induced by lithium augmentation. A case report. Br. J Psychiatry 1988 Dec; 153:828-30

Page 8 of 14 Phone: 1-888-TRUEHOPE July 23, 2003

Source: A Report on the use of Psychiatric Medications—Their Safety and Efficacy: Providing a Detailed Meta-Analysis" by *Truehope*, 2003

[33] Suraya Y., et al., Lithium neurotoxicity. Med J Malaysia 2001 Sep;56(3):378-81

[34] Howland R.H., Induction of mania with serotonin reuptake inhibitors. J Clin Psychopharmacol 1996 Dec;16(6):425-7

[35] Dorevitch A., et al., Fluvoxamine – associated manic behavior: a case series. Ann Pharacother 1993 Dec;27(12):1455-7

[36] Tueth M.J., Emergencies caused by side effects of psychiatric medications. Am J. Emerg Med. 1994 Mar;12(2):212-6

[37] Black DW, et al., Depersonalization syndrome induced by fluoxetine. Psychosomatics 1991 Fall;32(4):468-9

[38] Van Scheyen JD., et al., Clomipramine – induced mania in unipolar depression. Arch Gen Psychiatry 1979 May;36(5):560-5

[39] Reiss AL., et al., Carbamazepine – induced mania in two children: case report. J Clin Psychiatry 1984 Jun;45(6):272-4

[40] Hurowitz Gl., et al., Antidepressant – induced rapid cycling: six case reports. J Clin Psychopharmacol 1993 Feb;13(1):52-6

[41] Berk M., et al., Antidepressant induced mania in obsessive compulsive disorder. Eur Neuropsychopharmacol 1996 Mar;6(1):9-11

[42] Henry C., Et al., Antidepressant – induced mania in bipolar patients: identification of risk factors. J Clin Psychiatry 2001 Apr;62(4):249-55

[43] Hall KL, et al., Neuroleptic malignant syndrome due to olanzapine. Psychopharmacol Bull. 2001 summer,35(3):49-54

[44] Berardi D., et al., Clinical risk factors for neuroleptic malignant syndrome. Hum Psychopharmacol. 2002 Mar;17(2):99-102

[45] Viejo LF., et al., Risk factors in neuroleptic malignant syndrome. A case-controlled study. Acta Psychiatr Scand. Jan;107(1):45-9

[46] Frey R., et al., Fatal poisonings with antidepressant drugs and neuroleptics. Analysis of a correlation with prescriptions in Vienna 1991-1997

[47] Fux M., Emergence of depressive symptoms during treatment for panic disorder with specific 5-hydroxytryptophan reuptake inhibitors. Acta Psychiatr Scand. 1993 Oct;88(4);235-7

[48] Aysegul Y., et al., Do Antidepressants Induce Rapid Cycling? A Gender-Specific Association, J Clin Psychiatry 2003;64:814-818

[49] Becker D., et al., Risperidone, but Not Olanzapine, Decreases Bone Mineral Density in Female Premenopausal Schizophrenia Patients. J Clin Psychiatry 2003;64:761-766

[50] Janssen Ortho Warning: TOPAMAX, Reports of Hyperthermia in patients treated with TOPAMAX.

[51] Lantz MS. Serotonin syndrome. A common but often unrecognized psychiatric condition. Geriatrics. 2001 Jan;56(1):52-3

[52] Azaz-Livshits T. Paroxetine associated hepatoxicity: a report of 3 cases and a review of the literature. Pharmacopsychiatry. 2002 May;35(3):112-5

[53]Gandhi T.K. et al., "Adverse Drug Events in Ambulatory Care" NEJM, Vol. 348:1556-1564, April 17, 2003 Number 16.

[54] Reuters: "Prescription Drug Side Effects Hit 1 in 4", April 18, 2003

[55] Schachter B et al. (2001). How efficacious and safe is short-acting methylphenidate for the treatment of Attention–Deficit Disorder in children and adolescents? *CMAJ, 27*, 165.

[56] Ricaurte GA et al. (1984). Further evidence that amphetamines produce long lasting dopamine neurochemical deficits by destroying dopamine nerve fibers. *Brain Res 303*, 359-64

[57] Ricaurte GA (1992). Neurotoxic amphetamine analogues: Effects in monkeys and applications for humans. *Ann NY Acad Sci, 648*, 371-82

[58] Gitlin MJ, Swendsen J, Heller TL, Hammen C (1995). Relapse and impairment in bipolar disorder. *Am J Psychiatry, 152*, 1635-40

[59] Licht RW, Vestergaard P, Rasmussen NA, Jepsen K, Brodersen A, Hansen PE (2001). A lithium clinic for bipolar patients: 2-year outcome of the first 148 patients. *Acta Psychiatr Scand, 104*, 387-90

[60] Fava GA, Bartolucci G, Rafanelli C, Mangelli L (2001). Cognitive-behavioral management of patients with bipolar disorder who relapsed while on lithium prophylaxis. *J Clin Psychiatry, 62*,556-9

[61] Csernansky JG, Mahmoud R, Brenner R (2002). A comparison of risperidone and haloperidol for the prevention of relapse in patients with schizophrenia. *N Engl J Med, 346*, 16-22

Page 9 of 14 Copyright © Truehope Nutritional Support Ltd Phone: 1-888-TRUEHOPE July 23, 2003

Source: A Report on the use of Psychiatric Medications—Their Safety and Efficacy: Providing a Detailed Meta-Analysis" by *Truehope*, 2003

[62] Byrne SE, Rothschild AJ (1998). Loss of antidepressant efficacy during maintenance therapy: possible mechanisms and treatments. *J Clin Psychiatry 59*, 279-288.

[63] Tollefson GD (1993). Adverse drug reactions/interactions in maintenance therapy. *J Clin Psychiatry, 54* (8 Suppl), 48-58.

[64] Stewart JW, Quitkin FM, McGrath PJ, Amsterdam JM, Fava J, Fawcett F, Reimherr J, Rosenbaum C, Beasley, C, Roback, P (1998). Use of pattern analysis to predict differential relapse of remitted patients with major depression during 1 year of treatment with fluoxetine or placebo, *Arch Gen Psychiatry, 55*, 334-443.

[65] Sharma V (2001). Loss of response to antidepressants and subsequent refractoriness: diagnostic issues in a retrospective case series, *J Affective Disorders, 64*, 99-106

[66] Scott-Levine, Newton PA – Based on more than 2.04 billion prescriptions. Year 2000www.rxlist.com

[67] Arana G. et al., Alprazolam- induced mania: two clinical cases. Am J Psychiatry 1985 Mar;142(3):368-9

[68] Reddy J. et al., Alprazolam – Induced Hypomania. Aust N Z J Psychiatry. 1996 Aug;30(4):550-2

[69] Compendium of Pharmaceuticals and Specialties (CPS) Thirty-Fifth Edition (2000) Pages 187-188 Canadian Pharmacists Association.

[70] Health and Welfare Canada, The Effects of Tranquillization: Benzodiazepine Use In Canada, published by authority of The Minister of National Health and Welfare, 1982

[71] Preskorn SH & Denner LJ (1977). Benzodiazepines and withdrawal psychosis. *JAMA, 237*, 36-38

[72] Covi L, Lipman RS, Pattison JH, Derogatis LR, and Uhlenluth E H (1973). Length of treatment with anxiolytic sedatives and response to their sudden withdrawal. *Acta Psychiatrica Scandinavia, 49*, 51-64

[73] Pevnick J S et al. (1978). Abrupt withdrawal from therapeutically administered diazepam, *Archives of General Psychiatry, 35*, 995-998

[74] Petursson H & Lader MH (1981). Withdrawal from long-term benzodiazepine treatment, *Br Med J, 28*, 643-645.

[75] Marks J. *The Benzodiazepines - use, overuse, misuse, abuse*. Lancaster UK: MTP Press, 1978.

[76] DTB (Anon), (1985). Some problems with benzodiazepines, *Drug & Ther Bull, 26*, 11-12.

[77] Benzodiazepine dependence syndromes and syndromes of withdrawal. In Hallstrom C (Ed): *Benzodiazepine Dependence* (Oxford University Press, 1993)

[78] Tyrer et al. (1981). Benzodiazepine withdrawal symptoms and propranolol, The Lancet, 520-522

[79] Greenblatt DJ et al. (1978). Dependence, tolerance, and addiction to benzodiazepines: Clinical and pharmacokinetic considerations. *Drug Metabolism Reviews, 8*, 13-28

[80] Perault MC, Favreliere S, Minet P, Remblier C (2000). Benzodiazepines and pregnancy, *Therapie*, 55, 587-95

[81] Longo L.P., Johnson B, Addiction: Part 1. Benzodiazepines-Side Effects, Abuse Risk and Alternatives. American Family Physician. April 1, 2000

[82] Finnegan L., United Nations Report, Jan 1, 1979 "Pathophysiological and behavioural effects of the transplacenta neonates of narcotic dependent mothers"

[83] Harlow BL, Cramer DW (1995). Self reported use of antidepressants or benzodiazepine tranquilizers and risk of epithelial ovarian cancers: Evidence from two combined controlled studies (Massachusetts, United States). *Cancer Causes Control, 6*, 130-134

[84] Dalton et al. (2000). Antidepressant medications and risk for cancer. *Epidemiology 11*, 171-176

[85] Health and Welfare Canada, The Effects of Tranquillization: Benzodiazepine Use In Canada, published by authority of The Minister of National Health and Welfare, 1982 Page 49

[86] Health and Welfare Canada, The Effects of Tranquillization: Benzodiazepine Use In Canada, published by authority of The Minister of National Health and Welfare, 1982

[87] H Ashton, Benzodiazepines, "How They Work and How to Withdraw". University of Newcastle, Jan 2000

[88] Lawlor DA et al. (2000). Re: "antidepressant medication use and breast cancer risk". Am J Epidemiol 152: 1105.

[89] IMS Health Canada as reported in the National Post & Globe and Mail - March 29, 2001

[90] Tonks A (2002). Withdrawal from paroxetine can be severe, warns FDA. *BMJ 324*, 260

Page 10 of 14 Phone: 1-888-TRUEHOPE July 23, 2003

Source: A Report on the use of Psychiatric Medications—Their Safety and Efficacy: Providing a Detailed Meta-Analysis" by *Truehope*, 2003

[91] FDA Website:
www.fda.gov/medwatch/safety/2001/dec01.htm#paxil

[92] Hirose S (2001). Restlessness related to SSRI withdrawal, *Psychiatry Clin Neurosci 55*, :79-80

[93] Pinzani V et al. (2000). Venlafaxine withdrawal syndrome: report of six cases and review of the literature, *Rev Med Interne 21*, 282-4

[94] Agelink MW, Zitselsberger A, Kleiser E (1997). Withdrawal symptoms after discontinuation of venlafaxine, *Am J Psychiatry*, *154*, 1473-1474.

[95] Amsden GW, Georgian F (1996). Orthostatic hypotension induced by sertraline withdrawal, *Pharmacotherapy*, *16*, 684-686.

[96] Anderson IM, Tomenson BM (1995).Treatment discontinuation with selective serotonin reuptake inhibitors compared with tricyclic anti-depressants: a meta-analysis. *Brit Med J*, *310*, 1433-8.

[97] Antonuccio DO, Danton WG, DeNelsky GY, Greenberg RP, Gordon JS (1999). Raising Questions about Antidepressants, *Psychotherapy and Psychosomatics*, *68*, 3-14.

[98] Bakker A (1999). Severe withdrawal symptoms with fever upon stopping paroxetine (letter, in Dutch), *Ned Tijdschr Geneeskd*, *143*, 1795, discussion 1795-6.

[99] DK Arya, Withdrawal after discontinuation of paroxetine (letter), *Aust NZ J Psychiatry*, October 1996, 30 (5), 702

[100] Baldessarini RJ, Viguera AC, Tondo L (1999). Discontinuing psychotropic agents (comment on Healy and Tranter, 1999) *J Psychopharmacol*, *13*, 292-293.

[101] Barr LC, Goodman WK, Price LH (1994). Physical symptoms associated with paroxetine discontinuation (letter). *Am J Psychiatry*, *151*, 289.

[102] Belloeuf L, Le Jeunne C, Hugues,FC (2000). Paroxetine withdrawal syndrome [Article in French], *Ann Med Interne (Paris) 151* Suppl A,A52-3.

[103] Benazzi F (1996). Venlafaxine withdrawal symptoms, *Can J Psychiatry*, *41*, 487.

[104] Benazzi F (1998). SSRI discontinuation syndrome related to fluvoxamine, *J Psychiatry & Neuroscience*, *23*, 94

[105] Benazzi F (1998). Nefazodone withdrawal symptoms, *Can J Psychiatry*, *43*, 194-195

[106] Benazzi F. (1998). Sertraline discontinuation syndrome presenting with severe depression and compulsions, *Biol Psychiatry*, *43*, 929-930

[107] Black DW, Wesner R, Gabel J (1993). The abrupt discontinuation of fluvoxamine in patients with panic disorder. *J Clin Psychiatry*, *54*, 146-9

[108] Black K, Shea C, Dursun S, Kutcher S (2000). Selective serotonin reuptake inhibitor discontinuation syndrome: proposed diagnostic criteria, *J Psychiatry Neuroscience*, *25*, 255-261.

[109] Bloch M, Stager SV, Braun AR, Rubinow DR (1995). Severe psychiatric symptoms associated with paroxetine withdrawal. *Lancet*, *346*, 57.

[110] Boyd IW (1998). Venlafaxine withdrawal reactions, *Med J Aust*, *169*, 91-92

[111] Bryois C, Rubin C, Zbinden JD, BaumannP (1998). [Withdrawal syndrome caused by selective serotonin reuptake inhibitors: apropos of a case]. In German. *Schweiz Rundsch Med Prax*, *87*, 345-348.

[112] Haddad P (1998). The SSRI discontinuation syndrome, *J Psychopharmacology*, *12*, 305-313.

[113] Haddad P, Anderson I (1999). Antidepressants aren't addictive: clinicians have depended on them for years (comment on Healy and Tranter, 1999). *J Psychopharmacol*, *13*, 291-298.

[114] Huffstutler SY (1998). Management of antidepressant withdrawal reactions, *J Am Acad Nurse Pract*, *10*, 161-165.

[115] Pacheco L, Malo P, Aragues E, Etxebeste M (1996). More cases of paroxetine withdrawal syndrome, *Brit J Psychiatry*, *169*, 384.

[116] Parker G, Blennerhassett J (1998). Withdrawal reactions associated with venlafaxine. *Aust N Z J Psychiatry*, *32*, 291-4.

[117] Pollock BG (1998). Discontinuation symptoms and SSRIs (letter), *J Clin Psychiatry*, *59*, 535-537.

[118] A comparison of the post-marketing safety of four selective serotonin reuptake inhibitors including the investigation of symptoms occurring on withdrawal, *Br J Clin Pharmacol*, 1996, 42, 757-763.

[119] Pyke RE (1995). Paroxetine withdrawal syndrome. *Am J Psychiatry*, *152*,149-50.

Page 11 of 14 Phone: 1-888-TRUEHOPE July 23, 2003

Source: A Report on the use of Psychiatric Medications—Their Safety and Efficacy: Providing a Detailed Meta-Analysis" by *Truehope*, 2003

[120] Reeves RR, Pinkofsky LR (1996). Lhermitte's Sign in paroxetine withdrawal, *J Clin Psychopharmacol*, *16*, 411-412.

[121] Nathan RG, Kinney JL (1985). Long-Term Dependence on Antidepressants (letter), *Am J Psychiatry*, *142*, 524

[122] Zajecka J, Tracy KA, Mitchell S (1997) Discontinuation symptoms after treatment with serotonin reuptake inhibitors: a literature review, *J Clin Psychiatry*, *58*, 291-297.

[123] Young A, Haddad P (2000). Discontinuation symptoms and psychotropic drugs (letter), *The Lancet*, *355*, 1184

[124] Wolfe RM (August 1997). Antidepressant withdrawal reactions, *American Family Physician*, *56* (2).

[125] Young AH, Currie A (1997). Physicians' knowledge of antidepressant withdrawal effects: a survey, *J Clin Psychiatry*, *58* (suppl 7), 28-30.

[126] Wincor MZ (1998). Withdrawal symptoms associated with abrupt discontinuation of SSRIs, *J Am Pharm Assoc (Wash)*, *38*, 500-501.

[127] Walker-Kinnear M, McNaughton S (1997). Paroxetine discontinuation syndrome in association with sertindole therapy, *Brit J Psychiatry*, *170*, 389.

[128] Wade GS (2000). Controlled withdrawal for psychotropic drugs, *Lancet*, *355*, 1822-1823.

[129] Vergouwen AC, Kuipers T (1999). Severe withdrawal symptoms with fever upon stopping paroxetine (letter, in Dutch), *Ned Tijdschr Geneeskd*, *143*, 1794-5, discussion 1795-6.

[130] Health Canada, Paxil Warning, July 15, 2003 http://www.hc-sc.gc.ca/hpfb-dgpsa/tpd-dpt/paxil_pa_e.html

[131] Benazzi F., Pyschotic Mania in Bipolar 2 - Depression Related to Sertraline Discontinuation. Canadian Psychiatric Association, August 2002,

[132] Szabadi E (1992). Fluvoxamine withdrawal syndrome. *Brit J Psychiatry*, *160*, 283-284.

[133] Strickland GM, Hough DW (2000). Unilateral facial numbness and visual blurring associated with paroxetine discontinuation (letter), *J Clin Psychopharmacol*, *20*, 271-272

[134] BBC News – Anti Depressant Safety Reviewed. Jan 8, 2003. http://news.bbc.co.uk/1/hi/health/2635181.stm

[135] Stahl MM, Lindquist M, Pettersson M, Edwards IR, Sanderson JH, Taylor NF, Fletcher AP, Schou JS. Withdrawal reactions with selective serotonin reuptake inhibitors (SSRIs) as reported to the WHO system, *Eur J Clin Pharmacol*, *53*, 163-169

[136] BBC News Patients may sue over anti-depressant. http://news.bbc.co.uk/1/hi/health/2041430.stm

[137] Rosenstock HA (1996). Sertraline withdrawal in two brothers: a case report. *Int Clin Psychopharmacol*, *11*, 58-9.

[138] Rosenbaum JF, Fava M, Hoog S L, Ascroft R C, Krebs W B (1998). Selective serotonin reuptake inhibitor discontinuation syndrome: A randomised clinical trial, *Biol Psychiatry*, *44*, 77-87.

[139] Rojas-Fernandez C, Gordon J (1998). Selective serotonin reuptake inhibitor discontinuation syndrome: putative mechanisms and prevention strategies (letter), *Can J Psychiatry*, *43*, 523-524.

[140] Menecier P, Menecier-Ossia L, Bern P (1997). Fluoxetine dependence and tolerance. Apropos of a case (English abstract, French text), *Encephale*, *23*, 400-401.

[141] Mathew T (Chair, ADRAC), SSRIs and withdrawal syndrome, Neonatal Disorders. *Australian Adverse Drug Reactions Bulletin*, 15, 1, November 1996, 2.

[142] Maixner SM, Greden JF (1998). Extended antidepressant maintenance and discontinuation syndromes. *Depress Anxiety*, *8* Suppl 1, 43-53

[143] BBC News Prozac may encourage suicide. May 22, 2003 http://news.bbc.co.uk/1/hi/health/758763.stm

[144] Louie AK, Lannon RA, Ajari L J (1994). Withdrawal reaction after sertraline discontinuation (letter). *Am J Psychiatry*, *151*, 450-1.

[145] Macbeth R, Rajagopalan M (1998). Venlafaxine withdrawal syndrome, *Aust NZ J Med*, *28*, 218.

[146] Louie AK, et al., (1998) Venlafaxine withdrawal reactions. Am J Psychiatry, 151, 450-1

[147] BBC News Antidepressant can be addictive. http://news.bbc.co.uk/1/hi/programmes/panorama/2321545.stm

[148] Buckley NA Fatal toxicity of serotoninergic and

  July 23, 2003

Source: A Report on the use of Psychiatric Medications—Their Safety and Efficacy: Providing a Detailed Meta-Analysis" by *Truehope*, 2003

other antidepressant drugs: analysis of United Kingdom mortality data *BMJ* 2002;325:1332-1333 Dec 7, 2002

[149] Johnson H, Bouman WP, Lawton J (1998). Withdrawal reaction associated with venlafaxine, *Brit Med J, 317*, 787.

[150] Lehrman N. The SSRI Conference in Philadelphia, Oct 24, 2003

[151] ABC News May 24, 2001 "Falling Off Prozac" http://abcnews.go.com/sections/living/DailyNews/ssri000524.html

[152] Yapp P, Ilett KF, Kristensen J H, Hackett LP, Paech MJ (2000). Drowsiness and poor feeding in breast-fed infant: association with nefazodone and its metabolites, *Ann Pharmacocother, 34*, 1269-1272

[153] Nijhuis IJ, Kok-Van Rooij GW, Bosschaart AN (2001). Withdrawal reactions of a premature neonate after maternal paroxetine (letter), *Arch Dis Child Fetal Neonatal Ed, 84,* F77-78

[154] Stiskal JA, Kulin N, Koren G, Ho T, Ito S (2001). Neonatal paroxetine withdrawal syndrome (short report of four cases), *Arch Dis Child Fetal Neonatal Ed, 84*, F134-F135. See comment (and author's response) by Ibister et al. in *Arch Dis Child Fetal Ed*, 2001, Sept, 85(2), F147-148

[155] Spencer, MJ (1993). Fluoxetine Hydrochloride (Prozac) Toxicity in a Neonate. *Pediatrics,* 92, 721-2.

[156] Mohan CG, Moore JJ (2000). Fluoxetine toxicity in a preterm infant, *J Perinatol, 20,* 445-446.

[157] Nordeng H., et al., Neonatal withdrawal syndrome after in utero exposure to selective serotonin reuptake inhibitors. Acta Paediatr. 2001 Mar;90(3):288-91

[158] Bertolin G., et al., Akathisia due to risperidone withdrawal: two clinical cases. Actas Esp Psiquiatr 2002 May-Jun;30(3):195-7

[159] Van Harten PN. Drug-induced akathisia. Ned Geneeskd 2002 Jan 19;146(3):110-4

[160] Chong SA., et al., Clinical characteristics and associated factors in antipsychotic-induced akathisia of Asian patients with schizophrenia. Schizophr Res 2003 Jan 1;59(1):67-71

[161] Brune M, The incidence of akathisia in bipolar affective disorder treated with neuroleptics – a preliminary report. J Affect Disord 1999 May;53(2):175-7

[162] Lima AR., et al., Anticholinergics for neuroleptic – induced acute akakthisia. Cochrane database Syst Rev. 2002;(3):CD003727

[163] Kim JH., et al., Subjective emotional experience and cognitive impairment in drug-induced akathisia. Comp Psychiarty 2002 Nov-Dec; 43(6):456-62

[164] Lipinski JF, Mallya G, Zimmerman P, Pope HG (1989). Fluoxetine-induced akathisia: Clinical and theoretical implications. *Journal of Clinical Psychiatry, 59*, 339-42.

[165] Fava M., et al., Suicidality and fluoxetine: is there a relationship? J Clin Psychiatry. 1991 Mar;52(3):108-11.

[166] Leong GB., et al., Neuroleptic – induced akathisia and violence: a review. J forensic Sci 2003 Jan; 48(1):187-9

[167] Teicher MH., et al., Antidepressant drugs and the emergence of suicidal tendencies. Drug Saf. 1993 Mar;8(3):186-212

[168] Kasantikul D., Drug induced akathisia and suicidal tendencies in psychotic patients. J Med Assoc Thai. 1998 jul;81(7):551-4.

[169] Healy D., Lines of evidence on the risks of suicide with selective serotonin reuptake inhibitors. Psychother Psychosom. 2003 Mar- apr;72(2):71- 9

[170] Anderson GM., et al., Serotonin and suicidality: the impact of fluoxetine administration. Acute neurobiological effects. Isr J Psychiatry Relat Sci. 1995;32(1):344-50

[171] Lancon C., et al., Fluoxetine, akathisia, and suicide. Encephale. 1997 May-June;23(3):218-23

[172] Hamilton MS, Opler LA (1992). Akathisia, suicidality, and fluoxetine. *Journal of Clinical Psychiatry, 53,* 401-6

[173] Tueth M.J., Akathisia causing suicide attempts in patients taking fluoxetine (prozac) J Emerg Med. 1993 May-Jun;11(3):336-7

[174] Rothschild AJ., et al., Re-exposure to fluozetine after serious suicide attempts by three patients: the role of akathisia. J clin Psychiatry. 1991 Dec;52(12):491-3

[175] Cem Atbasoglu, et al., The relationship of akathisia with suicidality and depersonalization among patients with schizophrenia. J Neuropsychiatry clin Neurosci 2001 Summer; 13(3):336-41

[176] Tueth MJ., Revisiting fluoxetine (Prozac) and suicidal preoccupations. J. Emerg Med. 1994 Sep-Oct;12(5):685-7

Page 13 of 14 Copyright © Truehope Nutritional Support Ltd Phone: 1-888-TRUEHOPE July 23, 2003

Source: A Report on the use of Psychiatric Medications—Their Safety and Efficacy: Providing a Detailed Meta-Analysis" by *Truehope*, 2003

[177] King RA., Serotonin and suicidality: the impact of acute fluoxetine administration: Serotonin and suicide. Isr J Psychiatry Relat Sci. 1994;31(4):271-9

[178] Drake RE, Ehrlich J (1985). Suicide attempts associated with akathisia, *American Journal of Psychiatry*, 499-501.

[179] Hindmarch I, Kimber S, Cockle SM (2000). Abrupt and brief discontinuation of antidepressant treatment: effects on cognitive function and psychomotor performance, *Int Clin Psychopharmacol, 15*, 305-18

[180] Zubenko G. et al., Antidepressant – related akathisia. J Clin Psychopharmacol 1987 Aug; 7(4):254-7

[181] U.K. Department of Health , June 10, 2003 http://www.info.doh.gov.uk/doh/intpress.nsf/page/2003-0223?OpenDocument

[182] Press Release June 10, 2003, Prime Ministers Office , #10 Downing Street, London, England

[183] Teicher MH, Glod C & Cole JO (1990). Emergence of intense suicidal preoccupation during fluoxetine treatment, *American Journal of Psychiatry, 147*, 207-10.

[184] King RA, Riddle MA, Chappell PB, Hardin MT, Anderson GM, Lombroso P & Scahill L (1991). Emergence of self-destructive phenomena in children and adolescents during fluoxetine treatment, *Journal of the American Academy of Child and Adolescent Psychiatry, 30*, 179.

[185] www.rxlist.com Listed side effects.

[186] Wehr TA, Goodwin FK (1979). Rapid cycling in manic-depressives induced by tricyclic antidepressants, *Arch Gen Psychiatry, 36*, 555-9

[187] Nelson JC, et al (1979). Exacerbation of psychosis by tricyclic antidepressants in delusional depression., *Am J Psychiatry, 136*, 574-6

[188] Zis AP et al. (1979). Tricyclic-induced mania and MHPG excretion. *Psychiatry Res, 1*, 93-9

[189] www.rxlist.com Listed side effects

[190] Huang CL., et al., Zolpidem-induced distortion in visual perception. Ann Pharmacother, 37(5):683-6 2003

[191] Galder R., et al., Zolpidem: the risk of tolerance and dependence according to case reports, systematic studies and recent molecularbiological data. Fortschr Neurol Psychiatr, 69(12):592-6 2001

[192] Aragona M., Abuse, dependence, and epileptic seizures after Zolpidem withdrawal, a review and case report. Clin Neuropharmacol, 23(5):281-3, 2003

[193] Vartzopoulos D. Dependence on Zolpidem in high dose. Int Clin Psychopharmacol, 15(3): 181-2 2000

[194] Freudenreich O., Zolpidem-related delirium: a case report. J Clin Psychiary, 61(6):449-50 2000

[195] Lennkh C et al. (1998). Occurrence of trazodone – induced delirium. *Int clin Psychopharmacol, 13*, 225-8

[196] Jabeen S (1991). Trazodone – induced transient hypomanic symptoms and their management. *Br J Psychiatry, 158*, 275-8

[197] Knobler HY et al. (1986). Trazadone-induced mania. *Br J Psychiatry, 149*, 787-9

[198] Pae CU., et al., Association of lose dose trazodone treatment with aggravated angle glaucoma. Psychiatry Clin Neurosci, 57(1): 127-8 2003

[199] Rettman KS., et al., Hepatoxicity after short-term trazodone therapy. Ann Pharmacother, 35(12): 1559-61 2002

[200] Patterson DE., et al., Speech dysfunction due to trazodone – fluoxetine combination in traumatic brain injury. Taylor and Francis Health Sciences Vol 11, Number 4/ Apr 1, 1997

Page 14 of 14 Phone: 1-888-TRUEHOPE July 23, 2003

Source: A Report on the use of Psychiatric Medications—Their Safety and Efficacy: Providing a Detailed Meta-Analysis" by *Truehope*, 2003

from the TREHOPE Website

Research

Our first goal at TrueHope Institute is to raise funds for additional scientific studies in the area of nutritional supplementation for the treatment of mental illnesses. Many advances have already been made in this new and exciting area of study and we are dedicated to supporting this ongoing effort.

In 1997, Dr. Bonnie J. Kaplan, a behavioral research scientist with the University of Calgary began studying a nutrient formulation called EMPowerplus that was specifically designed to support the central nervous system. After years of extensive study, she made the following statement: "If substantiated in controlled trials, the normalization of the mentally ill via nutrient supplementation would be the most significant breakthrough in the field of mental illness since the beginning of time."

Dr. Kaplan has been joined by, Dr. Bryan Kolb, published author and leader in the study of brain cell regeneration, Dr. Charles Popper, a well published Harvard University researcher, Dr. Miles Simmons, clinical psychologist and published researcher and others in spearheading research that has been published in refereed medical journals. Dr. Kaplan and her colleagues have shared their published studies and independent clinical trial results with medical professionals around the world and continue to be directly involved with researching the effects of EMPowerplus. There is a groundswell of support for their work and the inroads they are making in this revolutionary treatment of mental illness.

We are assisting in the expansion of the research effort but need considerable financial support to accomplish this task. Performing randomized controlled trials and other types of research studies cost approximately two million dollars per study. Our goal is to sponsor several studies to add to and complete the body of evidence that could change the face of mental illness forever.

Published Research on EMPowerplus

1. Improved Mood and Behavior During Treatment with a Mineral-Vitamin Supplement: An Open-Label Case Series of Children *The Journal of Child and Adolescent Psychopharmacology* Volume 14, Number 1, 2004

2. Nutritional Approach to Bipolar Disorder *The Journal of Clinical Psychiatry* 64:3, March 2003

3. Treatment of Mood Lability and Explosive Rage With Minerals and Vitamins: Two Case Studies in Children *The Journal of Child and Adolescent Psychopharmacology* Volume 12, Number 3, 2002

4. Effective Mood Stabilization With a Chelated Mineral Supplement: An Open-label Trial in Bipolar Disorder *The Journal of Clinical Psychiatry* December 6, 2001 Edition

5. Letter to the Editor, Dr. Charles Popper Harvard Mclean Hospital *The Journal of Clinical Psychiatry* December 6, 2001 Edition

Summaries of Published Research

The idea that effective mood stabilization can be achieved through the use of vitamins, trace elements and amino acids is advanced in a study conducted by a team of researchers from the University of Calgary, Alberta's Faculty of Medicine. The results of the ongoing study are published in the latest edition of the Journal of Clinical Psychiatry. The same edition also contains a commentary by Dr. Charles Popper, MD, a psychopharmacologist from Harvard University. Dr. Popper also has patients in his clinical practice who are taking the nutritional supplement.

The subject of the research is Empowerplus, a nutritional supplement formulated by the Synergy Group of Canada Inc.

In an Abstract entitled: 'Effective Mood Stabilization with a Chelated Mineral Supplement: An Open-Label Trial in Bipolar Disorder," the study's author, Bonnie J. Kaplan, PhD, explains the therapeutic benefit of the use of a nutritional supplement to treat bipolar disorder. Dr. Kaplan is a research psychologist who studies mood and behavioral disorders and a Professor in the Department of Pediatrics, University of Calgary. She is also Director of the Behavioral Research Unit at the Alberta Children's Hospital.

Dr. Kaplan and colleagues at the University of Calgary, along with Dr. Richard C. Ferre (Salt Lake City , Utah), conducted a 6-month open-label trial with 14 patients diagnosed with bipolar disorder, aged 19–46 years, who were taking an average of 2.7 psychotropic medications each at study entry.

The intervention is a broad-based nutritional supplement (Empowerplus) of dietary nutrients; primarily trace minerals and vitamins, administered in high doses. The supplement has 36 ingredients, 33 of which are natural dietary minerals and vitamins including calcium, iron, magnesium, zinc, copper, potassium, and various vitamins such as A, C, D, E, and several B vitamins.

At study entry and periodically thereafter, patients were assessed with the Hamilton-Depression Scale (Ham-D), Brief Psychiatric Rating Scale (BPRS), and the Young Mania Rating Scale (YMRS). The results of the study demonstrated symptom reductions ranging from 55% to 66% on the outcome measures, while the need for psychotropic medications decreased by more than 50%.

Dr. Kaplan wrote about the outcomes: "The effect size for the intervention was large (>.8) for each measure and the number of psychotropic medications decreased significantly to a mean of 1.0 (from 2.7). In some cases, the supplement has replaced psychotropic medications and the patients have remained well. Side effects (i.e., nausea) have been infrequent, minor, and transitory."

Based on these findings, Dr. Kaplan concludes: "Some cases of bipolar illness may be ameliorated by nutritional supplementation."

"We have seen significant improvement in the mental health of the participants taking part in this study," says Kaplan. "Our early findings certainly warrant further exploration of this supplement as a new treatment for mood and temper problems. In fact, a randomized, placebo-controlled trial in adults with bipolar I disorder is currently underway, two more have been funded, and we have completed some open trials in children," she added.

In an article that accompanied the research, Dr. Kaplan provided an overview of the study's methodology, as well as a discussion of the various factors relevant to the impact of the nutritional supplement on behavior. She made the following points:

- "Solid scientific research shows that many dietary nutrients, including minerals and vitamins, are essential for normal brain function… Less is known about the role of trace elements but there is considerable evidence that these too may be essential for normal brain function. Zinc provides a good example…"
- "The evidence supporting the importance of minerals and vitamins in central nervous system functioning provided some scientific support for our interest in studying a supplement that is gaining considerable clinical attention in Canada and in many areas of the United States. Described herein are the data collected in open trials of the first, consecutive and unselected 11 cases of bipolar disorder in adults evaluated on this supplement and followed for at least six months, testing the hypothesis that a broad-based nutritional supplement that emphasizes trace minerals would help stabilize mood."
- "We have been exploring the possible clinical benefit of a broad-based nutritional supplement consisting of 36 items, primarily minerals. The data reported here provide the first, preliminary scientific validation of the supplement's efficacy, and suggest that further research is warranted. "
- "Although much additional research is needed…our preliminary data and the general clinical experience of psychiatrists who are monitoring patients in our trials indicate that the supplement has a beneficial psychotropic effect and is not acting in only an adjunctive manner."

- "No problematic adverse effects were encountered from the nutrient supplement. Patients generally reported a subjective sense of improved well being when taking the supplement, and several patients described this well-being as feeling more normal than what they had experienced with psychotropic medication. "
- "Regardless of the mechanisms involved, the findings reported here suggest that the amelioration of mood instability with broad spectrum nutritional interventions warrants further exploration."

David Hardy and Tony Stephan responded to the study results: "This study is an important step in the evolution of our efforts to help the mentally ill. While we have seen similar results with the participants in our open-label series, we knew it was crucial to the supplement's wider legitimacy to have its performance measured and scrutinized in a scientific setting. We are grateful to the University of Calgary and to Dr. Popper for taking the time to study the supplement's impact on the mentally ill. The decision to research the supplement was entirely theirs and the beneficiaries of this work will be the mentally ill."

The Alberta Children's Hospital Foundation and the Alberta Science and Research Authority supported this study.

Letter to the Editor—Dr. Charles Popper

Journal of Clinical Psychiatry Articles

December 6, 2001 Edition

In his commentary on Dr. Kaplan's research titled, Effective Mood Stabilization With a Chelated Mineral Supplement: An Open-label Trial in Bipolar Disorder, Dr. Charles Popper shared his observations from his clinical practice:

"My interest in this nutrient mixture was initially sparked by a case in my clinical practice. A 10-year-old with bipolar disorder was referred for treatment of severe temper tantrums, which had lasted for two to four hours daily for four months. The well-nourished child had no prior psychiatric history or treatment. After 2 days on the nutrients, his tantrums showed significant improvement, with the father-psychiatrist reporting a "complete" absence of outbursts or even irritability at 5 days. After 2 weeks, the available supply of the nutrient supplement was exhausted, and tantrums returned within 48 hours. A similar supplement, containing most of the same ingredients, was then started and produced a moderate improvement, which parents and teachers estimated as 60% of the original effect. When restarted on the original formula, the symptoms were judged to have again responded completely. This naturalistic A-B-A-C-B trial caught my attention because of the full stabilization without psychiatric medications and the absence of observed adverse effects."

"I proceeded to cautiously conduct additional trials of the Hardy-Stephan nutrient supplement. Among 22 patients who clinically met criteria for bipolar disorder, 19 cases showed what I judged to be a positive response (2 mild, 7 moderate, 10 marked improvement). Among the 15 drug-treated patients, 11 patients have been stable for 6–9 months without psychiatric medications. These observations are consistent with Kaplan's open-label findings..."

The fact that Dr. Popper's results were consistent with Dr. Kaplan's is indeed encouraging news, particularly since his symptom reduction rate was 86%, with a significant percentage of drug-treated patients (73%) stable, without psychiatric medications.

Dr. Popper also calls for more study into 'nutrition-behavior' reactions. "Even allowing for the usual overestimation of effects in open-label series, these preliminary findings raise interesting questions about nutrition-behavior interactions. Kaplan's open-label report justifies her now on-going controlled study, whose outcome appropriately precedes pursuing questions of mechanism of action and parsimony."

"(My) observations are consistent with Kaplan's open-label findings, but leave open questions of safety. Even though it contains only "natural" ingredients and is not under FDA purview, the Hardy-Stephan nutrient supplement should be examined in controlled empirical research—just as new pharmacological agents are—to properly assess adverse effects and potential risks. Psychiatrists do not normally think of vitamins or minerals as modifiers of the effects of psychiatric medications, but the early anecdotal experience with this nutrient supplement suggests that there may be strong micronutrient-medication interactions. This mineral-vitamin supplement seems to generally potentate the clinical properties of psychiatric drugs. Most patients in Kaplan's study could be managed with less medication after the nutrient supplement was added" he wrote.

Dr. Popper also signaled the need for more study into 'transitioning' patients from medications to micronutrients. "In my observations, transitioning patients from medications to micronutrients is exceedingly tricky to manage. Introducing micronutrients too quickly can increase the adverse effects of medications, including agitation, while withdrawing psychiatric medications too quickly can result in symptom exacerbation. Often, both increased adverse effects and symptom resurgence are seen at once. Much more data is needed about how to "transition" patients who are currently taking psychiatric medications."

Synergy welcomed these observations: "Based on our knowledge and experience we fully concur with Dr. Popper's cautionary note. As the nutritional supplement normalizes the brain's chemistry, it is critical that clinicians and their patients be aware of these interactions. That is why we consistently urge participants to work with their clinicians in order to ensure safe and effective monitoring. We strongly recommend that those desiring to reduce or eliminate psychotropic medications be under competent medical supervision," they said.

In closing his article, Dr. Popper said: "If Kaplan's preliminary findings are confirmed in controlled research, and if safety studies are favorable, what then? What if some psychiatric patients could be treated with inexpensive vitamins and minerals rather than expensive patented pharmaceuticals? Or if some doses of psychiatric drugs could be reduced by the concurrent use of nutrients? The economic implications, for individual patients and for the pharmaceutical industry, are difficult to overlook. For now, micronutrient treatments and other nutritional approaches remain in a very early scientific stage of investigation. Depending on how this line of research develops, clinicians and researchers may need to re-think the traditional bias against nutritional supplementation as a potential treatment for major psychiatric disorders."

4

Phony Food That Makes Us Sick

by Helke Ferrie

Truly, the Earth shall yet become a house of healing!"

—F. NIETZSCHE,
Thus Spake Zarathustra, 1885

The World Debates the Meaning of *No!*

Bill C-51 is intended to amend the Food and Drugs Act and, therefore, addresses not only the issues of pharmaceutical drugs and natural health products, but also the "modernization" of food safety. Making our food both safe and nutritious would, of course, require as mandatory that it not contain antibiotics, hormones, pesticides, genetically engineered products, and that food producing animals would not be fed rendered slaughterhouse waste. These "Five Pillars of Food Safety," as Dr. Shiv Chopra calls them, are actually the bare minimum of what is required to build a healthy population. The finer points of soil rehabilitation and agricultural techniques that cooperate with nature instead of strip-mine it, are yet another issue all together. First things first—we are in the midst of an emergency requiring our full attention; we might have to leave the finer points for the second half of the century.

Bill C-51 does not show any evidence of working towards this bare minimum of what is needed to establish food safety. It is the absence of any reference to food safety issues that makes the bill even more pernicious. Indeed, the word safety is conveniently not even defined or elaborated upon—as if drug or NHP safety is understood in the same way by one and all. What Health Canada under the administration of the last four prime ministers has shown by its actions as being considered safe has so far been mostly criminal negligence.

Food safety is the elephant in the room the government tries to ignore, even though everybody else in the whole wide world is gawking at its enormity. Wild and outright silly, yet dangerous rhetoric, which is the verbiage of bills C-51 and C-52, is not going to divert people's attention from that immense elephant.

There isn't even a hint at defining food safety and quality in these scientifically validated terms. In fact, we now have to fight for our right to decent food, just as so many other countries have done. The very first thing to do is to throw out both C-51 and C-52—not just amend them, because they are Codex-cloned pig's ears and beyond all hope of becoming a silk purse.

These days, most of us feel a sense of dread and embarrassment when we find out, from time to time, what our government has done on the international stage. Being a Canadian is a bit like being the parent of a teenager who is into drugs. When the telephone rings you hope and pray it's not the police again. Well, the feds did it again, and here is where and how. The why is as mysterious as the inner workings of the minds of one's juvenile delinquent kid.

Most people are familiar with the existence of the Intergovernmental Panel on Climate Change; its reports are not something purely academic, but attention must be paid to them by the entire family of nations. Discussion, debate, dissenting views, endorsements are all part of the process these reports set in motion—but you can't ignore the process.

There is a parallel organization of this type, also convened by the United Nations, and it is devoted to agriculture. It is called the International Assessment of Agricultural Science and Technology Development (IAASTD). The purpose of its four-year $10 million project is to do for hunger and poverty what the Intergovernmental Panel on Climate Change is mandated to do for global warming. From

April 7 to 12, 2008, representatives of the governments of 63 countries gathered in Johannesburg, South Africa, to debate the future of agriculture on the basis of IAASTD's first report; it was the result of three years' work by hundreds of scientist who wrote it. All those scientists were chosen by the 63 governments involved. At this meeting in April, 60 countries endorsed the report—only three refused to do so, and in fact walked out of the meeting.

Those three countries were Canada, the US and Australia.

Not only did these three countries refuse to accept their own, hand-picked scientist' report, they also ignored the demand of their own people.

The reason given was that the report was "unbalanced and one-sided," even though these countries had sent only those scientists in whom they themselves had placed perfect trust. Ah! Integrity is a treacherous quality! Governments can pick scientists, but they can't (always) make them lie. Faced with the evidence of world agriculture, they marched to the drummer of empirical science instead of the din of government policy.

The report concluded that "the ecological footprint of industrial agriculture is already too large to be ignored." The writer for *Gene Ethics*, observed on June 5, 2008, that this report also makes it clear that "the agriculture of the future is one that works with nature and the people—not against them."

The IAASTD report specifically points out that "genetically engineered crops are highly controversial and will not play a substantial role in addressing the key problems of climate change, biodiversity loss, hunger, and poverty."

From now on, the conclusions of the IAASTD report will be a "key reference point for the future of agriculture and impact UN and World Bank projects around the world." Since this report promotes the trend away from genetically engineered crops towards truly sustainable techniques, Canada, the US, and Australia have once again shown that they simply do not understand the meaning of No! All three are ignoring their own people and the IAASTD report's recommendation that "governments should recognize consumer preference with respect to GE crops, protect farmers' seed rights, and ensure that no cross contamination takes place."

A month earlier, Monsanto suffered a landmark defeat in the courts when it had to agree on March 19, 2008, to pay all the clean-up costs of the Roundup ready canola that contaminated Percy Schmeiser's fields. This sets an important precedent because it is now legally established that patented plants can be potentially trespassers and when they become contaminants must be treated like a pollutant. This decision will also ensure that all those farmers currently threatened by Monsanto's legal actions for having GE seeds drift into their non-GE fields, will have their own, natural, crops protected.

Back in the 1990s, without his knowledge, Schmeiser's fields had been contaminated with Monsanto's GE canola for which Monsanto sued him on the grounds of patent infringement. Schmeiser was forced to destroy all his own saved seed, which he had developed through natural breeding methods over four decades, because it might contain drift GE seeds which he didn't "own," of course. In the US and elsewhere farmers experienced what Schmeiser had and were totally ruined by Monsanto's aggressive actions and exploitation of antiquated patent laws. In 2004 Schmeiser lost his case in the Supreme Court of Canada because current patent law is unable to rule upon human inventions that replicate themselves, such as GE plants. Leaving antiquated patent laws behind, the far more rigorous and older laws governing liability now kicked in at last and redefined GE seeds as trespass—genetic trespass, but trespass nevertheless.

Back in 2004, the Supreme Court judges ordered the Canadian government to amend patent laws to reflect this new technological reality—which has so far not happened yet.

Schmeiser won the "alternate Nobel" last year, Sweden's Right Livelihood Award, for having "given the world a wake-up call about the dangers to farmers and biodiversity everywhere from the growing dominance and market aggression of companies engaged in the genetic engineering of food crops."

On July 24, 2007, the Public Patent Foundation (PUBPAT) in the US announced that the US Patent and Trademark Office had agreed with their legal challenge and rejected four patents held by Monsanto which are key to their production of genetically modified crops (US patents nos. 5,164,316; 5,196,525; 5,322,938; and 5,353,605). They were originally granted for the so-called "cauliflower mosaic virus" (CaMV) which was discovered in the 1980s as the tool by which foreign genes can be successfully implanted elsewhere. The methods that were subsequently developed throughout biotechnology were based on this virus' unique ability to be the Trojan horse of genetics.

This development regarding patents does not bode well for dreams of world dominion. Jeffrey Smith related in his 2007 book (discussed below) the following: When GM seeds were a rising star in 1999, Arthur Anderson Consulting Group (later colleagues in the Enron scandal) told Monsanto executives that their ideal future was just around the corner, namely "a world in which all commercial seeds are genetically modified and patented." Anderson worked on a plan to make this reality for Monsanto. One graph shown at a meeting of one of Monsanto's competitor's offices "projected a 95% replacement of all natural seeds with GM varieties in just five years" (i.e. 2004).

That dream was challenged when PUBPAT got involved, observing that Monsanto's "ruthless persecutions have fundamentally changed farming" and that the "result has been nothing less than an assault on the foundations of farming practices and traditions that have endured for centuries in this country and millennia around the world, including one of the oldest, the right to save and replant crop seeds." They filed a request for re-examination of these patents on September 29 last year. When PUBPAT challenges a patent, that patent tends to be reversed about two-thirds of the time. Re-examination showed that Monsanto did not have the right to these crucial patents, because the actual owners of the intellectual property rights to this CaMV technology are the scientists who invented it—they neither filed a patent application nor were they party to the ones Monsanto finally obtained. (www.pubpat.org/monsantovfarmers93rejected.htm)

A year earlier, in May 2006, the European Patent Office had revoked Monsanto's species-wide patent on genetically engineered soybeans.

This patent was granted in 1994, before any GMO products had appeared on the market, and covered all varieties of soy and had until now been "the broadest species patent ever granted on plants and seed" (www.no-patents-on-seeds.org).

The founders of the European Union would have been very surprised had they been told that unifying Europe would be challenged most by food sand drugs. The EU Constitution has not yet been ratified; this is a long process. Getting that many ducks in one row will take a long time and will require an unknown number of concessions and also a great many burial ceremonies for countless hatchets accumulated over at least a thousand years of bickering. The immense problems caused by the EU *Directive* and its practical execution by the Codex Alimentarius committee, was discussed earlier. While that fight is still going on, the GE issue has come to a head with a vengeance.

"America's masterplan to force GM foods on the world" isn't working out, wrote the UK's *Guardian* on February 13, 2006. At that time, the US, Canada, and Argentina had taken the European Union to the WTO court for refusing to import GMO foods. This court is secret, but the thousand-page ruling was leaked and shows that the EU's crime had not been, as alleged, untimely response to international trade law requirements; instead, the EU countries were accused by the WTO as having "politicized" this trade process by refusing GMO foods on *scientific* and *safety* grounds raised by the European population. In other words, the people of Europe wanted to debate this food issue, not just open their shopping bags and then their mouths when told to do so. Public debate is Enemy N. 1 to modern trade ambitions.

Dubbing the EU "the coalition of the un-willing," *The Guardian* observed: "There is little the WTO can do," especially since the EU spokesperson stated that the WTO court decision "will not alter the system within which the European Union makes decisions on GMOs." (*New York Times*, Feb.8) Significantly, in the spirit of the judgment given in the Truehope case in Canada, the EU had decided that the harm GMOs could do to people and animals could be far greater than the harm done by disobeying the WTO court.

On October 31, 2007, *Business Week* reported that Austria, Cyprus, Denmark, France, Germany, Greece, Hungary, Latvia, Lithuania, Luxembourg, Ireland, Italy, Malta, Poland, and Slovakia all agreed that they should have the right to forbid GE crops within their borders. Most of them already have laws forbidding them as well as the importation of foods that might be thus contaminated. However Estonia, the Netherlands, Sweden, and the UK voted against those GE-"phobic" countries. The European Commission promised to announce a plan of action on this messy internal dissent by February 2008. However, given all those EU countries were also involved in the IAASTD exercise, the European Parliament in Brussels opted for caution and has done nothing so far.

Forcing something down somebody's throat (or into any other orifice) often meets with some astonishing resistance.

Indeed, it looks increasingly as if North America is becoming disconnected from the rest of the world, which either mistrusts GM products or is at the very least ambivalent towards this technology. Venezuela has become the first country in our hemisphere to ban GMOs outright. In April 2007, president Hugo Chavez passed a law that prohibits the planting and sale of any genetically engineered plants, declaring such crops "contrary to the interests and needs of the nation's farmers and farm workers." He also announced the creation of a large seed bank, which will maintain and promote indigenous seeds for peasant movements right around the world. (*Green Left Weekly*, May 5, 2007)

Meanwhile, in Canada, by now 97% of us don't want GE foods, as poll after poll has shown, no matter who conducted it. Four Prime Ministers in a row (Mulroney, Chretien, Martin, Harper), even though they are familiar with both official languages, simply haven't understood this very simple message.

Below are some observations made by Mike McBane of the Canadian Health Coalition in his book *Safety Last*! (2003) This book serves perfectly as a detailed commentary on bills C-51 and C-52, even thought this was written five years ago. Remember, we have been through this exercise of selling out the health of Canadians over and over again. *Safety Last* in 2003 was a commentary on the so-called *Smart Regs* Health Canada had composed in an effort to con us into accepting that the Food and Drugs Act needs modernizing, when most of us just wanted it and its Regulations enforced. Health Canada's *Smart Regs* treated biotechnology as something that needed promoting, and then they ran into a few problems with some venerable authorities, such as the Royal Society of Canada. Here are some of Mike McBane's observations:

> "Several years *after* genetically modified (GM) food was mixed into 75% of all Canadian processed food, Health Canada asked an Expert Panel of the Royal Society (RSC) to evaluate its safety. The Panel found that Canadians are not being adequately protected from the risks of genetically modified foods and other biotech products. The safety of GM food has never been established by science [*by 2008 its lack of safety has become very nicely established*]. The RSC said the biotechnology industry must demonstrate the safety of their product *before* it can be approved. The expert panel called for the immediate application of the Precautionary Principle in the regulation of food biotechnology **under the existing legislative and regulatory framework**. Health Canada questioned the "factual validity" of the Panel and refused to act on any of its key recommendations.

- The Expert Panel report says: *"...New technologies should not be presumed safe unless there is a reliable scientific basis for considering them safe. The Panel rejects the use of 'substantial equivalence' as a decision threshold to exempt new GM products from rigorous safety assessments on the basis of superficial similarities because such a regulatory procedure is not a precautionary assignment of the burden of proof." ... "The Panel finds the use of 'substantial equivalence' to exempt GM products from rigorous scientific assessment "to be scientifically unjustifiable and inconsistent with precautionary regulation of the technology.*

- European Union policy is to accompany life sciences research with research on safety aspects of the new technology generated. The government of Canada conducts no research on the safety of biotechnology. According to a senior Industry Canada official, testing for safety would be counter-productive in light of the government's 'see no evil' biotechnology policy. Health Canada has all but eliminated its capacity for independent scientific research on product safety. The policy is to leave this responsibility to industry. The fox is now in charge of the chicken coup. Canada has the audacity to take the EU to court over the moratorium it imposed on GMOs. The Canadian Trade Minister says the EU moratorium is not consistent with the WTO because it is "not based on scientific risk assessment"! Having force fed Canadians untested GM food, the government of Canada is now attempting to force Europeans to eat GM food against their will.
- Without a scientific risk *assessment* there can be no risk *management* to estimate the probable harm to persons and environments. In chemistry there is a science called toxicology which allows one to judge some risk. In biotechnology, there is no comparable science to assess risk of releasing live genetic organisms into the environment and into the food supply. In the absence of both science and risk management, Health Canada cannot regulate food biotechnology. Instead, the government of Canada promotes food biotechnology using the expertise of the public relations industry.
- The RSC Report found excessive secrecy among federal regulators about biotech safety and criticized the cozy relationship between regulators and the biotech industry. The panel also said the co-opting of biotechnology science in universities by commercial interests and the emphasis on secrecy contributes to the general erosion of public confi-

> dence in the objectivity and independence of the science behind the regulation of food biotechnology.

You are what you eat, but government and industry won't let you know what that is. A major function of the secrecy in Health Canada's regulatory system is to prevent accountability and public examination of regulatory decisions."

Faced with the people's rejection of GE foods, our government did two things: First, they killed bill C-517 (introduced April 3, killed May 5, 2008) which would have at least made labelling of this phony food mandatory. One does have to give the government credit for at least being consistent: they almost always follow the Americans. At the United Nations Food Standard Committee meeting held in Ottawa, May 1–5, 2006, the US tried, with Canada's full support, to force member nations to drop all labeling whatsoever, but this failed due to the resistance from Consumers International's representatives and from those who came from countries which have banned GMOs.

Second, the Conservatives decided now to bring in the troops, announcing, to all of us who complain about phony food and dangerous medicines, that the commencement of law and order is at hand. Bill C-51 and C-52 are to serve that purpose, as their wildly authoritarian and reality-challenged wording clearly shows.

It's the Big Stick approach that curiously always starts by ignoring constitutional rights. It acts like a bullying, incompetent parent suffering from some serious self-esteem issues, who threatens everyone in the household instead of going into rehab himself.

By the way, while governments tell us that labeling of such foods would be too cumbersome and an alarmist measure, the fact is they are already labeled. If you avoid processed foods, farmed fish, conventional soy and corn products, and especially cooking oils packaged in plastic bottles, you are almost GM safe. Now check produce stickers: conventionally grown foods have *four* numbers on the PLU code, while organics have *five* prefaced by a 9, GM fruit has five numbers as well, but prefaced by the number 8.

Yes–GM Foods Can And Do Make Animals And People Sick

Recently we were afforded a glimpse into what makes a biotech company tick. Jeffrey M. Smith of the Institute for Responsible Technology tells the story of Kirk Azevedo in his 2007 book *Genetic Roulette*. Robert Shapiro, Monsanto's charismatic CEO in the 1990s, known also for his devotion to daily Zen meditation practice, had inspired Azevedo by the company message of "saving the world through genetic engineering."

Azevedo decided: "Here we go! I can do something to help the world and make it a better place." Joining Monsanto in 1996, just as the first GE food plants were coming to market, he quickly rose in the ranks to become one of their top GM-cotton sales coordinators. To his astonishment, he found that Monsanto scientists were not required to consider safety assessments for their products; they focused exclusively on producing a new patentable plant of potential importance to world agriculture. Like kids with a Lego set, they were totally focused on producing new and exciting structures that could self-replicate and could also be patented. Azevedo pointed out to them that their newly created proteins, which have never existed in nature before and, therefore, are not embedded in the evolutionary web, had the potential to be allergenic or toxic or both, to other animals and plants or even people. His fears were simply dismissed as nonsense.

When he then suggested that they should check Monsanto's bovine growth hormone products for the potential of promoting prions, which cause Mad Cow Disease, he was met with blank stares. Soon everybody avoided him. "Anything that interfered with advancing the commercialization of this technology was going to be pushed aside," he concluded. Azevedo quit and became a chiropractor.

The industry mantra of "substantial equivalence" guided the thinking of GE scientists. Meanwhile, non-industry scientists worried about GMO technology and continued their investigations with some astonishing surprises.

European research has shown that the current problem of antibiotic resistant bacteria, and some of the new super-viruses, appear to have been promoted over the past decade by GM crops and the agricultural practices these crops require. This discovery implies the production of a systemic effect in animals promoted by the plants they eat. In biology this sort of discovery is an earthquake.

In May 2007, German researchers supported the earlier discovery and showed that genetically altered crops do not maintain their genetic integrity, as claimed by those who hold the patents on such altered crops. In fact, such altered plants seem to have little if any genetic integrity because the are not held together, as it were, by millions of years of evolutionary reinforcement. In fact, those foreign genes that reside and act in crops in which they did not evolve have now been shown to jump the species barrier. *The Observer* in the UK reported on May 28, 2008 the findings of geneticist Hans Heinrich Kaatz of Jena University which showed that "the herbicide-resistant genes [inserted into] rapeseed transferred across to the bacteria and yeast organisms inside the intestines of young bees." This finding, if supported by further and already ongoing research, would shatter the myth "substantially equivalent." Naturally evolved plants don't pass their genetic material on to other organisms; the whole point of DNA is to stay put and take care of its own context only. Genes taken out of the context within which they evolved appear to become loose canons in nature.

A parallel finding has also been made with regard to cloning animals. The propaganda would have us believe that cloning propagates the finest and the best, a sort of eugenics program for food producing farm animals—the best steak replicated forever and ever. However, that is not how those see it who actually are familiar with the processes involved. A guest editorial on the topic of "restoring public trust," especially with regard to the acceptance of cloned animals products, ran in the March 15, 2007, issue of *Genetic Engineering and Biotechnology News*. It quoted one of the leading cloning scientists in the world, Rudolph Jaenisch of the Massachusetts Institute of Technology: "You cannot make normal clones. The ones that survive will just be less abnormal than the ones that die early. There has been no progress—none—in the last six years in making cloning more safe."

Until last year, there were very few studies on GMOs and health. The most important one was by a scholar who himself worked in genetic engineering, Ardai Pusztai of Scotland's Rowett Institute. The government asked him to conduct routine safety studies mandated by food and drugs laws in the UK. He expected nothing unusual, being a genetic engineer himself. At the behest of Monsanto, he was fired when his results showed that GM potatoes caused pre-cancerous cell changes to all vital organs in rats.

Prince Charles, who also is the president of the British Medical Association, had Pusztai testify before the House of Lords. Since then, animal deaths on a large scale, and many instances of severe illness and deaths in humans, caused especially by Bt biotech crops and GE soy, have been reported from the Philippines, India, and from drug trials in the UK using recombinant drugs. Like Puzstai's rats, potentially fatal allergic responses were observed, and damage to many organs was also found (Institute for Science and Society, April 18. 2006, gmwatch.org Jan-June 2006, *Environmental Health Perspectives*, March 3). When genetically modified peas were tested on mice, their immune systems were severely damaged. (www.seedsofdeception.com)

In 2006, the Russian Academy of Sciences published research by Irina Ermakova which confirmed Pusztai's work. She fed pregnant rats Monsanto's Roundup Ready soy. The mothers were unharmed, but 55.6% of the offspring died within 3 weeks, compared to only 9% of normally fed pups; all GM-fed pups also showed significant reduction in weight. This prompted the American Academy for Environmental Medicine to join forces with the Institute for Responsible Technology and they called upon the US National Institutes of Health to commence immediately with safety studies of GE foods.

So far, biotechnology has produced nothing useful in medicine (let me know if you hear of something!). Some (financially profitable) gene therapy disasters are described by former *New England Journal of Medicine* editor, Dr. Jerome Kassier's in his extremely depressing book, *On The Take* (Oxford, 2005). Gene therapy has caused cancer, diabetes, and most recently the deaths of several participants in a UK drug trial (*The Guardian*, March 16, 2006 and gmwatch.org). On April 27, 2006 *Nature* reported on patients born with combined immune deficiency who, following successful biotech treatment to jump-start their immune systems, subsequently developed lymphoma (a T-cell leukemia). It was concluded that the biotech method itself was the cause.

It has often been said, that one needs a chemistry degree these days to know what foods to buy, and truly the best advice I can give to all, when entering the toxic waste dumps that we call supermarkets, is this: "Don't buy anything that contains substances you can't pronounce" and take Marion Nestle's book, *What to Eat*, with you in your shopping cart.

Fortunately, it is not necessary to have a degree in bio-chemistry to understand genetically engineered foods, because the logic that explains what's wrong with them is as profound as it is simple. Einstein often referred to the need for an important natural law to be fundamentally simple in order to be true. GMOs are an excellent case in point because they violate many interconnected laws of biology, and their harm can be empirically verified and tested: they fail to nourish because they poison complex systems of biology.

Jeffrey M. Smith is author of the international bestseller *Seeds of Deception* (2003). Now he has produced the most authoritative book yet available anywhere on the health risk involved with GMOs, *Genetic Routlette* (2007). Former UK Environment Minister, Michael Meacher MP, states in his introduction: "This is *the* authentic book on genetic modification that the world has been waiting for."

As executive director of the Institute for Responsible Technology (www.responsibletechnology.org) his expertise has helped several US States to regulate GMOs. He also advises governments around the world on this technology and has been very successful with his Campaign for Healthier Living in America. He knows the GMO world from the inside: he used to be the vice president of marketing communications for a GMO detection laboratory—a technology used constantly by the European Union to prevent GMOs from getting into their food supply. Indeed, the technology itself was invented by scientists who originally developed the techniques for creating GMOs; they became so troubled by the genii they had inadvertently let out of the bottle, that they set their minds to developing this highly effective and sensitive detection technology.

This book is introduced by a roll call of the brightest and the best in science, medicine, technology and politics, each adding their own experience to support the effort Smith has made to bring out all of this documented and verifiable information on GMOs' detrimental effects on the health of humans, animals, and the earth itself. We learn that soy allergies jumped by 50% in the UK right after the GM variety entered their food supply. It is known that entire sections of the amino acid sequence in GM soy are human allergens. Similarly, Bt toxin, which GE technology has made part of food crops, is associated with immune and allergic-type responses in humans, as has been documented especially in farm workers. Bt cotton has also caused reproductive problems in farmers.

The first time serious harm was observed, coming from a genetically engineered food substance, involved the well-known natural health product L-tryptophan. In its natural form, tryptophan is an essential amino acid found in milk, turkey meat and other foods. Being an "essential" amino acid means that it is an absolute requirement for life, and as such it interacts with a host of targets within the whole system. Messing with an amino acid means messing with everything.

Smith tells the story of how in the late 1980s a lot of people suffered sudden and extreme nerve pain, and their legs and arms filled with fluid; they also had trouble breathing. The Mayo Clinic discovered that the first few cases all had something in common: they had taken this amino acid as a supplement. Since amino acids are essential to life, such a supplement is inherently harmless. Then about 100 people died. Thousands of cases were reported and the symptoms were given the name eosinophilia myalgia syndrome (EMS). The *Journal of the American Medical Association* reported on July 11, 1990, that all these victims had in common the fact that they had taken GE-contaminated tryptophan pills; they were all traced to one manufacturer who had used genetically engineered bacteria: genes had been inserted into these bacteria to produce higher concentrations of this amino acid. Later *Science* reported this in more detail, which prompted the FDA to "blast" the authors for revealing this finding, because of the adverse "impact on the industry" these findings would have.

Smith's book is organized in such a way, that readers of all educational backgrounds and levels are guided through whatever is necessary for understanding what happens to a plant that is genetically modified, how that affects the soil, the water supply, the food-producing animals that are fed such altered plants, and what can happen also to people who eat those plants and animals. Detailed lists show which processed foods contain GE plants as well as the specific chemical details involved.

This book shows exactly *how* GMOs do harm, such as by promoting sterility, increasing infant mortality, provoking serious allergies, setting in motion cascades that result in organ damage, increasing vulnerability to childhood diseases, challenging and breaking down immune responses, harming the nervous system and—most importantly—why these foods do not nourish and never will be able to, no matter how sophisticated this technology might yet become. The sources provided will satisfy even the most obsessed reference hunter (like myself).

For all of us who wanted to know—really know—what this is all about, even the politics is carefully explained, and to satisfy those who thirst for justice in every argument, the point of view of those who champion GMOs is also carefully discussed. As for Health Canada, Smith tells us the following:

"Tracking down the impact of GM foods is even more difficult in North America where these foods are not labeled [*and one, therefore, does not have a control group for comparison, just as the GE industry requires to escape all liability*]. Regulators at Health Canada announced in 2002 that they would monitor Canadians for health problems from eating GM foods. A spokesperson said, 'I think it's just prudent and what the public expects...' But according to the CBC TV news on *Current Affairs*, September 25, 2006, Health Canada 'abandoned that research less than a year later saying that it was too difficult to put an effective surveillance system in place."

A copy of *Genetic Roulette* should go to every MP.

Sources & Resources:

Jeffrey M. Smith. *Genetic Roulette: The Documented Health Risks of Genetically Engineered Foods* Yes! Books, 2007, $31.95

M.-W. Ho & R. A. Steinbrecher, *Fatal Flaws in Food Safety Assessment: Critique of the Joint FAO/WHO Biotechnology & Food Safety Report*, Third World Network, 1998

M.-W. Ho et al, *Gene Technology in the Etiology of Drug-resistant Disease*, Third World Network, 1998

M.-W. Ho & L. L. Ching, *GMO Free: Exposing the Hazards of Biotechnology*, Vital Health, 2004

G. Merzer, *Mad Cowboy: Plain Truth From The Cattle Rancher Who Won't Eat Meat,* Touchstone, 1998

T. Traavik & Lim Li Ching. *Biosafety First—Holistic Approaches to Risk and Uncertainty in Genetic Engineering and Genetically Modified Organisms*, Tapir Academic Press, 2007

Section Home

Français • Print format

Publications - April 3, 2008 (Previous - Next)

Debates | Order Paper and Notice Paper | Journals

Options

Back to calendar | Hide Hyperlinks

39th PARLIAMENT, 2nd SESSION

EDITED HANSARD • NUMBER 071

CONTENTS

Thursday, April 3, 2008

Expand All | Collapse All

Source: How C-517 was Killed – Transcript of House of Commons Debate

The Acting Speaker (Mr. Royal Galipeau):
When we next return to the study of Bill C-50, the hon. member for Scarborough--Rouge River will have 10 more minutes.

It being 5:30 p.m., the House will now proceed to the consideration of private members' business as listed on today's order paper.

Private Members' Business

[Private Members' Business]

* * *

(1730)

[*Translation*]

Food and Drugs Act

[Table of Contents]

Mr. Gilles-A. Perron (Rivière-des-Mille-Îles, BQ)
moved that Bill C-517, An Act to amend the Food and Drugs Act (mandatory labelling for genetically modified foods), be read the second time and referred to a committee.

He said: Mr. Speaker, it is with emotion and pleasure that I speak to you and my colleagues in this House to express my point of view on genetically modified foods.

I would ask for your indulgence as I make a brief aside in my speech to commend two young people in my riding, Claire and Norbert. On December 11, they sent me an email, which I have before me, encouraging me to ensure mandatory labelling of genetically modified foods. Claire and Norbert even called me at my office and, together with their teacher, Marcel Parizeau—whom I salute this evening—invited me to discuss this with them. This was a very pleasant meeting. To my great surprise—you too will be surprised, Mr. Speaker—Claire and Norbert, who I met with at the Coeur à Coeur alternative school in Saint Eustache, are roughly 12 years old. I was surprised that young people that age had concerns about the food they eat.

I would also like to pay tribute to and thank my friend from Brossard—La Prairie, for supporting this bill.

Bill C-517 before us this evening is not an original bill. This is a topic that has been dear to the Bloc Québécois for many years. The hon. member for Drummond, in 1993 and 1994, had concerns about genetically modified foods. In 1999, my friend, Hélène Alarie—who is surely watching me this evening because I told her I was going to talk about this—tabled a bill in this House. By the way, Hélène was the first female certified agronomist in Canada. Ms. Alarie could speak at length about genetically modified organisms. I salute you, Hélène.

In 2001, an hon. Liberal member, Mr. Ciaccia—if my memory serves me correctly—tabled a bill calling on the government for mandatory labelling of genetically modified foods.

The summary of this bill reads:

> This enactment amends the Food and Drugs Act to make the Minister of Health responsible for establishing that a food or one or more of its components has been genetically modified. If it is established that a food or one or more of its components has been genetically modified, the Minister shall cause the name of the food to be published in the Canada Gazette. The Minister shall also prepare a list of all such foods and cause a copy to be sent at no cost to any one who requests it.
>
> No one may sell this food or a food product containing this food in a package unless a label is affixed to the package containing the following notice:

Source: How C-517 was Killed – Transcript of House of Commons Debate

This product or one or more of its components has been genetically modified—

In addition, no one may sell this food or a food product containing this food in a package unless a poster in the prescribed form has been placed near the food containing the following notice:

Genetically modified—

(1735)

The main goal of this bill is not to put genetically modified foods on trial, but to inform consumers about what they are eating and to give them a choice between consuming genetically modified foods or not. That is a democratic choice.

This is bound to be a very popular bill, and I invite all members of this House to read their local papers to find out what is going on and what their constituents want. Between 79% and 90% of Canadians—the average is 83%—want foods containing genetically modified organisms to be labelled. In the Quebec nation, 86% of people want labelling, and 80% of agricultural producers support implementing mandatory labelling standards. In my youth, there was a saying that went "What the people want, God wants". I would amend that by saying that what the people want, we, their elected representatives, want. This is what we, their elected representatives, want.

Another very important aspect of labelling is food safety. As a result of globalization—and we have examples—any type of food product can be found on our grocery store shelves and consumers may not know what it contains. For instance, there were cases of toothpaste that contained antifreeze. We must be careful. Therefore, there is also the issue of food safety. Given the lack of information about the medium- and long-term effects of GMOs, it is only natural to have concerns. You surely have concerns about the long-term effects, as I do.

In order to approve a transgenic product, the federal government relies on studies made by companies, which I will not mention, and merely reviews them. It does not conduct a systematic second assessment of all the plants and foods that are put on the market. Consequently, there is very little public or independent expertise in the evaluation of transgenic foods. The approval process must be more accessible and transparent in order to help the public better understand the risks and benefits associated with GMOs.

In March 2004, the government established a voluntary and ambiguous labelling policy.

(1740)

It is so ambiguous that no foods on our store shelves are labelled to indicate whether or not they contain GMOs. There are none; we can find none. The policy is so confusing, everything is so mixed up that it would be too complicated. If there are no genetically modified organisms in the food, the producer should not have any trouble labelling it. However, the voluntary labelling system is so complicated and confusing that no one even wants to start the process.

In four years, the voluntary labelling program has failed to yield any results. None. In September 2003, after four years of consultations, the Canadian General Standards Board published voluntary labelling rules for products containing GMOs. I will repeat that it was a compromise, a complex and unclear system of labelling, left to the discretion of the industry and, above all, not suited to the needs of consumers.

We have witnessed a part of history in the last couple of years. I would like to talk about José Bové, the Frenchman—as he is called—who spoke out against GMOs. After many battles, Mr. Bové was able to get France to ban all GMOs for human consumption. And so it started.

Mr. Bové served three or four months in prison. He has done it all. He had the nerve to destroy entire crops, but he won. Europe is currently looking at the possibility of banning any food destined for human or animal consumption that contains GMOs—genetically modified organisms.

What I find surprising is that only Canada, the United States and New Zealand have yet to take this position. Why are European countries and other countries throughout the world completely opposed to genetically modified organisms?

One benefit of labelling GMOs is that consumers will have relevant information about the products they

Source: How C-517 was Killed – Transcript of House of Commons Debate

are consuming, so that they can make an informed decision, a cultural decision, a personal decision or a religious decision. It is up to agricultural producers to ensure they have access to the markets by complying with the current national and international standards. This would open up the European market to wheat producers.

What is a GMO? All living organisms have a multitude of genes that determine the colour and shape of their fruits and leaves. A GMO is a living organism to which has been added one or more genes to give it a special characteristic. For example—

(1745)

[Table of Contents]

The Acting Speaker (Mr. Royal Galipeau):
It is with regret that I must interrupt the hon. member, but his time has expired. I tried to catch his eye, but he was too immersed in his speech.

The hon. member for Simcoe North has the floor for questions and comments.

[*English*]

[Table of Contents]

Mr. Bruce Stanton (Simcoe North, CPC):
Mr. Speaker, I enjoyed the member's presentation. I fully admit that Canadian consumers are very interested in food labelling and the importance of it as it relates to information that helps them make their choices about food.

Some 50 products have been approved by Health Canada and have gone through rigorous assessments in terms of their health safety. Only when these assessments have been completed will those products go on the market. Why should the member be concerned that these GM products need some additional labelling?

[*Translation*]

[Table of Contents]

Mr. Gilles-A. Perron:
Mr. Speaker, I would like to thank my colleague for his question. If I am not mistaken, he attended this afternoon's meeting of the Standing Committee on Veterans Affairs. It was his first time present, and he did well.

It is a bit like hiding one's head in the sand. How can we trust them, if it has been proven by departments and by everyone that the government does not have the means or methods for verification. It trusts the methods of companies like Monsanto, and looks only to see if the tests appear valid. That is crazy. We do not get a second opinion, no second opinion at all. We have to blindly trust the industry. Can we actually trust them?

Remember that the former U.S. Secretary of Agriculture said that the enormous pressure was put on him to approve genetically modified products. Even President Bush was pressured to accept GMOs.

Mr. Speaker, I am sorry, but I get very passionate whenever it comes time to—

[Table of Contents]

The Acting Speaker (Mr. Royal Galipeau):
The hon. member for West Nova for questions and comments.

[Table of Contents]

Hon. Robert Thibault (West Nova, Lib.):

Source: How C-517 was Killed – Transcript of House of Commons Debate

Mr. Speaker, I am very pleased that the hon. member for Rivière-des-Mille-Îles is presenting such a bill. Doing so demonstrates the maturity of the Bloc Québécois.

We must recognize that in order to protect Canadians, we need to have a strong, central government. The central government can tell merchants and retailers in the provinces, like Quebec, what must be found on the shelves, what must be displayed to inform citizens. It can go even further and tell them what language and even what words must be used—the specific nomenclature that must be used.

This is a acknowledgement of federalism, a recognition of Canada, and I congratulate him wholeheartedly.

[Table of Contents]

Mr. Gilles-A. Perron:
Mr. Speaker,—

[Table of Contents]

The Acting Speaker (Mr. Royal Galipeau):
The hon. member for Rivière-des-Mille-Îles must first realize that when the Speaker rises, he must wait.

[Table of Contents]

Mr. Gilles-A. Perron:
Mr. Speaker, my dear friend, I apologize.

[Table of Contents]

The Acting Speaker (Mr. Royal Galipeau):
Then he will have 90 seconds to respond to these comments. Then the axe will fall.

[Table of Contents]

Mr. Gilles-A. Perron:
Mr. Speaker, my dear friend, you just took some of my time.

I would like to respond to my colleague that it is not a question of sovereignty. It is a question of human well-being. Since 2001, Ontario has been calling for labelling. British Columbia and Quebec have also been calling for labelling. It falls under federal jurisdiction, so we must take care of it.

This does not mean that the government is running smoothly. This means that it is not running smoothly. The Conservatives are not doing their job, which is to take care of mandatory labelling.

(1750)

[Table of Contents]

Mr. Steven Fletcher (Parliamentary Secretary for Health, CPC):
Mr. Speaker, we are here today to discuss a private member's bill, Bill C-517, which was recently tabled in the House.

[*English*]

Bill C-517 proposes amendments to the Food and Drugs Act in order to require the mandatory labelling of all foods derived from a genetically modified organism or containing an ingredient derived from a genetically modified organism.

First of all, let me remind the House that Health Canada is responsible for ensuring that all foods, including foods derived from genetically modified organisms, are safe prior to entering the Canadian food system.

I would like to point out that this bill provides a narrower definition of genetically modified food than that which already exists under division 28 of the Food and Drugs Act, also referred to as the novel foods

Source: How C-517 was Killed – Transcript of House of Commons Debate

regulations.

Under division 28, "genetically modify" includes modifications obtained through the use of more traditional techniques, such as chemical mutagenesis and conventional breeding, as well as those obtained from modern biotechnology.

Health Canada regulates genetically modified foods as novel foods. The Food and Drugs Act and regulations have defined the concept of "novel food" to include those products derived through specific genetic modification.

This concept also encompasses foods that may have undergone a significant change in composition or nutritional value as a result of a manufacturing or packaging process, or any substance that does not have a history of safe use as a food.

The novel foods regulations permit Health Canada to assess the safety of all novel foods, irrespective of the method used for their development prior to their sale in Canada. Only after a novel food is determined safe for human consumption is it allowed to be sold on the Canadian market.

I would like to stress that amendments to the Food and Drugs Act as proposed in Bill C-517 would create a two tier system for genetically modified foods.

Depending on the method used in the development of the specific food, foods falling under the new definition would be required to be labelled to indicate the method of production, while others derived from more traditional modification methods, such as mutagenesis, would not be subject to mandatory labelling.

We have a rigorous process in Canada. Novel foods regulations require that Health Canada be notified prior to the marketing of any novel food in Canada so that a thorough safety assessment can be performed for each product.

The basis of these assessments by Health Canada scientists is a comparison of each novel food with a conventional counterpart and requires a critical evaluation of the scientific information and results of research studies provided in accordance with Health Canada requirements.

The information requirements are comprehensive. Typically, they include a complete description of the food product, its intended use, a molecular characterization of any novel traits, biochemical and compositional analysis, toxicological, nutritional and allergenicity data, and an estimate of dietary exposure and anticipated use patterns by the average consumer, including population subgroups where applicable.

The requirements are laid out in the Health Canada publication entitled "Guidelines for the Safety Assessment of Novel Foods". These guidelines were recently updated following public consultation.

The guidelines were revised to provide more detailed information about the pre-market notification procedure for novel foods in Canada, to provide more explicit guidance on the safety assessment data requirements for different types of novel foods, and to reflect advances in science and technology.

The revised guidelines are also consistent with guidance documents developed at the international level with respect to the assessment of genetically modified foods.

(1755)

[*Translation*]

The Government of Canada believes that protecting the health of humans and of Canada's environment is the primary consideration of the regulatory system.

[*English*]

As I have mentioned before, only those foods demonstrated to be safe for human consumption are permitted into the market place.

This bill calls on the Minister of Health to maintain a list of all genetically modified foods, publish the list in the *Canada Gazette*, and post it on the Internet so anyone who requests it can see it.

Source: How C-517 was Killed – Transcript of House of Commons Debate

This requirement is unnecessary as Health Canada already publishes a list of approved novel foods and decision documents which describe how regulatory authorities determined the safety of each new product and why certain conclusions were reached. It is all on the website.

Also available on Health Canada's website are decision summaries for each new product, the new novel foods regulations and guidelines, along with fact sheets and answers to frequently asked questions to aid in understanding this subject.

The Government of Canada is committed to sharing information with Canadians on how it regulates products of biotechnology.

In addition, Health Canada and the Canadian Food Inspection Agency, or CFIA, have launched a project to post information about products that are under review on the CFIA website.

As part of this notices of submission project, the public is provided with an opportunity to provide input on scientific matters relevant to the safety assessment of submissions from certain product developers who have requested safety assessments of novel foods or plants with novel traits.

Scientific questions or information is forwarded to Health Canada and CFIA evaluators for consideration in the assessment.

[*Translation*]

The subject of the bill is food labelling.

[*English*]

In Canada food labelling policies at the federal level are a shared responsibility of Health Canada and CFIA under the Food and Drugs Act.

Health Canada's responsibilities for food labelling fall within the department's mandate for health and safety issues. With respect to genetically modified foods, as with all foods, Health Canada's role is to identify the information required on the label of that food to ensure safe use.

Health Canada would determine what type of information is needed on the label to inform Canadians about these changes in the food. For example, in cases where the final food product has been intentionally modified in composition, such as increasing the level of a particular acid in canola oil, a different common name will be required to describe the oil.

Special labelling is required if changes occurred in the food that the consumer needs to be informed of for health and safety reasons, such as major compositional or nutritional changes.

[*Translation*]

Once again, genetically modified foods cannot be sold in Canada unless it has been proven that they are safe to eat.

[*English*]

Special labelling would not be used in place of a thorough safety assessment.

Apart from safety concerns, there are important trade issues that need to be looked at. Mandatory labelling would be required for genetically modified foods where safety concerns such as allergies and compositional or nutritional changes are identified. The labelling would be required to alert consumers in any case and the statements could not be misleading.

Let me say that mandatory labelling would require that all parts of the production chain participate, regardless of the nature of the products or consumer preferences. This would have major trade implications and costs.

(1800)

[*Translation*]

Source: How C-517 was Killed – Transcript of House of Commons Debate

[Table of Contents]

Hon. Robert Thibault (West Nova, Lib.):

Mr. Speaker, it is a pleasure for me to rise in this House and take part in this extremely important debate. First, I would like to congratulate the two members who spoke before me and added much to the debate. I would also like to congratulate the Parliamentary Secretary for Health on the quality of his French, which is steadily improving and which he is using more and more. I do have some concerns, however, about some of what he said.

I agree with him that Health Canada is doing a very good job of making sure that the foods on the Canadian market are safe and meet the highest international scientific standards, even though mistakes can occur. Some will say, however, that even with these assessments, genetically modified organisms can negatively impact Canadians' health, especially because we do not know how they interact with one another in growing children. It will take someone who knows more about organic biology or organic chemistry than I do to determine who is right.

What we can do is deal with what comes under our responsibility. In that regard, I agree with the member for Rivière-des-Mille-Îles that if consumers and parents are informed, they can make decisions they deem appropriate, in light of information and instructions they can follow. It is true that we are seeing young people in our schools who are taking an interest in these issues and discussing them.

There are some problems, however. The parliamentary secretary raised some valid points. In Canada, there are already about 50 genetically modified products on the market that have been approved, are in circulation and can be consumed on their own or are used to produce another food. This can present problems when it comes to marketing products and also for parents or consumers, who need to know the level of risk. Solutions to these problems must be found.

I support the member's bill because I agree with its purpose. It may yet be amended, but I believe that the member has to table this kind of bill in the House because of certain things the government has done. Like the member who spoke before me, I was once the parliamentary secretary for health. I had to explain which measures the government took and why the government did not decide to impose labelling. Even so, that is no reason not to consider it in the future.

[*English*]

That being said, we have to recognize that there are some problems in the food chain. If we say that all products that have genetically modified components in them must be labelled, we would be labelling so much on the shelves of our stores that the labelling would become meaningless. Canola oil is a GMO and it is omnipresent in the production of other foods. In the instance of aquaculture it may be that the entrance part of the feed, being an animal or plant, was partly produced using some GMO that might be one-thousandth of one per cent.

If that is not defined in the regulations, then that can become a problem, in that we could over label or end up not labelling enough. That is not defined in the bill as presented by the member. This is a subject for debate and questions. What is it? Is it a product that is 100% GMO? Is it a product that is at a certain percentage? How do we define that? How do we do it? At the health committee we can hear from experts who perhaps can help us.

This is not the ideal. The ideal would be that we would do this through regulation rather than through a bill, that we would make a minor amendment to the act so that it compels the minister to create the regulations. The regulations can be modified as market conditions or scientific conditions change a lot faster than bringing it back to this House in a bill to modify it. That is a problem.

I recognize the point of the member that if we do not do it through a private member's bill, we may not do it at all. That is an issue that will have to be debated at the committee to see if there is a way to do it under the current regulations that would meet the desired effects of this bill without creating stand-alone legislation, to do it through the regulatory process.

That would be the wise way for us to proceed. We have huge industrial and agricultural interests in this country and other areas that have an interest in this, that would want to make sure that we do not disadvantage ourselves when it comes to the products that we are competing against in our very own

Source: How C-517 was Killed – Transcript of House of Commons Debate

market and in other markets.

Other countries could say that when 50% of the product is manufactured from GMO it has to be labelled as GMO. However, in Canada a product that is 10% GMO would have to be labelled as such. Consumers would see on the same shelf a competing product from another country with 40% GMO not labelled as GMO. We would be producing a product that has less GMOs in it, but it would have a competitive disadvantage because the consumer would believe that it was all GMO and that the other product was not, whereas actually more GMO entrants were included within that competing product from another country. We have to consider the point the parliamentary secretary raised. It is a valid point. We have to consider our trade relationships and where we are in relation to other countries.

Our party has advanced a grown in Canada initiative with four major actions. This would play well within its intent.

We should design regulations under the current Consumer Packaging and Labelling Act to clarify the definitions of "made in Canada", "product of Canada" and create a separate "grown in Canada" label for 100% Canadian grown products.

We should work with farmers and agri-food value chain partners to create a non-profit governing body that would manage and implement a voluntary "grown in Canada" label that would identify 100% Canadian grown products and work with CFIA to establish an audit process to maintain label integrity.

We should establish a grown in Canada marketing fund with two major objectives.

We should provide marketing grants to local farmers' markets and other buy local initiatives in communities across Canada.

We should develop a marketing campaign informing Canadian consumers of Canada's strong record of farm initiatives for environmental sustainability, food safety and others.

We should develop a grown in Canada toolkit, a series of knowledge and development programs where farm and industry organizations work in partnership with the government to develop information and business extension tools.

(1805)

[*Translation*]

I could go on about this, but we all understand the problems associated with buying products labelled as made in Canada. These products, food or otherwise, can be made entirely in other countries and just packaged in Canada.

Recently, there were problems with toothpaste and pet food. Labels indicated that the products came from Canada or the United States, markets that people are familiar with and that comply with food safety standards. However, the products inside the packages were from China and did not comply with safety standards. We saw what happened as a result.

It is important to answer all of these questions. My time is up, but there is still a lot to discuss. We will have to continue this discussion in the Standing Committee on Health.

Once again, I would like to congratulate the member on introducing this bill, as well as all of the members who took part in the debate.

[*English*]

[Table of Contents]

Mr. Nathan Cullen (Skeena—Bulkley Valley, NDP):
Mr. Speaker, it is with some pleasure that I enter this evening's debate. Obviously this is an issue that the New Democrats hold near and dear to our hearts as the history has been recounted in this place.

[*Translation*]

Source: How C-517 was Killed – Transcript of House of Commons Debate

Bill C-517 is almost, word for word, the same bill as the one introduced by my colleague for Winnipeg North during the 37th Parliament and then introduced by my colleague for British Columbia Southern Interior in this Parliament. This is a necessary and long overdue bill and I am pleased to support it.

[*English*]

To recount the history of how this bill has been making its way through this place steadily parliament after parliament, it seems clear to me and to many others that it is a response by politicians representing different parties to a need expressed by Canadians.

(1810)

This bill attempts to allow people a greater certainty to have as much information as possible on the products they are buying for their families, the food they are consuming. Many people have approached me and I am sure many of my colleagues in this House have been approached as well. People are confused and concerned about what it is they are buying in the stores. They want to know what the chemicals and other ingredients that are listed on the back of products actually are.

Most folks are not organic chemists. Most folks do not spend a great deal of time researching on the Internet each chemical additive to the products they are buying. Certainly there are very few, even those who specialize in organic chemistry, who understand the interaction that occurs when chemicals come together and what it means for the consumer, for the human form and for our environment in general.

When we step into the realm of genetically modified foods and products, we step into an entirely new conversation. This conversation about what the consequences are has not been properly had in this Parliament, in many of our legislatures and in the homes of Canadians. We need to understand the ethical, moral and environmental implications of the genetically modified foods that we consume, the foods that we put on the table for our friends and family, foods that have been modified at the genetic level.

Of course many on the big agriculture side, the Monsantos of the world, will say that foods have been modified for centuries. They will say that they have been trying to make crops grow better under certain conditions by only picking out the wheat that grows best or the cow that produces the most milk and that that is a genetic modification. It is patently false to try to compare those two systems and assume that they are one.

On the one hand we are choosing from the herd the cow that might produce more milk. In this case the genetic modification of food is when a scientist comes along and pulls genes from an organism at the molecular level and replaces them with genes from an entirely different organism. Genes from salmon are being put into genes that are meant to grow corn. Genes from a whole myriad of organisms are being placed into other organisms.

There is a fundamental principle that is absolutely missing from the legislation that governs this country. That is the precautionary principle.

We were very proud last year that a bill that New Democrats put forward to ban a series of dangerous chemicals from products in Canada was debated and modified at the environment committee and passed unanimously in this place and went to the other place. It applied the precautionary principle as its foundation. It said that in the absence of 100% evidence, which is sometimes the excuse I have heard from Health Canada and Environment Canada officials, that we do not have 100% conclusive evidence on a thing and in the overabundance of evidence pointing us in a certain direction there is something to be worried about with a new chemical or product, the precautionary principle says that we must act in a cautious way because otherwise the full testing of that product is taking place with the public in the marketplace. That is not responsible government.

We often have debates in this place about what the real role of government should be, what should government do and what should it not do. In this case, the setting out of the basic rules and principles as to what will be safe and what will be considered unsafe is clearly a role for government, because at the individual consumer level it is impossible.

It is an impossibility to say that rampant individualism will rule the day and people will simply know enough and will have done enough research themselves that they will conduct themselves in a safe manner and will ensure that nothing unsafe will end up on their kitchen tables. It is foolish. Every day in this place

Source: How C-517 was Killed – Transcript of House of Commons Debate

Bill C-517 is almost, word for word, the same bill as the one introduced by my colleague for Winnipeg North during the 37th Parliament and then introduced by my colleague for British Columbia Southern Interior in this Parliament. This is a necessary and long overdue bill and I am pleased to support it.

[*English*]

To recount the history of how this bill has been making its way through this place steadily parliament after parliament, it seems clear to me and to many others that it is a response by politicians representing different parties to a need expressed by Canadians.

(1810)

This bill attempts to allow people a greater certainty to have as much information as possible on the products they are buying for their families, the food they are consuming. Many people have approached me and I am sure many of my colleagues in this House have been approached as well. People are confused and concerned about what it is they are buying in the stores. They want to know what the chemicals and other ingredients that are listed on the back of products actually are.

Most folks are not organic chemists. Most folks do not spend a great deal of time researching on the Internet each chemical additive to the products they are buying. Certainly there are very few, even those who specialize in organic chemistry, who understand the interaction that occurs when chemicals come together and what it means for the consumer, for the human form and for our environment in general.

When we step into the realm of genetically modified foods and products, we step into an entirely new conversation. This conversation about what the consequences are has not been properly had in this Parliament, in many of our legislatures and in the homes of Canadians. We need to understand the ethical, moral and environmental implications of the genetically modified foods that we consume, the foods that we put on the table for our friends and family, foods that have been modified at the genetic level.

Of course many on the big agriculture side, the Monsantos of the world, will say that foods have been modified for centuries. They will say that they have been trying to make crops grow better under certain conditions by only picking out the wheat that grows best or the cow that produces the most milk and that that is a genetic modification. It is patently false to try to compare those two systems and assume that they are one.

On the one hand we are choosing from the herd the cow that might produce more milk. In this case the genetic modification of food is when a scientist comes along and pulls genes from an organism at the molecular level and replaces them with genes from an entirely different organism. Genes from salmon are being put into genes that are meant to grow corn. Genes from a whole myriad of organisms are being placed into other organisms.

There is a fundamental principle that is absolutely missing from the legislation that governs this country. That is the precautionary principle.

We were very proud last year that a bill that New Democrats put forward to ban a series of dangerous chemicals from products in Canada was debated and modified at the environment committee and passed unanimously in this place and went to the other place. It applied the precautionary principle as its foundation. It said that in the absence of 100% evidence, which is sometimes the excuse I have heard from Health Canada and Environment Canada officials, that we do not have 100% conclusive evidence on a thing and in the overabundance of evidence pointing us in a certain direction there is something to be worried about with a new chemical or product, the precautionary principle says that we must act in a cautious way because otherwise the full testing of that product is taking place with the public in the marketplace. That is not responsible government.

We often have debates in this place about what the real role of government should be, what should government do and what should it not do. In this case, the setting out of the basic rules and principles as to what will be safe and what will be considered unsafe is clearly a role for government, because at the individual consumer level it is impossible.

It is an impossibility to say that rampant individualism will rule the day and people will simply know enough and will have done enough research themselves that they will conduct themselves in a safe manner and will ensure that nothing unsafe will end up on their kitchen tables. It is foolish. Every day in this place

Source: How C-517 was Killed – Transcript of House of Commons Debate

we pass security bills, crime bills and environmental legislation that we hope provides the rules and the framework in which industry and individual consumers can guide themselves, can participate in the rules. This place is a referee for what is fair and unfair, what is safe and unsafe.

There is another very important issue, and that is the reversal of the burden of proof. The industry, which profits from genetically modified foods, should be responsible for proving that its products are safe before putting them on the market, and not the government.

However, the onus of responsibility is somehow reliant upon government to prove a thing safe, to run the tests. We know scientists in Health Canada and Environment Canada, and it is not only this administration but with the previous administration as well, have brought forward concerns about genetically modified products. They have said that in certain circumstances they have had some scientific concerns. We know a number of things have happened to them, and promotion has not been one of them. They have been terminated. They have been threatened. They have been muzzled.

This goes beyond the ideology of one party or another. This goes to the safety of Canadians and the freedom of science to conduct itself in a rational way, to provide advice and guidance to the government of the day.

We know in recent magazines the government has been noted as a so-called enemy of science, fearful of the science. That was in relation to issues around climate change and the resistance to meet the preponderance of evidence saying the climate science was in and that we needed to conduct ourselves in a different way.

We have never seen this in the history of Parliament, in Westminster tradition, but the government is filibustering a private member's bill at committee, delaying, denying, stalling hour after hour, not letting the democratic will of this place and the country to be expressed.

Is there anything more fundamental than what we do here? It is to allow the free and fair exchange of ideas and debate, to allow the best ideas to come forward and to allow the will of Parliament to be expressed, the will of the voters who put us in this place and to whom we are responsible to conduct ourselves.

What do we see from the government? It simply does not like the bill put forward by the leader of the New Democrats, the member for Toronto—Danforth. Its response to disliking environmental legislation, environmental initiatives like this one, is to filibuster, delay, deny the existence of this and therefore abdicate its responsibility.

This is consistently why New Democrats have found a lack of confidence in the government, an inability to support it in its agenda. It conducts itself in a way that is unsupportable.

We feel that if genetically modified foods are a safe thing, if the government feels it has the science and the evidence on its side to say that this is safe, 100% guaranteed, then the labelling of such products, the identification of those products, should not be a problem. Consumers will then have a choice between a product that has been genetically modified or one that has not. Consumers will vote with their feet, will vote with their dollars and they will choose products that are safer for their families.

I urge all members from all parties to take this bill into consideration, to let their conscience guide them, to support it, allow it to see debate and eventual passage so we finally feel full confidence in the products that appear on our shelves and on our tables.

(1815)

[*Translation*]

[Table of Contents]

Mr. Marcel Lussier (Brossard—La Prairie, BQ):
Mr. Speaker, I am also very pleased to speak to this debate on Bill C-517, a private member's bill introduced by the member for Rivière-des-Mille-Îles, which would amend the Food and Drugs Act. The bill primarily deals with foods and food components for human consumption that are or that contain

genetically modified elements.

As the member for Rivière-des-Mille-Îles said, this is not the first time that the Bloc Québécois has tabled a similar bill in the House of Commons. On November 4, 1999, Hélène Alarie's Bill C-309 was adopted at first reading. In reading this, I am very surprised to see that in nine years, Parliament has not been able to produce legislation on labelling for GMOs.

Bill C-517 would make the labelling of GMOs mandatory. The new clause 7.3 proposed in the bill provides for a list of genetically modified foods to be made available to the public. The bill also provides for prison sentences and fines for any violators.

In the absence of information about the medium- or long-term impact of GMOs, it is natural to have concerns.

Canada has no standards in place to force mandatory labelling of foods containing GMOs, despite the demands and concerns of many consumers and the recommendations of many studies and reports. The federal government's policy of voluntary labelling remains a fiasco.

In September 2003, after four years of consultations, the Canadian General Standards Board reached a decision regarding the rules for voluntary labelling of products containing GMOs. According to lobby groups following the issue, a final compromise was reached that involved complex, ambiguous labelling left to the discretion of the industries and manufacturers.

On April 15, 2005, on the first anniversary of the implementation of voluntary labelling policies, Greenpeace, the Union des consommateurs, Équiterre and other environmental groups denounced the laxity of the measure, demonstrating that it is still impossible to find foods labelled as containing GMOs. Those groups even based their information on a Health Canada assessment, estimating that nearly 70% of processed products found in grocery stores in Quebec and Canada would contain GMOs.

Once again today, Greenpeace, in partnership with the Bloc Québécois and the Union des consommateurs, came to Parliament Hill to say that the contamination of cultures by GMOs concerns all agricultural producers.

Voluntary labelling standards have failed completely, according to Greenpeace, which also reminded us that 86% of Quebeckers are demanding or calling for mandatory labelling. Its consultations with agricultural producers in Quebec confirmed that over 80% of farmers also want mandatory labelling. We can therefore ask when the government will give consumers the right to know if their food products contain GMOs.

Greenpeace and the Union des consommateurs came here to ask the Canadian government to respect and ratify the Cartagena protocol on biosafety.

(1820)

They are also calling on the government to respect consumers' fundamental rights to know what is in the foods they eat. Some 40 countries around the world have already brought in mandatory labelling. The Union des consommateurs is demanding that research into biotechnology be continued and improved.

Today, at this press conference on GMOs, Canada's dairy producers and Quebec's Union des producteurs agricoles also lent their support. The president, Réal Gauthier, also came to represent the Laurentian and Outaouais dairy producers.

In his speech, the member for Rivière-des-Mille-Îles mentioned that he had two idols in his riding: Claire and Norbert. He happened to mention that he was talking about young people aged 11 or 12. Last year, I had the same experience in my own riding. Two young people, Thomas Drolet and James Cameron, also got involved at school and created an Internet site to inform the community and their classmates about the problem of GMOs. They also came here to the House of Commons to present a petition with over 2,000 names of people who support them and recognize the need for mandatory labelling of genetically modified foods.

These young people did their research. They learned about the issues, they did a lot of reading, and they consulted websites about GMO issues. They developed their knowledge of the subject and shared

Source: How C-517 was Killed – Transcript of House of Commons Debate

that knowledge through presentations in class. I am very surprised that these primary school children are so interested in health issues at such an important time in their lives, right before they go to secondary school. We should pay close attention to these young people and tell them that we will accede to their request concerning GMOs.

Bill C-517 is a bill that also focuses on future generations and seeks to ensure that they have the right to healthful food and can read the labels to find out exactly what they are about to eat. Twelve year olds can make choices too. The young people at Notre-Dame-de-Saint-Joseph school in La Prairie want to make informed choices. Some people might tell them to consult the government websites that list the 50 products. However, when people are buying products or eating chocolate bars, they need to know what they are eating. If the chocolate bar label says that the product contains modified organisms, young people will be able to freely choose what they want to eat.

Bill C-517 is about the future. It is for future generations, for the young people who are now asking us—urging us—to pass this new bill.

(1825)

[Table of Contents]

The Acting Speaker (Mr. Royal Galipeau):
The time provided for the consideration of private members' business has now expired, and the order is dropped to the bottom of the order of precedence on the order paper.

Source: How C-517 was Killed – Transcript of House of Commons Debate

Section Home

Français • Print format

Publications - May 5, 2008 (Previous - Next)

Debates | Order Paper and Notice Paper | Journals

Options

Back to calendar | Hide Hyperlinks

39th PARLIAMENT, 2nd SESSION

EDITED HANSARD • NUMBER 088

CONTENTS

Monday, May 5, 2008

Expand All | Collapse All

CANADA

House of Commons Debates

VOLUME 142	NUMBER 088	2nd SESSION	39th PARLIAMENT

OFFICIAL REPORT (HANSARD)

Source: How C-517 was Killed – Transcript of House of Commons Debate

Monday, May 5, 2008

Speaker: The Honourable Peter Milliken

The House met at 11 a.m.

Prayers

PRIVATE MEMBERS' BUSINESS

[Private Members' Business]

* * *

(1105)

[*English*]

Food and Drugs Act

The House resumed from April 3 consideration of the motion that Bill C-517, An Act to amend the Food and Drugs Act (mandatory labelling for genetically modified foods), be read the second time and referred to a committee.

[Table of Contents]

Mr. Rob Merrifield (Yellowhead, CPC):
Mr. Speaker, it is a privilege for me to rise in debate and add my voice on behalf of the people of Yellowhead in regard to this private member's bill, Bill C-517.

I have to qualify my remarks prior to proceeding. I have worked with genetically modified foods. I have farmed all my life. I have also worked with conventionally grown crops and have a background in understanding crop development, how species grow, and what benefits or risks may exist with regard to genetically modified foods, as I have had the experience of growing them for several years.

On first looking at this bill, the question has to be asked: what is the problem with labelling the food that is grown and products that are on our shelves in Canada? My argument is that whatever label goes on those products has to be accurate. It cannot be misleading. It must inform the consumer in Canada as to exactly what they are eating and the risks that may or may not be associated with foods.

This is where I would like to start my remarks, because Canada has some of the very best foods in the world. Canadians know that, but they need to be reminded, and I am reminding them here and now that we have some of the safest and best quality food products in the world. That is important, because so many in the population now do not grow their own foods. That generational shift has happened over the last couple of generations in Canada and around the world.

Therefore, it is more important now than ever before that the safety measures are in place to ensure that safety is never compromised. Health Canada and the Canadian Food Inspection Agency together have the mandate to make sure the products on our shelves are as safe as they can possibly be.

The OECD nations, as well as the World Health Organization and the FAO of the UN, all have worked together on genetically modified foods to make sure there are standards and an agreement not only in Canada but around the world and across many jurisdictions to make sure these products are safe.

The argument is this. If there is any health risk at all with genetically modified foods, we should not just label them but eliminate them. If there is not a risk, we should accept them and use them as an

Source: How C-517 was Killed – Transcript of House of Commons Debate

advantage for our crops and foods so that we provide them not only for Canadians but our trading partners.

It is also important to know that when a genetically modified food is put on our shelves or examined by either Health Canada or the Canadian Food Inspection Agency, there is an extensive seven year process of analyzing, assessing and determining whether the product meets the safety standards in Canada. It is very important to understand that.

Some labelling of our food is very important. We fully recognize that when it comes to allergens. Some foods contain allergens and it important to label them because they can cause serious health risks for consumers. We make sure those allergenic foods are labelled. It is very important to do so.

With what we are seeing with genetically modified foods development in Canada and around the world, it is crucial that we understand the risks and perhaps the benefits, because if we do not understand them, then we are really not fully understanding as consumers what we are trying to do.

My fear is that if we put a label on genetically modified foods the electorate would not quite understand what it means. In fact, I would suggest that there is a real strong debate, both in this room by many members of Parliament and by members of the public, as to what is a genetically modified food. Is it just a food that has been developed by taking better foods and the best of generation after generation to enhance the performance of that commodity? That is one way of doing it.

When a food is genetically modified, we can be looking for dealing with a pesticide that is much safer and easier to use. One way of genetically modifying some of the canolas that we have been working with is to spray a light amount of pesticide on them. Those plants that survive are bred to one another so that eventually a product is developed that is resistant to that herbicide or pesticide.

That is one way of doing it. We have seen some tremendous advancements in some of the canola products that we grow in Canada. In fact, canola is a Canadian product, and that is why I refer to it. It is our own invention, which has provided a tremendous product. It is one of the lowest saturated fat food products on the planet. Compared to corn, which is about 20% saturated fats, soy, which is about 15%, and palm oil, which is about 50%, canola is only 7%. It is a tremendous alternative to some foods we have.

While we are looking at labelling, I note that there is a massive debate going on in the House and across Canada as to whether we should get rid of trans fats. A perfect alternative to trans fats is to move to non-hydrogenated canola oil, which is 7% saturated fat rather than 50%.

As we move away from trans fats, we are looking for options that will be healthier for the population. I say that in the context of why it is so important that we label. We have moved to labelling on trans fats. Why? Because trans fats are not healthy and there is scientific evidence that they should not be in the marketplace. The food industry is checking itself by making sure the consumer is not having an overabundance of trans fats. We have moved so that at least 40% and probably closer to 50% of the trans fats are eliminated from our diet.

Genetically modified foods are different from that. After 14 years or more of those products being on our shelves, and after 20 years or more of genetically modified foods being in our products, there has yet to be scientific research that shows those novel foods are less safe than the conventional ones. In fact, the last study that I saw was out of Europe. Europe has not embraced genetically modified foods, although France is now starting to flirt with using genetically modified corn and so on, so it is progressing. To date, though, I would say that broadly the continent has said no, that it will shy away from genetically modified foods.

However, this study in Europe took place over 15 years for 400 different genetically modified products. The final analysis showed that the genetically modified food was healthier than the conventional foods, because much less pesticide was used. In the long run, the product was much safer as far as the health of the individual was concerned.

I am concerned as a farmer and as a Canadian about the amount of pesticides we use. When we use a genetically modified food we are using the highest of technology as far as the new pesticide products are concerned. There are virtually zero residuals. Some of the pesticides that I used to use on the farm had seven-year residuals. They would stay in the soil for seven years before they would break down. Some of the new ones now are neutralized on contact. There have been tremendous advancements in the safety of

Source: How C-517 was Killed – Transcript of House of Commons Debate

the technology of the pesticides that we use today compared to what has been used in the past.

Why is that important? Because this is not only about the safety of food. It is about the environment. If I have a concern about genetically modified foods, it does not lie in the safety of the food but in the environment. It is about making sure that we are not creating a "super plant" that could get away from us.

There are 10 groups of pesticides that we use. On the farm, we start by using one group. Then we get some resistance and a mutation in the plants and we have to go to a different group of pesticides to be able to counter that. Therefore, we have to make sure that the balance is there, that we do not grow a super plant that creates a problem in the environment and causes tremendous havoc in the agriculture community.

I am a little concerned about that with genetically modified foods, but I am also very confident that Health Canada and the Canadian Food Inspection Agency are watching that very closely. To date I have not seen a significant problem on that side of it. One of the reasons is that the technology has allowed for a terminator gene to be put in so that the new generation of those seeds is not allowed to reproduce and cause that kind of problem.

I said earlier that it is important to have truth in labelling. We must realize that 75% of the processed food on the shelves in Canada contains some degree of genetically modified foods or novelty foods. Therefore, if we are concerned about eating genetically modified foods, then there should be truth in labelling.

(1110)

The only reality and truth that we could find in labelling would be to use what is a growing industry, which is organic foods. Organic foods not only have virtually no genetically modified foods in them, but they have zero pesticides. The option is there for the consumer.

However, if we were to put a label of genetically modified foods on every product in Canada, we would be misleading the consumer. We would be saying to the consumer that we are a little concerned about genetically modified foods or we would not be putting this on a label, and that the foods do not meet all the safety standards, which they do.

I am all for truth and I am all for more information for the consumer, but it has to be real information. This piece of legislation, although well intended, is going in the wrong direction, I believe, because it makes this compulsory. I believe we need to make sure we have the options for the consumer. If consumers are nervous about genetically modified foods, they can go to organic foods. If not, then leave it the way it is.

(1115)

[*Translation*]

[**Table of Contents**]

Ms. Raymonde Folco (Laval—Les Îles, Lib.):
Mr. Speaker, I am honoured to participate today in the debate on Bill C-517, introduced by the member for Rivière-des-Mille-Îles. This bill amends the Food and Drugs Act to make the Minister of Health responsible for establishing that a food or one or more of its components has been genetically modified, and for preparing a list of all such foods for anyone who requests it, because the public must know.

As the member for Rivière-des-Mille-Îles said when he introduced his bill, this is not a new bill, since a few years ago, two other colleagues, including one from the official opposition, were already concerned about the mandatory labelling of genetically modified foods and organisms, commonly known as GMOs. Since 2001, Ontario has been calling for labelling; British Columbia and Quebec are calling for it as well.

The main purpose of Bill C-517 is to inform consumers about what they are eating, and to let them choose whether or not to eat genetically modified foods or food products. Therein lies the challenge. This is not about putting genetically modified foods or food products on trial; this is about the precautionary

Source: How C-517 was Killed – Transcript of House of Commons Debate

principle and fundamental information, and about protecting the consumer from any unknown risks or potential effects these types of foods could have on a person's health. As legislators, this is our duty.

This is about ensuring that consumers are safe, by giving them the opportunity to look at the nutritional information on labels of foods on the market, and to make an informed decision.

[*English*]

Genetically modified organisms, GMOs, could impact Canadians' health. We do not know today what could be the effect of GMOs, in the short term or the long term, on people's health and on the environment. Some scientists say that biotechnologically derived foods create or enhance diseases such as malaria, for example. Therefore, it is our responsibility as legislators to make sure that consumers have proper information on the food they buy and eat.

In Canada, there are already about 50 genetically modified products on the market. These have been approved by the government and can be consumed on their own or can be used to produce another food. We must also address the issue of the percentage of GMOs in the food and determine which level would require mandatory labelling.

In the European Union, for instance, traces of GMOs do not require mandatory labelling if they do not contain more than the threshold of 0.9% and only if their presence in the food is involuntary or accidental and technically inevitable.

[*Translation*]

This issue, like all environmental issues, does not concern just Canada, but the entire planet. I would like to point out that the European Union, which has ratified the March 2006 Cartagena protocol, already has mandatory labelling regulations.

In fact, the European Union has incorporated the Cartagena protocol, which came out of the meeting held from March 13 to 17, 2006, into its legislation. Signatories to the protocol commit to meeting a series of requirements pertaining to the international trade in GMOs intended for human or animal consumption.

Unfortunately, as our colleague proved a few minutes ago, the Conservative government still does not seem ready to take the necessary steps to make labelling mandatory for genetically modified foods or food products. On the contrary, the Conservative government continues to advocate voluntary labelling, which has been a complete failure because it has been left entirely in the hands of the agriculture and agri-food industries.

Proof of the government's bad faith can be found in an article that appeared in the *Ottawa Citizen* on April 4. The newspaper reports that Canada is opposed to the mandatory labelling recommended by the WHO, the World Health Organization, to inform consumers about the quantity of fruits, vegetables, whole grains and added sugars in modified foods.

The Codex committee on mandatory labelling, which was put in place by the WHO to develop international codes of practice and implement the WHO's food standards program, met at the end of April.

The members of the Canadian delegation, headed by the Canadian Food Inspection Agency, stated their position, which unfortunately is that Canada will not support the amendment put forward by the WHO that would encourage national governments and give them more power to require agri-food industries to reveal the percentage of ingredients that could pose a risk to human health in modified foods. Bill Jeffery, national coordinator of the Center for Science in the Public Interest, stated that Canada's position is indefensible.

The objective of the Cartagena protocol is to help regulate the transboundary movement, transfer, handling and use of any GMO that may have adverse effects on the conservation and sustainable use of biological diversity and pose risks to human health.

The protocol provides that international shipments of GMOs must be accompanied by documentation that clearly indicates the exact identity of the GMOs concerned. If the exact identity is not known, this documentation must clearly indicate "may contain GMOs".

This protocol affirms the precautionary principle, because it states the following:

Source: How C-517 was Killed – Transcript of House of Commons Debate

Lack of scientific certainty due to insufficient relevant scientific information and knowledge regarding the extent of the potential adverse effects of a living [genetically] modified organism on the conservation and sustainable use of biological diversity in the party of import, taking also into account risks to human health, shall not prevent that party [that is, the importing state] from taking a decision, as appropriate, with regard to the import of the living modified organism in question ... in order to avoid or minimize such potential adverse effects.

(1120)

[*English*]

The European Union's policy has two goals: first, to inform consumers, through labelling, about genetically modified organisms; and, second, to create a safety net due to the traceability of the GMO at every step of the manufacture and at the time the product is put on the marketplace.

[*Translation*]

The operative word in the European regulations is "traceability", that is, the ability to track GMOs and products made from GMOs at all stages of their marketing, throughout the production and distribution chain.

Traceability of GMOs allows the monitoring and checking of information given on labels, the monitoring of effects on the environment and the withdrawal of GMOs that are potentially dangerous for human or animal health.

In closing, some farm organizations claim that Bill C-517 will not improve food safety and will not provide increased consumer choice, and that it will be enough for consumers to rely on foods containing the Canadian organic label to ensure that the foods they buy do not contain genetically modified ingredients.

However, we must ensure that the so-called organic label is properly certified by an independent, authorized organization that guarantees that the food is 100% organic. The fact is, these days, we are seeing a proliferation of foods labelled as organic that contain very little or no organic ingredients.

(1125)

[*English*]

[**Table of Contents**]

Mr. Paul Dewar (Ottawa Centre, NDP):
Mr. Speaker, it is a pleasure to speak today to this important legislation.

I will begin my comments by noting that Bill C-517 is identical to Bill C-456 and Bill C-410. Bill C-456 was tabled by my colleague, our agricultural critic from B.C., and Bill C-410 was tabled by my colleague from Winnipeg.

I think the reason people are concerned about this issue, an issue with which our party has been seized and which has been our party's policy for a long time, is essentially from many points of view but it comes down to the right to know. In a democracy, it is extremely important to have transparency.

In terms of food safety, which has been an extremely important issue to Canadians and to people around the world recently because of many of the concerns around food safety, one of the things we need to invoke, as was mentioned earlier by another member, is the precautionary principle.

The precautionary principle, as it relates to GM, genetically modified foods, is that we have some tracking and predictability and at the end of the day we have not only sufficient information for consumers, but also for farmers, which is important.

We know that recent actions of the EU and other jurisdictions have required that GM be noted on all food products. We need to take that into consideration as to what the government's role is to help farmers, as well as consumers. On this side of the House, we believe, and have believed for quite a while, that requires legislation and, quite frankly, support.

Source: How C-517 was Killed – Transcript of House of Commons Debate

We have seen in the past that large agri-businesses have foisted certain products upon farmers, only to find out that sometimes these seeds during planting drift over to other farmers' fields, corrupting their product and their food. Once that happens, it can corrupt and infect a whole crop when these things are not tracked and traced.

Those stories are well-known. I am sure every member of the House is aware of scenarios where, through no fault of the farmers, they discover that some genetically modified seeds have blown over into their fields when they did not ask for them.

When we look at GM labelling and the importance of the consumers' right to know, it also applies to farmers.

When we look at the peer review on this, the independent testing of the environmental and health impacts of growing and eating GM food, it is important to apply the precautionary principle.

I would submit that if we look into policies of the government, certainly of Environment Canada which claims to invoke the precautionary principle, in rhetoric certainly, but we want to ensure it does that in practice.

What are some of the potential adverse effects of GM food consumption? They have to be taken into consideration. The jury is not out. The studies need to be done. Some government members in the House have posited the benefits of it. I have mentioned some of the concerns that have affected farmers. The EU has suggested that GM foods need to be labelled and that there needs to be a clear and transparent process around that. There is the market share for Canadians and for Canadian farmers, which is another reason.

I should note that Canadian companies like McCain have successfully removed GM ingredients in their potatoes, in this case. They were responding to market pressures. Let us not say that it cannot be done. It can be done in terms of tracking and, in this case, removing. However, what we believe must be done without compromise is to bring in the labelling.

I am sure members will be interested to note that the biosafety protocol for countries like Canada will soon require that we supply, as an exporter of GM foods, detailed information on GM products. These products are exported to about 141 countries around the world. It is not only the EU.

(1130)

Mandatory GM labelling would help Canada and its farmers to continue to have access to the markets. It is a right to know for citizens and consumers, and to help farmers gain access to markets. It is something to make sure that Canada is in line with other countries on a multilateral basis.

In Canada there have been many civil society groups and NGOs that have spoken out on this issue, such as the Canadian Biotechnology Action Network, the Saskatchewan Organic Directorate, the National Farmers Union and the Rideau Institute. The USC, which has its headquarters in Ottawa, has spoken out very strongly on this issue. I should note that one of the most prominent experts on this issue, Pat Mooney, has actually given advice to various Liberal and Conservative governments. He has been very clear on the concerns that he has about what GM foods do to our food supply and also the sources of seeds for our foods.

All of this should be taken into account. That is why we should be providing this legislation for Canadians, for our farmers, and to bring us up to speed on our international agreements and commitments.

It is also important to note that there are other pieces of legislation which touch on this. I would perhaps declare a conflict of interest here. I have a private member's bill that would not only ask that GM foods be labelled but that we also include meat products and what antibiotics are in the meat products. We want to know what rendered slaughterhouse waste was used and are there hormones in the food. These are the questions that Canadians have.

Canadians remember the mad cow crisis and the failure of our food system, notwithstanding the warnings from scientists at Health Canada that rendered feed would corrupt our meat system. Certainly

Source: How C-517 was Killed – Transcript of House of Commons Debate

that happened. Two years prior to the mad cow crisis one of our scientists, who blew the whistle, was fired for doing his job. We were told that if we did not keep an eye on rendered feed that was fed our cows that there would be an outbreak of mad cow disease. He told us that two years before the first case was detected. This scientists is still fighting the government in court because of his actions on blowing the whistle.

It is all about time. It is not about waiting any longer. If we are going to be competitive in the world and provide safe foods for our citizens, as well as an advantage in the export market, this is the bare minimum.

A member of the Liberal Party mentioned the issue of the Codex Committee on Food Labelling which has essentially been ignored by the government. This is another indication of the government not wanting to be a relevant actor on the international stage and following multilateral approaches in my opinion.

It is important that Canadians are in line with the international commitments and protocols that exist. The Codex Committee on Food Labelling is asking our government and other governments to bring forward legislation such as Bill C-517. It is another validation by a third party on why the bill should be passed.

I might add that I recently met with a group who is concerned about baby formula and the fact that it does not have sufficient labelling. We know that baby formula companies are going into hospitals and having access to new mothers and providing formula, instead of urging breastfeeding as the best way to feed babies. I thought those days were over. We know that there is not sufficient labelling on that formula.

The bill before us is the bare minimum for the international commitments that Canada has made for food safety for Canadians and for farmers gaining access to international markets. On this side of the House we strongly support the bill. We have supported the bill in the past and we will support it in the future. It is about time that the Conservative government passed this bill.

(1135)

[*Translation*]

[**Table of Contents**]

Mr. Bernard Bigras (Rosemont—La Petite-Patrie, BQ):
Mr. Speaker, it is with great joy that I rise today to speak to Bill C-517, An Act to amend the Food and Drugs Act (mandatory labelling for genetically modified foods).

I would like to begin by thanking my colleague from Rivière-des-Mille-Îles for introducing this bill. Once again, this shows that the Bloc Québécois is listening to what Quebeckers want, because in Quebec, between 80% and 90%—

An hon. member: Ninety-one percent.

Mr. Bernard Bigras: Ninety-one percent of Quebeckers want mandatory labelling. Though not unanimous, the vast majority of Quebeckers want it, so my colleague decided to introduce this critical bill. The purpose of the bill is to set up a transparent food system so that we know where the things we eat, the foods we put on the table, come from. If genetic modification has taken place, consumers will know about it before making these decisions.

I would also like to take this opportunity to pay tribute to a colleague who passed away over the weekend, the former member for Davenport, Charles Caccia. He was the environment minister a few years ago. He first came to the House in 1968 and, as an environmental warrior, he spent 36 years in this House trying to convince as many voters as possible that we need to protect the environment. A real fighter, in 2001, he introduced a bill for mandatory labelling. We must not forget that Charles Caccia, who died this past weekend, had been trying since 2001 to convince parliamentarians here to bring in this mandatory system. Unfortunately, the House rejected his bill, 126 votes to 91. This bill thus has a history.

I remember my former colleague, Hélène Alarie, the representative for Louis-Hébert, who was the first to get a motion passed about setting up this regulatory system. Unfortunately, the House of Commons has repeatedly rejected the new standards, which should be mandatory.

Source: How C-517 was Killed – Transcript of House of Commons Debate

What does Bill C-517 set out to do? First, the minister would be responsible for establishing that a food has been genetically modified. Second, the minister would also be responsible for preparing a list. Third, under the legislation, no one would be allowed to sell genetically modified products unless clear information is made available to the consumer indicating that the product or one or more of its components has been genetically modified.

How did we arrive at this legislative measure today? In 2004, the federal government did not pass a mandatory approach, as most Quebeckers and Canadians wanted, but a voluntary approach leaving it up to the industry to label genetically modified foods.

What does this voluntary system achieve? Four years later, because of this chance the industry has been given, we cannot identify any genetically modified products on our grocery store shelves. This proves that the federal government's voluntary approach has been a failure across the board.

What were these standards adopted by the Standards Council of Canada all about? The standard was that a product was considered genetically modified if more than 5% of its ingredients were the product of genetic modifications.

(1140)

The standard is 5%, while Europe has adopted a standard of 0.9%, or close to 1%. Similarly, the Quebec ministry of agriculture, fisheries and agri-food had proposed to the federal government, during consultations on GMO regulations, a standard of about 0.9%, in other words, a standard extremely similar to the European approach.

This 5% safety threshold adopted by the federal government is clearly inadequate for the people of Quebec, the government of Quebec and those who expect more transparency from the federal government.

There is something else to consider in the federal government's proposed figure. For products containing 5% genetic modifications or more, the product label would not use the term GMO, as prescribed in the international standard set out in the Codex Alimentarius. Instead, the term GE, or genetically engineered, or GEP, genetically engineered product, should be used. Again, the federal government's approach is nothing less than an attempt to disguise where the products on our shelves truly come from and what they truly contain.

In short, we should first remember that the proposed regulations are voluntary, and therefore implementation is at the discretion of industry. Second, the term used misleads Canadians. Third, the safety thresholds are too high; Quebec is asking for a lower threshold of almost 1%, like the one adopted by Europe.

As I said, this approach has failed. However, there are precedents. I am thinking of Russia and China, which have already adopted mandatory labelling of GMOs. Why am I bringing up these two precedents? Quite simply because our exports to Asian countries are on the rise. I am thinking of the wheat issue, for example. When the time came to approve Roundup Ready wheat in Canada, the Canadian Wheat Board advised against it because Canadian farmers would lose some of their market share.

Therefore, Canada should follow the move to make the international standard more transparent in order to avoid reducing market share for those goods it sells in Canada and abroad.

This morning, my Conservative colleague told us that a multitude of studies have shown that this does not pose a threat to our health or the environment. However, all these studies were conducted by the industry and the multinational known as Monsanto. The Royal Society of Canada established a few years ago that the only valid studies are independent studies. I invite our colleague, if he believes that this does not affect our health and the environment, to order this government to fund independent studies that will shed light on this issue.

In closing, I would say that this bill is essential because its main purpose is to better inform citizens about the products they eat. I would add that, contrary to what some would have us believe, this bill presents an economic opportunity for Canadian farmers to embrace and join the international movement to make labelling of transgenic products mandatory.

Source: How C-517 was Killed – Transcript of House of Commons Debate

(1145)

[*English*]

[**Table of Contents**]

Mr. James Bezan (Selkirk—Interlake, CPC):
Mr. Speaker, I am pleased to speak to Bill C-517 which seeks to require that all genetically modified food is labelled. As a representative of a riding with thousands of farmers and ranchers, I am opposed to this bill. As chair of the Standing Committee on Agriculture and Agri-Food, I also oppose this bill.

Technically speaking, Bill C-517 provides a much too narrow definition of genetically modified food, narrower than that which already exists in the food and drug regulations. Under the current regulations the term "genetically modified" includes modifications obtained through the use of traditional techniques, such as chemical mutagenesis and conventional breeding, as well as those obtained from modern biotechnology.

Bill C-517 would create a two-tiered system for GM foods. Depending on the method used in the development of specific foods, foods falling under the new definition would be required to be labelled to indicate the method of production, while others derived from more traditional modification methods, such as mutagenesis, would not be subject to mandatory labelling.

Health Canada regulates GM foods as novel foods. This encompasses foods that may have undergone a significant change in composition or nutritional value as a result of a manufacturing or packaging process. It also encompasses any substance that does not have a history of safe use as a food. Under the current legislation, the novel foods regulations permit Health Canada to assess the safety of all novel foods irrespective of the production method used prior to their sale in Canada.

We have a rigorous process in Canada. For instance, Health Canada must be notified prior to the marketing of any novel food in Canada so that a thorough safety assessment can be performed. The basis of this assessment is a comparison of each novel food with a conventional counterpart and requires a critical evaluation of the scientific information and results of research studies.

The information requirements are comprehensive. They include a complete description of the food product, its intended use, a molecular characterization of any novel traits, biochemical and compositional analysis, not to mention toxicological, nutritional and allergy data, and an estimate of dietary exposure and anticipated use by the average consumer.

The government is committed to sharing information with Canadians on how products of biotechnology are regulated. Health Canada publishes on its website a list of approved novel foods and decision documents which describe how regulatory authorities determine the safety of each new food product and why certain conclusions were reached. Other information, including Health Canada's guidelines for the safety assessment of novel foods, fact sheets, and answers to frequently asked questions are also available.

Health Canada and the Canadian Food Inspection Agency post information about products that are under review on the CFIA website. This provides the public with an opportunity to provide input on scientific matters relevant to the safety assessment of submissions from certain product developers.

Health Canada's responsibility for food labelling falls within the department's mandate for health and safety issues. As with all foods, special labelling of GM foods is required in cases where potential health and safety concerns, which can be mitigated through labelling, are identified during the product's pre-market safety assessment.

In Canada it is not mandatory to identify the method of production, including biotechnology, that is used to develop a food product. Nevertheless, a voluntary method of production labelling is permitted, provided it is truthful, not misleading and in compliance with all domestic regulatory requirements.

These principles are consistent with policy for all foods under the Food and Drugs Act. In general, food products that are demonstrated to be safe and nutritious are treated the same way as their traditional counterparts with regard to labelling requirements.

Source: How C-517 was Killed – Transcript of House of Commons Debate

Related to this is the CFIA's new regulations for organic products. The organic regulations will protect consumers against false organic claims and will govern the use of a new Canada organic logo.

The government is providing a competitive advantage for the Canadian organic sector and protecting consumers. Not only will Canadians be protected against deceptive and misleading claims on organic products, but the organic industry's capacity to respond to international and domestic market opportunities will be strengthened.

The Canada organic logo will be permitted for use only on those food products certified as meeting the revised Canadian standard for organic production and that contain at least 95% organic ingredients. Following a phase-in period, it will be mandatory that all organic products be certified for interprovincial and international trade.

(1150)

This government has taken further action to make sure that Canadian families can go to the grocery store knowing the food they purchase is safe. The Prime Minister announced a new food and product safety initiative on December 17, 2007 to ensure that we are ready to meet the new challenges of a global market. The government's food safety action plan will enhance the safety and reliability of food and health products by modernizing our system to better protect Canadians in our global environment.

The government is working hard to ensure our food safety system evolves to meet the challenges posed by increased volumes of trade, consumer demands and differing food safety frameworks among countries. We are delivering on our promises with $113 million provided in budget 2008 for the product and food safety initiative.

This government's approach is threefold. It focuses on managing risk along the food continuum. It prevents problems early on so that quick action can be taken. It no longer waits for threats to emerge before reacting.

As a government we are proud that we have one of the most stringent food safety systems in the world. Our plan recognizes that product safety is in everyone's interest and that everyone--Canadians, industry and government--has a role to play.

In conclusion, Canada's long-standing policy for the labelling of GM foods allows for the provision of information to consumers while avoiding the costs and potential trade implications associated with the implementation of the requirements of Bill C-517. We are taking steps to protect consumers in the marketplace without needlessly damaging the agriculture industry.

As a farmer, I believe that we should let the market dictate how we produce our food. Consumer driven initiatives will essentially dictate to us on how we move forward with our production methods. I believe voluntary labelling of genetically engineered foods is the correct way to move forward on this issue.

On the news we always hear about increasing prices for grain products, particularly the staples of wheat, rice and corn. Everybody keeps talking about a food shortage. We know we are in a tight supply. Now is not the time to start talking about turning back the clock and going back to an organic production system, which would actually short the marketplace and create even more increases in food prices.

Farmers will decide what is the best way to meet this new world demand and allow the consumers to choose what is best for them, whether that is GMO or non-GMO. My father grew organic crops for over 25 years because the market was there for that product. We received a good return on our investment in growing organic crops. We also know there is greater need out there that can only be met through new technology and improvements to our production systems. Farmers should be allowed to adapt those to make the most money they possibly can and feed the world.

[**Table of Contents**]

Hon. Wayne Easter (Malpeque, Lib.):

Mr. Speaker, how much time do I have?

[**Table of Contents**]

The Acting Speaker (Mr. Royal Galipeau):

The hon. member will be interrupted at noon, high noon.

[**Table of Contents**]

Hon. Wayne Easter:

Mr. Speaker, I speak to Bill C-517 with a great deal of concern, because while the intent sounds reasonable, there are other and better ways of addressing the intent of this bill.

The consequences of this bill would impose costs on Canadian consumers, producers and processors, either driving up the costs of food, or driving down producers' returns, or more likely both, and for what gain? This bill would do absolutely nothing for the safety of food and it would not really clarify choice for consumers.

As the member who spoke before me said, there are already regulations coming into effect that can give consumers that clarity of choice. That is the new Canadian certified organic system under the Canada Agricultural Products Act. When these new regulations come into effect on November 14 of this year, consumers can be assured that when they choose products carrying the Canada organic label they are choosing foods that do not contain products of biotechnology. Beyond that, if consumer demand is there, industry can use voluntary labelling--in fact, that was being done in Prince Edward Island with Island natural pork--as long as that labelling is truthful and abides by the laws of the land.

The bill, other than to say something is a genetically modified food, which to be honest happens in both natural breeding and scientific means, I think we ought to be blunt about it; it does actually cater to emotion and to people's fears about the unknown, and genetically modified foods are certainly a bit unknown. To be blunt, with this bill there is absolutely no gain in addressing those fears, but there is a tremendous cost. Let me turn to what some of the organizations have said.

The Canadian Seed Trade Association said:

> We believe that if enacted, the provisions of this bill could have a very detrimental effect on the ability of our members to continue to deliver innovative products.

The association went on to say, and this is important:

> [Our members] support the rigorous system of assessment in Canada, and expend many human and financial resources to participate in it. Biotechnology is likely the most scrutinized of all of the tools we use to bring innovation to agriculture and agri-food. New products derived from biotechnology are subject to the approval of three different government departments working with 5 different pieces of legislation and associated regulations.

It is very concerned. The bottom line is, who will pay these costs? The costs are substantial. Maple Leaf Foods and others in a letter stated:

> This Bill will impose hundreds of millions of dollars of unnecessary cost to the agri-food industry without providing any benefit to Canadian consumers.

The fact is producers and consumers will pay the costs of this mandatory labelling legislation. I would say the bill is a bad investment for no gain, other than to play on people's emotions. Let me list the organizations which have said they are strongly opposed to this bill. They are substantial and they represent a lot of investment in this country: CropLife Canada; Food and Consumer Products of Canada; Maple Leaf Foods; Canadian Egg Marketing Agency; Casco; Canadian Seed Trade Association; Canadian Horticulture Council; Quebec's food processors association, CTAC; UPA in Quebec, the major farm organization there; Canadian Federation of Independent Grocers; Food Processors of Canada; Canadian Meat Council; Saskatchewan Association of Rural Municipalities; Canola Council of Canada; Canadian Canola Growers Association, BIOTECanada, and the CFA.

(1155)

This is a substantial list of organizations. I underline the fact that these are not just organizations; they are also Canadian consumers who have the same concern about food as others in our society.

Source: How C-517 was Killed – Transcript of House of Commons Debate

Let me turn to a statement that was made by the member for Skeena—Bulkley Valley. He said:

> We need to understand the ethical, moral and environmental implications of the genetically modified foods that we consume, the foods that we put on the table for our friends and family, foods that have been modified at the genetic level.

I agree with that, but the bill would do absolutely nothing to deal with this concern. Others have raised questions about scientists not being able to speak out, and I agree with that fact. I faced that when I fought rBGH, the drug hormone being put into dairy cattle. We managed to get that specific product stopped. Yes, scientists were shut up, but the bill would do nothing to deal with that issue. Therefore, let us concentrate on where the real problem is rather than bring in a bill that requires mandatory labelling, but does nothing about what people perceive the problem to be.

The bill is not about a safety issue and it would do nothing to clarify what is in food. If consumers have a concern about GM foods, they can turn to their organic labelling product. Industry can also use voluntary labelling. Mandatory labelling will be costly, and I outlined many of those costs.

The bottom line is the bill would not do what it is intended to do. Therefore, I believe it should be stopped at this stage and our time should be invested in dealing with the real issues.

(1200)

[*Translation*]

[**Table of Contents**]

Mr. Gilles-A. Perron (Rivière-des-Mille-Îles, BQ):
Mr. Speaker, I am disconcerted to see a scaremonger, such as the one who just spoke, saying such things and frightening the public.

Let us talk about GMOs.

An hon. member: Oh, oh!

Mr. Gilles-A. Perron: I was polite, I kept quiet, so I would ask the member to do the same, please.

I am going to speak about GMOs. I have a quotation to read, since I have only five minutes left. I am quoting someone who knows a lot about GMOs:

> Frankly, I think there should have been more testing. But the biotechnology companies were not interested—they had invested a lot of money in developing their products.
>
> ...
>
> At that time, if you did not blindly accept rapid development in terms of biotechnology and GMOs, you were thought to be a Luddite. I was under a lot of pressure not to overregulate these products.

Who said that? Dan Glickman, the American Secretary of Agriculture under the Clinton administration.

Last week, when we banned baby bottles—small bottles for babies and infants—made of polycarbonate, the member for Mégantic—L'Érable, Secretary of State (Agriculture), said that when it comes to health and the health of our children, no cost is too high.

Seventy per cent of the producers in Quebec's UPA are in favour of labelling. What is more, 91% of Quebeckers and 83% of Canadians are in favour of labelling. We are talking about the health and safety of Canadians like you and me. I believe and I hope that the members in this House will remember, before they make a decision, that this could affect their re-election. When 83% of people are in favour, what should we do? We should listen to our constituents and say yes to mandatory labelling for genetically modified foods.

In closing, I would like to acknowledge two 12-year olds, Claire and Norbert, from the Cœur à cœur

Source: How C-517 was Killed – Transcript of House of Commons Debate

school in Saint-Eustache, who are firm supporters of mandatory food labelling.

[**Table of Contents**]

The Acting Speaker (Mr. Royal Galipeau):
It being 12:05 p.m., the time provided for debate has expired.

[*English*]

The question is on the motion. Is it the pleasure of the House to adopt the motion?

Some hon. members: Agreed.

Some hon. members: No.

The Acting Speaker (Mr. Royal Galipeau): All those in favour of the motion will please say yea.

Some hon. members: Yea.

The Acting Speaker (Mr. Royal Galipeau): All those opposed will please say nay.

Some hon. members: Nay.

The Acting Speaker (Mr. Royal Galipeau): In my opinion the nays have it.

And five or more members having risen:

The Acting Speaker (Mr. Royal Galipeau): Pursuant to Standing Order 93 the division stands deferred until Wednesday, May 7, immediately before the time provided for private members' business.

* * *

Source: How C-517 was Killed – Transcript of House of Commons Debate

C-517

Second Session, Thirty-ninth Parliament,
56-57 Elizabeth II, 2007-2008

HOUSE OF COMMONS OF CANADA

BILL C-517

An Act to amend the Food and Drugs Act (mandatory labelling for genetically modified foods)

FIRST READING, FEBRUARY 29, 2008

MR. PERRON

392149

Source: C-517

SUMMARY

This enactment amends the *Food and Drugs Act* to make the Minister of Health responsible for establishing that a food or one or more of its components has been genetically modified. If it is established that a food or one or more of its components has been genetically modified, the Minister shall cause the name of the food to be published in the *Canada Gazette*. The Minister shall also prepare a list of all such foods and cause a copy to be sent at no cost to any one who requests it.

No one may sell this food or a food product containing this food in a package unless a label is affixed to the package containing the following notice:

This product or one or more of its components
has been genetically modified

Ce produit ou un ou plusieurs de ses composants
ont été génétiquement modifiés

In addition, no one may sell this food or a food product containing this food in a package unless a poster in the prescribed form has been placed near the food containing the following notice:

Genetically modified

Génétiquement modifié

Source: C-517

2nd Session, 39th Parliament,
56-57 Elizabeth II, 2007-2008

HOUSE OF COMMONS OF CANADA

BILL C-517

An Act to amend the Food and Drugs Act (mandatory labelling for genetically modified foods)

R.S., c. F-27

Her Majesty, by and with the advice and consent of the Senate and House of Commons of Canada, enacts as follows:

1. Section 2 of the *Food and Drugs Act* is amended by adding, in alphabetical order, the following:

"genetically modified" « *génétiquement modifié* »

"genetically modified", with respect to a food or one of its components, means that the genetic make-up of the food or component has been modified by a technique that combines DNA fragments of the food or component with DNA fragments from another source in a way that could not occur without the use of modern technology.

2. The Act is amended by adding the following after section 7:

GENETICALLY MODIFIED FOOD

Duties of Minister

7.1 (1) The Minister is responsible for establishing, on the basis of scientific evidence, that a food or one or more of its components is genetically modified.

Publication in the *Canada Gazette*

(2) As soon as the Minister declares that a food or one or more of its components is genetically modified, the Minister shall cause the name of the food to be published in the *Canada Gazette*.

392149

Source: C-517

List

(3) The Minister shall prepare a list of all foods whose names have been published in the *Canada Gazette* under subsection (2) and shall cause a copy to be sent at no cost to any person who requests it.

Internet

(4) The Minister shall cause an electronic version of the list to be posted on a site of the Government of Canada that is generally accessible to the public through the Internet.

Access to the Internet

(5) The Minister shall ensure that an electronic version of any list posted on the Internet under subsection (4) is accessible at no cost, without a password, and in downloadable form.

Sale prohibited

7.2 Beginning on the sixteenth day following publication of the name of a food in the *Canada Gazette* under subsection 7.1(2), no person shall sell the food or a food product of which the food is a component in a package, unless a label is affixed to the package that contains the following notice:

This product or one or more of its components has been genetically modified

Ce produit ou un ou plusieurs de ses composants ont été génétiquement modifiés

Sale prohibited

7.3 Beginning on the sixteenth day following publication of the name of a food in the *Canada Gazette* under subsection 7.1(2), no person shall sell the food or a food product of which the food is a component, unless a sign in the prescribed form has been posted near the food that contains the following notice:

Genetically modified

Génétiquement modifié

3. Subsection 30(1) of the Act is amended by adding the following after paragraph (*e*):

(*e.1*) respecting the form of the label referred to in section 7.2 and the sign referred to in section 7.3;

Published under authority of the Speaker of the House of Commons

Available from:
Publishing and Depository Services
Public Works and Government Services Canada
Ottawa, Ontario K1A 0S5
Telephone: (613) 941-5995 or 1-800-635-7943
Fax: (613) 954-5779 or 1-800-565-7757
publications@pwgsc.gc.ca
http://publications.gc.ca

Source: C-517

C-517: How they voted

The following table lists how MPs voted on the recently defeated Bill C-517. Mouse over provinces to see the vote summary, click for the vote count.

To top

Alberta

Constituency	First name	Last name	Party	Vote
Calgary - Nose Hill	Diane	Ablonczy	Conservative	No
Edmonton - Spruce Grove	Rona	Ambrose	Conservative	No
Calgary West	Rob	Anders	Conservative	No
Vegreville - Wainwright	Leon	Benoit	Conservative	No
Wetaskiwin	Blaine	Calkins	Conservative	No
Lethbridge	Rick	Casson	Conservative	No

Source: C-517: How They Voted

Constituency	First name	Last name	Party	Vote
Edmonton - Sherwood Park	Ken	Epp	Conservative	No
Edmonton East	Peter	Goldring	Conservative	No
Calgary Notheast	Art	Hanger	Conservative	No
Edmonton Centre	Laurie	Hawn	Conservative	No
Edmonton - Strathcona	Rahim	Jaffer	Conservative	No
Fort McMurray - Athabasca	Brian	Jean	Conservative	No
Calgary Southeast	Jason	Kenney	Conservative	No
Edmonton - Mill Woods -Beaumont	Mike	Lake	Conservative	No
Macleod	Ted	Menzies	Conservative	No
Yellowhead	Rob	Merrifield	Conservative	No
Red Deer	Bob	Mills	Conservative	No
Calgary East	Deepak	Obhrai	Conservative	No
Calgary Centre - North	Jim	Prentice	Conservative	No
Edmonton - Leduc	James	Rajotte	Conservative	No
Calgary Centre	Lee	Richardson	Conservative	No
Medicine Hat	Monte	Solberg	Conservative	No
Crowfoot	Kevin	Sorenson	Conservative	No
Westlock - St. Paul	Brian	Storseth	Conservative	No
Wild Rose	Myron	Thompson	Conservative	No
Peace River	Chris	Warkentin	Conservative	No
Edmonton - St. Albert	John	Williams	Conservative	No
Calgary Southwest	Stephen	Harper	Conservative	Did not vote

To top

British Columbia

Constituency	First name	Last name	Party	Vote
Kootenay - Columbia	Jim	Abbott	Conservative	No
Delta - Richmond East	John	Cummins	Conservative	No
Okanagan - Coquihalla	Stockwell	Day	Conservative	No
Vancouver Kingsway	David	Emerson	Conservative	No
Fleetwood - Port Kells	Nina	Grewal	Conservative	No
Cariboo - Prince George	Richard	Harris	Conservative	No
South Surrey - White Rock - Cloverdale	Russ	Hiebert	Conservative	No

Source: C-517: How They Voted

Constituency	First name	Last name	Party	Vote
Prince George - Peace River	Jay	Hill	Conservative	No
Pitt Meadows - Maple Ridge - Mission	Randy	Kamp	Conservative	No
Saanich - Gulf Islands	Gary	Lunn	Conservative	No
Esquimalt - Juan de Fuca	Keith	Martin	Liberal	No
Okanagan - Shuswap	Colin	Mayes	Conservative	No
Chilliwack -Fraser Canyon	Chuck	Strahl	Conservative	No
Langley	Mark	Warawa	Conservative	No
Port Moody -Westwood - Port Coquitlam	James	Moore	Conservative	No
British Columbia Southern Interior	Alex	Atamanenko	NDP	Yes
Vancouver Island North	Catherine	Bell	NDP	Yes
North Vancouver	Don	Bell	Liberal	Yes
KelownaÑLake Country	Ron	Cannan	Conservative	Yes
Richmond	Raymond	Chan	Liberal	Yes
NanaimoÑCowichan	Jean	Crowder	NDP	Yes
SkeenaÑBulkley Valley	Nathan	Cullen	NDP	Yes
Vancouver East	Libby	Davies	NDP	Yes
Newton - North Delta	Sukh	Dhaliwal	Liberal	Yes
Vancouver South	Ujjal	Dosanjh	Liberal	Yes
Burnaby - New Westminister	Peter	Julian	NDP	Yes
Vancouver Quadra	Joyce	Murray	Liberal	Yes
Surrey North	Penny	Priddy	NDP	Yes
Victoria	Denise	Savoie	NDP	Yes
Burnaby - Douglas	Bill	Siksay	NDP	Yes
West Vancouver - Sunshine Coast - Sea to Sky Country	Blair	Wilson	Independent	Yes
New Westminister - Coquitlam	Dawn	Black	NDP	Did not vote
Abbotsford	Ed	Fast	Conservative	Paired
Vancouver Centre	Hedy	Fry	Liberal	Did not vote
Kamloops - Thompson - Cariboo	Betty	Hinton	Conservative	Paired

Source: C-517: How They Voted

Constituency	First name	Last name	Party	Vote
Nanaimo - Alberni	James	Lunney	Conservative	Did not vote

To top

Manitoba

Constituency	First name	Last name	Party	Vote
Selkirk - Interlake	James	Bezan	Conservative	No
Winnipeg South	Rod	Bruinooge	Conservative	No
Charleswood - St James - Assiniboia	Steven	Fletcher	Conservative	No
Dauphin - Swan River - Marquette	Inky	Mark	Conservative	No
Saint Boniface	Raymond	Simard	Liberal	No
Provencher	Vic	Toews	Conservative	No
Brandon - Souris	Mervin	Tweed	Conservative	No
Elmwood - Transcona	Bill	Blaikie	NDP	Did not vote
Churchill	Tina	Keeper	Liberal	Did not vote
Winnipeg Centre	Pat	Martin	NDP	Did not vote
Winnipeg South Centre	Anita	Neville	Liberal	Did not vote
Portage - Lisgar	Brian	Pallister	Conservative	Paired
Kildonan - St Paul	Joy	Smith	Conservative	Did not vote
Winnipeg North	Judy	Wasylycia-Leis	NDP	Did not vote

To top

New Brunswich

Constituency	First name	Last name	Party	Vote
Tobique - Mactaquac	Mike	Allen	Conservative	No
Madawaska - Restigouche	Jean-Claude	D'Amours	Liberal	No

Source: C-517: How They Voted

Constituency	First name	Last name	Party	Vote
Miramichi	Charles	Hubbard	Liberal	No
Beausejour	Dominic	LeBlanc	Liberal	No
Fundy Royal	Rob	Moore	Conservative	No
Moncton - Riverview - Dieppe	Brian	Murphy	Liberal	No
New Brunswick Southwest	Greg	Thompson	Conservative	No
St John	Paul	Zed	Liberal	No
Acadie - Bathurst	Yvon	Godin	NDP	Yes
Fredericton	Andy	Scott	Liberal	Did not vote

To top

Newfoundland / Labrador

Constituency	First name	Last name	Party	Vote
Humber - St Barbe - Baie Verte	Gerry	Byrne	Liberal	No
St John's East	Norman	Doyle	Conservative	No
St John's South - Mt Pearl	Loyola	Hearn	Conservative	No
Avalon	Fabian	Manning	Conservative	No
Randon - Burin - St George's	Bill	Matthews	Liberal	No
Bonavista - Gander - Grand Falls - Windsor	Scott	Simms	Liberal	No
Labrador	Todd	Russell	Liberal	Did not vote

To top

Northwest Territories

Constituency	First name	Last name	Party	Vote
Western Arctic	Dennis	Bevington	NDP	Yes

To top

Nove Scotia

Source: C-517: How They Voted

Constituency	First name	Last name	Party	Vote
Kings - Hants	Scott	Brison	Liberal	No
South Shore - St Margaret's	Gerald	Keddy	Conservative	No
Central Nova	Peter	MacKay	Conservative	No
Halifax West	Geoff	Regan	Liberal	No
Dartmouth - Cole Harbour	Michael	Savage	Liberal	No
Sydney Victoria	Mark	Eyking	Liberal	No
Halifax	Alexa	McDonough	NDP	Yes
Sackville - Eastern Shore	Peter	Stoffer	NDP	Yes
West Nova	Robert	Thibault	Liberal	Yes
Cumberland - Colchester - Musquodoboit Valley	Bill	Casey	Independent	Did not vote
Cape Breton - Canso	Rodger	Cuzner	Liberal	Did not vote

To top

Nunavut

Constituency	First name	Last name	Party	Vote
Nunavut	Nancy	Karetak-Lindell	Liberal	No

To top

Ontario

Constituency	First name	Last name	Party	Vote
Kitchener - Conestoga	Harold	Albrecht	Conservative	No
Niagara West - Glanbrook	Dean	Allison	Conservative	No
Ottawa West - Nepean	John	Baird	Conservative	No
London West	Sue	Barnes	Liberal	No
Brampton West	Colleen	Beaumier	Liberal	No
Thunder Bay - Rainy River	Ken	Boshcoff	Liberal	No

Source: C-517: How They Voted

Constituency	First name	Last name	Party	Vote
Leeds - Grenville	Gord	Brown	Conservative	No
Barrie	Patrick	Brown	Conservative	No
Wellington - Halton Hills	Michael	Chong	Conservative	No
Parry sound - Muskoka	Tony	Clement	Conservative	No
Thunder Bay - Superior North	Joe	Comuzzi	Conservative	No
Etobicoke North	Roy	Cullen	Liberal	No
Sarnia - Lambton	Patricia	Davidson	Conservative	No
Peterborough	Dean	Del Mastro	Conservative	No
Haliburton - Kawartha Lakes - Brock	Barry	Devolin	Conservative	No
York Centre	Ken	Dryden	Liberal	No
St Catherine's	Rick	Dykstra	Conservative	No
Haldimand - Norfolk	Diane	Finley	Conservative	No
Whitby - Oshawa	Jim	Flaherty	Conservative	No
Ottawa - Orleans	Royal	Galipeau	Conservative	No
Renfrew - Nipissing - Pembroke	Cheryl	Gallant	Conservative	No
Cambridge	Gary	Goodyear	Conservative	No
Simcoe - Grey	Helena	Guergis	Conservative	No
Willowdale	Martha	Hall Findlay	Liberal	No
Etobicoke - Lakeshore	Michael	Ignatieff	Liberal	No
Mississauga - Streetsville	Wajid	Khan	Conservative	No
Prince Edward Hastings	Daryl	Kramp	Conservative	No
Stormont - Dundas - South Glengarry	Guy	Lauzon	Conservative	No
Scarborough - Rouge River	Derek	Lee	Liberal	No
Oxford	Dave	MacKenzie	Conservative	No
Welland	John	Maloney	Liberal	No
Sudbury	Diane	Marleau	Liberal	No
Markham - Unionville	John	McCallum	Liberal	No
Bruce - Grey - Owen Sound	Larry	Miller	Conservative	No
Niagara Falls	Rob	Nicholson	Conservative	No

Source: C-517: How They Voted

Constituency	First name	Last name	Party	Vote
Northumberland - Quinte West	Rick	Norlock	Conservative	No
Carleton - Mississippi Mills	Gordon	O'Connor	Conservative	No
Durham	Bev	Oda	Conservative	No
London North Centre	Glen	Pearson	Liberal	No
Nepean - Carleton	Pierre	Poilievre	Conservative	No
Elgin - Middlesex - London	Joe	Preston	Conservative	No
Don Valley East	Yasmin	Ratansi	Liberal	No
Kitchener - Centre	Karen	Redman	Liberal	No
Lanark - Frontenac - Lennox and Addington	Scott	Reid	Conservative	No
Perth - Wellington	Gary	Schellenberger	Conservative	No
York West	Judy	Sgro	Liberal	No
Lambton - Kent - Middlesex	Bev	Shipley	Conservative	No
Brant	Lloyd	St. Armand	Liberal	No
Algoma - Manitoulin - Kapuskasing	Brent	St. Denis	Liberal	No
Simcoe North	Bruce	Stanton	Conservative	No
Huron - Bruce	Paul	Steckle	Liberal	No
Oak Ridges - Markham	Lui	Temelkovski	Liberal	No
Dufferin - Caledon	David	Tilson	Conservative	No
Halton	Garth	Turner	Liberal	No
Chatham - Kent - Essex	Dave	Van Kesteren	Conservative	No
York Simcoe	Peter	Van Loan	Conservative	No
Burlington	Mike	Wallace	Conservative	No
Oakville	Bonnie	Brown	Liberal	No
Oshawa	Colin	Carrie	Conservative	No
Glengarry - Prescott - Russell	Pierre	Lemieux	Conservative	No
Kitchener Waterloo	Andrew	Telegdi	Liberal	No
Mississauga - Erindale	Omar	Alghabra	Liberal	Yes
Timmins - James Bay	Charlie	Angus	NDP	Yes

Source: C-517: How They Voted

Constituency	First name	Last name	Party	Vote
Mississauga - Brampton South	Navdeep	Bains	Liberal	Yes
Vaughn	Maurizio	Bevilacqua	Liberal	Yes
Nickel Belt	Raymond	Bonin	Liberal	Yes
Hamilton Mountain	Chris	Charlton	NDP	Yes
Trinity - Spadina	Olivia	Chow	NDP	Yes
Hamilton Centre	David	Christopherson	NDP	Yes
Windsor Techumseh	Joe	Comartin	NDP	Yes
Ottawa Centre	Paul	Dewar	NDP	Yes
Brampton - Springdale	Ruby	Dhalla	Liberal	Yes
Don Valley West	John	Godfrey	Liberal	Yes
Mississauga East - Cooksville	Albina	Guarnieri	Liberal	Yes
Ajax - Pickering	Mark	Holland	Liberal	Yes
Thornhill	Susan	Kadis	Liberal	Yes
Scarborough - Agincourt	Jim	Karygiannis	Liberal	Yes
Toronto - Danforth	Jack	Layton	NDP	Yes
Bramalea - Gore - Malton	Gurbax	Malhi	Liberal	Yes
Hamilton East - Stony Creak	Wayne	Marston	NDP	Yes
Windsor West	Brian	Masse	NDP	Yes
London Fanshawe	Irene	Mathyssen	NDP	Yes
Ottawa South	David	McGuinty	Liberal	Yes
Beaches - East York	Maria	Minna	Liberal	Yes
Parkdale - High Park	Peggy	Nash	NDP	Yes
Nipissing - Timiskaming	Anthony	Rota	Liberal	Yes
Mississauga South	Paul	Szabo	Liberal	Yes
York South - Weston	Alan	Tonks	Liberal	Yes
Scarborough Southwest	Tom	Wappel	Liberal	Yes
Richmond Hill	Bryon	Wilfert	Liberal	Yes
Etobicoke Centre	Borys	Wrzesnewskyj	Liberal	Yes
Essex	Jeff	Watson	Conservative	Yes
Ottawa - Vanier	Mauril	Belanger	Liberal	Did not vote

Source: C-517: How They Voted

Constituency	First name	Last name	Party	Vote
St Paul's	Carolyn	Bennett	Liberal	Did not vote
Scarborough Centre	John	Cannis	Liberal	Did not vote
Sault St Marie	Tony	Martin	NDP	Did not vote
Scarborough - Guildwood	John	McKay	Liberal	Did not vote
Pickering - Scarborough East	Dan	McTeague	Liberal	Did not vote
Kingston and the Islands	Peter	Milliken	Liberal	Did not vote
Toronto Centre	Bob	Rae	Liberal	Did not vote
Davenport	Mario	Silva	Liberal	Did not vote
Newmarket Aurora	Belinda	Stronach	Liberal	Did not vote
Ancaster - Dundas - Flamborough - Westdale	David	Sweet	Conservative	Paired
Kenora	Roger	Valley	Liberal	Did not vote
Eglinton - Lawrence	Joseph	Volpe	Liberal	Did not vote

To top

Prince Edward Island

Constituency	First name	Last name	Party	Vote

Source: C-517: How They Voted

Constituency	First name	Last name	Party	Vote
Malpeque	Wayne	Easter	Liberal	No
Cardigan	Lawrence	MacAulay	Liberal	No
Egmont	Joe	McGuire	Liberal	No
Charlottetown	Shawn	Murphy	Liberal	Yes

To top

Quebec

Constituency	First name	Last name	Party	Vote
Jonquiere - Alma	Jean-Pierre	Blackburn	Conservative	No
Beaufort - Limoilou	Sylvie	Boucher	Conservative	No
Pontiac	Lawrence	Cannon	Conservative	No
Bourassa	Denis	Coderre	Liberal	No
Lotbiniere - Chutes de la Chaudiere	Jacques	Gourde	Conservative	No
Megantic - L'Erable	Christian	Paradis	Conservative	No
Pierrefonds - Dollard	Bernard	Patry	Liberal	No
Charlesbourg - Haute Saint Charles	Daniel	Petit	Conservative	No
Beauce	Maxime	Bernier	Conservative	No
Louis Saint Laurent	Josee	Verner	Conservative	No
Berthier - Maskinonge	Guy	Andre	Bloc Quebecois	Yes
Manicouagan	Gerard	Asselin	Bloc Quebecois	Yes
St Jean	Claude	Bachand	Bloc Quebecois	Yes
Papineau	Vivian	Barbot	Bloc Quebecois	Yes
Rosemont - Lapetite - Patrie	Bernard	Bigras	Bloc Quebecois	Yes
Gaspesie - Iles de la Madeleine	Raynald	Blais	Bloc Quebecois	Yes
Levis - Bellechasse	Steven	Blaney	Conservative	Yes
Compton - Stanstead	France	Bonsant	Bloc Quebecois	Yes
Chicoutimi - Le Fjord	Robert	Bouchard	Bloc Quebecois	Yes
Terrebonne - Blainville	Diane	Bourgeois	Bloc Quebecois	Yes

Source: C-517: How They Voted

Constituency	First name	Last name	Party	Vote
Sherbrooke	Serge	Cardin	Bloc Quebecois	Yes
Montmagny - L'Islet - Kamouraska - Riviere du Loup	Paul	Crete	Bloc Quebecois	Yes
Beauharnois - Salaberry	Claude	DeBellefeuille	Bloc Quebecois	Yes
Laval	Nicole	Demers	Bloc Quebecois	Yes
Laurentides - Labelle	Johanne	Deschamps	Bloc Quebecois	Yes
Laurier - Saint Marie	Gilles	Duceppe	Bloc Quebecois	Yes
Vaudreuil - Soulanges	Meili	Faille	Bloc Quebecois	Yes
Laval - Les Iles	Raymonde	Folco	Liberal	Yes
Chateauguay - Saint Constant	Carole	Freeman	Bloc Quebecois	Yes
Quebec	Christiane	Gagnon	Bloc Quebecois	Yes
Montmorency - Charlesvoix - Haute - Cote - Nord	Michel	Guimond	Bloc Quebecois	Yes
Notre Dame de Grace - Lachine	Marlene	Jennings	Liberal	Yes
Saint Maurice - Champlain	Jean-Yves	Laforest	Bloc Quebecois	Yes
Argenteuil - Papineau - Mrabel	Mario	Laframboise	Bloc Quebecois	Yes
La Pointe de Ile	Francine	Lalonde	Bloc Quebecois	Yes
Saint Bruno - Saint Hubert	Carole	Lavallee	Bloc Quebecois	Yes
Roberval - Lac Saint Jean	Denis	Lebel	Conservative	Yes
Abitibi - Temiscamingue	Marc	Lemay	Bloc Quebecois	Yes
Chambly - Bourduas	Yves	Lessard	Bloc Quebecois	Yes
Abitibi - Baie James - Nunavik - Eeyou	Yvon	Levesque	Bloc Quebecois	Yes
Brossard - La Prairie	Marcel	Lussier	Bloc Quebecois	Yes

Source: C-517: How They Voted

Constituency	First name	Last name	Party	Vote
Hochelaga	Real	Menard	Bloc Quebecois	Yes
Ahuntsic	Maria	Mourani	Bloc Quebecois	Yes
Gatineau	Richard	Nadeau	Bloc Quebecois	Yes
Brome - Missiquoi	Christian	Ouellet	Bloc Quebecois	Yes
Saint Leonard - Saint Michel	Massimo	Pacetti	Liberal	Yes
Joliette	Pierre	Paquette	Bloc Quebecois	Yes
Riviere des Mille Iles	Gilles-A.	Perron	Bloc Quebecois	Yes
Bas - Richelieu - Nicolet - Becancour	Louis	Plamondon	Bloc Quebecois	Yes
Hull - Aylmer	Marcel	Proulx	Liberal	Yes
Honore Mercier	Pablo	Rodriguez	Liberal	Yes
Lac Saint Louis	Francis	Scarpaleggia	Liberal	Yes
Jeanne Le Ber	Thierry	St-Cyr	Bloc Quebecois	Yes
Saint Hyacinthe - Bagot	Eve-Mary Thai	Thi Lac	Bloc Quebecois	Yes
Rinouski - Neigette - Temiscouata - Las Basques	Louise	Thibault	Independent	Yes
Shefford	Robert	Vincent	Bloc Quebecois	Yes
Alfred - Pellan	Robert	Carrier	Bloc Quebecois	Yes
Portneuf - Jacque - Cartier	Andre	Arthur	Independent	Did not vote
Richmond - Arthabaska	Andre	Bellavance	Bloc Quebecois	Paired
Trois Rivieres	Paule	Brunelle	Bloc Quebecois	Paired
Mount Royal	Irwin	Cotler	Liberal	Did not vote
Saint - Laurent - Cartierville	Stephane	Dion	Liberal	Did not vote

Source: C-517: How They Voted

Constituency	First name	Last name	Party	Vote
Montcalm	Roger	Gaudet	Bloc Quebecois	Paired
Repentigny	Raymond	Gravel	Bloc Quebecois	Paired
Riviere du Nord	Monique	Guay	Bloc Quebecois	Paired
Louis - Hebert	Luc	Harvey	Conservative	Paired
Vercheres - Les Patriotes	Luc	Malo	Bloc Quebecois	Paired
LaSalle - Emard	Paul	Martin	Liberal	Did not vote
Marc - Aurele - Fortin	Serge	Menard	Bloc Quebecois	Paired
Outremont	Thomas	Mulcair	NDP	Did not vote
Drummond	Pauline	Picard	Bloc Quebecois	Did not vote
Haute Gaspesie - La Mitis - Matane - Matapedia	Jean-Yves	Roy	Bloc Quebecois	Paired
Longeuil - Pierre Boucher	Caroline	St-Hilaire	Bloc Quebecois	Paired

To top

Saskatchewan

Constituency	First name	Last name	Party	Vote
Cypress Hills - Grasslands	David	Anderson	Conservative	No
Desnethe - Missinippi - Churchill River	Rob	Clarke	Conservative	No
Prince Albert	Brian	Fitzpatrick	Conservative	No
Wascana	Ralph	Goodale	Liberal	No
Souris - Moose Mountain	Ed	Komarnicki	Conservative	No
Regina - Lumsden - Lake Centre	Tom	Lukiwski	Conservative	No
Battlefords - Lloydminster	Gerry	Ritz	Conservative	No
Regina - Qu'Appelle	Andrew	Scheer	Conservative	No

Source: C-517: How They Voted

Constituency	First name	Last name	Party	Vote
Saskatoon - Rosetown - Biggar	Carol	Skelton	Conservative	No
Saskatoon - Humbolt	Bradley	Trost	Conservative	No
Saskatoon - Wanuskewin	Maurice	Vellacott	Conservative	No
Blackstrap	Lynne	Yelich	Conservative	No
Palliser	Dave	Batters	Conservative	Paired
Yorkton Melville	Garry	Breitkreuz	Conservative	Paired

To top

Yukon

Constituency	First name	Last name	Party	Vote
Yukon	Larry	Bagnell	Liberal	Yes

Source: C-517: How They Voted

5

A Manifesto for True Security and Prosperity

by Helke Ferrie

"Never doubt that a small group of thoughtful, committed citizens can change the world. It is the only thing that ever has."

—Margaret Mead

A manifesto is defined in the Oxford English Dictionary as "a public written declaration of principles, policies, and objectives." In this book two such declarations of principles have been presented. The two are incompatible. We have to decide which one we want.

Bills C-51 and C-52 announce to Canadians the government's objectives regarding the protection of the public from hazardous products and ensuring that the regulation of "therapeutic products" conforms to the stated objective of safe and effective drugs, natural health care products, and similar products, as well as safe foods. The definitions and justifications given for these bills are explicit in their intent to give maximal latitude in the arbitrary exercise of power to the Ministers of Health and Agriculture.

Another declaration published in this book is that which was put forward in 2006 by Justice Maegher when he ruled on the Truehope case. He asserted that the demonstrated needs of patients must take precedence over regulatory objectives and that the preeminence of these human needs is supported by common law and previous Supreme Court decisions. His decision not only drastically reduced the right of government to become involved in the regulation of novel therapeutic activities, but also established that potential harm to people must always seen as the greater harm to the public interest than the harm done to government's regulatory powers if these powers are disobeyed.

To put it another way, this judgment reaffirmed the right of people to practice civil disobedience and told the government that it and its regulatory agencies are intended to serve citizens, and that the primary duty of citizens is not obeying their governments and fulfill its regulatory objectives.

Nothing more ought to be said, actually. It is unfortunate that so much does have to be said, of which this book is merely a fraction. To have to tell yet another administration over the course of some twenty years to kindly remember that the government exists for the people—not the other way around—is really alarming.

To have to tell the Harper government that the government oversteps its competence as well as its constitutional rights when judging or pre-judging what is the proper practice of medicine, and what may be explored in medical research, is absolutely shocking. It is bizarre that Schedule A still exists in this form in 2008, listing specific diseases for which natural health products may not make any health claims. I say this is bizarre, because whatever health claims for natural products currently exist in the standard medical literature came from sources of the highest scientific integrity and are the stuff of modern biochemistry.

The classic example showing a government out of touch with reality is of course the Truehope case. The fact is, that one of the most severe illnesses known to psychiatry was successfully treated exclusively with nutritional medicine, while during that same period of time many leading psychiatrist in the world made it public that standard drug therapy generally used for bipolar disorder is far more harmful than nutritional protocols, and that these standard therapies are virtually all based on fraudulent industry-sponsored research.

It is a mystery that the government ignores or supports the stuff that can kill and now so often is based on fraud. Personally, I don't care in the least whether the reason for this is corruption, ignorance or a combination of the two. I once asked one of Canada's leading criminal and constitutional lawyers, Michael Code, formerly of Sack Goldblatt and Mitchell in Toronto and now at Osgode Hall: "Why would somebody *do* such a thing?" I was referring to some very nasty behavior by a medical regulatory agency with terrible consequences for very sick people (see the *Toronto Star*'s "Medical Secrets' series starting in 2001). His reply was: "Motive is irrelevant. You don't have to know why somebody commits a crime. You only need to prove that it is a crime." This observation has been a great comfort to me ever since, because this way of thinking anchors one in demonstrable facts and banishes the fretting, the sleepless nights, and the sense of being at the mercy of the absurd.

Returning to Schedule A, there are only 9 conditions on that portion of the list for which *resonabley* no health claims may be made for nutritional medicine; those 9 are conditions that tend to be surgical emergencies right from the start; nutritional medicine primarily focuses on chronic conditions anyway. The rest on that list of diseases, for which natural products may not make health claims, are now well-known to medical research as benefiting from natural products, and they are equally well-known to medical research as not benefiting much from drugs beyond symptom-control because those therapies are in part or wholly fraudulent—those are the drugs that are now the primary causes of death.

What really is unforgivable, and what gives the lie to the government's stated good intentions, is the fact that the descriptive terms for bipolar symptoms, namely "acute anxiety state," "acute psychotic disorder," and "depression" were retained in that Schedule A list one year *after* the Truehope decision was handed down! That is why the *Canada Gazette* issue of December 13/26th, 2007, was included for the readers of this book, so the reader can see what really happened. Not only does the government flaunt the right of patients' wishes, as to how they want to be treated for a serious disease that can totally wreck one's life, but the government even flaunts the courts to whom the whole of Parliament is subject! Canada is a constitutional democracy in which whatever happens, happens by the grace of the law. The courts are the final authority.

Everything else in this book has been provided as amplification of these two incompatible manifestos.

With regard to bill C-51, the only justification Health Canada and the Minister of Health can cite for this massive planned exercise and proposed immense expenditure, is the alleged liver toxicity of black cohosh (see letter to Prime Minister pages vii–xvii), a toxin found in some toothpaste (which may have happened, but no source is provided), and some material that treats erectile dysfunction and may have been found in a natural health product. No references are made to a lot of dead bodies, or even a joyous epidemic of innumerable uncontrollable erections.

The current Food and Drugs Act is perfectly capable of dealing with such possibly accidental occurrences and has the entire box of tools to enforce safety. The Act is written with safety as its top priority. How about using it? No bill C-51 is needed to give regulators these powers. Meanwhile, Health Canada has in my opinion totally failed to deal with the major and constantly on-going event, namely tens of thousands of people dying every year from the side effects of prescription drugs. For those merely "advisories" and "warnings" are posted on their websites and in the CPS (the FDA "blackboxes" such drugs). Some toothpaste or alleged herbal contamination incident, on the other hand, supposedly requires a totally revamped Act with enforcement powers that exceed those of the police.

If Health Canada's website www.healthycanadians.ca had mentioned the need to avoid in future such disasters as Vioxx, synthetic hormone replacement therapy, the whole family of deadly antidepressants, and fraudulent vaccines and stated that the large-scale deception practiced upon Canadians and government regulators by the pharmaceutical industry requires strengthening the Food and Drugs Act and its regulations—now *that* would have been realistic information most of us can relate to, especially if we have ever been on those drugs from pharma hell or lost a loved one to its products. Not a peep on that subject, though.

If furthermore, we were told that the Food and Drugs Act needs to be drastically renovated in order to stop the use of antibiotics, hormones in food-producing animals, pesticides, herbicides and fungicides, and the use of slaughterhouse waste as feed—now that, too, would have been a truthful exercise in bringing legislation up to date with current science. Not a peep about that either. In fact, "safety" isn't even defined.

With regard to bill C-52, which aims to protect Canadians against hazardous products here and from abroad, there is actually a positive list of items and substances which is appended to this bill. Listed are in specified contexts the following: jequirity beans, cellulose nitrate, polychlorinated biphenyls, 2,3dibromopropyl, 3,3'-dimethoxybensidine or any of its salts, hellebore, protoveratrine or veratrine, nitrobensaldehyde, nitrite under certain conditions, and urea formaldehyde in insulation products. This list is astonishingly short, given the enormity of the bill's implications for the increased powers of search and seizure and potential loss of liberties. Hence, we need to turn to Europe where they mean business, when it comes to banning toxins to protect their population from the effects of lucrative poisons.

(As an aside I should add, that while Europe has its expected share of human inconsistency because it also has that bizarre process guided by Codex Alimentarius, the difference between North America and Europe is that the Old Countries have very loud, noisy, eloquent and refreshingly disobedient citizens with long memories and lots of experience with the abuse of power. We can learn a lot.)

The following is an expanded and updated version of an article I published in December 2007 in *Vitality Magazine* and the Canadian Centre for Policy Alternatives *Monitor*. It describes the nature and effect of a new treaty that came into effect January 2008. It is called REACH which stands for Registration, Evaluation and Authorization of Chemicals. Dr. Shiv Chopra made me aware of Mark Schapiro's 2007 book on this treaty, for which the readers of this article will no doubt be as grateful as I am.

The New Green Superpower

The ancient Chinese believed that a cosmic force, the Will of Heaven, controlled the rise and fall of their imperial dynasties. When an emperor failed to act in accord with the laws of nature, also called the Tao, the Mandate of Heaven passed to a contender who founded a new dynasty.

Mark Schapiro, the director of the Center for Investigative Reporting in San Francisco, published *Exposed: The Toxic Chemistry of Everyday Products and What's at Stake for American Power* (Chelsea Green, 2007) in which he chronicles the fall of the American Empire and the passing of the Mandate of Heaven to the European Union as a result not of America's financially crippling and immoral wars, but rather because the US refuses to understand it is not a sound business strategy to poison one's own citizens for profit and demand that the rest of the world buy America's toxic products.

In 2000 the EU adopted the Precautionary Principle, first formulated in Germany in the early 1930s (Vorsorgeprinzip in German). It was adopted in 1982 by the United Nations, and the first international treaty based on it was the Montreal Protocol; it is also part of the 1992 Rio Declaration on Environment and Development.

Its 2006 EU wording is, in part: "Where ... there are reasonable grounds for concern for the possibility of adverse effects, but scientific uncertainty persists, ... priority will be given to human health and the environment, ...without having to wait until the reality and seriousness of those adverse effects become fully apparent."

In 2002, the EU put this ideal in practice and formally asserted that "sustainable and environmentally sound principles" would have to be as important for all industry as "competitiveness." By 2004 they had drafted the world's most comprehensive environmental laws, most of which came into force in January 2008. The US and the rest of the world have to obey, if they wish to trade with 495 million of the "wealthiest and best-educated consumers and producers in the world." According to the CIA's World Fact Book, Germany alone in 2005 surpassed the US in exports; the EU that year surpassed the US in gross domestic productivity and produces a third of the global economy, almost equal to the US and Japan combined.

European Union Regulators Go Green

In 2006, the EU informed the US that electronics may no longer contain the universally accepted toxic (and non-recyclable) ingredients mercury, cadmium, lead, chromium and two types of fire retardants. My iMac has most of those toxic metals in it; that of one of my friends in Germany does not. A spokesperson for the industry commented that ever since "we have been in reactive hell." The director of the Electronic Industry Alliance said: "If you are not compliant … your market is evaporating as we speak." Electronics was just one item. Cars are no longer allowed to use any toxicants either, which are usually found in the electric wiring, the synthetic seat materials, etc.. A General Motors spokesperson said: "We have been hit by a tsunami!"

The EU has a list of some 60,000 chemicals which are to be investigated to eliminate all those that are found to be cancer-causing, hormone-disrupting, birth defect promoting, fertility compromising, toxic to aquatic life, or damaging to the environment. This move is amazing because Europe, not the US, was the world's largest producer of toxic chemicals. It is their own industries they are cleaning up the most, and it is also the European scientists who are working overtime to find safe substitutes everybody in the world will use.

The Europeans have a word for their new attitude: "glocalism"—thinking locally and acting globally, the phrase antibiotic researcher and environmentalist Renee Dubois coined. What was once the Cold War's greatly feared "domino effect" (then attributed to communism and socialism), has now become reality in the sphere of environmental stewardship arising out of the socialism of the European Green Party that started this whole process in the 1970s. Now China, Japan, India, several South American countries have either already adapted their environmental laws to the EU, or are in the process of doing so. The EU is also pouring hundreds of millions of

Euros into helping these countries clean up their own technologies.

Brazil has taken the next logical step and identified the root cause of the global poison market, namely advertising. In January 2007, the world's fourth largest city, São Paulo, banned all outdoor advertising as part of their new "Clean City Law," and eliminated 15,000 billboards with the 70% approval of the city's population. (Imagine the quantum leap in aesthetics if the QEW and the whole of Toronto were free of those dreadful billboards!)

A similar attitude was evident when a French court dealt with farmers who had destroyed vast tracts of Monsanto's test fields growing genetically engineered corn: they were all acquitted on grounds of "self defense."

North America–The Toxic Dump

Meanwhile, Asian countries have to get rid of their existing stocks. They can't sell to Europe, so they sell their toxicant-laced products to the US and Canada—where it's still legal—and the clean stuff to Europe. Canada's proposed Consumer Safety Act is, unfortunately mostly hot air by comparison to REACH. The wee little list of toxins appended to the text of bill C-52 is funny by comparison. It does not list the scientifically supported poisons that may not be used anymore, such as lead in lipstick—to name one of the 60,000 possible items. It is of course up to the discretionary power of some enlightened Ministers of Health and Agriculture to zero in on any of these chemicals, but that's just it—C-51 and C-52 leave everything conveniently vague: anything may or may not happen. Canadians are to trust their government implicitly. Europeans chose to demand explicit explanations, and got them.

The EU assumes that government regulation in matters of public health and planetary survival is a good thing. Fancy that! In Canada, it seems to be only the NDP and the up and coming Greens who share this radical idea. By contrast, in Europe this idea is shared by the Conservatives and the Greens. The US was so horrified by the obvious consequences of this European attitude to business, the international affairs officer of the American Electrical Association actually exclaimed: "The EU must get the science out of politics!" Whenever the US is outraged, Canada runs to their aid, as they did when they joined the US and took the EU to court for refusing to accept GMO products, on the grounds of having "politicized" the process of acceptance—which is another way of objecting to informed citizens pointing out the science involved.

Dr. Shiv Chopra, our own Health Canada drug regulator who was fired by former Prime Minister Paul Martin for "insubordination" observed that "in Europe they listen to their scientists, while North American governments fight them." Martin had a point: Chopra and his colleagues, Drs. Haydon and Lambert, who were also fired, had steadfastly refused for two decades to subordinate themselves to corporate and government pressure to pass unsafe substances—doing which would have been in direct contravention of Canada's Foods and Drugs Act, but there was nobody home in the government to uphold it.

During the past couple of years, prior to REACH coming into effect, the US dispatched some 15,000 lobbyists to stop the European parliament from going green. One of them was none other than Colin Powell and his file was pesticides. All efforts failed; the laws passed. Schapiro quotes an EU diplomat: "...why should we listen? If we are to listen to the US, how would we explain to European citizens where the hundreds of chemicals in their bodies come from?" Schapiro sees these EU-led developments as a "convergence of 'green' and 'economy' which is "not utopian; it's more like *realpolitik* for the twenty-first century."

On the international scene, the Mandate of Heaven has withdrawn also from the US in every instance where the great laws of natural justice were at stake. The rest of the world simply ignored determined US opposition to the POPS treaty which successfully banned the sale and production of "the dirty dozen," the world's most hazardous substances. The same happened with the Kyoto and the Land Mine treaties, the establishment of the International Criminal Court, and the Basel Convention on Hazardous Wastes which outlaws dumping toxic wastes on Third World countries. Schapiro comments that these are all "human rights initiatives that have gained international legitimacy without American participation." In each case, the EU was the leader instead.

Science, being both a transcendent force as well as an enterprise that knows no borders, has placed the US in the ultimate of ironies: since the late 1990s, most of the policy decisions made in the EU are based on primarily American research. In fact, the leading US research institutions and even the FDA and EPA, whose databases are possibly the most comprehensive in the world, often simply bypassed their own regulatory agencies, and sent their reports directly to the European Commission—who wasted no time in using that information to help pass appropriate laws.

Canada has access to those data bases even more easily, but doesn't seem to make the same use of them as the Europeans have done.

This behavior on the part of American scientists so enraged those who cannot accept that the Mandate of Heaven is passing from them, that they have started to close the immense network of the Environmental Protection Agency's scientific libraries and destroy much of its contents. The Union of Concerned Scientists is hoping to stop this vandalism (go to www.ucsusa.org). There is an interesting parallel here to Prime Minister Stephen Harper's decision to shut down the public data base of access-to-information requests. All authoritarian regimes especially attack sources of free information flow; during the height of the Cold War in the former Soviet Union, it used to be a crime to own a duplicating machine (like those old Gestetner machines) and phone books were prized possessions of the few.

Meantime, Back In Canada

In Canada we still have cancer-causing hormones and antibiotics in our food-producing animals. Slaughterhouse waste is still being fed to herbivores exposing us to the risk of Mad Cow Disease. Our food is contaminated with pesticides and genetically engineered substances. We can't sell any of this to Europe. If this goes on, North America will become a toxic pariah.

The NDP seem to be the only ones consistently in touch with reality on these issues. There are two good bills before Parliament that have not yet been killed; every effort should be made to get them passed, which probably is only possible by throwing out this government first. Bill C-510 was introduced by MP Paul Dewar (NDP) on April 14, 2007, only a few days after C-51 and C-52 were introduced. Its text is reproduced in this chapter. C-510 is based on Dr. Shiv Chopra's Five Pillars of Food Safety, and since nutritious food is the fundamental prerequisite for health, one might as well call it also the Five Pillars of Health because safe food is only possible in a clean world.

Dr. Chopra writes in his book *Corrupt to the Core*: "It is our divine right as people of God and our constitutional right as people of Canada to eat and feed to our families the food that the earth produces naturally. Therefore, we demand all contaminants in our food supply to be banned by an Act of Parliament. The five items in question include: Hormones, antibiotics, genetically modified organisms (GMOs), rendered animal proteins, and pesticides."

When I interviewed MP Dewar about this bill he observed that what it wants to pass into law is actually "a no-brainer" because Canada needs Europe and Japan as trading partners.

The other important bill before parliament is C-448 which would make the development, use, and sale of terminator seeds illegal in Canada. The text of that bill is reproduced here as well.

While Europe is in high gear to save life on Earth, this government is embroiled in ethical inconsistencies that boggle the mind. It spends millions on supporting biotechnology and has so far not come out against terminator biotechnology, yet it has a bill before Parliament, C-484, that makes the unborn fetus a "person" by the backdoor. The bill would make it a double murder if a pregnant women is killed. The numbers of pregnant women being murdered in Canada is not exactly daily front-page news. The Federation of Medical Women of Canada is quite right in its assessment that this looks more like an underhanded way to start whittling away at diminishing Canada's legal protection of the right to reproductive choice (*Medical Post*, May 23, 2008) (Go to the Canadian Medical Association's website www.cma.ca and to www.fmwc.ca).

Whatever one's views maybe on the abortion issues, it is very curious that the Harper government does not see terminator technology as an abortion issue. It is a horrendous crime to kill a pregnant woman, but to program abortion of life into entire genera of food-producing seeds is to my mind every bit as disgusting.

Sources and Resources:

W. Wagner & R. Steinzor eds. *Rescuing Science from Politics*, Cambridge, 2006

Decent Medicine Or What We Want

The *security* we want is incompatible with secrecy. You can't be secure if you have no idea what you are eating and what the research is on a drug is recommended to you. Taking food and medicine on trust is potentially suicidal. It is a double-blind experiment of entirely the wrong kind, where both parties are injured: our doctors have been duped and thousands of us die every year because our doctors give them drugs they thought would be helpful. The same applies to government activities that do not involve the public's consent and knowledge, such as the Security and Prosperity Partnership whose "partners" are all industry representatives; we were not consulted on anything, but our regulatory systems are to be "harmonized" with those of the US and Mexico without our input. The latest polls show that 83% of Canadians do not approve of this at all. We also do not approve of being excluded from the "confidential agreements" Health Canada has entered into with the US and the European Medicine Agency in December 2007—when also that Order in Council was passed making that scientifically untenable law, under the pretext of prior consultations; see the discussion on the *Canada Gazette* earlier.

The prosperity we want and need cannot be defined in terms of citizens being customers who will only be able to buy whatever the government thinks is safe and good for them. Even if the production and sale of genetically engineered foods were to increase prosperity in the short run, none of us are willing to sacrifice the integrity of plant, animal and human genome activity for quick-fix short-term wealth. We are also not willing to increase the wealth of the manufacturers of useless toxic drugs at the expense of being "roadkill on the highway to profit," as Dr. Michelle Brill-Edwards, formerly of Health Canada, puts it so well. Most importantly, the prosperity of a nation depends on the freedom its citizens have to explore. Government involvement in determining the scope and nature of medical research is therefore out of the question. C-51 would stifle creativity and innovation as Health Canada already tried to do with Truehope. Do we really want a law that could arbitrarily stifle the exploration of an effective treatment for cancer just because it isn't along the lines of the traditional cut-burn-and-poison treatments?

In my view we need the following:

1. Both bills C-51 and C-52 cannot be amended. They must be withdrawn entirely, or else application must be made to the appropriate level of court to determine if the provisions and the intent of these bills are in accord with Canada's Charter of Rights and Freedoms.
2. These two bills need to be examined by experts in corporate law to determine if they are potentially in contravention of existing trade law. As discussed earlier, this approach was highly successful in Europe when draconian restrictions were proposed for natural health products through the EU *Directive* and Codex. The International Court of Justice found them to be in contravention of various internationally binding trade laws. It is highly likely that the same problems are going to be found here.
3. Schedule A of the Food and Drugs Act needs to be dropped entirely. Since the *practice* of medicine is under provincial authority anyway, there need be no fear that doctors will treat acute appendicitis with black cohosh. The 9 surgical

emergencies listed in that Schedule A are so well known to standard medicine that is it redundant to even bring them up at the federal level. All diseases listed in both parts of Schedule A are currently being researched by experts in all types of therapies and it is silly for Health Canada to make list of exclusion when the research itself is moving faster than Health Canada possibly can.

4. All information on drugs as well as natural products, which was used at Health Canada to approve them for use in Canada, must be freely available to the public so that we can find out what research was actually considered in this process. We already have the industry's CPS—but we do not have access to the process that led to a drug coming to market at Health Canada. This is the minimum of accountability we can expect. We are not stakeholders of therapeutic products—we are the recipients who wish to exercise informed consent.
5. The independent laboratories that Health Canada used to have, until then Minister of Health Alan Rock quietly disbanded them in 1997, must be reinstated so that we are not at the mercy of the information coming from the FDA, an agency that is going through even greater turmoil than Health Canada because the way in which medical research is compromised by industry interests in the US.
6. The user-fee system that has successfully made Health Canada "the best customer" of the drug industry, as a drug company resprentative informed Terrence Young, must be stopped. The money saved for Medicare by thus cleaning up the pharmaceutical market, increasing the sales of cheaper and safer generic drugs, and stopping the flow of questionable information will be so immense, that funding Health Canada and those government laboratories will be a mere flea bite.
7. The database of the Freedom of Information Registry must be re-opened and funded by the government, just as before. Many of the freedom-of-information requests made to this

office are health and environment related, and we need to know what they are, or have been, in order to be able to challenge government secrecy as effectively as possible.

8. Any current legislation affecting foods and drugs that contains the terms "risk management" must be changed to "risk assessment." The health and survival of Canadians is not a matter of management—it is an end, not a means, as the 18th century philosopher Emanuel Kant taught. Dr. Shiv Chora observes about both C-51 and C-52: "Provisions must be made to legislate Risk Assessment, in contrast to Risk Management, so that the manufacturers of the products in question are held liable for possible damage to public safety and the public interest."

Other than the dissenting voice of Conservative MP James Lunney, whose article is in chapter 1 of this book, the NDP seems to have the best understanding what bills C-51 and C-52 really are all about. Appended below are the remarks made on April 30th, 2008, by MP Judy Wasylycia-Leis (NDP). They sum up the issues perfectly.

39th PARLIAMENT, 2nd SESSION

EDITED HANSAR D • NUMBER 085

CONTENTS

Wednesday, April 30, 2008

C-51 – Food and Drugs Act

Ms. Judy Wasylycia-Leis (Winnipeg North, NDP):

Mr. Speaker, I am pleased to join in the first round of debate on Bill C-51, a bill to amend, in large measure, the Food and Drugs Act.

I bring to this debate a lot of skepticism but it is a healthy dose of skepticism based on the history of this whole aspect of Health Canada and our regulatory regime in Canada.

It will be no surprise to the House to learn that this is the fifth attempt by government in the last decade to overhaul the Food and Drugs Act. Four times before the Liberals attempted to do so and each time they failed. Why? They failed because the community spoke up and demanded more accountability from government and much clearer answers around accountability and regulatory authority.

Members will recall Bill C-80, a draft piece of legislation that was supposed to do much of what we have before us today. That bill was supposedly attempting to modernize our food and drug provisions, bring us into the 21st century and bring our rules and our regulations in line with modern day science.

It did not take too long for Canadians to quickly figure out that this was a ruse. It was an attempt to make Canadians believe the government would be on their side but was in fact loosening its hold over regulations, minimizing its role and moving us away from what has been an entrenched part of our history, and that is a bill that regulates the safety of food and drugs in such a serious manner that it is part of the Criminal Code.

That legislation operated on the basis of the do no harm principle, the precautionary principle, which means that we do not allow products on the market unless there is evidence that they are safe beyond a reasonable doubt. That is the do no harm principle. It is not the buyer beware principle. It is not the risk management model that we have seen with the Liberals before and with the Conservatives today.

There is a marked difference between the do no harm principle and the risk management model. Do no harm means that we put people and safety first. The risk management model means that we can only go so far in ensuring Canadians' safety so

Source: NDP versus C-51

we will allow the products on the market and then we will see what happens. It will be up to individual Canadians to determine whether or not it is worth taking the risk. It will be up to the corporations that produce the products to regulate themselves and decide if they are in line with the standards on paper.

The risk management model is not a proactive regulatory model that puts the needs and concerns of Canadians first. It is a model that puts the needs of big pharma, large corporations and global capital forces ahead of ordinary citizens. It is a model that makes guinea pigs out of Canadians.

We have had our share of offering up people as guinea pigs for large pharmaceutical corporations. I do not need to tell the House about the incidents in our past, especially when women were treated as guinea pigs. Thalidomide comes to mind as does Depo-Provera, breast implants and the list goes on.

We need to ask ourselves some questions. If we cut through all the rhetoric and tough talk about putting safety first and modernizing our system, are we better off? Are we any closer to the kind of system that Canadians thought we had and expected to have, which was abandoned by the Liberals?

It was abandoned when, in 1997, the former minister of health, Allan Rock, in his first gesture as minister of health, killed the federal drug laboratory, the only independent federal research lab in this country for testing on a post-market surveillance basis. It tested whether drugs that were on the market were safe and whether there were any negative consequences when that drug was combined with certain foods, other drugs or natural health products. It was a lab that performed a very important safety function in our country.

That was the beginning of a whole string of actions taken by the then minister of health, Allan Rock, and subsequent Liberal ministers of health to dismantle our regulatory system and move us away from the do no harm model toward a system where corporations pay for their drug approval processes. The bulk of the fees for our drug approval process comes from the corporations themselves.

Scientists at Health Canada have seen numerous incidents and they said that enough was enough. I think of Dr. Michèle Brill-Edwards who spoke up about being cornered to approve something she thought was not safe. She had to leave Health Canada to have any sense of integrity intact.

There were many others. Who can forget the whole group of veterinary scientists who stood tall about the tampering with food products and the adulteration and modification of veterinarian drugs? They were chastised, disciplined and lambasted by the Liberal government.

Whatever happened to the government being a bastion of independent, objective science that operated on the basis of the constituents it is supposed to serve? Whatever happened to government for the people, by the people and of the people? Nowhere is this more important than when it comes to the food we eat, the drugs we take because of medical conditions and the water we drink to sustain us and yet in those areas the government has abandoned us in large measure.

Today we are supposed to believe that the Conservative Government of Canada has such integrity, courage and vision that it is offering us a blueprint for a do no harm precautionary model around drugs and food. I bring to this debate a dose of healthy skepticism because I have seen nothing from the Conservatives to date that leads me to believe that the government is on the side of ordinary Canadian families and is not on the side, first and foremost, of the big corporations and their profit margins.

I have not seen that when it comes to housing, education, health care, women's equality, people with disabilities, the environment, jobs and child care. I have not yet seen the government stand up for Canadians

Mrs. Irene Mathyssen: Nor will we.

Ms. Judy Wasylycia-Leis: My colleague from London—Fanshawe says, "Nor will we". That is why I bring to this debate my concerns.

Source: NDP versus C-51

However, that is not to say that there are not some good provisions in this bill. I do recognize that the government has moved a significant distance from the days of the Liberals. Ironically, this legislation is more proactive than the Liberals ever presented to this House. However, it still has lots of problems and it still does not mean we will be supporting it but it is a step forward.

I would like to point to a couple of those initiatives. The bill has provisions for the recall of drugs and food products that have contaminants. The bill sets out hefty fines for corporations that do not reveal problems or side effects with drugs. There is new emphasis in this bill around ensuring that government has the tools to protect Canadians. I commend the government for those initiatives and I support those aspects of the bill that take us forward toward what I consider fundamental to this whole debate and that is a do no harm approach when it comes to food and drugs.

However, beneath those specific clauses and the fine words of the press release that the Prime Minister and the Minister of Health presented to Canadians about safety first, there are enough concerns to make me and others suspicious of what the government is all about and where it is trying to lead us.

We only need to look at a couple of the areas that we have heard about to date. I hear some of my colleagues on the Conservative benches chuckling. I do not think they would chuckle if they were to listen to the words of Dr. Barbara Mintzes, who has brought to the attention of the House a clause in the bill that appears to move the government closer to direct to consumer advertising. That is so well documented that some of the officials have already said that they acknowledge that is a problem and maybe it needs to be addressed.

Why is that important? Do we want to see another $6.3 billion added to our pharmacare bill? Do we want to see big pharma pushing their drugs on Canadians without scientific basis? Do we want to see full-blown advertising in this country, as is the case in the United States?

Is it not enough that we have this grey area where drug companies can find a loophole and advertise all they want the lifestyle and create the appearance of something helping this person without naming the drug. We need only to look at the Viagra ads. They are pretty clear and impressive and they have led to all kinds of people demanding prescriptions for certain drugs from their doctors without necessarily a basis in terms of either their condition or the science available.

Direct to consumer advertising is just one of the problems in the bill that will make us very cautious about supporting it. Unless this loophole is closed and there is a firm commitment from the government to absolutely close the door to direct to consumer advertising, which not only means where we are today but going back and closing the door in terms of the loophole, there is no way in the world we should support the bill because of the ramifications it would have for our entire health care system, a system where costs for pharmaceuticals are now outstripping all other aspects of the system.

I will give another example. We have heard mentioned in the Chamber today the words "lifecycle approach" to drug surveillance or "progressive licensing". It all sounds great, innovative and progressive but we need to realize that underneath it all there could very well be an agenda to speed up the approval of drugs at the front end and create the illusion of safety or the reality of safety at the other end.

However, what does it matter when we have already digested a drug that is not safe and has produced serious health consequences? Can it be that the government has listened to the drug companies when they say that they would rather deal with expensive lawsuits and pay out big money after being sued than to put in the money that is needed at the front end to ensure that the drugs are safe in the first place?

The real question we have to ask today is the one Alan Cassels and others asked in the media when the bill was released. Would this bill prevent another Vioxx? Would it stop a situation where hundreds of thousands of people are dying because they took a drug without realizing there were serious side effects unrelated to the condition for which they were taking it? What in this bill would stop that? Where is the inspection force? Where is the apparatus? Where is the infrastructure to make that happen? Where is the

Source: NDP versus C-51

commitment from the government to deal with contaminated drugs coming into this country? How will the government handle another heparin, a contaminated drug from China? Is it prepared to send inspection officers to manufacturers in China? Is it prepared to put surveillance officers at the border? Is it prepared to take seriously the side effects that Canadians talk about? Is it prepared to act the minute there are serious reactions to drugs?

I hope that is the case. I do not know if that is the case. I do not know if this bill would do that. I want to keep an open mind about that. When we get to committee, I want to ask those questions. Witnesses will testify. We are going to seriously study that aspect. The fundamental bottom line when it comes to this bill is, is it going to stop another Vioxx? That is the question. How will it do it? Will it do it in time? Will it really make drug companies provide the information that they may have held in secret which may reveal something? Would it have been able to get out of Merck Frosst the information around Vioxx that it kept secret that would have prevented hundreds of thousands of deaths?

Those are two areas of concern. There are others.

We have received hundreds of letters from people concerned about natural health products. We have been inundated with letters and communications expressing concern about this bill and whether or not there is a hidden agenda to bring natural health products under the rubric of drugs, after the huge battle we have had in this House for a decade to have a separate category for natural health products. This is something that the Conservatives took up with a vengeance some 10 years ago, which led to a health committee discussion and a report, which led to the establishment of a third category, which led to some reasonable approach to dealing with natural health products. Unfortunately, both the Liberals and the Conservatives since then have botched the whole plan. We now have hundreds of thousands of natural health products waiting in line to be assessed and licensed.

The question here is, is this a way to get around that? Is this an attempt to deal with the backlog like we have seen with immigration? Perhaps it is similar to the budget implementation bill and slipping immigration into that bill. We do not know.

Needless to say, when it comes to this area, there is nothing more important than how we protect people in terms of the drugs and the medications they have to take and the food they have to eat. It is the job of government to put safety first, to ensure that products on the market are as safe as possible. That means a proactive government, tough regulations, adequate resources, a government with the will to make safety fundamental and to put people before drug profits.

Mr. Brian Fitzpatrick (Prince Albert, CPC):

Mr. Speaker, I was astounded to listen to the member's presentation and the one from the Bloc as well. I have come to the conclusion that maybe we should have a special law that prohibits big corporations from distributing and selling prescription drugs to NDP members and their supporters, and maybe Bloc members as well, because we would not them to take something they feel is unscientific and would not have any benefit.

Let us be clear. For every drug cleared through the clinical trial process, there are literally thousands of drugs that do not get to first base. This is not a slam dunk process and it costs an awful lot of money. There are a lot of other safeguards. The EU has a clinical process that is very tough. The Japanese have one that is very tough. The Americans have one that is very tough. If manufacturers fail in the United States, they get through the entire process and get a drug approved but if they make a mistake, they can be financially ruined by the American tort system.

However, for members of this House to say that we are just allowing drugs on to market without any due diligence or any comprehension for public safety and that there is some great conspiracy between members of Parliament and the drug companies to foist all these poisonous and toxic drugs on people is total nonsense. I cannot believe the member actually believes that. I do not want to disagree too strongly with her opinion because it might insinuate that I am challenging her intelligence.

Source: NDP versus C-51

Ms. Judy Wasylycia-Leis:

Mr. Speaker, this is a very serious matter, not a laughing matter. It has to be debated in the context of the health and well-being of Canadians. I make my comments with all seriousness and based on significant input from many Canadians.

As I also said, we will pursue every one of those concerns at committee to determine the legitimacy. No one is making generalizations without basis in fact. No one is casting aspersions without any reason.

We are here today with one of the most important pieces of legislation this Parliament has seen in a long time. We are questioning on the basis of evidence that has been provided to us. I do not need to tell anyone how many Canadian lives are put at risk every day because we do not have an adequate safety system right now. All I have to do is read through the papers and list off numerous cases.

Maybe the member is interested in this one, if he is not interested in some of the others. It is a recall order for a product for erectile dysfunction. This is Libidus, an unauthorized product promoted on the manufacturer's website as treating erectile dysfunction, saying it does not produce health risks. Well it does. Where is the government?

How about Evra, a birth control product for women, a patch that produces blood clot risks. Why is that? Why are young women at risk right now as we speak?

What about the drug to quit smoking that came out not too long ago, Champix, which produces all kinds of psychiatric side effects?

What about as I mentioned, heparin, in which contaminants were found after production in China?

What about all of these examples? Does it not matter? Should Canadians not feel safe? Is that not what we are here for? It is not to put people at the will of the marketplace and let them take chances. It is about trusting government, and if we cannot trust government when it comes to the safety of the drugs we have to take and the food we have to eat, then when can we trust government?

Mr. Steven Fletcher (Parliamentary Secretary for Health, CPC):

Mr. Speaker, unlike my colleague from Prince Albert, I actually love the loony left. The loony left allows average Canadians to see the ridiculousness of the arguments. I commend the member on the passion of her case, but I think the member knows that she is mistaken on numerous points including the suggestion that products or drugs coming onto the market are less safe. This bill does not deal with that. The drugs that have come onto the market are under the same regime with or without this bill. That is important for the member to know.

On the issue of direct consumer advertising, the member also knows that this government is in court to prevent direct advertising of pharmaceuticals to the Canadian market. The member knows that and this bill in fact strengthens the government's position on that.

I would also like to read to the member proposed section 2.3 of the bill:

> The purpose of this Act is to protect and promote the health and safety of the public and encourage accurate and consistent product representation by prohibiting and regulating certain activities in relation to foods, therapeutic products and cosmetics.

We can see that the intent is in the best interests of Canadians. I would ask the member to put aside the worries about the black helicopters, put away the tinfoil hats and come to committee with an open mind. All the other parties are. We are. If there are reasonable suggestions for amendment, we will listen to them. Will the member come to committee with an open mind and listen to the facts and read the bill for what it is, an improvement to the health and safety of Canadians?

Ms. Judy Wasylycia-Leis:

Source: NDP versus C-51

Mr. Speaker, you will know that I have already said that we come to this whole process with an open spirit, wanting to know if in fact the substance of the bill meets the rhetoric of the government. We enter the process willingly and with open minds.

I just wish the hon. member were open to some of the concerns being raised because when he suggests that this is about the loony left speaking, he is insulting thousands of Canadians across the country who are raising concerns. He is actually casting aspersions on Dr. Mary Wiktorowicz. He is casting aspersions on Joel Lexchin, on Dr. Barbara Mintzes, on Dr. Steve Morgan and Alan Cassels, many people who came to our committee and expressed their concerns. So, I hope he is open and I hope he is willing to actually amend the bill when those concerns have been substantiated.

Hon. Larry Bagnell (Yukon, Lib.):

Mr. Speaker, another one upon whom the Conservatives could have cast aspersions is one of my constituents who asked questions. I wanted to ask the government, but it is not putting up any speakers, just the minister who introduced the bill, so I cannot ask the questions. Maybe the member could answer just three concerns that this constituent put forward.

Will this new law be used to abuse and punish special interest groups, minorities, religious groups or others? Why do the bureaucrats want seizure warrants without judge approval? With fines being increased a thousand times and seizing authority without a warrant, is Bill C-51 meant to bankrupt and silence its target audience?

Ms. Judy Wasylycia-Leis:

Mr. Speaker, those are all questions that need to be addressed by the government and vetted at committee. I certainly hope the member will encourage those who have raised these concerns to present them in writing to the committee or in fact to attend our committee hearings.

I hope that we will have a wide open, serious, indepth review of the bill in terms of all of its aspects, because when it comes to judicial oversight and RCMP investigations, as he has mentioned, these are very serious issues. When we are talking about direct to consumer advertising, progressive licensing, natural health products, oversight, investigative forces and discretionary powers, all of those issues are critically important in an area of such fundamental importance.

Source: NDP versus C-51

Section Home

Home

C-510

Second Session, Thirty-ninth Parliament,

56-57 Elizabeth II, 2007-2008

HOUSE OF COMMONS OF CANADA

BILL C-510

An Act respecting the labelling of food products

FIRST READING, FEBRUARY 15, 2008

MR. DEWAR

392110

Source: Bill C-510

2nd Session, 39th Parliament,
56-57 Elizabeth II, 2007-2008

HOUSE OF COMMONS OF CANADA

BILL C-510

An Act respecting the labelling of food products

Her Majesty, by and with the advice and consent of the Senate and House of Commons of Canada, enacts as follows:

SHORT TITLE

Short title

1. This Act may be cited as the *Food Products Labelling Act*.

INTERPRETATION

Definitions

2. The following definitions apply in this Act.

"genetically modified organism" « *organisme génétiquement modifié* »

"genetically modified organism" means an organism whose genetic material has been altered using genetic engineering techniques causing the expression of modified traits in the organism.

"Minister" « *ministre* »

"Minister" means the Minister of Health.

REGULATIONS

Regulations

3. Despite anything in the *Food and Drugs Act* or the regulations made under that Act, the Minister shall, within nine months after the day on which this Act comes into force, make regulations providing

(*a*) that no person shall sell a meat product or poultry product that has been produced using hormones, antibiotics or rendered slaughterhouse waste unless a label is affixed to the package, meat product or poultry product clearly showing that the meat product or poultry product has been produced using hormones, antibiotics or rendered slaughterhouse waste; and

(*b*) that no person shall sell any food product that has been produced using pesticides or genetically modified organisms unless a label is affixed to the package or food product clearly showing that the food product has been produced using pesticides or genetically modified organisms.

Published under authority of the Speaker of the House of Commons

Available from:
Publishing and Depository Services
Public Works and Government Services Canada

Source: Bill C-510

C-448

First Session, Thirty-ninth Parliament,
55-56 Elizabeth II, 2006-2007

HOUSE OF COMMONS OF CANADA

BILL C-448

An Act to prohibit the release, sale, importation and use of seeds incorporating or altered by variety-genetic use restriction technologies (V-GURTs), also called "terminator technologies", and to make a consequential amendment to another Act

---

FIRST READING, MAY 31, 2007

Source: Bill C-448

1st Session, 39th Parliament,
55-56 Elizabeth II, 2006-2007

HOUSE OF COMMONS OF CANADA

BILL C-448

An Act to prohibit the release, sale, importation and use of seeds incorporating or altered by variety-genetic use restriction technologies (V-GURTs), also called "terminator technologies", and to make a consequential amendment to another Act

Preamble

WHEREAS Canada is a signatory to the Convention on Biological Diversity;

WHEREAS the Conference of the Parties to the Convention on Biological Diversity have (by paragraph 23 of decision V/5, section III, Genetic Use Restriction Technologies) recommended that "in the current absence of reliable data on genetic use restriction technologies, without which there is an inadequate basis on which to assess their potential risks, and in accordance with the precautionary approach, products incorporating such technologies should not be approved by Parties for field testing until appropriate scientific data can justify such testing, and for commercial use until appropriate, authorized and strictly controlled scientific assessments with regard to, inter alia, their ecological and socio-economic impacts and any adverse effects for biological diversity, food security and human health have been carried out in a transparent manner and the conditions for their safe and beneficial use validated";

AND WHEREAS the Government of Canada wishes to prohibit variety-genetic use restriction technologies (V-GURTs) in order to protect the nation's farmers, national food security and the

391407

Source: Bill C-448

environment by ensuring that "terminator seeds" cannot be released, sold, imported or used within Canada;

NOW, THEREFORE, Her Majesty, by and with the advice and consent of the Senate and House of Commons of Canada, enacts as follows:

SHORT TITLE

Short title

1. This Act may be cited as the *Terminator Seeds Ban Act*.

INTERPRETATION

Definitions

2. The following definitions apply in this Act.

"contravention" « *contravention* »

"contravention" means any contravention of this Act or the regulations that may be proceeded with in accordance with the *Agriculture and Agri-Food Administrative and Monetary Penalties Act*.

"environment" « *environnement* »

"environment" means

(*a*) air, land and water;

(*b*) all layers of the atmosphere;

(*c*) all organic and inorganic matter and living organisms; and

(*d*) the interacting natural systems that include components referred to in paragraphs (*a*) to (*c*).

"import" « *importation* »

"import" means to import into Canada.

"Minister" « *ministre* »

"Minister" means the Minister of Agriculture and Agri-Food.

"release" « *dissémination* »

"release" means any discharge or emission of terminator seeds into the environment or exposure of terminator seeds to the environ-

Source: Bill C-448

ment, and includes the growing and field-testing of plants containing V-GURTs as part of their genetic structure.

"seed" « *semences* »

"seed" means any plant part of any species belonging to the plant kingdom, represented, sold or used to grow a plant.

"sell" « *vente* »

"sell" includes agree to sell, or offer, keep, expose, transmit, send, convey or deliver for sale, or agree to exchange or to dispose of to any person in any manner for consideration.

"terminator seed" « *semence Terminator* »

"terminator seed" means any seed or plant containing V-GURTs as part of its genetic structure.

"use" « *utilisation* »

"use" means the planting or cultivation of terminator seeds resulting in a release.

"variety-genetic use restriction technologies" or "V-GURTs", or "terminator technologies" "« *technologies de restriction de l'utilisation des ressources génétiques affectant les variétés* », « *V-GURT* » *ou* « *technologies Terminator* »

"variety-genetic use restriction technologies" or "V-GURTs", or "terminator technologies", means molecular technologies

(*a*) that use tools such as recombinant DNA technologies and genetic engineering aimed or designed to result in a seed or plant whose ability to reproduce — including the ability to germinate or mature to the reproductive stage — is blocked or otherwise compromised; and

(*b*) that involve the utilization or insertion of molecular mechanisms, including genetic sequences, capable of acting as switches aimed at activating or deactivating, through external inducers such as environmental or chemical inducers or through inducer lines — that is, the activation or establishment of the V-GURTs mechanism by crossing two transgenic plant lines — genes involved in the seed's or plant's ability to reproduce, including the ability to germinate or mature to the reproductive stage.

Source: Bill C-448

HER MAJESTY

Binding on Her Majesty

3. This Act is binding on Her Majesty in right of Canada or a province.

PROHIBITIONS

Prohibited products

4. Notwithstanding any other Act of Parliament or a regulation made thereunder, no person shall release, sell, import or use any terminator seed.

REGULATIONS

Regulations

5. The Governor in Council may make regulations generally for carrying the purposes or provisions of this Act into effect, and in particular, but without limiting the generality of the foregoing, may make regulations

(*a*) for classifying V-GURT components and for prescribing the composition, quality and character of V-GURTs;

(*b*) prescribing any thing that is to be included or not to be included in the definition "V-GURTs" in section 2;

(*c*) prohibiting the release, use, sale or importation of V-GURTs; and

(*d*) prescribing procedures for the destruction or disposal of seeds modified by V-GURTs.

OFFENCES AND PUNISHMENT

Contravention of Act or regulations

6. (1) Every person who, or whose employee or agent, contravenes any provision of this Act or any regulation made under Section 5

(*a*) is guilty of an offence punishable on summary conviction and liable to a fine not exceeding $1,000,000 or to imprisonment for a term not exceeding six months, or to both; or

(*b*) is guilty of an indictable offence and liable to a fine not exceeding $5,000,000 or to imprisonment for a term not exceeding two years, or to both.

Source: Bill C-448

Offence by director or officer of corporation

(2) Where a corporation commits an offence under this Act or the regulations, any director or officer of the corporation who authorizes or acquiesces in the offence or fails to exercise due diligence to prevent its commission is guilty of an offence and liable to the punishment provided for in subsection (1).

Offence by employee or agent

(3) In a prosecution for an offence under this Act, it is sufficient proof of the offence to establish that it was committed by an employee or agent of the accused, whether or not the employee or agent is identified or has been prosecuted for the offence.

Limitation period

(4) Proceedings by way of summary conviction in respect of an offence under this Act may be instituted at any time within two years after the time when the subject-matter of the proceedings becomes known to the Minister.

Minister's certificate

(5) A document purporting to have been issued by the Minister, certifying the day on which the subject-matter of any proceedings became known to the Minister, is admissible in evidence without proof of the signature or official character of the person appearing to have signed the document and is evidence of the matters asserted in it.

Source: Bill C-448

CONSEQUENTIAL AMENDMENT

R.S., c. P-4

PATENT ACT

7. Subsection 27(8) of the *Patent Act* is replaced by the following:

What may not be patented

(8) No patent shall be granted for

(*a*) any mere scientific principle or abstract theorem; or

(*b*) any modified DNA sequence or construct, or any plant or other organism containing such a DNA sequence or construct, where that DNA sequence or construct is the variety-genetic (i.e., DNA) basis for a GURT (genetic use restriction technology) or GURT application, including one designed to result in an organism whose ability to reproduce, including the ability to germinate from seed or mature to the reproductive stage or develop to produce viable seeds, is blocked or otherwise compromised.

Source: Bill C-448

RESOURCES

Tools for Action

WRITE A LETTER to your own MP protesting these bills. Always ask for a reply! Always make sure the bottom of your letter indicates that you also sent copies of it to

- the big national newspaper editors
- your local papers and to
- the leader of the Opposition (if your MP is Conservative; if not, to the PM and the leaders of the other parties)

Make an **APPOINTMENT with your MP** to discuss these bills: ***do not take No! for an answer.*** If he or she tells you they are already committed to oppose it, ask for that in writing.

- Always go with friends who share your concerns: do not go alone. You must have witnesses to your visit.
- Take Shawn Buckley's two legal opinions on C-51 and C-52 with you and give those to your MP. Download them from www.nhppa.org
- If your MP refers you to the government's website www.healthycanadians.ca make it clear that you do not believe the information on that site, with respect to bills C-51 and 52, because all its assertions are completely contradicted by Buckley's legal opinion and by the facts of the 2006 *Truehope Case* as it transpired in court. Make it clear that you want an assurance these two bills will be killed—absolutely, dead.

If a **PETITION** is being circulated in your area, sign it, make copies of the petition text and get signatures in your own workplace or from your friends and family. To get details on how to do a petition, contact the NHPPA via their website.

Order more copies of **THIS BOOK** and distribute or sell them. Remember, this book was published for the purpose of financially supporting the NHPPA's legal and activist work to stop these bills and make the government, thereby, accountable. Orders through the NHPPA website www.nhppa.org and www.stopc51.com or e-mail helke@sympatico.ca (the publisher) or fax 519-927-9542 with an order request.

Photocopy and fill in the **PATRON PLEDGE** reproduced here to become a member of the Natural Health products Protection Association and to support their work on behalf of all of us.

Organize or assist an already organized **PUBLIC DEMONSTRATION** in your area.

For all information on C-51 and C-52

www.nhppa.org
Home of Natural Health Products Protection Association

www.stopc51.com
website for Canada's effort to stops both C-51 and 52

www.healthcoalition.org
Home of the Canadian Health Coalition

For information on GMOs based on non-industry-funded science:

www.seedsofdeception.com

www.responsibletechnology.org

For correct information on CODEX and related issues:

www.alliance-natural-health.org
Home of the European resistance to Codex

www.iahf.com
Home of the International Association or health Freedom

To read the House of Commons Debates on C-51 and C-52:

Go to www.parl.gc.ca

Click on **LEGISINFO** and follow the leads... You need to be in: 39th Parliament, 2nd Session which began Oct. 16, 2007

C-51 dates:
First Reading debates took place on April 8, April 30, May 1, 2008

C-52 dates:
First Reading on April 28, Second Reading on May 1, 2008
This bill was referred to the Standing Committee on Health.

Standing Committee on Health

Letters may be addressed "To the Members of ...."
Phone 613-992-7974
Standing Committee on Health
House of Commons
131 Queen Street, Sixth Floor
Ottawa, ON, K1A 0A6

Committee Members reachable by E-mail

Chair: Smith.J@parl.gc.ca

Members: Bennett.C@parl.gc.ca, BrownPa@parl.gc.ca, Davidson.P@parl.gc.ca, Fletcher.S@parl.gc.ca, Kadis.S@parl.gc.ca, Malo.L@parl.gc.ca, Thibault.R@parl.gc.ca, Tilson.D@parl.gc.ca, Wasylycia-Leis.J@parl.gc.ca

Everybody else in Parliament

Abbott.J@parl.gc.ca, Albrecht.H@parl.gc.ca, Allen.M@parl.gc.ca, Allison.D@parl.gc.ca, Anders.R@parl.gc.ca, Anderson.Da@parl.gc.ca, Batters.D@parl.gc.ca, Benoit.L@parl.gc.ca, Bezan.J@parl.gc.ca, Blaikie.B@parl.gc.ca, Blaney.S@parl.gc.ca, Boucher.S@parl.gc.ca, Breitkreuz.G@parl.gc.ca, Brown.G@parl.gc.ca, Bruinooge.R@parl.gc.ca, Calkins.B@parl.gc.ca, Cannan.R@parl.gc.ca, Carrie.C@parl.gc.ca, Casson.R@parl.gc.ca, Charlton.C@parl.gc.ca, Chong.M@parl.gc.ca, Clarke.R@parl.gc.ca, Clement.T@parl.gc.ca, Cullen.N@parl.gc.ca, Comuzzi.J@parl.gc.ca, Cummins.J@parl.gc.ca, Cuzner.R@parl.gc.ca,, DelMastro.D@parl.gc.ca,Devolin.B@parl.gc.ca, Doyle.N@parl.gc.ca, Dykstra.R@parl.gc.ca, Epp.K@parl.gc.ca, Faille.M@parl.gc.ca, Fast.E@parl.gc.ca, Fitzpatrick.B@parl.gc.ca, Gallant.C@parl.gc.ca, Goldring.P@parl.gc.ca, Goodyear.G@parl.gc.ca, Gourde.J@parl.gc.ca,

Gravel.R@parl.gc.ca, Grewal.N@parl.gc.ca, Hanger.A@parl.gc.ca, Harris.R@parl.gc.ca, Hawn.L@parl.gc.ca, Hiebert.R@parl.gc.ca, Hinton.B@parl.gc.ca, Jaffer.R@parl.gc.ca, Jean.B@parl.gc.ca, Julian.P@parl.gc.ca, Kamp.R@parl.gc.ca, Keddy.G@parl.gc.ca, Keeper.T@parl.gc.ca, Khan.W@parl.gc.ca, Komarnicki.E@parl.gc.ca, Kramp.D@parl.gc.ca, Lake.M@parl.gc.ca, Lauzon.G@parl.gc.ca, Layton.J@parl.gc.ca, Lebel.D@parl.gc.ca, Lemieux.P@parl.gc.ca, Lukiwski.T@parl.gc.ca, Lunney.J@parl.gc.ca, MacKenzie.D@parl.gc.ca, Maloney.J@parl.gc.ca, Manning.F@parl.gc.ca, Mark.I@parl.gc.ca, Masse.B@parl.gc.ca, Mathyssen.I@parl.gc.ca, Mayes.C@parl.gc.ca, Menzies.T@parl.gc.ca, Merrifield.R@parl.gc.ca, Mills.B@parl.gc.ca, Miller.L@parl.gc.ca, Minna.M@parl.gc.ca, Moore.J@parl.gc.ca, Moore.R@parl.gc.ca, Murphy.B@parl.gc.ca Norlock.R@parl.gc.ca, Obhrai.D@parl.gc.ca, Pallister.B@parl.gc.ca, Petit.D@parl.gc.ca, PoiliP@parl.gc.ca, Preston.J@parl.gc.ca, Priddy.P@parl.gc.ca, Rajotte.J@parl.gc.ca, Reid.S@parl.gc.ca, Richardson.L@parl.gc.ca, Schellenberger.G@parl.gc.ca, Shipley.B@parl.gc.ca, Skelton.C@parl.gc.ca, Sorenson.K@parl.gc.ca, Stanton.B@parl.gc.ca, Storseth.B@parl.gc.ca, Sweet.D@parl.gc.ca, Thompson.M@parl.gc.ca, Trost.B@parl.gc.ca, Tweed.M@parl.gc.ca, VanKesteren.D@parl.gc.ca, Vellacott.M@parl.gc.ca, Wallace.M@parl.gc.ca, Warawa.M@parl.gc.ca, Warkentin.C@parl.gc.ca, Watson.J@parl.gc.ca, Williams.J@parl.gc.ca, Yelich.L@parl.gc.ca

The Prime Minister's Office

Office of the Prime Minister
80 Wellington Street
Ottawa, On, K1A 0A2
e-mail: pm@pm.gc.ca
613-992-4211 in Ottawa
403-253-7990 Constituency office

The Media

You can get contacts for all media outlets in Canada by going on www.canada.com

That way you can find the details of your own local paper and radio and TV stations.

Globe & Mail— 416-585-5243 Paul Taylor, Medical Health Editor
444 Front Street West, Toronto, M5V 2S9

Toronto Star—Medical Health Editor
1 Yonge Street, Toronto, ON, M5E 1E6

Ottawa Citizen—Editor, Scott Anderson, 1101 Baxter Road, Ottawa, K2C 3M4

CBC—416-205-5808 Box 500, Station A, Toronto, ON, M5W 1E6

NATURAL HEALTH PRODUCTS PROTECTION ASSOCIATION

There's more than one way of looking at health

Patron Pledge

In becoming a patron of the NHPPA, I, ___________________________________, pledge the following:
(print name)

I support the Natural Products Protection Association in their mission of maintaining my rights to the natural health products of my choice, from the manufacturers of my choice, from the businesses of my choice, and from the practitioners of my choice.

I support the NHPPA in their mission to maintain my fundamental right to health information from any sources I find credible.

I support the NHPPA in their mission to oppose any agency's authority to restrict my choice in reading, watching, or listening to any information whatsoever that I find of value in my judgement.

I support the NHPPA in their mission to ensure that my Charter rights are not accidentally extinguished by the actions, well intentioned or otherwise, of over-zealous lawmakers or regulators.

I support the NHPPA in their efforts to forge working relationships with like-minded organizations in other nations facing similar threats to their personal choices in self-care, and grant them full authority to represent me in any legal, governmental, or international affairs where decisions may be made that affect my health.

I support the NHPPA with my financial contribution of $20 (twenty) dollars, and include an extra donation of $_____________ to further support them in their efforts, (to be receipted).

Signed: ____ Date:________________

Method of payment:

Visa / MC card #___________________ expiration:_______ Name on Card:____________________________
(circle one) (print name)

Checks – please mail to: NHPPA, #2 953 Laval Cres., Kamloops, BC, V2C 5P4

I consent to receiving emails or other communications from time to time from the NHPPA to keep me abreast of developments in their mission, and to contact me if need be.

Email Address: ________________________________

Mailing Address: ______________________________ Phone # __________________________

____

____

For further information please visit: www.nhppa.org info@nhppa.org

Source: Patron Pledge

Suggested Reading: Verifiable and Uncompromised

It may come as a surprise to learn that reliable and uncorrupted information on food and medicine is easily available and also easily understood. The truth is always simple and lies are always complicated.

The persistent lies (often innocently repeated) which are necessary to understand for what they are, namely ruthless sales pitches, are generally found in the *negative* catch words such as "unproven," "untested," "unregulated," of "unknown efficacy," "not based on sound science," "potential toxicity"; or in *positive* propagandistic assertions, such as "medical breakthrough," "life-saving new technology," "safe and effective," "based on sound science," "eradicating world hunger," "approved by Health Canada," and so on.

What follows here is a two-part information kit: the first consists of a list of the "Top Ten Books," the "Top Six Documentaries" and the "Top Five Medical Periodicals" all of which anybody can understand and most people can easily afford. Everybody should read or see this material and thereby learn to understand the nuts and bolts of the corruption that endangers our food, medicine, and science. As a public service, you may consider taking this list to your local library and request that these items be added to their holdings as soon as possible; once these items have arrived, organize a reading group and viewings of the documentaries.

The second part has a more extensive list of important books and documentaries for those who want to dig deeper in a specific area of interest. This does not pretend to be in any way exhaustive. Many of these authors endured serious hardships because they refused to sell their souls to industry or politics. A new breed of writers has evolved: scientists who go directly to the general reader, because those who should be guarding public health have themselves largely sold out or are muzzled. The line between self-help books and rigorous, honest science is fast disappearing. These are Public Guardian Scientists.

Top Ten Books

S. M. Wolfe, MD et al. *Worst Pills Best Pills.*

A book as well as a monthly newsletter from Ralph Nader's Public Citizen's Health Research Group. Annually updated (or available by subscription), this book provides the latest information on safety and efficacy issues and problems regarding side effects and drug interactions not generally found in the drug information manufacturers make publicly available. Therefore, prescribing physicians don't even know these facts. The editor of this publication, Dr. Sidney Wolfe, is justly famous for his successes in getting toxic drugs off the market. Nobody should fill a prescription until the latest issue of this publication has been consulted.

D. Healy, MD. *Let Them Eat Prozac*, Lorimer, 2003.

The author was one of the experts on whom government regulators relied in order to get Prozac and the other drugs in that class of SSRIs (selective serotonin re-uptake inhibitors) on the market. In this book Dr. Healy, a UK professor of pharmacology and psychiatry and world-renowned historian of pharmacology, tells the story of how even he and other experts were deliberately misled by doctored information about the actual facts concerning the safety and efficacy of antidepressants. He also describes the criminal complicity of the regulatory agencies with corporate interests, specifically with regard to these drugs. This book started the process of re-evaluation and eventually obtaining full access to the raw data gathered at the original trials. Today we know that SSRIs are neither safe nor effective, no better than placebo, that their long-term use may cause cancer, diabetes, and increase the risk of suicide. In fact, due to the more recent research by Dr. Healy' and others we also know that the entire serotonin hypothesis, on which these drugs are based, has never been verified.

R. Moynihan & A. Cassels. ***Selling Sickness: How the World's Biggest Pharmaceutical Companies Are Turning Us All Into Patients.*** **Nation Books, 2005.**

Ray Moynihan is an Australian medical science journalist and Alan Cassels is a pharmaceutical policy researcher at the University of Victoria, BC. In this book they describe ten medical conditions which the pharmaceutical companies invented and how they systematically duped or browbeat the medical profession into cooperation by infiltrating guide line committees. Those phony conditions include high cholesterol, depression, menopause, attention deficit disorder, and more. They are at best *symptoms* of conditions which remain untreated and undiagnosed because symptom control is far more lucrative than the cure of the underlying condition would be. The always dubious and often deadly properties of the blockbuster drugs involved in each condition are discussed as well.

L. Armstrong, G. Dauncey & A. Wordsworth. ***Cancer: 101 Solutions To A Preventable Epidemic*****, New Society, 2007**

The authors are internationally known Canadian cancer and environmental writers and health activists. This book is a first in that it tackles the world's cancer producing industries whose products are in our food, medicines, air, and soil. None of them are necessary, but in an economic system such as this one, cancer is simply collateral damage. What is unusual also about this book is the fact that it identifies the sources, shows how to avoid them, what to do to stop cancer before it starts, find alternative sources of goods and services, offer an outline of a health-promoting economic system and documents all this with first-rate scientific research. Every assertion and suggestion in this book is based on verifiable scientific information.

P.D. Blanc, MD**.** ***How Everyday Products Make People Sick: Toxins at Home and in the Workplace.*** **University of California Press, 2007.**
The author is a professor of medicine at the University of California in San Francisco and holds the chair for occupational and environmental medicine. The unholy alliance between regulatory systems and the lucrative business of poisons is laid out here and explained so as to be of practical use. What the previously mentioned books have done for psychiatric drugs, corruption of medical diagnosis, and cancer, this book does for the whole range of toxins that cause many other conditions, ranging from autoimmune diseases to infertility.

C. Bryson. ***The Fluoride Deception.*** **Seven Stories Press, 2004.**
The author is an award-winning investigative reporter who probed the science underlying fluoride toxicity and interviewed the medical researchers working in that field. The story of how one of the world's most dangerous toxins wound up in our toothpaste and drinking water with the full complicity of the medical profession, governments and regulatory agencies is told here and solidly supported by the exhaustive scientific research finally available today. In 2007 the American Academy of Sciences published their review on fluoride which supports ending the use of this carcinogen and neurotoxin. Anyone with teeth should read this book.

D. Kirby. E*vidence of Harm: Mercury in Vaccines and the Autism Epidemic—A Medical Controversy.* **St. Martin's Press, 2005**
Since this *New York Times* medical science journalist wrote this book, a lot more evidence has appeared showing how ineffective and dangerous most vaccines are. Today we know that almost all currently used vaccines are potentially neurotoxic, especially to children whose immune systems are not yet fully developed. Kirby's discussion of the then available evidence has since been validated beyond probably his own wildest dreams. The claims made by pharmaceutical companies about vaccines are largely false, and the information doctors get comes from questionable science not verifiable or supported by the results

in the our vaccinated populations. This book is for the more shock-resistant reader.

M.R. Werbach, MD. *Textbook of Nutritional Medicine.* Third Line Press, current edition.
Nothing is as astounding as a visit into medical practice that cures people, not just controls their symptoms. There are many textbooks of this type. This one just happens to be especially accessible to the general reader even though the fine print—the immense bibliographies of mainstream medical research following the discussion of each disease—is the most astounding information of all. Each disease is discussed in terms of its known causalities and non-toxic therapeutic options, and the treatment modalities are then rated according to how much available mainstream science exists to support such therapy. This book provides a reference outline, a starting point for a rational approach to illness, and is most helpful when consulted together with the latest current research. Since standard, pesticide-laden supermarket produce and processed foods are neither nutritious nor health-promoting, leave alone healing, reading a textbook such as this makes it very clear just how important *real* food is for health.

M. Nestle. *What to Eat.* North Point Press, 2006.
This book should be in every shopping cart and be consulted while shopping! The author is a professor of nutritional science at New York University. Having served as a policy advisor to the US government's Department of Health and Human Services, she is intimately acquainted with the ruthless tactics the five giant food retailers use to ensure shareholder satisfaction—and nutritional science be damned. Her science advisory work for the FDA also gave her an insider's view of how government and corporations undermine public health interests. She teaches the reader how to decode the nutritional disinformation as she takes the reader through the local supermarket—aisle by aisle, shelf by shelf, product by product.

J.M. Smith, Genetic Roulette: *The Documented Health Risks of Genetically Engineered Foods.* Yes! Books, 2008.
This book should be placed on every MP's desk with the request to read it before voting on bills C-51, 52, 448, and 517. What the scientists from around the world document here should lay to rest, once and for all, that GMOs are safe. After reading this book, the next time your MP puts a fork-full of food cooked with GE canola in his or her mouth, some disturbing thoughts might helpfully interfere with the gastric juices forced to deal with that stuff. What is especially interesting is the fact that many of the scientists reporting on GMOs in this book are themselves experts in the prerequisite technology and realized through their work that "improving" on Nature is a very bad idea for human health.

Top Six Documentaries

The Corporation, 2005. The 2-disc special edition. An exploration of the psychopathic properties of our economic paradigm.

The Gerson Miracle, 2004. An exploration of the science, protocols and results of the nutritional cure for most cancers.

We Become Silent, 2005. A half hour documentary on the United Nations Codex Alimentarius Committee.

The Future of Food, 2004. On GMO foods—politics, health, regulatory failures, truthful and corrupt science.

The two disk set on the politics and science of dentistry produced by dentists and dental surgeons: ***Rooted: A scientific Look at the Dangers of Root Canal Therapy*** (2006) and ***Quecksilber: The Story of Dental Amalgam*** (2004)

Available via Google, www.amazon.com and often also through local Blockbuster outlets.

Top Five Medical Periodicals

Journal of Orthomolecular Medicine published quarterly by the International Society for Orthomolecular Medicine, 16 Florence Ave. Toronto, ON, Canada, M2N 1E9, www.orthomed.org

Founded in 1970 by Dr. Abram Hoffer, JOM publishes original research in nutritional medicine as well as analyses of advances in such research. Its annual international conferences are held alternately in British Columbia and Ontario.

Dr. Sherry Rogers' *Total Wellness* monthly newsletter for patients, available through www.prestigepublishing.com or 1-800-846-6687.

This is the most thoroughly researched, carefully sourced and comprehensive medical newsletter, designed for patients, currently available. It discusses the latest, the best and the worst in drugs and therapies of every kind, and gives comprehensive explanations of how nutrients work, what toxins do, which detoxification protocols work for what conditions, and how to evaluate medical interventions. The author has four decades of experience practicing environmental and nutritional medicine. She is the author of many excellent books. Every household should subscribe to this newsletter.

The Townsend Letter for Doctors and Patients: The Examiner of Alternative Medicine, published monthly in the US, available through www.townsendletter.com.

Written by practicing physicians and researchers in a style that patients can understand, but resourced so the specialist has access to the primary publications, this journal surveys everything that is going on in medical and food research throughout the spectrum of medical practice. It also fearlessly exposes the current regulatory mess.

PloS Medicine (Public Library of Science—Medicine)
A free on-line publication that has no advertising of any kind. It was founded by medical Nobel laureate and former director of the National Institutes of Health, Harold Varmus, together with "No Free Lunch," an association of medical students dedicated to freeing medicine of Big Pharma control.

Open Medicine
Also free on-line and without advertising for drugs. It was more recently co-founded by Dr. John Hoey, for many years editor-in-chief of the *Canadian Medical Association Journal.*

Digging Deeper

The following publications have proven to be most important. They are arranged by subject matter. Almost without exception, either the authors themselves or the sources consulted are mainstream—but financially uncompromised. That said, it is recommended that all encounters with health professionals, and the assertions made by regulatory bodies, should be tested first against the information in the following totally mainstream publications: you can't afford to be ill without them!

Harrison's Principles of Internal Medicine. The current edition is the seventeenth.

This hefty textbook is the primary source of everything mainstream in internal medicine. Here is the "classic" stuff: the basic biochemistry of a disease process, the detailed symptom descriptions, the mainstream therapies (usually drugs, of course). Without this fundamental text—and despite its many serious flaws and contaminations from industry—neither doctors nor patients know in which waters they are sailing. In my own research, *Harrison's* is always the first stop. For medicine this book is much like the parliamentary debates on a proposed bill: silly or profound, one needs to know what the acknowledged issues are. Conducting a comparison is especially interesting: take a disease you are familiar with and compare what *Harrison's* authors said about it ten, twenty, or fifty years ago. You will be amazed! The further back you go towards the 19th century boundary, when Sir William Osler wrote its first edition (*The Principles and Practice of Medicine*, 1892) the more useful nutritional and life-style advice you will find.

CPS: Compendium of Pharmaceuticals and Specialties: The Canadian Drug Reference for Health Professionals, published annually by the Canadian Pharmacists Association, in print for 101 years. Available on-line, in all pharmacies, and in every doctor's office.

Nobody should fill a prescription without first reading the relevant entry in this book. Here one finds everything that the industry admits to publicly as well as the Health Canada advisories and warnings that the public and medical science forced upon our government. If you don't understand the high-tech jargon, ask your pharmacist or your doctor and go to Google. Informed consent is the law and means you are entitled to an explanation. By the time you have read the information provided here, you might decide being ill is often preferable and time and a good naturopath may be the best courses of action.

P. Ross & J. LaValle. *The Nutritional Cost of Prescription Drugs*, Morton, 2004.

Compiled by professional pharmacists, this is a handy volume (about $10 on amazon.com) for the general reader and informs about the *essential* nutrients pharmaceutical drugs deplete. If you must or want to take prescription drugs, at least you know what to supplement with to avoid the worst side effects.

P. Ross et al. ***Drug-Induced Nutrient Depletion Handbook, 2nd Edition***, Lexi-Comp's Clinical Reference Library (look for current edition), published by the American Pharmaceutical Association and Natural Health Resources.

This is the professional version of the above-mentioned book and quite costly. It provides for each drug (and its specified essential nutrient depletion) the references in the standard medical literature. Because this information is so vast, the book has to be used in conjunction with its website which is constantly updated. This book all by itself gives the lie to the constantly repeated assertion that there is no research or information on the clinical efficacy and safety of essential nutrients and their known requirements in health and disease.

On Big Pharma

M. Angell, MD. ***The Truth About the Drug Companies, How They Deceive Us, And What To Do About It.*** Random, 2003. Dr. Angell was the editor of the *New England Journal of Medicine* for almost two decades.

C. Dean, MD. ***Death by Modern Medicine.*** Matrix Verite, 2005

S. Ellison. ***Health Myths Exposed.*** Author House, 2005

R. Fitzgerald. ***The Hundred-Year Lie: How Food and Medicine Are Destroying Our Health***, Dutton, 2006

M. Goozner. ***The $800 Million Pill: The Truth Behind the Cost of New Drugs.*** University of California Press, 2004

N.M. Hadler, MD. ***The Last Well Person: How to Stay Well Despite the Health-Care System.*** McGill's Queen's University Press, 2004. A professor of medicine, who frequently testified before the US Congress, takes on all the sacred cows of modern high-tech and drug medical therapies to help you escape from its worst effects.

J.P. Kassirer, MD. ***On The Take: How Medicine's Complicity With Big Business Can Endanger Your Health.*** Oxford University Press,

2005. A professor of medicine from Yale University and former editor of the *New England Journal of Medicine* examines the corruption in the medical profession.

M. Loe. ***The Rise of Viagra: How the Little Blue Pill Changed Sex in America.*** New York University Press, 2004.

The Olivieri Report. The Report of the Independent Inquiry by the Canadian Association of University teachers. Lorimer, 2001

M. Petersen. ***Our Daily Meds: How the Pharmaceutical Companies Transformed Themselves into Sick Marketing Machines and Hooked the Nation on Prescription Drugs.*** Sarah Crichton Books, 2008

J. Robinson. ***Prescription Games: Money, Ego, and Power Inside the Global Pharmaceutical Industry.*** McClelland & Stewart Ltd, 2001. A breath-taking book; especially helpful in showing how the various international trade agreements and the World Trade Organization figure in distorting and controlling our choices in therapies.

R. Smith. ***The Trouble With Medical Journals.*** Royal Society of Medicine Press, 2006. The former editor of the *British Medical Journal* and president of the British Medical Association explains why medical journals cannot be trusted and how they are financially enslaved by Big Business.

W. Wagner & R. Steinzor eds. ***Rescuing Science From Politics: Regulation and the Distortion of Scientific Research.*** Cambridge University Press, 2006. Should be required reading for anybody dealing with Health Canada.

J. Washburn. ***University Inc. The Corporate Corruption of Higher Education.*** Basic Books, 2005.

Drug Deals: The Brave New World of Prescription Drugs. National Film Board of Canada documentary, 2001

Money Talks: Profits Before Patient Safety and Side Effects. 2006, www.sideeffectsthemovie.com. Two documentary films produced by a former drug rep. They explore the relationship between doctors and drug companies

Big Bucks Big Pharma. Documentary, 2006 documentary by Media Education Foundation, www.mef.org

Vaccines: The Risks, the Benefits, the Choices and *Vaccines: What CDC Documents and Science Reveal*, both 2003 by Dr. Sheri J. Tenpenny. www.nmaseminars.com

Cancer

B. Bishop. *A Time to Heal: Food as Medicine—The Way to Heal 'Incurable" Cancer*. First Stone, 2005

D. Davis. *The Secret History of the War on Cancer*. Basic Books, 2007. Director of the Center for Environmental Oncology at the University of Pittsburg and a member of the US National Academy of Sciences.

S.S. Epstein. *Cancer-Gate: To Win the Losing Cancer War*. Baywood, 2005. The story of the National Cancer Institute's and the National Cancer Society's complicity with the industries that produce the best-known carcinogens. Epstein is an oncologist and public health expert at the University of Chicago. He spearheaded the banning of DDT and, in collaboration with Dr. Shiv Chopra, a Health Canada scientist at the time, helped to stop the use of bovine growth hormone in Canada and the EU.

G.B. Faguet. *The War on Cancer: An Anatomy of Failure*. Springer, 2005. A cancer researcher from the national Institutes of Health, Faguet reveals the truth behind the mythology of current cancer statistics and the fact that almost all standard treatments do not work or even prolong life.

M. Gerson MD. *A Cancer Therapy: Results of Fifty Cases & The Cure of Advanced Cancer by Diet Therapy*. Gerson Institute (1952), Sixth edition 2002

C Gerson & B. Bishop. *Healing the Gerson Way: Defeating Cancer and Other Chronic Diseases*. Totality Books, 2007

S.D. Kaur. *The Complete Natural Medicine Guide to Breast Cancer.* Robert Rose, 2003.

R. W. Moss. *Questioning Chemotherapy*, Equinox, 2000.

S. Steingraber. *Living Downstream: An Ecologist Looks At Cancer And The Environment.* Addison Wessley, 1997

S. Steingraber. *Having Faith: An Ecologist's Journey to Motherhood.* Perseus, 2001

H. Strauss & B. Marinacci. *Dr. Max Gerson: Healing the Hopeless.* Quarry health Books, 2002.

H.G. Welch, MD. *Should I Be Tested For Cancer? Maybe Not And Here's Why.* University of California Press, 2004.

Psychiatry and Mental Health

P. R. Breggin, MD. *Toxic Psychiatry.* St. Martin's Press, 1991

D. Healy, MD. *The Anti-Depressant Era.* Harvard University Press, 1997.

D. Healy, MD. *The Creation of Psychopharmacology*, Harvard University Press, 2002.

Abram Hoffer, MD. *Adventures in Psychiatry: The Scientific Memoirs.* Kos, 2005

J.M. Larason. *Depression-Free Naturally.* Ballantine, 1999

D.J. Rapp, MD. *Is This Your Child's World?* Bantam, 1996. On ADHD, asthma, allergy etc.

GMOs and Food Issues

S. Allport. *The Queen of Fats: Why Omega-3s Were Removed From The Western Diet and What We Can Do To Replace Them.* University of California Press, 2006

R. L. Blaylock, MD. *Excitotoxins: The Taste That Kills.* Health Press, 1997

T. C. Campbell. , MD, Benbella, 2005
S. Cox. *Sick Planet—Corporate Food and Medicine.* Pluto Press, 2008
R. Cummins & B. Lilliston. *Genetically Engineered Food: A Self-Defense Guide for Consumers.* Marlowe, 2000
J. Higdon. *An Evidentiary-Based Approach to Dietary Phytochemicals.* Linus Pauling Institute Series, Thieme, 2007
J. Higdon. *An Evidence-based Approach to Vitamins and Minerals.* Linus Pauling Instiute Series, Thieme, 2003
M.W. Ho & L. L. Ching. *GMO Free: Exposing the Hazards of Biotechnology.* Vital health, 2004.
C. Holdrege & S. Talbott. *Beyond Biotechnology: The Barren Promise of Genetic Enginering.* University of Kentucky, 2008
M. Nestle. *Food Politics: How the Industry Influences Nutrition and Health.* University of California Press, 2002
M. Nestle. *Safe Food: Bacteria, Biotechnology and Bioterrorism.* University of California Press, 2004
M. Pollan. *In Defense of Food: An Eater's Manifesto.* Penguin, 2008.
W. A. Price DDS. *Nutrition and Physical Degeneration,* 50th anniversary edition. Weston Price Foundation, Keats, 1989
P. C. Ronald & R.W. Adamchak. *Tomorrow's Table: Organic farming, Genetics and the Future of Food.* Oxford university Press, 2008
U. Ravnskov MD. *The Cholesterol Myth: Exposing the Fallacy that Saturated Fats and Cholesterol Cause Heart Disease.* New Trends Publishing, 2000
E. Schlosser. *Fast Food Nation.* Houghton Mifflin, 2001
M. Simon. *Appetite for Profit; How the Food Industry Undermines our Health and How to Fight Back.* Nation Books, 2006
T. Traavik & L. L. Ching. *Biosafety First.* Academic Press, 2007. The definitive basic science text book.
P. Weirich ed. *Labeling Genetically Modified Food: The Philosophical and Legal Debate.* Oxford university Press, 2007
K.G. Wenzel, MD & R. J. Pataracchia, ND. *The Earth's Gift to Medicine: Minerals in Health and Disease.* Kos, 2005

Supersize Me, 2004. The famous documentary that showed how fast foods cause disease.

The Genetic Takeover or Mutant Food. National Film Board of Canada, 2000

Clone Inc. National Film Board of Canada, 2000

Deconstructing Supper. Moving Images, 2002

Politics

M. Barlow. *The Fight of My Life: Confessions of an Unrepentant Canadian*. Harper Collins, 1998

M. McBane. *Ill-Health Canada: Putting Food and Drug Company Profits Ahead of Safety*. Canadian Centre for Policy Alternatives, 2005

B. J. Richards. *Fight for Your Health: Exposing the FDA's Betrayal of America*. Truth and Wellness Books, 2006

D. J. Savoie. *Court Government and the Collapse of Accountability in Canada and the UK*. University of Toronto Press, 2008

S. Tipps ed. *Codex Alimentarius: Global Food Imperialism*. Foundation for Health Research, 2007

ACKNOWLEDGMENTS

This year is the 60th anniversary of the Universal Declaration of Human Rights. It is still very necessary to reaffirm those universal rights, and this is one such occasion. Perhaps this book is a small contribution to celebrating this anniversary. Without some important helpers this little book would not have been possible in such a hurry.

I would like to thank **Dr. James Lunney**, Conservative MP for Nanaimo-Alberni for his courage and dedication to natural health which he displayed by giving me permission to print his 2003 his article on Health Canada and his proposed bill C-420.

Dr. Shiv Chora has spent much time over the years, explaining to me the difference between risk assessment and risk management , as well as given me an insider's view of Health Canada by asking me to publish his book, *Corrupt to the Core.* Knowing him is to be engaged in a constant education.

Mike McBane of the Canadian Health Coalition very kindly allowed me to use large sections from his book *Safety Last*, for which I am very grateful.

Croft Woodruff, as always, kept me in touch with all the details of the perfidy going on in the world. Without his immense research, which he shares so gallantly with me and so many other lucky people, nothing I do would be possible.

Peter Helgeson of Strauss Herbal and **Ian Stewart** of Truehope kept me informed about the Truehope case over a long time and patiently explained the intricate details of Health Canada's published materials to me. They were guides through a labyrinth.

Bonita Polin, the Canadian Coordinator of the Global Recognition Program for Multiple Chemical Sensitivity (www.mcs-global.org) provided me with the invaluable information on public reactions to bills C-51 and C-52 .

Eleanor Johnston sent me a copy of Donald J. Savoie's new book, *Court Government and the Collapse of Accountability in Canada and the*

United Kingdom just as I began working on this book. It was just what the doctor ordered! Many questions were answered by this thoughtful analysis of what's gone wrong with our government.

Beth Crane of Heidy Lawrance Associates did the impossible by getting this book out in time for the Toronto event on June 26, 2008, for which heartfelt thanks.

Julia Woodford of *Vitality Magazine* not only published my article on these two bills in the June issue, but asked so many questions that the article became better with every re-write. Her generalship is most appreciated.

Joe D'Addario, president of *Nature's Emporium*, the ultimate holistic super (!) supermarket in Newmarket, Ontario (905-898-1844) at 16655 Yonge Street, where one learns how to be healthy, for his generous financial assistance in getting a copy of this book to each and every Member of Parliament.

Coach, Helen and **Jill Hewlett** of Aurora, Ontario, and Canadian Youngevity, which markets essential minerals (1-866-727-2191) for their kind and ongoing assistance in generating publicity for the problems involved with bill C-51.

Dr. Robert Ferrie, who is my husband of nearly 40 years and who proofreads almost everything I write, insists on clarity in every detail, and eggs me on to improve the eloquence of my habitual dissent. Whatever mistakes I made are not his fault; whatever is good in my writing is fueled by his constant appreciation.

Caledon, Ontario,
June 2008

"Over the past 30 years, I have reviewed several hundred books in this new field of nutritional medicine. Of these, two dealing with minerals stand out. The first by Carl Pfeiffer called *Mental and Elemental Nutrients* published in 1975 — and this one. This book is well organized and reads well... I do recommend that every person dealing with health have this book in his or her library... Physicians who pay attention to the properties of these minerals and use them in their practice will be surprised and pleased at how much better their patients will be."

— From the Foreword to this book by Dr. A Hoffer, Prof. Emeritus (psychiatry) University of Saskatchewan, founder of the International Society for Orthomolecular Medicine. Editor-in-Chief of The Journal of Orthomolecular Medicine, author of many books.

"This book is as essential as the minerals it talks about. The word "trace" hides the enormous importance of these minerals that work in concert and are essential for maintaining health. This could not be further from the truth. Indeed, I would suggest, that this book should be understood as a most useful survey of all that is essential 'beyond calcium'.

We need all the minerals in sufficient quantities to replace what we no longer get in our food, which is grown on factory farms that do not use mineral fertilizers. Most plants may look fine, but they no longer provide all that we need for good health. Medical and nutritional research now shows that the current epidemic of chronic diseases is in large part due to chronic mineral deficiencies throughout the population. The list of diseases is as long as the list of minerals that are necessary for human functions: diabetes because of lack of chromium; cancer and AIDS for want of selenium; thyroid disease due to lack of iodine; immune deficiency because there is not enough zinc in the soil, and much more.

— Carolyn Dean, M.D., N.D., board member of the Canadian College of Naturopathy, author of *The Miracle of Magnesium*, Random, 2003.

ISBN 0-9731945-5-3

6" × 9" | 200 pages | PB | $25.00

PRAISE FOR:

Corrupt to the Core

Dr. Shiv Chopra

"Shiv Chopra is a Canadian hero. He was guided by science to conclusions that were not politically convenient. I'm grateful that he was not deterred and continued to speak out. Do you think our governmental institutions keep our health and best interests as their uppermost priorities? Read this eye opening book for a shocking answer."

—**David Suzuki**, Canadian environmentalist and geneticist

"Shiv Chopra is a hero. So are his five scientist colleagues who took on the powers at Health Canada's food inspection bureau. My best memory of Shiv is sitting on a platform with him and Ralph Nader at a huge conference in Ottawa called "Science in the Public Good" when, after receiving our "Whistleblower of the Year" award, he announced to the audience that he would whistle blow "again and again and again" until the abuse stopped. Ralph Nader doubled over with laughter and declared that in all his years as a rabble-rouser, he had never heard anyone announce publicly, in advance, that they were going to blow the whistle."

—**Maude Barlow**, Chair, *Council of Canadians*,
recipient of the Swedish Right Livelihood Award

"The cancer of corporate corruption of science and safety regulations is becoming a major threat to the planet's health and to public health. Dr. Shiv Chopra's book describes a leading scientists' witnessing of this corruption. His courageous writing provides a dose of resilience to all who care about the integrity of science, the independence of government regulations from corporate influence, and the freedom of citizens from hazardous food and medicines."

—**Vandana Shiva**, Environmental activist in India,
recipient of the Swedish Right Livelihood Award

"As scientists and public citizens, both Dr. Shiv Chopra and I have fought for the freedom of science and government from corporate corruption ... I have been privileged to have been, and to continue to be, his legal advisor in those areas. Dr. Chopra and his colleagues seek to uphold the law: the law that requires that drugs, which are allowed or maintained to be used by Health Canada, must meet the human safety requirements of the Food and Drugs Act and its Regulations. I admire his tenacity, his love for the law, his love for science ... I am amazed that, in spite of all that has been thrown at him, he continues to pursue these issues without bitterness and with a determination ..."

—**David Yazbeck** of Ottawa-based law firm
Raven Cameron Ballentyne & Yazbeck

Dr. Shiv Chopra' s name has become synonymous with food safety. Dr. Chopra and some of his fellow scientists waged many battles over many years against a succession of Canadian federal ministries of health—theft employer.

With full support of The Professional Institute of the Public Service of Canada—a 50,000 member union of scientific and professional public service employees, Dr. Chopra and his colleagues refused to approve various harmful drugs to be used in meat and milk production. Despite the political pressures to do otherwise, and holding fast to sound science, they did better than the gambles that a series of prime ministers and health ministers played with public safety.

Time and again the federal courts supported Dr. Chopra and his fellow scientists and ruled against government attempts to shut them up. Also, time and again the government overruled these scientists to feed corporate greed and allowed dangerous drugs to enter food production. Yet, today, the dangers of these drugs are internationally recognized and many countries have forbidden their use for such purposes. In 1999, Bovine Growth Hormone was barred in Canada and in the European Union, which was due essentially to Dr. Chopra's negative findings on this drug going back to 1988. Since 2000, the United States government has been trying unsuccessfully to withdraw market approval for a very seriously hazardous antibiotic, Baytril for which regulatory compliance in Canada was rejected by Dr. Chopra in 1995.

Here is the full account of how government corruption endangers the public food supply and how Dr. Chopra and his colleagues fearlessly continue to "to speak truth to power." Here is also the story of how the elected representatives in both Canada and USA are more interested in protecting industrial profits and trade, instead of the public's health. The stories told here for the first time include products like Revalor-H, Baytril, Bovine Growth Hormone, Silicon Breast Implants, and slaughterhouse waste to cause the biggest ruin of health safety—Bovine Spongiform Encephalopathy (BSE) or "mad-cow disease."

Everybody who eats should read this book.

The general reader learns from his book to:

- identify health hazards in the home and work-place environments and what to do about them
- find help through a comprehensive resource section covering everything from pesticides to food allergies, electromagnetic fields, holistic dentistry, safe building materials, how to become a practitioner in environmental medicine and much more
- recognize warning signs that indicate probable environmental illness and how to find medically reliable help

Readers who are health professionals may use this book

- to find the references from the mainstream medical literature covering the field of environmental toxins and the treatment of environmental illness
- basic treatment and detoxification protocols for patients with environmental illness

ISBN 0-9731945-0-2
6" × 9" | 368 pages | PB | $25.00 | 2003

Anybody who bought this book may purchase the following at a 10% reduction. State in your order that you saw the informaton on the book of your choice in this book.

KOS
Publishing

Order form

KOS can be contacted at the address given below to obtain more information or to place an order for any of our publications.

KOS PUBLISHING INC.
1997 Beechgrove Road,
Caledon, Ontario Canada L7K 0N3
Tel: (519) 927-1049 Fax: (519) 927-9542
Email: helke@sympatico.ca

Name: ______________________

Address: ______________________

City: ______________________

Prov./State: ______________________

Postal/Zip Code: ______________________

Telephone: ______________________

Email: ______________________

Date: ______________________

Payment: ○ Cheque ○ Visa ○ Master Card

Name on Card: ______________________

Card #: ______________________

Expiry Date: ______________________

Signature: ______________________

ISBN	TITLE	QTY.	PRICE	TOTAL
978-0-9731945-8-6	What Part of *NO!* Don't They Understand?*		$20.00	
0-9731945-0-2	Healing the Planet		$25.00	
0-9731945-5-3	The Earth's Gift to Medicine		`$25.00	
0-9731945-7-X	Corrupt to the Core PB		$30.00	
0-9731945-7-X	Corrupt to the Core HC		$40.00	
Shipping Charges: 1 title $6.00, for each additional title add $3 plus gst. Bulk orders of 10 copies or more of any one title receive a 50% discount on books only, regular shipping and taxes apply.			Sub-Total	
			Taxes	
			Total	

*No discounts. Profit for legal action.